HERMANN GILIOMEE

The Rise and Demise of the Afrikaners

TAFELBERG

Tafelberg,
an imprint of NB Publishers,
a division of Media24 Boeke (Pty.) Ltd.,
40 Heerengracht, Cape Town, South Africa 8000
www.tafelberg.com

© 2019 Hermann Giliomee

All rights reserved.
No part of this book may be reproduced or transmitted in any form or
by any electronic or mechanical means, including photocopying and recording,
or by any other information storage or retrieval system,
without written permission from the publisher

Set in 10,5 on 15,5pt Dante
Cover design by Michiel Botha
Book design by Nazli Jacobs
Edited by Russell Martin
Proofread by Eugenie du Preez
Index by George Claassen
Printed and bound by CTP Printers

First edition, first impression 2019
ISBN: 978-0-624-08671-0
Epub: 978-0-624-08672-7
Mobi: 978-0-624-08673-4

CONTENTS

Note

The dog that did not bark: A word in advance

Introduction

Section 1: The making of apartheid   1

1. Non-racial Afrikaner politics and the 'coloured vote': The non-racial franchise and Afrikaner and coloured identities, 1910–1994   3
2. The making of the apartheid plan, 1929–1948   32
3. 'Survival in justice': An Afrikaner debate about apartheid   58
4. Ethnic business and economic empowerment: The Afrikaner case, 1915–1970   83
5. 'Bantu Education': Apartheid and mass black education   115

Section 2: Attempting to share power without losing control   137

6. BJ Vorster and the sultan's horse   139
7. The Botha quest: Sharing power without losing control   147
8. The Botha quest: Changing everything, except the way we think   159
9. 'Great expectations': President PW Botha's Rubicon speech of 1985   167
10. Breyten's outrage   202
11. The elusive search for peace   218

Section 3: Losing power   235

12. Surrender without defeat: Afrikaners and the South African 'miracle'   237
13. Admit defeat and seek an independent cultural space   266
14. Mandela and the last Afrikaner leaders   270

Section 4: An elite abandons its people   **295**

  15. Stellenbosch University turns against itself: A reply to Professor Wim de Villiers's dismissive attitude to the university's history   297

  16. The rise and decline of Afrikaans as a public language and the possible demise of the Afrikaners   304

Books by Hermann Giliomee   326

References   327

Index   354

NOTE

All the chapters except the last one have been published before and are republished here with the permission of the original publishers. They appear here as they did originally, aside from minor editing. Chapter 13 first appeared in the newspaper *Rapport* and was translated from the Afrikaans. The last chapter has not been published before, but an earlier version of it was presented to a conference at Leuven University, Belgium, with the theme of 'The Internationalisation of Universities and the National Language'.

Chapter 1: *African Affairs*, 94, 375 (April 1995)

Chapter 2: *Journal of Southern African Studies*, 29, 2 (2003)

Chapter 3. *Comparative Studies in Society and History*, 36, 3 (1994)

Chapter 4: *South African Journal of Economics*, 76, 4 (2008)

Chapter 5: This chapter appears in the forthcoming volume *Making Society a Better Place to Live: A Festschrift for Charles Edward Simkins* (in publication)

Chapter 6: *Frontline*, November 1983

Chapter 7: *Leadership SA*, 1983

Chapter 8: *Leadership SA*, 1984

Chapter 9: *New Contree*, 55 (May 2008)

Chapter 10: *Tydskrif vir letterkunde*, 46, 2 (2009)

Chapter 11: *Optima*, 36, 3 (1988)

Chapter 12: *Daedalus*, 126, 2 (1995)

Chapter 13: *Rapport*, 2 February 1997

Chapter 14: *New Contree*, 72, 5 (2015)

Chapter 15: *Rapport*, 16 September 2018; and Politicsweb blog, 18 September 2018

Chapter 16: Presented to a conference at Leuven University, 4 May 2018

The dog that did not bark:
A WORD IN ADVANCE

This book collects some of my journal articles written between 1980 and today. They deal with the perils of reform, the strange end of the policy of apartheid, which Afrikaners during the middle decades of the century had seen as a radical survival plan, and the birth of an unstable new order that may spell the end of the Afrikaners as a community over the next twenty-five years.

For the sake of preserving the flavour of the times, I have kept the articles in the form in which they were originally published. I make a single exception in order to correct a major error on my part. This is because the article on President PW Botha's ill-fated 1985 Rubicon speech has the potential of distorting, at a critical juncture, the history of contemporary South Africa.

The facts are as follows. On 2 August 1985, two weeks before PW Botha was scheduled to make a widely anticipated speech (later called the Rubicon speech), an informal cabinet meeting took place at the Sterrewag facility in Pretoria. The goal was to discuss some bold new reforms that could possibly break the deadlock in constitutional negotiations with the internal black leadership. The meeting was secret, no minutes were kept, and the participants were asked to speak freely.

Chris Heunis, the minister responsible for constitutional reform, proposed a cabinet that included internal black leaders, while Pik Botha, Minister of Foreign Affairs, advocated the unbanning of the ANC and the freeing of Nelson Mandela and other imprisoned ANC leaders.

Everyone found it strange that there was no response from President Botha, who was feared for his curt, and often rude, rejection of proposals that clashed with mainstream NP policy. Immediately after the meeting, Pik Botha flew off to Europe to alert Western leaders to the major structural reforms that, according to him, were imminent. The President did not object to the visit.

Two weeks later Botha gave a shocking speech from which all major reform proposals were omitted. On television screens across the world he came across as a hard-bitten reactionary leader. Political reform had received a lethal blow.

The question was: what prompted Botha's sudden rejection of the Sterrewag proposals? In my research for an article in the historical journal *New Contree*, which appeared in 2007, I investigated the rumour that had done the rounds, even among cabinet ministers, that Botha suffered a major stroke in the mid-1980s.

In my research I interviewed two neurosurgeons whom Botha consulted. One of them saw Botha in 1989 after the stroke that would lay him low for three months. He told me Botha's condition was so serious that he had considered it inadvisable that the President continue in his job.

I then interviewed another neurosurgeon, who examined Botha early in 1985. He showed me a letter Botha sent to him at the end of March 1985, thanking him for his services. I did not ask this surgeon what his diagnosis was, because I simply assumed that he had also treated Botha for a stroke.

Much later, after a controversy had erupted about my allegation concerning a first stroke, this neurosurgeon told me that when he saw Botha in 1985, the President was suffering from a nervous twitch in the face, which many lay people mistakenly assumed to be the effect of a stroke.

In my original interview with this neurosurgeon I had asked him, and some other doctors, what treatment they would prescribe for patients who suffered a stroke. They replied that it was imperative to avoid any interaction that caused stress and anxiety.

PW Botha in fact had suffered no stroke in 1985. Without telling anyone, he simply decided to listen to the speeches at the Sterrewag meeting instead of his standard response – slapping down anyone uttering what he considered a political heresy.

'The dog did not bark', as Sherlock Holmes once tellingly remarked about a certain mystery, but no one in the NP cabinet got the reason for Botha's silence right. Nor did anyone ask the President outright why he had kept quiet. The political consequences were momentous. It meant nothing less than the collapse of the Botha government's credibility.

I am still being punished for my wrong assumption about Botha's silence. The *Mail & Guardian* published an excerpt from this passage in my 2007 article and it still appears today under my name on its blog.

A WORD IN ADVANCE

For me as a historian, it taught a valuable lesson about the cunning of history. Political actors are not programmed and politics never take a predetermined course. The attraction of history is that it is so full of sudden twists and turns no one anticipated. Humility about the extent of our ability to really know the past is one of the best traits a historian can develop.

Hermann Giliomee

INTRODUCTION

The rise of Afrikaner nationalism, of Afrikaans as a literary language, and of apartheid had their roots in the 1920s and 1930s. This period in South African history can be described as a testing time, as is the case today, ninety years later. Similarly to today, a profound organic crisis, affecting both the political and economic systems, then threatened to wreck the state. In a despairing mood General Jan Smuts wrote: 'There has never been such a test to our economic civilisation and it is still a question whether we can pull through without serious challenge to our spiritual heritage.'[1]

The 1929 election, the central event of the first chapter of this book, was a close contest. All parties accepted the Cape's non-racial franchise, as entrenched in the Union Constitution of 1909, and the National Party won in Stellenbosch because of its coloured support. Behind the scenes, political leaders were exploring the possibilities of an alternative political system that would factor in the growing numbers of people moving from the black reserves to find work in the towns and cities. When Smuts of the South African Party and Hertzog of the National Party privately exchanged views, Smuts proposed a qualified franchise based on occupation and income or salary, enabling a 'decent' white unskilled worker earning the standard minimum wage to qualify. Coloured and black people who met this requirement would have to pass an additional 'civilisation test for non-Europeans'. Hertzog rejected the proposal because it would exclude unskilled and unemployed whites. Most of these were Afrikaners. In the 1930s a quarter of all Afrikaners were considered poor whites, without the means to maintain a 'white living standard'.

The late 1920s and early 1930s saw South Africa in the grip of a set of profound crises. The 1929 crash of the New York stock exchange produced a major economic crisis, which in South Africa was compounded by a prolonged drought and the government's initial refusal to devalue the currency. In 1930 JH Hofmeyr,

INTRODUCTION

who would soon become the major voice of liberalism in Parliament, published a book entitled *Coming of Age*, to commemorate the Union of South Africa reaching 'adulthood'. In his contribution Hofmeyr identified three causes of the 'present discontents'. First was the lack of national unity between the two white language communities. Secondly, there were major defects in the economic structure. It was an illusion, Hofmeyr wrote, that South Africa was a rich country with vast mineral resources and boundless agricultural possibilities. The gold mines, the only reliable source of foreign exchange, were a wasting asset, the manufacturing sector was sluggish, and agriculture 'no easy oyster for man's opening'. The country was in a race against time to provide food and work for a rapidly growing population. Thirdly, there was the factor of racial demography, giving rise to the white fear that 'ultimately black numbers will tell' in the struggle for power. Hofmeyr wrote: 'The native – . . . whom he, the white man, has crushed into submission – will he not do him some evil yet?'[2]

By the 1930s the reserves were no longer able to sustain their populations, and black people in growing numbers were moving into the towns and cities. Most black students attended schools founded by British or American churches using English as medium and inculcating British values. In the Orange Free State, less than 10 per cent of black students attended the Dutch Reformed Church's mission schools. Afrikaner ministers and missionaries tried to attract more black students to DRC schools and churches, where their mother tongue would be the main means of communication and where pupils would learn to cherish their own heritage.[3]

The first written record of the term 'apartheid' dates back to 1929. In a journal covering the proceedings of a conference of the Free State DRC on missionary work, held in Kroonstad, the Rev. Jan Christoffel du Plessis wrote: 'In the fundamental idea of our missionary work, and not in racial prejudice, one must seek an explanation for the spirit of apartheid that has always characterised our [the DRC's] conduct.' By apartheid Du Plessis meant that blacks had to be uplifted 'on their own terrain, separate and apart'. Blacks and whites had to worship separately to 'ensure the survival of a handful of [white] people'.[4]

Owing to the devastation of the Anglo-Boer War and the crisis of subsistence farming, thousands of Afrikaners flocked to the cities in the first three decades of the century. Here they found people of British or Jewish descent virtually

INTRODUCTION

monopolising the non-agricultural sectors of the economy. Afrikaner entrepreneurial activities were extremely modest. In 1936, when the future business leader Albert Wessels arrived in Johannesburg, he found only three Afrikaner businesses of any significance: the publishing company Afrikaanse Pers, with its struggling pro-United Party daily, *Die Vaderland*; the bank Volkskas, on the second floor of an old building; and a shop for men's clothes, soon to fold. In 1937 the Johannesburg newspaper *Die Transvaler* estimated that there were in total only twenty Afrikaner enterprises in the city.[5] The educational standards of Afrikaners were low, and Afrikaner workers struggled to compete for work. A 1933 study reported that out of a 100 who started school, only eight completed matric and fewer than three went on to university.

Section one of this book (chapters 1–5) deals with the development of Afrikaner nationalism and with apartheid as a survival plan. Chapter 1 discusses the coloured vote, which white Afrikaners generally accepted in the 1910s and 1920s. Dr DF Malan, Cape leader in General Hertzog's National Party, and Dr HF Verwoerd, a professor at Stellenbosch University, considered the poverty of Afrikaner and coloured people as of a similar kind, requiring similar solutions. Coloured support helped the NP to win the Stellenbosch seat in the 1929 general election.

The situation changed in the early 1930s when Hertzog and Smuts joined forces to found the United Party (UP) and Malan formed the Purified National Party. Concluding that the UP, as a broadly based party, would attract virtually all coloured voters, Malan and his followers did an about-turn and vigorously promoted a separate voters' roll for coloured people. They claimed it would 'improve' race relations, but the opposite happened. An exclusive Afrikaner identity and culture emerged after coloured people had been disfranchised. The same would happen in the Southern states of the US after the 1890s.

'The making of the apartheid plan' (chapter 2) analyses the main influences on apartheid, considered one of the radical ideologies of the twentieth century by the American scholar A James Gregor. The aggressive policies that the NP government implemented to segregate the coloured community deeply troubled NP van Wyk Louw, the leading Afrikaans poet, who was then living in the Netherlands. Chapter 3 discusses the essay, first published in 1952, in which he asked: 'Can a small *volk* survive for long if it becomes hateful, even evil in the

INTRODUCTION

eyes of the best of its members and also to people outside its fold?' The *volk*, he warned, ran the risk of losing the allegiance of a critical number of intellectuals if it yielded to the 'temptation' of abandoning the quest for 'survival in justice' and preferred 'mere survival'. Although he died in 1970 just before apartheid began to crumble, Louw's words continued to haunt Afrikaners. FW de Klerk cited Louw in his victory speech after the referendum of 1992, which was taken as a firm white renunciation of apartheid.

Chapters 4 and 5 deal with two critically important tests the Afrikaner nationalists faced: whether they could advance economically without patronage by the ruling party (chapter 4), and whether they could put in place a system of segregated mass education (chapter 5). Economically, Afrikaners indeed made steady progress. Between 1938 and 1975 the Afrikaner share of the private sector grew in mining from 1 per cent to 18 per cent; in manufacturing and construction from 3 per cent to 15 per cent; and in trade and commerce from 8 per cent to 16 per cent. Chapter 5 discusses the first twenty years of Bantu education, which was introduced in 1954, and which is often seen as the most disastrous legacy of apartheid.

Section two (chapters 6–10) discusses the NP attempts at political reform between the mid-1970s and the mid-1990s. It tries to show how attempts to remove the nationality of black South Africans amounted to squandering limited time and why the effort to 'share power without losing control' met with little success. Chapter 9 describes what happened behind the scenes prior to PW Botha's Rubicon speech and why it was a disaster that, for all practical purposes, meant the end of reform from above.

The third section (chapters 11–15) investigates the difficulties in finding a solution that would satisfy both white and black, and examines the interaction between Nelson Mandela and the last four Afrikaner leaders.

For the first ten years after 1994 South Africa seemed well positioned to make the transition to a prosperous democratic society. But from 2008 on, South Africa started to slide. As in 1930, when Jan Hofmeyr wrote his essay, the prospects for South Africa seemed dire. The hope of minorities that the Constitutional Court would resolve the ambiguities with respect to language rights, affirmative action and redress has been all but dashed. As chapter 11 argues, South Africa shares the fate of Northern Ireland and Israel of intractable conflict that makes real peace very difficult. Times will remain trying.[6]

INTRODUCTION

Finally, there is chapter 16, which discusses the rise of Afrikaans from a vernacular with low status to one of only four languages that in the twentieth century had become the bearer of a particular intellectual tradition. It explains how university managements between 2002 and 2016 stealthily allowed English to supplant Afrikaans as medium of instruction, squandering a rich cultural heritage.

Simply put, Stellenbosch University failed the test of character. It was not the state but Afrikaners in leading positions that decapitated the language and, in the process, made it much harder for sections of the coloured Afrikaans-speaking people to recover from the ravages of apartheid. History will judge them harshly.

I wish to thank Flip Smit, a friend, leading educationist and demographer, for discussing with me the state of the universities in South Africa. My wife and *lewensmaat* Annette encouraged me in writing on the issue of Afrikaans, which we both care about deeply. Thanks also to Erika Oosthuysen, my publisher at Tafelberg, for her patience and unwavering support. It is to her that I dedicate the book.

HERMANN GILIOMEE
Stellenbosch
Spring 2018

SECTION ONE

The making of apartheid

1.

Non-racial Afrikaners and the 'coloured vote': The non-racial franchise and Afrikaner and coloured identities, 1910–1994

Although we all know that democracies can wither and die, the temptation is strong to see democratisation as a broad, inexorable process that swells to establish ever greater rights and freedoms. For this reason analysts have tended to concentrate more on the extension than the contraction of the franchise.[7] One of them is Alexis de Tocqueville, who observed:

> When a nation modifies the elective qualification, it may easily be foreseen that sooner or later that qualification will be entirely abolished. There is no more invariable rule in the history of society: the further electoral rights are extended, the greater is the need of extending them, for after each concession the strength of democracy increases, and its demands increase with its strength . . . no stop can be made short of universal suffrage.[8]

White politicians in the American South and South Africa would of course prove Tocqueville wrong. Nevertheless, the contraction of the franchise into a Herrenvolk democracy was not inevitable. C Vann Woodward's *The Strange Career of Jim Crow* has vividly demonstrated how for nearly twenty-five years after slavery ended, black Southerners enjoyed the right to vote and suffered less harsh forms of segregation than would later be the case.[9]

The same was true of the Western Cape. In the late nineteenth century the coloured people had to make their way through a thicket of discriminatory practices but at least their vote was sacrosanct. Cape political leaders made it clear that the Cape Colony would refuse to join the Union of South Africa in 1910 if the constitution did not entrench the Cape's non-racial franchise. Nevertheless, a wave of what Woodward calls 'white supremacy extremism' overwhelmed Southern blacks in the period 1890 to 1910 and the coloureds of the Cape Province in the period 1930 to 1956.[10] The wave did not recede in the South until the 1960s and in South Africa until the 1990s.

This chapter briefly looks at the contraction of the democratic franchise in the American South before it investigates the period of multi-racial electoral competition in the Cape Province between 1910 and 1929. The last part discusses the expansion of the franchise in the early 1990s and the election of 1994 in which most coloured people supported the National Party – the very party which had disfranchised them earlier.

The franchise and ascriptive identities

Under what circumstances do franchise extension and contraction occur? It will be anachronistic to apply Seymour Martin Lipset's thesis about the requisites for the consolidation of democracy in the modern world. J Morgan Kousser's study of franchise contraction in the American South between 1880 and 1910 applies a lesser known Lipset formulation to earlier times. Lipset writes that a state's legitimacy, which he defines as a 'believed-in title to rule', has been most secure 'where the society could admit the lower strata to full citizenship, to rights of participation in the economic and political systems, and at the same time allow the traditionally privileged strata to keep their status whilst yielding power'.[11] Kousser concludes that such a solution was impossible in the South at the end of the nineteenth century because the elite denied the lower strata's moral right to take part in society's affairs. Considered 'political automatons' who had 'no will of their own' and 'easily corruptible', they were deemed to have no right to the vote or to equal citizenship. What the sentiments in effect meant was that these voters, despite being bribed or intimidated, refused to vote for Southern Democrats.

When they set out in 1890 to disfranchise blacks, Democratic Party leaders were determined not to take away the vote of any whites.[12] As the disfranchisement movement gained momentum, however, some states added qualifications which struck at whites and blacks alike. Standards of literacy and property qualifications were set in a way which excluded the indigent across racial lines. The payment of poll tax, which was made a requirement in all states, did not allow for the same loopholes as those which accompanied literacy and property tests. The precise effect of the exclusionary devices is difficult to judge because they interacted with other political processes. However, the figures for the state of Louisiana give some indication of their impact. Registered white voters dropped from 164,088 in 1897 to 91,716 in 1904 and registered black voters from 130,344 to 1,342.[13]

The exclusion of indigent whites was not simply a case of unintended consequences. It was rather the result of attempts by whites of intelligence and wealth to establish their control. Their grab for power was accompanied by an upsurge of anti-democratic theorising which proclaimed the poor and the illiterate unfit to participate in politics. Governor Oates of Alabama spoke for many in the upper classes when in 1901 he declared that he favoured eliminating 'all those who are unfit and unqualified, and if the rule strikes a white man as well as a negro let him go. There are some white men who have no more right and no more business to vote than a negro and not as much as some of them.'[14] Disfranchisement devastated the poorer whites. An observer of registration in the Virginian mountains remarked:

> It was painful and pitiful to see the horror and dread visible on the faces of the illiterate poor white men who were waiting to take their turn before the inquisition . . . This was horrible to behold, but it was still more horrible to see the marks of humiliation and despair that were stamped on the faces of honest but poor white men who had been refused registration and who had been robbed of their citizenship without cause.[15]

The next few decades saw the readmission of whites to the Southern political system, but that of blacks had to wait until the 1960s. Black admission did not come about because the traditionally privileged strata were more ready to absorb the lower strata. They tended to believe that the civil rights movement was mainly the result of outside agitators and that Southern blacks preferred segregation. Confronted by a resolute Federal government, however, they accepted integration and electoral competition in a remarkably short time.[16]

The history of segregation in the South between 1865 and 1910 shows there is no 'natural' form of race relations. Unless bound by laws and social conformity pressure, people will react differently to different political situations. A comparative perspective also illuminates the primacy of political rather than class considerations in the establishment of a system of racial exclusion. Woodward argues convincingly that while economic and social change prepared the way for the introduction of a comprehensive and systematic system of segregation from the 1890s onwards, the basic motives were political. The new system promoted the political interests of not so much whites as a collectivity but of the elites of a particular party, the Southern Democrats. Subsequently the exclusion of blacks became the basis of the South's political system and of white unity. This raises major questions about the issue of ethnic or racial identity and the way in which this impacts on the functioning of a democratic system. Social identity theory holds that group membership offers information to members about who they are. For the poorer Southern whites of the 1890s there was no consistent information about what group they belonged to. What they were being told about their own status was negative or contradictory. Indeed, it can be argued that the criteria for group membership had not yet been established.

How are the criteria formulated by which groups establish norms for likeness and unlikeness? Donald Horowitz declares flatly that this is still 'a wholly unexplored process'. He cautions that the significance of the cultural mix as a determinant of political identity has probably been vastly overemphasised. It is more likely that adaptations in a group's culture *follow* or *accompany* rather than precede changes in the way in which an elite defines a group's political identity. The vital element in identity change is not the broad modernisation or industrialisation process but whether the political context favours the expansion or contraction of an ethnic boundary. To quote Horowitz at some length:

> The moving force of assimilation and differentiation is the sense of similarity and difference from others sharing the space. As the importance of a given political unit increases, so does the importance of the highest available level of identification immediately *beneath* the level of that unit, for that is the level at which judgements of likeness are made and contrasts take hold. There seems to be a kind of 'Parkinson's Law' at work by which group identity tends to expand or contract to fill the political space available for its expression.[17]

If Horowitz is correct, the intensification of segregation and the contraction of democratic freedoms result less from class struggles than from battles among political elites about the best ways of promoting their own or their party's prospects. Whether they resort to the politics of exclusion depends in the first place not on their historical and cultural identities but on the opportunities for sectional political gain which extension or contraction of the franchise offers. Culture can be pushed into the service of either.

Fluid Cape identities

In the American South, as we have seen, the contraction of the franchise and the rise of a virulent racism were the products of a recrudescence of anti-democratic thought which was quite prepared to sweep poor whites aside along with blacks. In the colonial situation of the Cape, by contrast, the rise of segregation was driven by a determination to salvage poorer whites by incorporating them fully into the social system and by excluding Africans. The fate of the coloured people would be determined not by their racial identity but by the political interests of the ruling political party.

In the Cape Colony the fear of the poorer whites losing caste first became an issue of serious public concern in 1892. Previously the attitude of elites in the dominant group had been that 'the poor (also the white poor) would always be with us'; now, however, they felt that something had to be done about white poverty. At the 1893 Afrikaner Bond congress a speaker declared that the issue was of utmost importance for Afrikaners: 'it was a question of survival'. At the same occasion SJ du Toit, founder of the Bond, stated: 'The whites are the aristocracy of the land. We dare not let them sink lower than the black.'[18]

In 1894 the liberal politician John X Merriman, who wielded great influence among Cape Afrikaners, also expressed the fear that white poverty was a drain on white power, which could result in the destruction of minority rule. While there was genuine concern about the poor there was an overriding anxiety about the socio-political implications of white poverty.[19] Merriman, for instance, stated: 'The white population was a minority in the country, but they must be a dominant minority if they were to live there at all, and if their brethren were to sink into the slough, as they saw them doing, it would be impossible to maintain their position of dominance.'[20]

During the first three decades of Union the problem arose whether coloureds, along with the poor whites, should be uplifted to strengthen the dominant group. Especially in the Cape Peninsula no clear-cut division existed between whites and coloureds, whose lower classes lived interspersed. A Labour Party pamphlet of 1915 stated that it was 'impossible in thousands of cases... to say definitely whether, judged by appearance alone, a given individual is a Coloured or a white man'. It added that there were some people 'occupying some of the highest positions in the land' who passed for white despite their 'obvious characteristics of known mixed descent'.[21] Two decades later official reports would also stress the fluidity of colour. The 1936 census takers complained that so many coloured parents tried to have their children enumerated as 'whites' that it was impossible to arrive at an exact figure for coloureds. Another report stated that the degree of whiteness determined whether someone could pass for a European; a lighter skin also brought a higher status among those within the coloured community unable to pass for white.[22]

Despite this fluidity there always were politicians like the prominent Nationalist Bruckner de Villiers who could say: 'Kind with kind: white with white, coloured with coloured, native with native.'[23] Yet no consensus existed about who the coloureds were. In the last quarter of the nineteenth and the first quarter of the twentieth century some whites used the term 'coloured people' for all non-European people – not unlike the usage current in North America. The 1892 Cape census, for instance, declared that the Cape population 'falls naturally into two main classes, the European or White and Coloured'.[24] There were also two other ways in which the term was used. One was to describe the various categories of non-Bantu-speaking blacks, including 'Hottentots', 'Malays' and 'Cape boys', as coloureds, and the other was to reserve it for only those people whose ancestors were slaves brought to the Cape from the East, particularly Malays.[25]

The catch-all designation of 'coloured' for all people of mixed descent became popular as the authorities increasingly established an intermediate category between Europeans or whites and 'raw natives'. The latter were subject to pass laws and the colour bar in industry and who had to live in locations on the perimeters of the major cities.

Were the coloureds also Afrikaners? No simple answer was possible because the term 'Afrikaner' was also a contested one. In the eighteenth and nineteenth centuries it was occasionally used to designate slaves or ex-slaves born in southern Africa but more frequently for whites whose highest loyalty was to the region rather than the Dutch or British metropole. Almost all Dutch- or Afrikaans-speaking colonists and a large section of English-speakers embraced this identity. In the second half of the nineteenth century liberal English-speakers began to reject it because, as James Rose Innes observed, the term Afrikaner implied 'a view on the native question which I cannot share'.[26] By contrast the jingoist *Cape Times* spurned the term because it was originally applied to 'the half-bred offspring of slaves and even in a word the mark of slavery is detestable'.[27]

Between 1910 and the mid-1930s the relatively mild form of Afrikaner nationalism appropriated the term, but many nationalists refused to give it an exclusive ethnic connotation. In 1929, for instance, *Die Burger* wrote in an editorial: 'As a *volk* we have a task to perform in the service of nationalism. It is not the task of English-speakers or Dutch-speakers; it is the task of all who are Afrikaners, [all] who have the spark of nationalism.'[28] Coloured people were not normally called Afrikaners although most spoke a form of Afrikaans. Nevertheless, in election campaigns Afrikaner politicians were quick to extend the term to these people if they thought this would bring them votes.

The Union constitution, which granted the vote to both Africans and coloureds in the Cape, thwarted the designs of white supremacists until the 1930s. Together, coloureds and Africans formed 9.6 per cent of the Cape electorate in 1910, rising to 20.8 per cent in 1921. In the nine constituencies of the Cape Peninsula 'non-European' voters (of whom the overwhelming majority were coloured) made up more than a quarter of the electorate.[29] This concentration of voters meant that the coloured vote of the Western Cape would be decisive in any closely contested election. As in the pre-1890 American South, white supremacist politicians refrained from attacking this vote for fear of damaging their party's prospects. There was also another factor which served to safeguard the votes of coloureds. White political leadership generally saw them as allies in the larger struggle between whites and Africans. In 1908 Lord Selborne, one of the British architects of Unification, warned that it would be sheer folly to classify coloureds together with Africans 'and by treating them as Natives to force them away from their natural allegiance to the whites and to make common cause with the Natives'. Selborne observed that a wise policy was 'to give Coloured people the benefit of their white blood – not to lay the stress on the black blood but to lay the stress on the white blood and to make any differentiation of treatment between them and whites the exception and not the rule'.[30]

The South African Party, which ruled South Africa from 1910 to 1924 first under Louis Botha and then under Jan Smuts, differentiated between whites and coloureds, on the one hand, and Africans, on the other. When Botha in 1914 met a delegation of the main coloured party, the African Political Organisation (APO), he told them that the only way of resolving the franchise issue was to restrict the African vote but to incorporate the coloureds into the white political system. Coloured people, he continued, 'were civilised and it was impossible to force them back'.[31]

The founder and leading spirit behind the APO, Dr Abdullah Abdurahman, was ambivalent about where to draw the line of identity and political division. Founded to fight the denial of the franchise to all people who were not white, the organisation first stressed black unity. At the APO's 1909 conference Abdurahman said that by the term 'coloured' he meant 'everyone who was a British subject in South Africa, and who was not a European', and committed the APO to fighting for the 'absolute equality of opportunity to every man to rise and progress in the scale of civilisation'.[32]

Threats to the coloured people both from above and below soon forced the APO to reconsider its attempt to rally all blacks. It became primarily concerned with defending coloured civil rights against white supremacists, and with promoting the social upliftment of the coloured people as part of the struggle to claim full citizenship with whites. As growing numbers of unskilled coloured workers were squeezed out of their jobs by lower-paid African workers, Abdurahman urged them to form coloured trade unions.[33] Reluctantly the elite began propagating a distinct coloured identity as an expedient, short-term manoeuvre, something which could be abandoned once a more liberal spirit prevailed in white politics.

The white division between pro-Empire political parties and an Afrikaner party provided the small section of coloured people registered as voters (some 5.4 per cent in 1921) with a choice between quite different political and cultural identities. The APO aligned itself first with the pro-Empire, exclusively English-speaking Unionist Party and subsequently with the SAP, which in 1921 absorbed the former. Its fortnightly publication, *APO*, used English for at least three-quarters of the edition, with the Dutch section confined to the back pages. The choice of language medium was an important act in the establishment of an identity. From its humble beginnings Afrikaans was making rapid strides in winning recognition among white Afrikaans-speakers as a respectable language fit for public discourse. The *APO* nevertheless shunned it as being representative of lower-class status.[34] An *APO* editorial advised coloureds to

> endeavour to perfect themselves in English ... the language which inspires the noblest thoughts of freedom and liberty, the language that has the finest literature on earth and is the most universally useful of all languages. Let everyone ... drop the habit as far as possible, of expressing themselves in the barbarous Dutch that is too often heard.[35]

The most remarkable feature of the APO was nevertheless a political column 'Straatpraatjes' (Street talk), published in Cape Dutch/Afrikaans under the pseudonym of Piet Uithaalder. Its author was Abdurahman, a man who in public displayed a very negative attitude towards the language. Using this medium, he tried to redefine the political identity of Afrikaans-speaking coloureds who were in the process of becoming urbanised, while also attempting to persuade already urbanised coloureds to accept these people in their ranks.

In his first column Uithaalder introduced himself as a cattle herder from the Kat River settlement who had recently arrived in Cape Town and who was without a permanent job. 'Well, friends,' Uithaalder wrote, 'let me introduce myself. Piet Uithaalder is my name, I am unknown but I am one of the race so do not despise me.'[36] Uithaalder becomes a travelling reporter who attends the sessions of Parliament, registers outrage over the Afrikaner 'backvelders' from the northern provinces dominating Parliament, pours scorn on the attempts to use European descent as a code word for superior status and white privilege, rails against discrimination in education against coloureds, and excoriates those whites like farmers, politicians and publicans who use liquor to keep coloureds dependent, exploit their labour and use them as 'voting fodder'. Significantly, Uithaalder's foil in the column is Stoffel Francis, also a former cattle herder who had mastered English, 'the language of Shelley, Milton and Tennyson'. He clearly is the model figure – someone who was educated and was thus aspiring to the 'civilised status' which liberal whites considered to be the prerequisite for equal rights.[37]

In contrast to Abdurahman's pro-Empire, pro-English strategy there were attempts by Afrikaner nationalist politicians to rally the coloureds behind a pro-South Africa, pro-Afrikaner banner. To win support they often used the term 'Afrikaner' to include coloureds, prompting Abdurahman to comment scornfully: 'The election is near and now one can hear of brother Afrikaner and fellow men, and the tot [of wine].'[38]

The NP opposition and the coloured vote, 1914–1924

Founded by General JBM Hertzog in 1914, the National Party (NP) from the start competed for the coloured vote. Despite opposition from his northern followers to political and economic equality between whites and coloureds, Hertzog refused to commit the party to wide-ranging discrimination against the coloureds. At the founding congress he objected to a proposal which elevated white workers to a special status, saying that sympathy and non-partisanship was the key to success, including in one's relations with coloured labourers.[39]

Hertzog stressed that the coloureds had to enjoy the same political and economic rights as whites. There could be no question of segregating them in these spheres, he said. They had to be treated 'honestly' and as friends. In the Cape Province all that needed to be done was 'to keep the natives away from the Coloureds', then the problem would solve itself. In 1919 he explained to delegates to the Free State NP congress: 'They [the coloured people] were not natives. They are born and educated in the midst of white civilisation and particularly among Dutch-speaking Afrikaners and they feel that the interests of the Dutch-speaking Afrikaners were their interests.'[40]

Someone who spoke in similar vein was DF Malan, leader of the Cape NP and editor of *Die Burger*. He depicted widespread poverty among Afrikaners and coloureds as an identical problem, the solution for which was to separate them from the Africans:

> For the Coloured, segregation was not possible but also unnecessary. The Coloured with the level of civilization he has already acquired constitutes no danger to the whites. If the Coloured realises that his interests and those of the white man are identical he will also make the right use of his vote to protect both himself and the white ... With the right counselling and sympathetic treatment the Coloured could become the bulwark and safeguard of the whites and white civilisation.[41]

Both Hertzog and Malan nonetheless rejected social integration between whites and coloureds. They did so primarily on the grounds that social segregation would induce educated coloureds to accept 'what they were' and prompt them to concern themselves with the rehabilitation of their 'own'. As Hertzog phrased it: 'The place of the educated Coloured is under his own people and not with the White man. He must serve his *volk*. That is true of the Afrikaner too: as soon as someone pretends to be something different from an Afrikaner we lose all respect for him.'[42] Leading Cape Nationalists, most particularly Malan, JHH de Waal and Bruckner de Villiers, used white rejection of social integration to develop their own ambiguous strategy towards the coloureds. On the one hand they hoped to attract coloured voters by pledging the party to pursue political equality for coloureds. On the other hand they urged coloureds to develop their own racial identity and promote their distinctive communal interests through institutions founded by themselves. In contrast to Hertzog, who rejected tampering with the coloured vote, Malan as early as 1919 proposed a separate roll for coloured voters to choose their own (white) representatives.

In 1919 the Cape NP embarked on a concerted effort to win coloured support. The leadership approached some APO dissidents who had broken with Abdurahman because of his support for the Unionists and his demand for the extension of the franchise to all blacks. They were asked to support the NP and some were offered employment in the newly founded Afrikaner insurance company, Sanlam. In October 1919 the APO dissidents formed the United Afrikaner League (UAL), pledging to support the NP and the principle 'Africa for the Afrikaner'. It appealed for equal economic opportunity and education for coloureds but gave no backing to the proposal for separate coloured representation.[43] The extent of popular support for the UAL is unknown.

Of greater historical interest was the UAL's NP-sponsored publication, *The Clarion*, a weekly paper set up in opposition to the APO and its publication. This paper claimed that it was owned, managed and edited by coloureds, but there is strong circumstantial evidence that it was published by *Die Burger*. Most of the paper was written in English except for those articles about coloured identity, which appeared anonymously or under a pseudonym in polished Afrikaans. Ostensibly authored by coloureds writing letters to the editor, most were probably the work of *Die Burger* journalists or NP politicians. Rather than an authentic articulation of identity, the articles should be considered primarily as an attempt by Afrikaner cultural entrepreneurs to break down the APO's pro-Empire, pro-English coloured identity and to construct in its place a (segregated) pro-Afrikaans, pro-NP identity for coloureds. As such, they represent an important elaboration of NP ideas about race and ethnicity.

Read together, the contributions on the issue of identity displayed a particular line of thinking. Firstly, there was an open acknowledgement of the fluidity of racial and ethnic identities. As one of the correspondents, 'Kleurling', remarks: 'Some of us are totally white and once we have reached this level both sides [Afrikaans-speaking and English-speaking whites] are keen to claim us, but when we are yellow or brown we have trouble.'[44] In the second place there was an attempt to model the construction of a coloured identity on that of the Afrikaners, who were then in the process of successfully mobilising politically on the basis of a putative pure racial identity and the Afrikaans language. An unsigned article in Afrikaans under the heading 'The coloured as entity' exhorted coloureds to be proud of their history, strive towards unity and guard against racial degeneration. It observed: 'Once whites became aware that they were dealing with a community who was pure and elevated in it [*sic*] sphere they would extend a helping hand to Coloureds who wished to attain an ideal along the lines of developing on their own. The result would be that their political power would be greater.'[45]

Ultimately the attempt to develop a single line of thought broke down because it was impossible to develop consensus about the significance of racial differences. A letter written by someone with the pseudonym 'Pure me' took issue with 'The coloured as entity', arguing that culture weighed heavier than race. The author declared boldly:

> It is my contention that, should we wish to speak of the Coloureds as an entity, it is more the tie of language which binds us than the tie of blood. The Coloureds are Afrikaners who speak the Afrikaans language and nothing else... Now that the Afrikaans language is increasingly becoming a written language, the Coloureds feel themselves to be of greater worth. Even the Bible is now printed in Afrikaans. We feel very glad and grateful about this.[46]

The obstacles to constructing a distinctive coloured identity were formidable. Coloureds laboured under a dual disability: their mixed descent and their supposed lack of cultural development. A correspondent wrote that whites despised coloureds despite the fact that both the English and Dutch had procreated them. To overcome this burden, coloureds had to develop their own culture by promoting Dutch or Afrikaans as their own language. The correspondent continued: 'We must learn to speak Dutch in our houses with our children and take it further in the schools. This would prove a strong foundation for unity among our generation.'[47] Yet another correspondent exhorted coloureds to use Afrikaans. 'This would indicate', he continued, 'that the Coloured community still has a soul which finds expression in their own language. We should guard against allowing the usefulness of speaking English becoming a matter of despising one's own. We should remember the saying "*Die taal is gans die volk*" (Language constitutes the entire *volk*). A *volk* without a language is an impossibility.'[48]

The Clarion also grappled with the question whether coloureds should accept a form of political self-segregation in order to advance their own interests more successfully. It published an editorial calling for a system in which coloured people would elect their own (coloured) representatives on a separate voters' roll. It pointed out that by using the existing electoral formula coloured voters would be able to elect 17 representatives and hold the balance of power between the white parties. 'Yes', it said, 'we fight for nationalism among the Coloureds... respect for our race, the education of our children, the rehabilitation of our *volk* and our economic advancement.'[49]

This was a long-term vision to which the NP accorded a lower priority than winning coloured support in the following election. *The Clarion* often published articles in which Nationalist MPs appealed to interests which white and coloured Afrikaans-speakers shared. In one of these articles the Nationalist MP and Afrikaans writer JHH de Waal painted a picture in which the arch-enemy was British 'imperialists', the 'mining capitalists', the 'selfish fortune-seekers' and 'birds of passage'. Against them stood the 'permanent population' of which the coloured section was an indispensable part. De Waal's objection to the APO was that it aided the former against the latter, setting 'the Coloured population against their fellow-Afrikaners who speak the same language, have the same love for South Africa, have mostly the same history and interests, are hoodwinked by the same friends ... and find themselves in virtually all respects in the same position'.[50] De Waal accused the *APO* of spreading the same false stereotypes about the Afrikaners as the British imperialists did, depicting them as slave-holders and racists who wished to bring coloureds under the heel of Afrikaner republicanism and slavery. De Waal struck a sensitive chord when he said that the imperialists wanted to open the gates to British immigrants, who would take the bread out of the mouth of the 'sorely tried sons of the soil', both white and coloured.[51] Despite worsening unemployment, the Prime Minister had announced that the country would see large-scale British immigration. In the election of the 1920s the NP made much of this issue in addressing coloured audiences.

By the time of the 1921 election *The Clarion* had become openly pro-NP. J Grainger Rossouw issued a call to 'Coloured Afrikaners' to vote for the NP. He declared:

> Your vote is to decide whether you hand over your tools to the Immigrants and kill your family by starvation or to stand shoulder to shoulder with those who say: 'Africa and all its interests for the Afrikaners' ... Let us say, Nationalist, in spite of your bitter prejudice against our people we are going to trust you and put our lives in your hands.[52]

Occasionally articles from *Die Burger* were reprinted which argued that the political alienation of coloureds from Afrikaners was a recent phenomenon. They claimed that once the Afrikaner Bond won power in the Cape Colony's parliament in 1898, its policies had proved so acceptable that the coloured vote helped it to clinch marginal seats.⁵³ The articles wanted to counter the APO's construction of coloured history and identity in a way that presented the Afrikaners entirely in a negative light. They called for a new narrative which told of the bonds between slaveholders and their slaves which had continued after slavery and of farmers donating large sums of money for the Rhenish Mission church in Stellenbosch. 'The history of our old Boland and Boland *volk* is worth researching again', wrote a correspondent. 'Let our old people dust off the old stories and tell them to produce not alienation but *toenadering* [rapprochement] between the white and Coloured Afrikaners.'⁵⁴

The NP was unsuccessful in the 1921 election and *The Clarion* immediately afterwards ceased publication. The NP nevertheless did not give up on the coloured vote. Just before or just after the 1924 election Malan, De Villiers and other Cape NPs helped coloured dissidents to form the Afrikaanse Nasionale Bond (ANB). The DF Malan papers at the University of Stellenbosch contain a draft document of 21 pages in Malan's handwriting of the ANB's constitution. It reflects much of the *Clarion*'s confused thinking about concepts such as race, *volk*, nation and coloured identity. It stated that the ANB identified itself 'with the aspirations of the South African *volk*' and represents more specifically 'the non-European population'. The three 'main races' (whites, coloureds and natives) had an inalienable right to be considered component parts of the South African *volk*.⁵⁵ The ANB would promote both political equality and a spirit of independence and self-respect among coloureds. It demanded segregation to protect white and coloured persons with a civilised standard of living against unequal and unreasonable competition from Africans. The ANB's publication *Die Bond*, which appeared only in 1926, paid far less attention to the issue of Afrikaans culture than had *The Clarion*. After pointing out in the first issue that only five per cent of coloureds in the Cape Peninsula understood Dutch, it used virtually only English in the few other issues which appeared.⁵⁶

To complement the ANB, the Cape NP leadership also helped to found an insurance company, the Kleurling Versekeringsmaatskappy (the Coloured Insurance Company), and a separatist church, the Volkskerk. The ANB leadership did not disappoint the NP. It echoed the party's concern about social segregation and a distinctive coloured identity. 'We want', its leader declared, 'to build up a race that the Europeans would be proud of.' The ANB rejected *samesmelting* (fusion) between coloureds and Africans because it wanted 'to look after, first of all, our own', and 'cultivate a spirit of national pride' in co-operation with whites. In evidence to a select committee of Parliament it proposed that the term 'coloured' in a bill before the House be changed to 'Eurafrican'.[57] By 1928 the Bond's membership was estimated by Abdurahman at 10,000.

The Pact government and the coloured vote, 1924–1932

The NP contested the 1924 election in the Pact alliance with the Labour Party. Using Hertzog's policy of equal political and economic rights for coloureds with whites rather than the argument for separate coloured representation, the alliance attracted some coloured support in its electoral victory.[58] After the election *Die Burger* wrote that the most educated coloureds voted against the Smuts government.[59] Heading up the Pact government, Hertzog immediately embarked on implementing his policy of segregation. It had two objectives: rehabilitating poor whites and safeguarding white survival through disfranchising Africans. For the NP, rehabilitation of the white poor was a priority because it believed that their large numbers threatened continuing white domination. 'It was in order to deal with [poor whiteism]', declared Hertzog just after taking power, 'that he advocated his so-called segregation policy.'[60] It nevertheless was common cause between Smuts's South African Party (SAP) and the NP that the rehabilitation of indigent whites should not occur at the expense of the coloureds. As Smuts phrased it just after the election, he had no objection to such a scheme, but 'in helping our poor whites . . . we must see that no injustice is done to any other section of the community'.[61]

The NP was bound by its election promise to put coloureds on an equal footing with the whites.[62] Prime Minister Hertzog stated that whites and the 'more civilised' coloureds would enjoy preference on the railways and in other public works over 'the less civilised native'. Coloureds would be treated equally with whites in all aspects of economic policy, down to Land Bank loans for coloured farm settlements.[63] But the NP's desire to uplift whites and more particularly Afrikaners outweighed its commitment to equal treatment for coloureds. In the provision of social services the new government was prepared to spend more on coloured welfare but it also declared that the quite different living standards of whites and coloureds justified a lower level of government service to the latter.

For the government, economic equality meant the acceptance that coloureds, along with whites, had a higher claim than Africans on jobs in the industrial economy. This did not mean equal access or, for that matter, equal wages.

Despite the 'civilised labour' policy, which granted a privileged position to whites and the more educated and skilled coloureds on the railways and in other public works, government circulars made it clear that juvenile white labour had to be given preference where possible. In 1926 a cabinet minister announced that it was never the intention to pay coloureds equal wages, adding: 'The Coloured man is different from the white man in his standard of civilization . . . and must be treated accordingly.' Ten years later the Mayor of Johannesburg told a government commission that he interpreted the 'civilised labour' policy to mean the employment of whites.[64]

Other disabilities continued to weigh heavily upon the coloureds. Because education was not made compulsory for coloureds, only 785 coloured children as against 13,128 white children in 1927 completed the first year of secondary education – the educational standard which the Apprenticeship Act of 1921 laid down for entry to trades. As a result the large majority of coloured youths were excluded from skilled work. Coloured workers could resort to undercutting wages but this was made much more difficult by Acts passed in 1924–5 which provided the means for establishing uniform wages for certain categories of work. These Acts pushed up minimum wages and prompted employers to pay the higher wages to whites.[65] The effect of all this was that coloureds in both the public and private sector received wages half or less than half of those of their white counterparts.[66]

The Pact government nevertheless brought some improvements for coloureds. On the mines new opportunities opened up because certificates of competency could now be issued to coloured as well as white men. NR Veldsman, leader of the ANB, held this up as evidence that the government regarded the coloured man as a 'civilised man', and 'an integral part of the civilisation of the country'.[67] In industry the number of coloured workers increased by 9 per cent as against 14 per cent for whites during the last half of the 1920s. *Die Burger* claimed that the number of coloured workers on the railways doubled during the first four years of the Pact government while those of whites trebled, but these figures are contradicted by other sources.

Coloured children at school increased by 30 per cent and the amount spent on coloured education by approximately 60 per cent.[68] But despite the increased spending, the differentials between white and coloured education remained the same. The government introduced old age pensions for coloureds as well as whites, but while the maximum for whites was £30, that of coloureds was only £18.[69]

Africans fared worse under the 'civilised labour' policy, but the gap between the somewhat more privileged coloureds and Africans at the bottom of the ladder began to narrow because of intensifying discrimination against all who were not white. A commission found that while the coloured elite identified with European values and standards, they strongly sympathised with Africans 'as sharing with them the lot of a suppressed people with whom in many ways they can make common cause'.[70]

It was the other leg of Hertzog's segregation policy, disfranchising Cape Africans, which would ultimately destroy the NP's commitment to political and economic equality for coloureds. With African children outnumbering white children in the Cape Province by nearly two to one, Hertzog believed that if the African vote was not taken away, white civilisation in the longer run would be handed over to the 'tender mercies of barbarism'.[71] However, the political fortunes of the NP were as much at stake as the future of 'white civilisation'. The NP calculated that Africans voting as a bloc for the SAP handed that party between 12 and 17 seats on a platter. Even if this estimate was an exaggeration, it could hardly be denied that the African vote, which was projected to double over the next fifteen years, could materially affect the outcome of a general election. In the 1924 election the NP country-wide won only eleven more seats than the SAP, while in the Cape Province the SAP enjoyed a seven seat majority over the NP.

With the provincial councils controlling schools, this meant, in the words of *Die Burger*, that black voters would decide the future of white children's education.[72] Even the more liberal *Cape Times* warned that the African vote would eventually mean 'either a Parliament dominated by black voters or the break-up of Union possibly by way of a bloody civil war'.[73]

The segregation package proposed by Hertzog entailed putting African voters on a separate roll and, as some form of exchange, allowing Africans in all four provinces to acquire more land and choose seven white parliamentary representatives. Coloured men in the Cape and Natal would retain their franchise while coloured men in the Free State and Transvaal would be allowed to elect one white representative. Over the longer run the NP leadership envisaged extending the franchise to coloured women along with white women and to give the full franchise to coloureds in the ex-republics. 'It would be foolish', Hertzog noted, 'to drive the Coloured people into the arms of the enemies of the Europeans – and that will happen if we expel him, if we allow him eventually to come to rest in the arms of the native.'[74]

It was the fear of Africans which prompted the party to propose the extension of the vote to a non-white group although most of the group opposed it. Hertzog needed the support of Smuts and the SAP for pushing his package through Parliament. Confronted by opposition both on his right and his left, Smuts hesitated. 'I see nothing but darkness before me, and unless I see clear light I shall not walk a step.'[75]

In talks Hertzog and Smuts groped for ways to reach a compromise. Both wanted to expand the white political base on the basis of culture rather than race, but both thought that all whites were 'civilised' and, as such, entitled to vote. Both believed that although there were large numbers of coloureds who deserved the vote, many others were in no respect superior to 'raw natives' and thus not entitled to equal rights with whites. However, they could reach no agreement on where to draw the electoral line among people who were not white. Hertzog favoured a blanket exclusion of Africans while Smuts in his confidential talks with Hertzog held up the ideal of a common franchise all over South Africa which would not involve any colour distinctions. It would be a qualified franchise based on occupation and income or salary, and the qualifications had to be high enough to exclude the great mass of Africans. In addition to this common qualification there also had to be an education and civilisation test, 'the presumption being that the European was civilised and that the Non-European had to prove his adoption of European civilisation'.[76] In public Smuts declared to the APO: 'to my mind there is only one principle. That is the one enunciated many years ago by Mr Rhodes – the principle of equal rights for all civilised men.'[77] Yet in a speech during the 1929 election campaign he denied that the SAP favoured an equal franchise for whites and Africans alike in a system of qualified voting. He added: 'The natives do not claim and the whites certainly will not concede any such claim.'[78]

Hertzog's segregation proposals were also fraught with difficulties. Recounting a conversation with Hertzog, Arthur Barlow wrote that the NP leader, in thinking about extending the coloured vote to the north, contemplated some kind of 'stud book'. He was after 'the more educated people among Malays and the Cape Coloureds . . . He wished to build up a sort of *herrenvolk* among these people.'[79] Even more difficult was the task of drawing a line between coloureds and Africans, something the NP had all along believed was essential for carrying out its policy of incorporating coloureds politically and economically with whites. But how to distinguish between Africans and coloureds? Hertzog pretended it was a simple matter. On one occasion he said: 'The Coloured person, except that he is brown, has practically nothing in common with the native.'[80] Given the fluidity of coloured identity, it was in fact an infinitely more intricate matter, and the failure to find an acceptable definition for the coloureds was soon to lead the NP to abandon its commitment to political equality for them.

In February 1929, while the election campaign was already under way, the government proposed two interdependent bills, the one disfranchising Cape Africans and the other extending the vote on a limited basis to coloured men in the northern provinces – the Transvaal and Free State. The latter bill introduced 'revision boards' with a duty to provide a list of coloured voters and remove Africans from it. The definition of a coloured was vague and full of loopholes. Opposition speakers pointed out that in terms of the law it was possible that one brother in a family could be defined as a coloured and another as an African. Smuts declared that the distinction was 'absurd and arbitrary'.[81] Even more important, it became clear in the parliamentary debate that coloureds in the Cape Province were also required to appear before a board to be certified as eligible voters. Opposition speakers pointed out that if a 'superior civilisation' was the only qualification for the vote, coloureds were entitled to vote in exactly the same way as whites – as had always been the case.[82]

In the 1929 election campaign the NP made a determined effort to capture the coloured vote. The party firstly based its appeal for support on policies that benefited coloureds. At ANB meetings speakers observed that more had been done during the previous five years for coloured education than in the past fifteen years. At APO meetings some speakers were not prepared to condemn the Pact government unreservedly and made special mention of the inclusion of coloureds when the Pact government introduced old age pensions. In the second place the NP tried to drive a wedge between coloureds and Africans, who were penetrating the Western Cape in growing numbers. It argued that racial equality threatened coloureds most because they were in so much weaker a position than whites. Already they were being squeezed out of jobs which had previously been exclusively theirs. It was in the mutual interests of whites and coloureds to stand together, the NP declared.[83]

The NP was returned to power in the 1929 election and won the seats of Stellenbosch and Paarl with coloured support. The coloured supporters of Bruckner de Villiers, who won Stellenbosch, even carried him shoulder-high up the steps of Parliament and deposited him in the lobby amidst the cheers of the Cape Nationalists.[84] However, the party was greatly disappointed with the coloured backing it had received. *Die Burger* estimated that in the urban seats of the Cape Province, less than 10 per cent of the coloureds voted NP. By contrast, more than 60 per cent of SAP support in these seats came from coloureds and Africans. After the election Paul Sauer, a leading NP member, told an ANB congress: 'The services of the Government during the past five years had merited better support from the Coloured community.'[85] But why did the NP not do better? It had in fact bestowed more socio-economic patronage on the coloureds than any previous government. Three of the ANB leaders, Veldsman, Azared Gamiet and Christian Dantu, are described by the historian Richard van der Ross as influential men in their community. During the election of 1929 the ANB held several large meetings.[86] The NP did not publicly analyse the main causes of its failure to win coloured support, but an important reason undoubtedly was the proposed revision boards, which would register coloured voters on the basis of descent. Speaking in the debate on the bill which introduced revision boards, Smuts observed that coloureds were unanimous about retaining the status quo rather than embarking on the 'dangers and doubts of the policy embodied in the bill'.[87]

In the aftermath of the election Malan also pointed to this factor. Referring to the attempt to separate coloureds and Africans, he said that SAP 'misrepresentations' had made the coloureds afraid of the NP.[88] 'The Coloureds were told that they would have to go to court to prove their parentage . . . In this way prejudice had been created among the Coloured against the government's policy under which the Coloureds would really be favourably treated.' Coloured people, Malan continued, should go to the polls not as coloured men but as citizens of South Africa. The idea of separate representation had to be rejected because 'it would lead to the creation of a definite racial group'.[89] But the problem would not go away. In the debate on the Women's Enfranchisement Bill of 1930, which extended the vote to white but not coloured women, Hertzog declared that coloureds were excluded partly on account of white prejudice and partly because Parliament had failed to agree on a definition of a coloured person. The bill, first tabled in 1926, extending the vote to coloured people in the northern provinces, did define a coloured,[90] but had to be withdrawn because the Pact failed to get the necessary two-thirds majority to pass it. Speaking in the debate on the Women's Enfranchisement Bill, Hertzog said: 'We can only give rights to the coloured person if we know who a coloured person is . . . However much I may wish or not wish the coloured women to have the franchise, we cannot do it, because the necessary stipulations, as to who is a coloured person and who is a native, have not been put on the statute book.'[91] In fact the government had already given up three years previously when it banned sexual intercourse between whites and Africans, but exempted coloureds from the Act. In 1931 the Franchise Laws Amendment Act introduced universal suffrage for white men in the Cape but retained the existing educational and property qualifications for coloured and African men. As a result of these two Acts the proportion of coloured voters in the Cape Province dropped from 11 per cent to 6 per cent.

The NP's switch meant the end of the road for the ANB. The disillusioned members dissolved the organisation. Its leader, W le Grange, denounced both coloured 'radicals' and Malan for his betrayal of coloureds.[92] The number of coloured voters remained stagnant until Malan's government removed them from the common voters' roll in the 1950s.

So the process of coloured disfranchisement began. Hertzog's move in 1930 was not a volte-face as historians have often claimed. Fearing African numbers, he and Malan had all along insisted on the separation of Africans from coloureds through some form of classification as a precondition for incorporating coloureds. Nor was coloured exclusion the outcome of a rising tide of racism. Coloureds in fact had experienced a lowering of the barriers of race under the Pact government. In his draft constitution for the ANB, Malan committed the organisation to fighting against unequal treatment, and De Villiers said at a public meeting during the 1929 campaign that where coloureds and whites were employed next to each other, ability rather than race should determine remuneration.[93]

In the 1929 election the NP discarded its Pact ally, the (white) Labour Party, which De Villiers pejoratively called a 'wooden leg', hoping to compensate for this by winning coloured support.[94] Even the rejection of the NP by coloured voters in the 1929 election must not be given too much weight as an explanation for the NP reneging on its promise to extend the coloured vote. At the Cape NP congress, held three months after the election, Malan rejected a proposal for separate representation for coloureds. Arguing that coloured and white interests were identical, he rejected a system whereby coloureds had to vote according to their own racial interests.[95] Coloured disfranchisement occurred above all because the contraction of the vote developed a dynamic of its own. Reduced to a mere six per cent of the Cape electorate, the coloured vote had become quite insignificant. When Malan and several other Cape NPs broke with Hertzog in 1933–4 to form a 'Purified' NP, they could propose separate representation for coloureds without any real costs.

The fact that the new line of political demarcation was not preceded by an upsurge in racist thinking or a more exclusive definition of ethnic identity confirms Horowitz's suggestion that the contraction of boundaries is not so much the product of the cultural mix of a particular group but of the calculation that party leaders in democratic systems make about gains which can be achieved by exclusion. It was after the political abandonment of the coloureds that the Afrikaner nationalist intelligentsia embarked vigorously on the project of proclaiming an exclusive Afrikaner identity. The secret organisation of the Nationalist elite, the Afrikaner Broederbond, took on a new lease of life to propagate the idea of Afrikaner domination of South Africa. Afrikaans writers, poets and historians now strongly identified with the ethnic movement which gathered momentum in the 1930s. It championed the language of Afrikaans as a modern, European, white language, not something which had developed as a medium of communication for whites, slaves and Khoikhoi over nearly three centuries. During the time of the Pact government, Malan and De Waal publicly thanked Muslims in Cape Town for maintaining Afrikaans by the turn of the century when whites had abandoned it.[96] During the 1930s such sentiments were no longer expressed in Nationalist circles. The emphasis was now on the historical exclusivity of the Afrikaners, and their culture. Democratic politics determined culture, not culture democratic politics.

Franchise expansion

For 60 years after the legislation of the early 1930s, the coloured community faced a whirlwind of disfranchisement, enforced residential segregation, race classification and a ban on sexual intercourse with whites. With overwhelming majorities, successive generations of Afrikaner leaders endorsed these policies as being necessary for them to control the state and for coloureds to discover and develop their own 'identity'. At the same time, however, apartheid failed to obliterate the idea of white and coloured Afrikaans-speakers sharing the same identity and interests. In certain respects the system even strengthened it. The NP, which won power under Malan in 1948 and held it until 1994, made great play of the western part of the Cape Province as an area where coloured as well as white labour had to enjoy preference over Africans. The NP government also insisted that urbanising coloureds attend (segregated) Afrikaans schools, thus reversing the trend of anglicisation. Many Afrikaans-speakers harboured a degree of scepticism about apartheid for coloureds for the simple reason that it was patently absurd to believe that they could ever have a separate political destiny. In polls taken in the 1970s about half of the Afrikaners indicated that they considered an Afrikaans-speaking coloured as an Afrikaner. Several Afrikaans writers and academics propagated a non-racial definition of Afrikaner identity. For quite different reasons the Afrikaner nationalist elite, just like the coloured intelligentsia, rejected a racially inclusive definition of the term Afrikaner.[97]

While coloured people were in no hurry to declare themselves Afrikaners, a remarkable political convergence occurred between them and the Afrikaners between the early 1980s and the first fully inclusive election of 1994. The political development facilitating this process was the NP split of 1982. When the NP leadership decided to bring coloureds back into Parliament (separate representation for them was introduced in the late 1950s and abolished in the late 1960s), a conservative NP faction under Andries Treurnicht objected to any dilution of political apartheid. The NP leadership took the view as expressed by the editor of the party's propaganda sheet that 'we must at any price align the Coloured people as a bloc of 2.5 million behind the Whites to broaden our power base and thus avoid turning them over to a black power situation'.[98] Although the Tricameral Constitution of 1983 was a severely contested issue, many coloured people gave the NP credit for its willingness to split over the issue of coloured parliamentary representation.

A second development that made for convergence was the socio-economic advance of coloured people. Coloured fertility dropped from over 6 per cent in the late 1960s to under 3 per cent in the late 1980s. Patronage under the Tricameral Parliament also facilitated coloured progress. More than 100,000 houses were built in the period 1984 to 1993. Education improved significantly. The number of children in secondary school increased by a third while the number of successful matriculants doubled. Between the early 1970s and early 1990s the mean income of the top 60 per cent of coloureds increased by about 20 per cent.[99] Far from becoming radicalised, most coloured people wanted to protect the gains they had made.

The third development was a rapid, often chaotic influx of close to a million Africans into the Cape Town metropolitan area during the 1980s. The severe shortage of houses and lack of good schools for Africans caused coloureds to fear that their homes and schools were at risk. There was also the perception that under an African National Congress government, Africans would be favoured by both the state and private employers to the detriment of coloureds.

Once multi-party negotiations had started in 1990, the NP realised it would desperately need coloured votes in a future non-racial election.[100] The NP leadership now promptly embraced a non-racial definition of the term Afrikaner and branded as racists those conservatives who clung to an exclusive definition. In a joint sitting of the white, coloured and Indian chambers of Parliament, the NP's Transvaal leader, Barend du Plessis, asked: 'Are those Hon. [coloured] members sitting there not Afrikaners?' Treurnicht responded that the Afrikaner people had been known for more than two and a half centuries as the Afrikaans-speaking whites of South Africa. This prompted Du Plessis to state: 'They [the coloureds] speak the way we do. They believe the way we do. They live the way we do. Why does he say they are not Afrikaners? He says he is not a racist.'[101]

While in 1929 the NP did not win much more than 10 per cent of the coloured vote, in the 1994 'liberation election' roughly two-thirds of coloureds in the Western Cape voted for the NP as against not more than a quarter who voted for the ANC and not more than 5 per cent who voted for the Democratic Party (DP). A straight comparison between the elections of 1929 and 1994 is not possible since the 1929 election was fought not only over the issue of race but also over South Africa's relationship with Britain, on which both the SAP and the APO put a high premium. Nevertheless, some comparative points seem in order. To start with the hypothesis of Lipset cited at the beginning of this chapter, the Afrikaners in the early 1990s were much more ready to entertain the idea of extending the vote to coloureds than they had been in the early 1930s. Sixty years previously there were large numbers of destitute and poorly educated Afrikaners and coloureds who were in direct competition with each other. By the early 1990s, in contrast, the Afrikaners of the Western Cape had largely become a settled middle class whose superior education as a result of the apartheid system gave them a head start over coloureds and Africans in the marketplace. The Afrikaner and larger white community now eagerly welcomed as allies the coloureds, whose embourgeoisement was well under way.

There are also some other comments which can be made about the election campaigns in the Western Cape in 1929 and 1994. In both elections the coloured vote was considered crucial, but in 1929 the coloureds formed only 10 to 15 per cent of the Cape Province vote while in 1994 they formed 57 per cent of Western Cape voters. In 1929 the APO and the ANB campaigned separately for the SAP and NP respectively, and the two parties held segregated meetings for coloured voters. In 1994 there were no separate coloured political organisations, and the NP, ANC and DP spent most of their resources in the Western Cape on canvassing coloureds. At public meetings outside the African townships, coloureds formed the majority of the audiences. There were a few endorsements by predominantly coloured organisations – the largest Muslim body and some trade unions backed the ANC while an alliance of Pentecostal churches supported the NP – but they did not seem to have affected the outcome.

The way in which party support linked up with different segments in the coloured population also needs to be examined. In 1929 the SAP drew support from the English-speaking coloureds while spokesmen for the NP after both the 1924 and 1929 elections declared that the party managed to attract 'the more developed' coloureds.[102] In the absence of concrete evidence, one can only presume that the NP following consisted mostly of Afrikaans-speaking teachers. In 1994 the NP targeted the less qualified coloured workers vulnerable to competition. Abe Williams, the coloured politician highest on the NP list, repeated the message that Africans would get jobs ahead of coloureds. He asked: 'Are we going to pay a price yet again because of the colour of our skin? Are we going to pay a price because we speak Afrikaans, not Xhosa?'[103] For better qualified coloureds this appeal fell on deaf ears. The ANC far outstripped the NP among coloured graduates and did slightly better among matriculants. By contrast, the NP drew four times more support than the ANC among those with a Standard 8 or less.[104]

A final comment can be made about the vote and social identity. In 1929 the APO propagated an identity which was pro-Empire and pro-English and anti-racist and anti-Afrikaner. But the SAP was only interested in the coloureds at election time while the ANC wanted the APO as an ally in its struggle but made it clear at the conferences which Abdurahman organised between 1927 and 1934 that it would not allow the ANC to be supplanted as 'the leader of the native people'.[105] The APO was thus compelled to mobilise a coloured identity. Ironically the organisation was successful precisely when a white party like the NP wanted to use the state to compel coloureds, a group with such fluid boundaries, to assume a distinct statutory identity. It was probably the main reason for the NP's failure in 1929 to make any headway among coloured voters.

But many people in a vulnerable group like the coloureds may want a strong ally which can fend for it in the divided society of South Africa. Writing in the mid-1980s, Richard van der Ross noted that the ANB's spirit had not died out altogether. Basic to the ANB's politics was the assumption that 'the British were here only temporarily or for their own interests' and that the coloureds' best interests were served by aligning themselves with the 'Boers' with whom they had so many things in common. 'While less refined [the Boer] was at heart more sincere and honest in his dealings with the Coloured people.'[106] The untold suffering and injury inflicted by apartheid would put these feelings to a severe test, but with South Africa starkly polarised racially by the end of the 1980s and the beginning of the 1990s, coloured people saw themselves as being compelled to choose sides between whites and Africans, and between the NP with its Afrikaans image and the DP with its English image.

In the election campaign of 1994 the ANC tried its best to persuade coloureds that it was the natural champion of liberation and non-racialism. As a movement which rejected any political expression of ethnicity, the ANC had great difficulty coming to terms with coloured identity. Almost all its coloured representatives were people who did not want to be considered coloured. Its vague and contradictory message of non-racialism appealed primarily to the thin upper layer of well-educated coloured people without any job insecurity. For most coloureds, especially the less educated, the ANC's identity was revolutionary, English and black, while that of the DP represented wealth and Englishness. Van der Ross, who was one of the DP's candidates, concluded that coloureds decided that 'they had a greater affinity for De Klerk than Mandela and for the Afrikaners than the English'.[107]

The NP projected itself as a party that was Afrikaans, conservative and committed to maintaining both white and coloured identities and interests. It even offered itself as a vehicle for coloured mobilisation. Anwar Ismael, a coloured NP organiser, articulated a new sense of coloured empowerment as follows: 'We [the coloured people] are the majority here and we shall determine the course of the election. We speak Afrikaans, we live as conservatives, attend church and raise our children on traditional values. Hence we are National Party. The Xhosa of Transkei and the ANC are the real settlers here. The ANC with its black profile and Communist cloak repels us.'[108] De Klerk and other NP leaders frequently apologised to the coloured community for the hurt and suffering apartheid had caused. At the same time they urged coloureds to see the election as a vote for the future, not the past. For the NP leadership the past was another country. After the 1992 Cape NP congress, which was the first one attended by coloured and African members, the Cape leader, Dawie de Villiers, said in private: 'We were there united as a group – I cannot imagine that it ever had been different.'[109]

Conclusion

The political lines of demarcation in the case of both the American South and South Africa's Western Cape remained fluid for a considerable period after the abolition of slavery. While both blacks and indigent whites were disfranchised in the American South, white demographic weakness in South Africa generated a quite different response. Here the determination to 'save' poor whites was the driving force behind the segregationist policies of the 1920s and 1930s.

What is striking in both the United States and South Africa is that democratic politics shaped culture and ideology rather than the other way round. Extreme racism only engulfed the American South after 1890 when the process of franchise contraction was well under way.[110] In the Western Cape the 'purified' Afrikaner culture and identity only made headway after the coloured vote had been emasculated in 1931. In both these regions a redefinition of the boundaries of the political system and of white interests and values set black democratic rights back for many decades. Yet once political exigencies forced Southerners and Afrikaners to open up the political system, social identities again became fluid. This made possible the vigorous competition for votes which is the essence of democracy.

2.

The making of the apartheid plan, 1929-1948

For a concept that has dominated South African politics for the past fifty to sixty years, some aspects of apartheid have a remarkably obscure history. To start with the simple question: where and how did the term originate? Hexham records an early but eccentric use of the term in Potchefstroom in 1905.[111] Davenport and Saunders accept the view of Nic Rhoodie that the term originated during the 1930s in the Transvaal in the circles in which MC de Wet Nel, a later cabinet minister, moved.[112] Both these ascriptions ignore the much stronger claim of the Rev. JC du Plessis that he was responsible for the first recorded use of the term in the sense in which it became accepted in the 1940s. In 1929, while a Dutch Reformed Church (DRC) minister in the Orange Free State, he addressed a DRC conference on the 'native question' held in Kroonstad. Rejecting a missions policy that offered blacks no 'independent national future', he pleaded for Christianity to be introduced in a way that fitted the African 'character, nature and nationality'. He said, 'In the fundamental idea of our missionary work and not in racial prejudice one must seek an explanation for the spirit of apartheid that has always characterised our [the DRC's] conduct.'[113]

It was only in the early 1940s that the idea of apartheid crystallised. *Die Burger* first used the term 'apartheid' in 1943 when it referred to the 'accepted Afrikaner viewpoint of apartheid'.[114] In January 1944, DF Malan, speaking as leader of the opposition, became the first person to employ it in the South African Parliament. A few months later he elaborated, 'I do not use the term "segregation", because it has been interpreted as a fencing off (*afhok*), but rather "apartheid", which will give the various races the opportunity of uplifting themselves on the basis of what is their own.'[115]

There also exists no consensus on what the policy represented in the larger scheme of things. Was it simply an extension of the 'traditional' policy of segregation and a marginal refinement of the racial ideology that justified segregation? Was it a modern ideology justifying Afrikaner domination in an era of decolonisation? Or was it something deviant that appealed to the same racist obsessions as those of the Nazis and to a heretical interpretation of the Bible that had never been used before?

Shortly after the 1948 election, Arthur Keppel-Jones, a young liberal historian, unequivocally declared that apartheid was simply a warmed-up version of segregation. 'One of the psychological curiosities of our history is the sudden substitution of the word apartheid for the word segregation, which means the same thing.' It was a case of 'same firm, same product, new label'.[116] More than fifty years later, a general history expressed almost the same opinion: 'It was really an elaboration of earlier segregationist traditions derived partly from Stallardism, partly from the thinking of Broederbond circles in the 1930s.'[117] The historian Legassick proposed a variation on the theme in suggesting that apartheid was an adaptation of traditional labour policy and practices to an economy whose base had shifted from mining to manufacturing.[118] O'Meara argues that apartheid developed as a plan to secure a stable and cheap labour supply for farmers and the emerging class of Afrikaner capitalists.[119] Posel's work opened up a new perspective in depicting apartheid as a policy and ideology largely shaped by post-1948 struggles within the Nationalist movement.[120] But she, too, saw conflicts over the labour supply and influx control as of paramount importance rather than the quest to find a justification for Afrikaner political domination.

The analysis by AJ Gregor was one of the first to project apartheid as a novel, post-Second World War ideology that went well beyond a justification for labour control in the specific South African circumstances. Written in the mid-1960s as part of a study of radical ideologies, it depicted apartheid as a secular social and political ideology typical of the twentieth century. 'It advances its own normic model of man and society, defends its models by appeals to science and experience, and employs that model in justificatory arguments in support of policy.'[121] Norval argued that apartheid was about formulating 'a new moral language' with which to legitimise the project of radically restructuring society. Whereas segregation worked with the notion of race, the essence of apartheid was the family, the community and the ethnic group formed by both racial descent and the *volkseie* – the beliefs, customs, language and history of a community.[122] Where Norval emphasises the *volkseie*, Dubow highlights Christian Nationalism as the core concept in the new moral discourse; both attach considerable importance to the racist thought of Geoff Cronjé and others.[123]

Table 2.1: Percentage responses to the question whether the basic idea of apartheid was good (2001)

	True	Not true	Don't know
All South Africans	39	55	6
Afrikaners	65	29	6
White English	36	60	4
Xhosa-speaking	18	73	9
Zulu-speaking	25	65	10

Although they are not discussed in the existing literature, GBA Gerdener, the main mission strategist of the Dutch Reformed Church, and NP van Wyk Louw, the premier man of Afrikaans letters, had, I would argue, a more lasting influence than any of the so-called Afrikaner nationalist intellectuals in constructing apartheid as an idealistic project, or what Louw called a liberal nationalism as the basis for 'survival in justice'.[124] Louw taught in the Education Department at the University of Cape Town during the 1930s and 1940s while Gerdener was one of the founders of the DRC (black) Mission Church in the Transvaal in the early 1930s. He arrived in Stellenbosch at the end of the decade to take up a chair at the Theological School. These two men, together with Albert Geyer, Phil Weber and Piet Cillié (successive editors of *Die Burger* in Cape Town),[125] and Hendrik Verwoerd, formulated apartheid in its most sophisticated guise.

Van Zyl Slabbert, liberal academic and politician, remembers 'the excitement, even the thrill' of students when this variant of apartheid ideology was explained during his student years at the University of Stellenbosch in the early 1960s. With African states all over the continent becoming independent, apartheid looked like an indigenous, post-colonial response. As an ideology it had 'a coherence and systemic quality' which could not be dismissed as racism; it made 'logical sense and addressed some very prickly moral issues'.[126]

It is the idealistic variant of which Slabbert spoke that accounts for the resilience of the apartheid idea, even while most commentators think it is quite dead and discredited. At the end of 2001, the Institute for Reconciliation and Justice, founded to carry on the work of the Truth and Reconciliation Commission, asked in a poll for responses to this statement: 'There were certainly some abuses under the old apartheid system, but the ideas behind apartheid were basically good.' Surprisingly large proportions in all communities still thought the basic idea had been sound, with only a third of Afrikaners believing it was bad.[127] Table 2.1 gives the responses in full.

The poll question did not define apartheid, but it can be assumed that the African or coloured respondents did not yearn for undiluted white supremacy, but rather for the more refined apartheid version of the 1980s. According to this, each population group as designated by apartheid was held responsible for its 'own affairs', with representatives from each group sharing in decision-making about 'general affairs'. Other polls show that members of apartheid's statutory groups at present consistently name someone from their own group as their most popular leader.

Finally, there are the approaches that emphasise the way in which apartheid deviated from the mainstream teachings of the Christian church and Western European liberal democratic experience. Moodie sees apartheid as conceived largely by exponents of a 'neo-Fichtean' romantic nationalism. He links this *volksnasionalisme* to German nationalism and National Socialism, and calls the belief that God made the Afrikaner people the object of his saving activity a 'Christian heresy'.[128] A recent study by Furlong makes the same connection between German and Afrikaner radical nationalism. It argues that Malan's National Party (NP), a paramilitary mass movement called the Ossewabrandwag (OB) and Oswald Pirow's New Order (NO) formed an 'interconnecting web'. The Nationalists in the Transvaal, in particular, while never becoming a Nazi-style movement 'in a real sense', represented a 'hybrid variant' of 'authoritarian and populist ingredients, reminiscent, although never an exact facsimile, of European fascism'. The study makes a strenuous and often tortuous effort to underline the similarities between apartheid and Nazism, for instance between apartheid's proscription of interracial sex and the Nazi race laws.[129]

This chapter will first look at Afrikaner nationalism in the northern and southern parts of the country in the 1930s and 1940s. It argues that the development and dissemination of apartheid as the operational ideology of Afrikaner nationalism was a project that originated in the church in the Orange Free State and in political and academic circles in the Western Cape rather than in the Transvaal-based Afrikaner Broederbond. It discusses this with reference to the debate in DRC mission circles, the efforts of the Cape NP and *Die Burger* to find a counter to the ideology of the ruling United Party (UP), and the intellectual contributions of Afrikaner academics in Stellenbosch and Cape Town.

A tale of two regions

There are two particularly strange features in the historiography of Afrikaner nationalism and the rise of the apartheid ideology during the 1930s and 1940s. The first is the assertion by Moodie and Furlong of a linkage between the Afrikaner nationalist movement and German nationalism of the 1930s. No one can quibble about the Ossewabrandwag and the New Order, but Malan's NP and the Afrikaner Broederbond are painted in similar, albeit more muted, colours. At a superficial level, the assertion may seem plausible. In the Transvaal, several prominent members of the Nationalist intelligentsia actively involved in elaborating a new racial ideology had Nazi sympathies, yet they later became stalwart members of the NP and the Afrikaner Broederbond establishment. This was true of LJ du Plessis, perhaps the most influential of all Broeders, HG Stoker, the leading Calvinist thinker, Piet Meyer, deputy secretary of the Bond, and Geoff Cronjé. They all published books and articles whose thinking resembled Nazi ideology.[130]

Yet any serious analysis must reject the linkage between German and Afrikaner nationalism, and André du Toit correctly comments that it is 'tenuous at best'.[131] From early 1942, before the apartheid plan had crystallised, Malan and other NP leaders, including Hendrik Verwoerd and JG Strijdom, had unequivocally rejected National Socialism as an alien import into South Africa, and had re-endorsed parliamentary democracy. The major Afrikaner church expressed a similar view. *Die Kerkbode*, influential official journal of the DRC, declared in March 1941 that 'the Church could never associate itself with any form of state domination or intervention as is found in the European totalitarian system, which undermines the Church in its freedom'.[132] In 1945, a day after Germany capitulated, *The Star*, which had been very critical of the NP during the war, declared, 'We do not suppose Dr Malan and disciples were ever Nazis at heart, or that they had any real affection for the Hitler regime.'[133]

In introducing apartheid legislation, the Nationalist leadership made it clear that their point of reference was the American South. Piloting through Parliament the Prohibition of Mixed Marriages Bill of 1949, Eben Dönges, Minister of the Interior, justified it by reference to the existence of a similar law in thirty states in the US.[134] In the two most important studies of the 1950s, those of Patterson[135] and Carter, little or no reference is made to a possible linkage between Nazism and apartheid. It is tempting to speculate that historians who made the comparison in the last quarter of the twentieth century suffered from the ailment Harrison Wright called 'the burden of the present'. With their much firmer comparative grasp than Furlong, sociologists Adam and Van den Berghe have dismissed comparisons with the totalitarian states in Central Europe, the latter arguing: 'Apartheid attempts to compartmentalise the country and perpetuate distinct racial and ethnic groups. A much closer parallel to South Africa than Nazi Germany or Fascist Italy is the southern part of the United States at the height of Jim Crow.'[136]

This theme links up with the historiography's other strange feature. This is the assumption in the studies of Moodie, O'Meara, Dubow and Furlong that northern-based intellectuals, most prominently Diederichs, Meyer, Stoker and Cronjé – Moodie's 'neo-Fichteans', Dubow's Christian Nationalists and Norval's Potchefstroom intellectuals – developed the apartheid ideology, and then succeeded in having it accepted by the NP national leadership, Afrikaner churches and the Afrikaner academic community. How this process actually worked is never really spelt out, but it seems as if there are two main assumptions: firstly, the Afrikaner Broederbond acted as the agency that spread and gained acceptance for these views across the country; secondly, the publications of the academics were extraordinarily influential.

Common sense suggests that this is implausible. After the political realignment of 1933–4, the NP at the national level was tightly controlled by DF Malan and a small group of advisors in the Western Cape; this continued until 1954. Nasionale Pers, publisher of *Die Burger* in Cape Town, towered over the other Afrikaans press companies and enjoyed such close personal ties with Malan that its editor was allowed to attend meetings of the NP's parliamentary caucus. With a considerable financial stake in the company that published *Die Transvaler*, the Cape NP leadership curbed Verwoerd when he advocated a republic too strenuously, a step that the northern intelligentsia strongly resented. To compound matters, Afrikaner financial power was concentrated in the south, with a growing proportion of Afrikaner savings attracted by Sanlam, the Cape Town-based insurance company, leaving little for aspiring Afrikaner entrepreneurs in the north.

Malan became a member of the Broederbond in 1933, but played no active role in it. None of his closest advisors – the circle includes Albert Geyer, editor of *Die Burger*, Willie Hofmeyr and Bruckner de Villiers, who served on the boards of Nasionale Pers and Sanlam, and the politicians Paul Sauer and Frans Erasmus – were members of the Broederbond. Geyer, who wielded great political influence, dismissed Diederichs, a key northern thinker, as a 'Nazi through-and-through'.[137] There is simply no evidence that the writings of Diederichs, Meyer, Cronjé and the Potchefstroom academics were taken particularly seriously in the south.

The leading Afrikaner nationalists in the south who shaped the apartheid ideology formed part of a relatively settled bourgeoisie. Unlike their counterparts in the north, they had been in contact for more than a century with English financial and commercial capitalism. There was no large, impoverished Afrikaner working class, and the two white communities had developed a tradition of a mutual tolerance. DF Malan, the Cape leader, disliked the neo-Calvinist obsession of the Potchefstroom-based Doppers with their 'pure' doctrine and abstract 'points of departure'.[138] He thought of the Afrikaners as having evolved as a distinct people, with their own religion, church, language and nationality, as the result of a particular historical process. In the Cape tradition, Malan, until the end of the 1920s, used the term 'Afrikaner' both inclusively, to denote 'all patriotic whites', and exclusively, for a particular ethnic group.

On the racial issue, the north tended to be dogmatic, rigid and uncompromising, with a strong overlay of racism. The south was much more ambiguous and very often hypocritical. Theoretically, coloured people could, over the long term, become part of the dominant group, but in practice they were held at arm's length. The southern Nationalists were racial pragmatists, sceptical of utopian solutions or biblical justifications of racial discrimination. They wanted to defend white supremacy by keeping different options open. Hard-core racism was a red herring that complicated the task of choosing between strategic alternatives.

The intelligentsia, prominent among whom were Albert Geyer and Phil Weber of *Die Burger*, the sociologists JFW Grosskopf and RW Wilcocks, who wrote reports for the Carnegie Commission, GBA Gerdener, HB Thom and AC Cilliers (and, later, PJ Schoeman, Nic Olivier, Barney van Eeden, PJ Coertze and Jan Sadie), were not attracted at all by the perversions and aberrations of Nazi scholarship or politics. Their frame of reference was the mainstream scholarship emanating from the Netherlands, Britain, the US and pre-Nazi Germany. They tended to use the term 'Afrikaner' in both an exclusive, ethnic sense and an inclusive sense that embraced white English-speakers. They tended to eschew talk of an 'organic nation'. Until the outbreak of the Second World War and the controversy about South Africa's participation, these academics were split right down the middle between Malan and Hertzog in their party affiliation. Subsequently, the overwhelming majority supported Malan and the construction of apartheid.[139]

The case of Hendrik Verwoerd is instructive. After his studies at Stellenbosch he spent 1926 in Germany and part of 1927 in the US before returning to South Africa for an academic career. There is no evidence that he had agreed with the racial ideology of the National Socialists in Germany. His lecture notes and memoranda at Stellenbosch stressed that there were no biological differences between the larger racial groups (or, for that matter, between Europeans and Africans), and since there were no differences, 'this was not really a factor in the development of a higher social civilisation by the Caucasian race'.[140] Like many of his colleagues, he was captivated by the new 'scientific' approach to curing social ills. In the US, attempts to address these questions through scientific inquiry and management were heralded as 'social engineering'. Afrikaner social scientists were attracted to this enterprise. During a visit to South Africa in the mid-1930s, Lord Hailey observed that 'South Africa regards itself as USA in the making'. Far from being a product of Nazi-style deviance, apartheid developed within the mainstream of pre-Second World War racism and social engineering enthusiasms in the West.

Contrary to the main assumption in the literature, the northern-based Afrikaner Broederbond and intellectuals influenced by Nazi thinking, in fact, contributed relatively little to the making of the apartheid plan. In 1934, a Bond sub-committee recommended 'comprehensive mass segregation' for blacks, but this did not differ significantly from mainstream segregation. The Bond established a sub-committee on the racial issue, but this could not report significant progress. Leading Bond members attended meetings of an Afrikaanse Bond vir Rassestudie, founded in 1935, but it foundered a few years later.

The 1938 Broederbond general conference (called the Bondsraad) felt that since a white consensus on policy towards blacks had already been formulated in legislation, their attention had to focus on policy towards coloureds. The Bond's Executive Council asked a sub-committee to identify an organisation to study the racial problem 'on behalf of Afrikanerdom'. But this request 'landed in the doldrums', as a Broederbond document noted.[141] In 1940, LJ du Plessis, one of the most prominent Broederbond academics, did not use the word 'apartheid' in an article on the 'native question'. He called segregation 'the national policy' which had not yet been fully implemented 'because Afrikanerdom had not yet had the chance to carry it out'.[142] Where the Broederbond, with its large contingent of teachers, lecturers and church ministers, did play a prominent role was in promoting Christian National education.

In 1944, the Bond organised a conference of cultural activists, academics and church leaders on the racial question. While some broad policy guidelines were suggested there, no practical policy was formulated. Two years later a plan had still not crystallised, and the Broederbond intelligentsia in the north were largely dispirited. Albert Hertzog, a Broederbond stalwart, despondently told the Bond's Executive Council in August 1946, '[The] Afrikaner people is without inspiration . . . and without that no power can emanate from it.' A year later he wrote in his diary that the NP was divided between a conservative Cape group and an idealistic northern group, among whom were Hendrik Verwoerd and JG Strijdom. He added: 'Unfortunately they are half-baked idealists who, except for a few vague principles, do not propose a major new direction.'[143]

At a 1947 Broederbond conference, basic disagreements about key aspects of racial policy surfaced. Speakers resigned themselves to the fact that Africans would remain part of the white socio-economic system for a long time. After the meeting, Bond secretary Ivan Lombard called the proceedings 'depressing', because no solutions had been suggested for the numerous problems identified. Ernst Stals, who enjoyed unrestricted access to the Broederbond archives for his unpublished study of the organisation, notes that the Broederbond agreed with, and supported, apartheid, but it did not develop and formulate it.[144]

We can now turn to the other, more important, sources from which the apartheid ideology drew.

'The spirit of apartheid': the DRC's faith

By 1930 the DRC had a broad record of missionary activity in countries such as Rhodesia, Kenya and the Sudan. However, its missionary efforts among Africans in South Africa itself lagged behind. The exception was the black DRC in the Orange Free State. Here, the white DRC, which formed an independent synod in 1864, continued to be influenced by the white DRC in the Cape, which had made missionary work one of its main activities. By 1910, the DRC in the OFS had 14 missionaries working for it and had established 40 mission congregations with a total of 6,839 members. In that year, the white church founded a separate DRC for its black (African) members, using the already existing Mission Church for coloured people as its model.

By the 1920s, there was no prominent figure in the DRC in any of the provinces who advocated extending the practice of segregated schools, parishes and churches to political rights and representation. Indeed, Johannes du Plessis (no relation of JC du Plessis), a towering figure in the DRC in the field of missions, rejected any attempt to use the DRC approach as a justification for political or economic discrimination. In 1921, Du Plessis edited a volume with contributions from ten leading figures in DRC missionary circles who tried to defend the DRC against the charge of DDT Jabavu, an influential black academic, that it was 'an anti-native church'. The book admitted that the DRC record with respect to black South Africans was not impressive, but pointed out that it was the only large church in the country that had to rely exclusively on local funding for missionary work. While the authors regarded segregation as a 'most excellent theory', they were, as Richard Elphick has pointed out, 'more aware of the ambiguities, contradictions and pitfalls of segregation than many English-speaking theorists'.[145]

Within the church, a conservative reaction had made itself felt by the end of the 1920s. A leading representative was JG (Valie) Strydom (no relation of the later Prime Minister), who became secretary for missions of the DRC in the OFS. He would later become one of the leading exponents of what he called 'apartheid as the DRC's missions policy'. At a 1927 meeting organised by the DRC Federal Council, and attended by Afrikaans, English and black church leaders, it was suggested that the aspirations of the small Westernised African elite be accommodated. Strydom replied as follows: 'All natives were not as calm and intelligent as those present were. If they were, he would say, "Give them a chance."' But he felt that they were unable to resist the pressure from more black radicals.[146]

The 1929 conference in Kroonstad, where the Rev. JC du Plessis made the first recorded reference to apartheid, took place against the background of three challenges emanating from the African community. During the 1920s, the Industrial and Commercial Workers' Union of Africa rallied masses of Africans to fight under the trade union banner. It mainly concentrated on urban constituencies, but in some Free State districts it tried to recruit farm workers. By the end of the 1920s, notes Bradford, 'the [Kroonstad] district was seething with rumours of pending unrest'.[147]

The second challenge had deeper roots. Since the 1890s, the Ethiopian movement had formed independent churches that attracted large numbers of Africans frustrated by the fact that all the main Christian churches were loath to advance Africans in leading positions. As early as 1905, a DRC missionary in the Free State had published a pamphlet in which he observed that the Ethiopians wanted to make themselves entirely independent from whites. It was an attempt to dig 'a gulf of hatred' between whites and blacks.[148] JC du Plessis, in his 1929 speech, expressed alarm over the spread of Ethiopianism, which was shared by other speakers. One asked, 'Who is today the best friend of the white man in the land? The native who got his education from the DRC. He is the greatest opponent of political agitators.'[149]

The third challenge was the demand for black education. The DRC lagged far behind the other churches in the provision of education to African and coloured children. DRC missions provided primary education for both, but no form of secondary education for Africans. By contrast, South African missions of English-speaking origin were educating nearly nine secondary school pupils per missionary.[150] The question of the type of religious instruction and education that the churches offered had become a burning issue. Between 1892 and 1902, Gustav Warneck, the most important German mission theorist, had published his magnum opus in three volumes which stressed the importance of converting the community at large to Christianity, and of establishing national churches that preserved both mother tongue and traditional customs. These churches had to be self-supporting, self-governing and self-propagating. But from the 1920s the English-speaking churches, both local and foreign, steadily moved towards the ideal of a common society and promoted this by providing mission education that stressed Westernisation and the central importance of a good command of the English language. For DRC mission strategists such as JC du Plessis and Valie Strydom, missions, education and politics had become intertwined. In his preface to the volume in which the proceedings of the Kroonstad conference were published, Strydom stated, 'By providing to the native the right kind of Evangelisation and the right kind of learning the danger of assimilation will be removed.'[151]

This was the kernel of the apartheid idea. For its proponents, privilege or exclusivity could be justified by finding a policy that concentrated on the *eie*, or that which was one's own, and which promoted what Du Plessis called the *self-syn*, or being oneself.[152] Implicit in this was the view that only identification with one's own ethnic community was authentic. Du Plessis envisaged the development of autonomous, self-governing black churches as a counter to English missionaries, who tried to produce converts by copying 'Western civilisation and religion'.

The Kroonstad conference decided to draft a mission policy and submit it to the synod of the Free State DRC in 1931. At this meeting, the church rejected *gelykstelling* or racial levelling and, with it, race degeneration and 'bastardisation' as 'an abomination to every right-minded white and native'. Yet DRC policy also affirmed that the 'native' possessed a soul of equal value in the eyes of God and that he was, on a certain level, the equal of whites. But equality in the hereafter certainly did not mean any social equality in this world. To justify its rejection of *gelykstelling*, the church proposed that blacks develop 'on their own terrain, separate and apart'.[153]

At a meeting in 1935 of the Federal Council of the DRC in all four provinces, a common missions policy was formulated. The church was firm in its view that 'education must not be denationalised', but must be based on the group's national culture, giving a prominent place to its language, history and customs. It called for Africans and coloured people to be assisted in developing 'into self-respecting Christian nations'. Two aspects were new. For the first time, coloureds were brought into the scheme as a separate nation. Secondly, the church laid stress on the equal worth of all 'self-respecting nations', whereas prior to 1935 it had emphasised the equal worth of all *individuals* before God.[154]

By the 1930s, those concerned with formulating the DRC missions policy were extending their ideas to areas beyond religious organisation. Again, it was Free State ministers who took the lead. Valie Strydom vigorously propagated the idea of Christian National education, which had to imbue the black child with respect for the history, customs and culture of the ethnic community in which he or she was born. But the idea that black people primarily formed separate nations rather than constituting a single black race or nation had not yet crystallised. In territorial terms, the apartheid scheme had in fact not yet moved much beyond segregated suburbs. Strydom was influenced by segregation in the US and the idea of black separatism expounded by some black leaders in South Africa. In 1937 he addressed a North Carolina audience and, after his return, wrote of 'the policy of apartheid here in our land and the United States of America'. He held up the American South, with its segregated schools, churches and suburbs, as a model to be emulated for both coloured people and Africans in South Africa.[155]

As NP leaders groped towards a policy, they began to claim that the apartheid system was built on the precedent set by the major churches in South Africa, which willingly provided segregated education for African and coloured people. In 1947, DF Malan, leader of the NP, remarked that 'It was not the state but the church that took the lead with apartheid. The state followed the principle laid down by the church in the field of education for the native, the coloured and the Asian. The result? Friction was eliminated. The Boer church surpasses the other churches in missionary activity. It is the result of apartheid.'[156]

From the second half of the 1930s, the United Party government moved towards segregated residential areas for people who were not white, but some church ministers also wanted the state to go further and proclaim whites-only suburbs. A leading role was taken by GBA Gerdener, Professor of Missiology at the University of Stellenbosch, whose father and father-in-law were both Rhenish missionaries, and who was himself profoundly influenced by the work of German missiologists, particularly Gustav Warneck.[157] Gerdener combined several strands in the church's thinking about apartheid. Apartheid, he wrote in his journal, *Op die horison*, 'required a Christian and generous political approach'. It was based not on race or colour alone but on colour 'paired . . . with language, tradition and lifestyle'. It did not imply a social hierarchy but a 'relationship of equals on separate terrains'. He did not accept biblical justifications of apartheid, and would soon deplore the use of that word, but to him *eiesoortige ontwikkeling* (autochthonous development) was a policy that had merit and promised to be of value to all parties. It met the demands of Christian trusteeship and served Afrikaner interests, while bringing to blacks the message of Christ. 'Autochthonous development', he wrote, 'serves not only our survival as a white nation, but in particular also our missions policy.'[158] Soon, Gerdener and Valie Strydom clashed. Strydom tended to insist on apartheid simply as a way to exclude blacks; Gerdener tended to be much more idealistic about the developmental potential of the proposed policy.

In 1939, Gerdener endorsed segregated residential areas for coloured people as well as Africans. In 1942 he became chairman of the Federal Mission Council (FMC) of the DRC. Policy towards missions and pseudo-scientific race theory soon became intertwined. When the FMC petitioned the government to introduce segregation, it inserted into its 1942 submission a memorandum by a Canadian biologist, HB Fantham, who maintained that the coloured offspring of white–black intermixture displayed negative social and mental characteristics. In a 1943 meeting between an FMC delegation and Prime Minister Smuts, the delegation requested a ban on racially mixed marriages. Smuts rejected this, declaring that 'the line between white and coloured people in many instances could not be drawn'.

The government was more sympathetic to the demand for residential segregation. Gerdener supported this, but differed from most other Nationalists in urging that coloured people should not be compelled to move to these townships. He seemed to think that residential segregation could be implemented fairly. At a 1945 conference of the DRC Sendingkerk (for coloureds), he demanded that coloured townships had to be 'one hundred per cent with respect to privileges and facilities'.[159] In 1947 the FMC, which was very much guided by Gerdener, developed the apartheid idea in greater detail. It proposed segregated townships for coloured people with the same facilities as those provided to whites, where coloured people would develop 'the greatest responsibility towards themselves'. With respect to Africans, the FMC proposed a policy that aimed at protecting them against exploitation and ensuring their development 'in their own territory and their own towns'.[160]

Gerdener was also the only non-politician who was a member of the Sauer Commission, which finalised the NP's position on apartheid prior to the 1948 election. The Sauer report of 1947, commissioned by the NP, recommended a strict form of Christian National education for black students in line with their 'ethnic nature', aptitude and background which would make it possible 'to cultivate Bantu-worthy [sic] citizens'.[161]

In 1948, the synod of the Transvaal DRC accepted a report that took as its starting point the 1935 missions policy and used the Tower of Babel and the Old Testament history of Israel as justifications for apartheid. In 1949, the Cape DRC synod gave a slightly more circumspect endorsement of apartheid. Its main argument was based on historical precedents. It referred to the 1857 DRC synod decision to condone segregated worship, as well as to the existing segregation of schools, and to the church's missions policy laid down in 1935. Apartheid, the synod declared, did not mean oppression or black inferiority but a 'vertical separation' in which each population group could become independent.[162] As Richard Elphick remarks, church leaders were enthralled by their utopian vision of separate peoples, each with their own mission, and they would continue to justify the unjustifiable, thus paving the way for the politicians.[163]

'An idea that one can bow down before': Apartheid as secular doctrine

Although the word was not yet used, the first secular formulations of what would become apartheid can be traced to the mid-1930s. After the fusion of the two main political parties in 1934 the NP, as a small opposition party, had little chance of attracting coloured (or African) voters, who were in any case reduced to a small proportion of Cape Province voters after the enfranchisement of white women. The Cape NP needed a modernised version of paternalism to defend a more extreme policy of white supremacy than that of the UP.

An opportunity arose when the government appointed a commission of inquiry into the coloured population, which was to be headed by Professor Johannes du Plessis. When he died early in 1935, he was replaced by RW Wilcocks, a professor at Stellenbosch and a member of the earlier Carnegie Commission on poor whites. The new commission found acute poverty among the overwhelming majority of coloured people, due to wide-ranging discrimination by government, employers and trade unions. Segregation against coloured people had intensified and had failed to deliver opportunities for them above the level of manual labour. The 'civilised labour' policy, which was supposed to benefit them as well, had aggravated their position. It had accelerated the trend among coloured people 'to pass for white'.

In the contributions of the three Afrikaner members of the commission and of the three Stellenbosch professors who gave testimony, a common thread could be discerned. They posited the existence of a coloured race, urged a demarcation in housing schemes between white, coloured and 'native' areas, and recommended special sections in government departments to look after coloured interests. While the other commissioners, among them Dr Abdullah Abdurahman, advocated common political rights and equal pay for equal work, the Afrikaners proposed the extension of 'civilised labour' to coloured people.

The testimony of Verwoerd to the commission provided the outlines of the emerging apartheid ideology. He used coloured poverty as a justification for increased discrimination against Africans in the Western Cape. He argued that Africans posed a threat to coloured people and poor whites alike in the competition for work opportunities. The real home of Africans was in the reserves, a view he also expressed to the *volkskongres* on the poor white issue, held in 1934.[164]

Another key moment was the 1936 parliamentary debate on the Cape African franchise. Here, DF Malan, NP leader, and his party opposed the purchase of more land for the African reserves, as proposed in the bill. Funds should go instead to buying land for white tenants, sharecroppers and *bywoners*. The acquisition of land by blacks had to happen 'on their own initiative and according to their own real needs'.[165] With the doubling of the reserves a fait accompli, Malan and his followers had to reconsider their views. They soon proceeded to make a virtue of necessity.

Three different academic approaches to legitimising apartheid can be discerned: the first was based on historical claims, the second on ethnic differences, and the third on racial differences. The historical argument was that whites and blacks had arrived simultaneously in the territorial boundaries of the current South African state and that the Voortrekkers had followed a policy of 'isolation' and territorial separation. Liberal historians easily dismissed this view. Afrikaner historians such as HB Thom were closer to the mark when they claimed that resistance to *gelykstelling* (social levelling), originating in the status distinctions of the Dutch East India Company, remained a central idea in Afrikaner political thinking.[166] Indeed, apartheid embodied this idea, with a remarkable correspondence existing between its statutory groups and the status groups introduced by the Dutch at the Cape.

One of the first Afrikaner scholars who stressed ethnic difference as a basis for policy was the anthropologist Werner Eiselen, who argued that the real task in South Africa was not the solution of a race problem but 'the creation of effective arrangements for the peaceful existence of different ethnic groups'.[167] The first book (it was more an extended pamphlet) promoting a policy called apartheid written in social science language was authored by three Stellenbosch academics, PJ Coertze (a lecturer in anthropology), FJ Language (lecturer in 'native administration') and BIC van Eeden (lecturer in Bantu languages). The acknowledgement in their preface of Gerdener's influence highlights the marriage of the ideas of mission strategists and secular nationalists. They proposed that blacks had to be steadily withdrawn from the white economy, and transferred to the territories where they 'belonged', with white labour taking their place. Only those blacks 'absolutely necessary' were to be permitted to remain. The study also advocated the regeneration of traditional institutions in the reserves where Africans could administer themselves, preserve their customs, and restore discipline and all 'that was healthy in the *volkseie*'.[168]

The novelist Joseph Conrad remarked that in order to dominate people, one has to have an idea – something one can 'set up, and bow down before and offer a sacrifice to'.[169] What redeemed apartheid in the eyes of the Nationalist intelligentsia was the idea that the Afrikaners were prepared to grant (the Afrikaans word, *gun*, is much stronger) everything to blacks that they demanded for themselves.[170] Like the Afrikaners, Africans would have their own schools, churches, residential areas, homelands and governments on which they could put their own cultural imprint. Nationalists persuaded themselves that apartheid would be implemented much more 'positively' than segregation, particularly because Afrikaner nationalists had waged a long and bitter struggle against attempts to assimilate them to English ways.[171]

It was within the context of an emphasis on culture that the ideology of Christian National education developed. Here at least, the Broederbond, with its large contingent of teachers, lecturers and church ministers, played a prominent role.

A racist policy without racists?

While Eiselen and others stressed culture as the foundation of Christian National education and the political programme of the Nationalists, another section of the Nationalist intelligentsia emphasised race. Invariably their point of departure was 'racial purity' as the foundation of white supremacy. It is sometimes suggested that such ideas were derived from Nazi ideology that swept through Germany in the 1920s and 1930s. However, National Socialism had few adherents among the local intelligentsia. There was broad support in South Africa for 'race purity', even among liberals, including Alfred Hoernlé and the editorial committee of *Forum*, but the biological variant of racism remained a fringe phenomenon.

Piet Cillié, together with Hendrik Verwoerd the most articulate apartheid apologists, wrote in 1952 that 'South Africa was remarkably free from racial mythologies'. For him, the Afrikaners' desire to survive was a far stronger and more indestructible feeling than race prejudice. 'Like the Jews in Palestine and the Muslims in Pakistan, the Afrikaners had not fought themselves free from British domination only to be overwhelmed by a majority of a different kind. Eventually we shall give that majority its freedom, but never power over us ... They [the blacks] will not get more rights if that means rights over and in our lives.'[172] These can be seen as self-serving statements, but LE Neame, liberal editor of the *Cape Argus* and author of a book on apartheid, made the same point. Writing from a comparative perspective, he took issue with the argument that apartheid was based solely on the claim that the white race was inherently superior to all others. An unreasoning prejudice against colour was not the root of the matter. The problem is 'national rather than pigmental . . . The motive is not detraction but defence.'[173]

The Nationalist academic with the most explicitly racist thesis, both in terminology and in the practical suggestions he offered, was Geoff Cronjé, a Pretoria sociologist. Perhaps because his books appeared just before the 1948 election, analysts have mistakenly thought that he was an influential figure. But he had stronger ties to the extra-parliamentary, pro-Nazi Ossewabrandwag movement than to the NP during the war years, and had no standing in DF Malan's inner circle. (He was one of the few Nationalist academics who declined to send a submission to the commission that drew up the Sauer report.) He went much further in the expression of his racial obsessions than almost any other Nationalist academic – JM Coetzee calls him 'crazy'[174] – but how much his ideas resonated at a grass-roots level still has to be examined.

The strongest and most enduring part of apartheid ideology was the construct of liberal nationalism and the associated appeal to an ethical form of survival. Here, the most articulate exponent was NP van Wyk Louw, the leading intellectual in the Nationalist movement. He was initially attracted to National Socialism but abandoned it by the end of the 1930s. As with General Hertzog and many others, his faith in Westminster-style liberal democracy and its acceptance of majoritarianism received a severe shock in 1939 when General Smuts took South Africa into the war on a split vote. However, he did not reject the fundamental liberal principles of liberty and equality.

In seeking a solution to the racial issue in South Africa, his point of departure was the impasse in the country and the impossibility of applying the principles of Westminster-style democracy there. 'It was the typical tragic situation of history: two "rights" [the white and the black right to self-determination] which confronted each other implacably.' There was a 'balance of power': blacks had their numbers; whites, particularly the Afrikaners, held the upper hand, politically, economically and militarily. The 'stalemate' could be resolved either by the 'ploughing under' of the smaller group or by the 'separate development' of each, which he claimed represented a peaceful solution.

He was stimulated by a 1939 lecture by Alfred Hoernlé, which was subsequently widely discussed among Nationalist academics. Hoernlé discerned three future political possibilities for South Africa. They were: *parallelism*, in which different races would be subjected to a 'master group', *assimilation*, in which all racial differences would be obliterated, and *separation*. He described the last as 'a sundering or dissociation so complete as to destroy the very possibility of effective domination' by another group. The third option was ethically sound, but Hoernlé, like Jan Hofmeyr, thought that whites would refuse the enormous sacrifices that would be required to make it a reality.[175]

Louw promoted Hoernlé's option of 'separation' as a possible solution to South Africa's racial problem. In 1946 he wrote: 'For Nationalism to be based on a true political principle it has to be true for everyone.' Accordingly, the recognition of the nationalist principle for the Afrikaners logically had to be extended to all other national groups in South Africa. Hence, 'we [the Afrikaners] should not speak of ourselves as the *volk* [nation] of South Africa, but as one of the *volke* of South Africa.'[176] By 1948 Louw was envisaging four white and four black separate states in southern Africa. But he left the whole question of the actual division of land obscure, and it was only in the 1960s that he made a brief reference to the 'two halves of this large country of ours' to which whites and blacks laid claim.[177]

Louw's words were double-edged. In the 1960s and the early 1970s, apartheid apologists used formulations and imagery very similar to those he had first used in the mid-1940s. But at the same time, his conception of Afrikaners as forming only one of several co-equal *volke* over the longer run undermined the ideology of white supremacy.

Yet the real reason why Louw's political ideas outlived him was the ethical dimension he introduced into the debate about Afrikaner survival. He did this by using the evocative phrase *'voortbestaan in geregtigheid'* – survival in justice – and by insisting that national death might be preferable to a form of ethnic survival based on injustice.

He identified three kinds of *volkskrisisse*, or national crises – situations in which the very existence of the ethnonational group was at stake.

- When the Afrikaners were overwhelmed by external military might or 'ploughed under' by mass immigration, as some pro-British politicians proposed. Louw was referring to the defeat of the Boer republics at the hands of the British in the Anglo-Boer War of 1899–1902, and the subsequent attempt by Sir Alfred Milner to establish an English-speaking majority in the white population by way of state-sponsored mass immigration.
- When a great number of the Afrikaner people doubted in themselves 'whether we ought to survive as a *volk*'. Afrikaners might still survive individually and some might even prosper, but they would no longer constitute a distinctive *volk*: they 'would be absorbed in either an Anglo-Saxon or Bantu-speaking nation'.
- 'When some time in the future a great number of our people would come to believe that we need not live together *in justice* [Louw's emphasis] with other ethnic groups; when they come to believe that mere survival is the chief issue, not a just existence.'

In a vivid passage he posed this question: 'Can a small *volk* survive for long, if it becomes hateful, even evil in the eyes of the best of its members and also to people outside its fold?' The *volk*, he warned, ran the risk of the withdrawal of allegiance by a critical number of intellectuals if it yielded to the 'final temptation' of abandoning the quest for 'survival in justice' and preferred 'mere survival'. In the case of a small nation like the Afrikaners, this could have a fatal effect. But he did not despair that ultimately Afrikaner survival would come to be based on moral values. As he phrased it: 'I believe that the greatest, almost mystical crisis of a *volk* is that in which it is reborn and re-emerges young and creative; the "dark night of the soul" in which it says: "I would rather go down than survive in injustice."'

Because Louw remained a staunch member of the Afrikaner Broederbond and supporter of apartheid, he has been judged negatively.[178] Ultimately, however, his status as a critic revolves around the question whether he could envisage a point where the *volk* deserved to go under. In his essay, Louw refused to go down the route of ethnic survival at all costs. His argument about survival in justice was a moral argument. Put differently, the Afrikaner people were not entitled to use extreme measures to maintain their hold on power.

There was ultimately no justification for a policy aimed at ensuring survival that constantly and consistently flouted liberal values. Louw died too early – in 1970 – for us to know whether he would have denounced nationalism and apartheid. During the 1980s, André du Toit and other members of a new generation of Afrikaner academics could, in urging the abandonment of apartheid, draw on Louw's work to do so.[179] In the end, the seemingly parallel lines of liberalism and liberal nationalism did meet.[180]

The crystallisation of apartheid

In May 1944, DF Malan and his closest political associate, Paul Sauer, offered the first extended defence of apartheid in Parliament. Their ideas were far removed from the racial ideology and xenophobia propounded at this time on the continent of Europe. Instead they were firmly rooted in the Cape Afrikaner experience of slavery, with its ideology of paternalism, and British colonialism, with its stress on indirect rule and trusteeship. In his first mention of the term 'apartheid', Malan called for a republic based on the policy of 'apartheid and trusteeship, made safe for the white race and the development of the non-white race, according to their own aptitude and abilities'.[181] As the historian Kenneth Robinson points out, British notions of trusteeship were influenced by the thoughts of a seminal liberal thinker, John Stuart Mill. Mill argued in 1859 that rule by a dominant country or 'by persons delegated for that purpose' was as legitimate as any other, if it facilitated the transition of a subject people to a higher state of improvement. In 1921, Lord Lugard, the most famous of British African governors, expressed the trusteeship idea in his book *Dual Mandate* as follows: Europe was in Africa for 'the mutual benefit of her own classes, and of the native races in their progress to a higher plane'. He believed the benefits could be made reciprocal. This was the 'dual mandate', the title of Lugard's book.[182]

In his 1944 speech, Malan pointed to the failure of ostensibly liberal systems to deal fairly with subordinate people. Eighty years after the victory of the North in the American Civil War, blacks in the South could still not vote and were subject to 'lynch law'. In Australia, the government took Aboriginal children away from their parents and brought them up as Europeans in special hostels. When the Aborigines failed to assimilate, the Australian government reverted to a policy of allowing them to elevate themselves 'on the basis of what is their own'. Malan's solution was couched in the classic terms of paternalism and trusteeship. Subordinate people had to be helped to develop that which was their own, and to climb the ladder of civilisation according to their own aptitude and capacity. At present they were unhappy because they had nothing that was their own. They could only be made happy if opportunities were created that enabled them to improve themselves. That meant establishing segregated townships with their own doctors, nurses, clerks and policemen. White, coloured and African communities could live alongside each other in 'friendship and co-operation with each other'.[183]

In the same debate, Paul Sauer poured scorn on the idea that the western part of the Cape had become more integrated. Forty years earlier, he said, it was still possible for coloureds to complete their education in a white school. 'Today such a thing is inconceivable. I cannot imagine that there is a single high school that would permit this today.' He called for a 'realistic policy' that would prevent Africans or coloured people from encroaching on areas where whites lived or worked. Only once racial competition had been ruled out would whites be willing to assume a sympathetic attitude towards coloured aspirations.[184]

In 1945, a party commission appointed by Malan recommended a policy of social, industrial and political apartheid with respect to coloured people, but argued at the same time that this would have to bring about a real improvement in their conditions.[185] In the same year, the NP accepted apartheid as its official racial policy. From 1946, *Die Burger* acted as the 'mass ventilator' of apartheid.[186] In 1947, Malan appointed Sauer to head a party commission to turn apartheid into a comprehensive racial policy. Also on the commission were three NP parliamentarians and the ubiquitous GBA Gerdener as the only non-politician. His presence symbolised apartheid's fusion of racial and mission policy.

The way in which the Sauer Commission went about its task illuminates the NP's grass-roots character. It did not invite representations from corporate bodies, such as the agricultural unions or Afrikaner business. It thought that the need to secure Afrikaner survival outweighed the need to accommodate Afrikaner interest groups. Secondly, the Afrikaners of the 1940s and 1950s attached great importance to culture and learning.[187] They did not look to businessmen or wealthy farmers to justify apartheid but to ministers, academics, professional men and senior journalists. The academics had to incorporate insights from their respective fields, and representatives of the party had to report back on what the people wanted.

Accordingly, the commission sent out a circular, inviting opinions, to all elected representatives of the party, all chairmen and secretaries of the party's district councils, all 'well-disposed' Afrikaner lecturers at universities and other 'knowledgeable experts and interested persons'. The last were mostly farmers, church ministers and missionaries. Some 5,000 circulars were sent out, and about 500 replies were received. Some of the academics who responded were appointed to sub-committees. The commission's report, published late in 1947, was incorporated into the NP platform for the 1948 election.[188]

The report combined the dual nature of NP thinking: both racist and 'ethnicist', both religious and secular. It formulated an antinomy that formed the bedrock of apartheid thinking: 'There are two policy directions towards non-whites: on the one hand there is the apartheid policy; on the other hand there is the policy of *gelykstelling* [social levelling], propagated by Communists and others who favour race-mixing.' To justify the rejection of 'equal rights and opportunities', the report used terminology very similar to that first employed in the DRC during the 1930s: 'It was decreed by God that diverse races and *volke* should survive and grow naturally as part of a Divine plan.' The report even incorporated a section on missions policy, which clearly was drafted by Gerdener: 'The Gospel has to be taught to all *volke* and population groups as part of the calling of the Christian church.' The aim of mission work was 'self-governing, self-supporting and self-propagating churches'.

The Sauer report has been extensively discussed and need not detain us here. The whole thrust of the report was the elimination of 'surplus' black labour, not black labour as a whole, and the channelling of sufficient labour to the mines, farms and industry.[189] The report clearly hoped that temporary or migrant labour would provide the bulk of the new labour demand. However, this clashed with the demand of organised Afrikaner business and agriculture for workers who had settled in the cities with their families. The report did not try to resolve this clash. In this sense, then, the report did not constitute a blueprint for apartheid to which all Afrikaner nationalists subscribed, but rather reflected the contradictory tendencies in the Nationalist movement.[190]

The idea of ten black ethnic groups each with its own homeland was a later elaboration. In 1950 Albert Geyer, ex-editor of *Die Burger* and then High Commissioner in London, mooted the idea that black authorities form a central council to discuss matters common to all the reserves, and the introduction of machinery for 'close contact and consultation' between such a council and the government. Hendrik Verwoerd, Minister of Native Affairs, rejected the idea because he felt that competition would develop between such a council and Parliament.[191]

English-speaking South Africans shared the NP's determination to maintain white domination. On the eve of the election, Keppel-Jones, whose 1947 book, *When Smuts Goes*, painted a dark picture of South Africa should the NP ever come to power, argued that the main concern of whites in general was 'not to be submerged in the oncoming tide of black race. If they were to remain a separate people then they must retain their dominant position.'[192] The kind of segregation that most English-speakers supported was less aggressive and blatant than that of the NP. They did not agree with crude manifestations, such as segregated suburbs and the racial sex laws. As the wealthier white community, they could buy their apartheid and, unlike the Afrikaners, did not have to worry about a large section in their community that had just escaped from acute poverty.

Apartheid indeed had a 'dogmatic intensity', as Saul Dubow points out, but its suppleness is underrated.[193] Nelson Mandela maintains that the NP fought the election on the twin slogans of: 'The kaffir in his place' and 'The coolies out of the country'.[194] But there never were any such slogans.[195] The NP leadership had no desire to upset ministers and other apartheid theorists who believed in the capacity of apartheid to uplift people. What it did was to promise that South Africa would remain a 'white man's country'. Unlike the UP, with its liberal wing led by Jan Hofmeyr, the NP spoke with one voice in promising to keep South Africa a 'white man's country'.

Apartheid was a flexible operational ideology for Afrikaner nationalism, attracting both those wanting to keep down all those who were not white and those who wanted to rehabilitate them and recognise their human dignity – single-minded and double-minded segregationists, a term Alfred Hoernlé first used. The latter – in the literature they are called the apartheid visionaries or idealists, but here they are called the apartheid theorists – took the initiative.

They had no argument with the apartheid hard-liners that the racial omelette in the common area had to be unscrambled, or with the argument that those who were not white had to be denied political rights. But in two vital areas they differed: the theorists wanted whites to reduce their dependence on black labour, and launch a dramatic development programme for the reserves to justify the denial of black rights in the common area. The Tomlinson Commission, which started its work in 1950, would attempt to reconcile the two in the process of fleshing out apartheid that began soon after the 1948 election.

Conclusion

The study of apartheid's origins has had a strange career. During the first two decades of the apartheid system, serious scholars or journalists only rarely referred to its supposed Nazi roots and affinities, or depicted it as a major deviation from the Scriptures. From the early 1970s, a distinct change occurred. This was due firstly to the intensification of the international anti-apartheid struggle that, in its ideological campaign, stressed the Nazi analogy and the theme of a crime against humanity, as well as the heretical nature of apartheid. Anachronistic projections also had a distorting effect. Because Nic Diederichs, Piet Meyer, Hendrik Verwoerd and Geoff Cronjé as individuals, and the Afrikaner Broederbond as an organisation, enjoyed strong influence in the 1960s, it was assumed that the same was true in the 1930s and early 1940s.

In actual fact, both the Bond and the members of the Afrikaner intelligentsia in the north contributed little to the apartheid plan that took shape in the decade prior to 1948. The Cape NP, *Die Burger* as a newspaper and the nationalist intelligentsia of Stellenbosch were by far the most influential forces at work. In their rejection of the liberal alternative, they stressed the failure of political integration in the American South. Their thinking was squarely in the mainstream of conventional Western racism and imperialism, with a heavy emphasis on paternalism, indirect rule and trusteeship. The fact that apartheid had very little to do with National Socialism but was instead deeply rooted in South Africa, nowhere more so than in the Western Cape with its long history of slavery and colonial rule, largely accounts for the resilience of the apartheid idea, still evident in a recent (2001) poll.

3.

'Survival in justice':
An Afrikaner debate about apartheid

Within nationalist movements a tension typically exists between group demands for ethnic self-preservation and the more universal demands of religious belief, professional commitment or academic vocation which confront particularly the intelligentsia in the group. Ethnic politicians tend to argue that decades or centuries of oppression or the anticipated disastrous consequences of a loss of self-determination make loyalty to the group and its leadership's strategies a matter of overriding importance. It is usually exceptional individuals, often poets or novelists, who in times of crisis issue the challenge that survival be reconciled with universal values and prevailing international political norms.

While the 'national-popular' critic (to use Antonio Gramsci's term) is usually an oppositional figure, he is not a disinterested observer on the sidelines. He is involved in two ways: he wants to tell his truth to a particular national audience, and he is concerned not only with the survival of the group but also the ethical quality of that survival. There is a claim to a higher patriotism, a refusal to pursue a survival that violates the values the group professes to share. This chapter looks first at how social critics grappled with the theme of ethnic survival in Israel, French Algeria and Yugoslavia before turning to a discussion of criticism from within Afrikaner ranks of the policy of apartheid.

The project of national-popular criticism: General perspectives

In his excellent book, *The Company of Critics*, the American philosopher Michael Walzer studies eleven modern 'connected critics' of the twentieth century, ranging from Gramsci through Martin Buber, George Orwell and Albert Camus to Breyten Breytenbach. Walzer's critics do not rail abstractly against the injustices or perversions of the world at large; they strive to be effective in the national-popular mode. They speak the language of the cultural group to which they belong, casting the people, their troubles and the possible solution to their troubles within the framework of a national history and culture. As Walzer formulates it:

> The form of attack will vary with the character of his culture, but he is likely to pay close attention to national history, finding in his people's past... a warrant for criticism in the present. In this sense, the biblical prophet was a national-popular intellectual: he spoke to the hearts of his people even when he was most harshly critical of their behaviour.[196]

The critic is not a ruling party loyalist, but neither is he a detached observer. He is someone who exploits his connections to the group. If his stand is one of absolute opposition or undifferentiated antagonism, there is little chance that people will listen to him. There must be some form of loyalty, some commitment, some constructive involvement. His task is not only, as Walzer says, to expose 'the false appearances of his own society'. He must also give expression 'to his people's deepest sense of how they ought to live'.[197]

Apart from Breytenbach, two of Walzer's social critics (and his interpretation of them) are of particular relevance to a discussion of the Afrikaner *volkskritiek*. The one is the Jewish philosopher Martin Buber and the other Albert Camus, a son of the white (pied-noir) Algerian community. Resident in Israel from 1938, Buber criticised the idea of a sovereign nation state for Jews in a land they shared with Arabs. Instead of simply filling the land with Jewish immigrants and building a separate state, a modus vivendi first had to be reached with the Arabs also living there. Two rights were in contention: the right of the Jews for a land of their own and what Buber called the Arabs' 'inalienable right' to remain.[198] Instead of simply recognising the conflict as a tragedy which had to play itself out, he proposed a bi-national Jewish–Arab state based on economic co-operation and political compromise within a common territory.

Although this was a highly unpopular stand to take for someone living in Israel in the 1930s and 1940s, Buber persevered because for him something higher than Jewish survival was at stake. He wrote: '[No] nation in the world has this [self-preservation and self-assertion] as its only task, for just as an individual who wishes merely to preserve and assert himself leads an unjustified and meaningless existence, so a nation with no other aim deserves to pass away.'[199] He foresaw that in the absence of a Jewish–Arab political accommodation, Israel 'would have to apply its best forces to military activity, instead of applying them to social and cultural enterprise'.[200]

Yet Buber never stopped believing in the possibility of reconciling the Jewish right to a secure existence in Palestine with the demands of justice and equity. Arguing that Israel was chosen to respond to God's demand for 'truth and righteousness', he set up Hebrew humanism in opposition to Jewish nationalism.[201] However, he took issue with Mahatma Gandhi, who declared that Palestine belonged to the Arabs and that it was therefore 'wrong and inhuman to impose the Jews on the Arabs'.[202] In Buber's view, the Arab and the Jewish claims were equivalent. He could not renounce the Jewish claim because 'something higher than the life of our people is bound up with this land, namely its work, its divine mission'.[203] Yet he categorically rejected Gandhi's formula that 'Palestine belongs to the Arabs'. Arabs themselves had conquered the land with an intent to settle. No portion of the earth can ever be exclusively claimed: 'Conquered land is . . . only lent even to the conqueror who has settled on it – and God waits to see what he will make of it.'[204]

Camus's pieds-noirs of Algeria represented an oppressive minority. Camus belonged, so a Tunisian intellectual wrote in 1957, 'to a minority that is historically in the wrong'.[205] Having grown up poor in French Algerian society, Camus strongly criticised sections of his native community but could never accept the judgement that the community was condemned beyond redemption by its colonial history.[206] The task of the critic was not to desert historical struggles nor to serve 'the cruel elements' in these struggles but to remain what he is 'to favour freedom against the fatalities that close in upon it'.[207]

Camus's conceptualisation of justice was a negotiated solution by the two peoples in Algeria based on absolute equality. Although this was rejected by the overwhelming majority of French Algerians, he insisted on a 'natural solidarity' with 'one's family', hoping that 'it will survive at least and, by surviving, have a chance to show its fairness'.[208] He rejected the FLN demand for Algerian independence and sovereignty because in his view that meant the destruction of the pied-noir community. It was in this context that he posed this simple antimony of justice and love: 'I believe in justice, but I will defend my mother before justice.'[209] He added: 'If that is not honour and true justice, then I know nothing that is of any use in this world.' Living safely in Paris, Camus could not bring himself to utter words which would expose his family and friends in Algeria to increased terrorism.[210]

Finally, there is also a relevant example from contemporary times. The context is the 'ethnic cleansing' carried out in 1992 and later by Slobodan Milošević and other Serbian nationalist strongmen. Their stated object was to secure Serbian survival amid the Serbophobia of other peoples by carving a Serbian state out of the old Yugoslav federation.[211] In practice it became a matter of removing non-Serbs from Serbian-claimed territories by force and intimidation through measures that included mass starvation and mass murder. One of Milošević's Serbian opponents turned out to be Dobrica Ćosić, a novelist considered to be the father of post-communist Serbian nationalism. He had helped write a manifesto that said all Serbs had the right to live in one state, and he was appointed by Milošević as first president of the Federal Republic of Yugoslavia in 1992. As the fighting dragged on in Bosnia in the latter half of 1992, revulsion at Serbian aggression overcame Ćosić. Alluding to five hundred years of domination by Ottoman Turks and then the catastrophic wars against Germany during the twentieth century, Ćosić said that his country's fatal curse had been that the world offered Serbia no alternative but 'capitulation or war – a slave or a grave'. But, Ćosić said, the world had changed. 'This time the answer should be in a negation of that slogan. Neither capitulation nor war; neither a slave nor a grave. Survival is in peace, and this can only come through a policy that is far-sighted and imaginative.'[212]

In South Africa, although the context is quite different from that in Palestine, Algeria and Yugoslavia, the debate among Afrikaners about survival in justice has a similar ring in many ways. The conditions, however, have been quite different. The Afrikaners were squeezed between the economically advanced group, the white English-speakers, who dominated the private sector of the economy, and the disenfranchised African majority, who were subjected to severe racial discrimination. In 1948, the National Party (NP), the vehicle of Afrikaner nationalism, won power. For many years its greatest emphasis was on securing the future existence of the Afrikaner group through apartheid and increasingly repressive security legislation. By the end of the 1970s, however, the Afrikaners had been transformed into a relatively secure middle-class people. At that time the idea of survival at all costs and by any means came under increasing attack by Afrikaner intellectuals. Together with black resistance and world pressure, the desire of Afrikaners to be recognised as part of the international community played an important role in the decision of the NP at the end of the 1980s to open negotiations with the liberation organisations for an inclusive democracy. In this intra-Afrikaner debate the seminal influence was the writings of NP van Wyk Louw on the theme of survival in justice.

Victory without salvation: 1946 to 1976

NP van Wyk Louw rose into prominence in the 1930s as the pre-eminent Afrikaans poet, playwright and national-popular critic. His writings in this decade were influenced by the Afrikaner nationalist movement, which sought to capture power by mobilising against British cultural imperialism and advocating apartheid as a policy designed to secure survival for Afrikaners and, even more so, for whites. Louw's play *Die dieper reg* (The higher right) was a justification of nationalism in view of the suffering Afrikaners had experienced in their history. His collection of essays, *Lojale verset* (Loyal opposition), propagated *volkskritiek* from a position of solidarity with the nationalist movement.

In 1950 Louw left South Africa for eight years to occupy the chair of South African literature, history and politics at the Gemeentelijke Universiteit of Amsterdam. Although still deeply committed to the welfare of the Afrikaner people, Louw now wrote more from the periphery of the group. The influences brought to bear upon him were quite unlike those to which his fellow writers were exposed in South Africa. In post-war Amsterdam there was above all the traumatic coming to terms with the Holocaust which had wiped out the greater part of the Jewish community in the Netherlands. There was the impending fall of the Dutch colonies in the East Indies, which had been founded before the Cape Colony. There was also Buber's visit to the Netherlands in 1946, which attracted great attention. Buber's theme, that Israel must be redeemed through righteousness, was one that Louw would grapple with in his own context.

In 1950 Louw published five seminal essays on the theme of 'Culture and

Crisis' in the popular weekly, *Die Huisgenoot*. A perceptive Jewish commentator, Henry Katzew, called these essays 'the highest Afrikaner thought on survival'. He endorsed the review of Piet Cillié, editor of the daily newspaper supporting the NP, *Die Burger*. Cillié described Louw as an 'intellectual midwife' whose essays contain 'the most important ideas, reflections and doubts that in recent years have been working within earnest South Africans, but particularly Nationalist Afrikaners'.[213] This judgement was correct, for in decades to come no serious debate about survival would take place in Afrikaner circles without at least a ritualistic bow to Louw's essays.

Writing in the immediate aftermath of the NP's momentous victory in 1948 and the introduction of the first apartheid laws, Louw identified three kinds of *volkskrisisse* – situations in which the very existence of the ethnonational group was at stake. Firstly, when Afrikaners were overwhelmed by military might such as their defeat in the Anglo-Boer War of 1899–1902 and the subsequent attempt by Lord Milner to establish an English-speaking white majority through state-sponsored mass immigration. The second crisis would arise when a great number of Afrikaner people doubted in themselves, and the third when 'a great number of our people would come to believe that we need not live together *in justice* [Louw's emphasis] with other ethnic groups; when they come to believe that mere survival is the chief issue, not a just existence.'[214]

Louw argued that for a *volk* which was small in numbers, like the Afrikaners, the challenges posed by the second and third crises were as severe as that of the first.[215] In the second, but more particularly in the third crisis, the response of intellectuals was of particular importance. If a *volk* yielded to the 'final temptation' of preferring mere survival to survival in justice, the withdrawal of allegiance by a critical number of intellectuals could have fatal effects. Louw posed the question: 'Is it possible for a small *volk* to survive for long if it becomes hateful or even evil in the eyes of the best people in – or outside – its ranks?'[216] Louw did not despair of the hope that ultimately ethnic survival could be based on moral values. As Louw phrased it: 'I believe that the greatest, almost mystical crisis of a *volk* is that in which it is reborn and re-emerges young and creative; the "dark night of the soul" in which it says: "I would rather go down than survive in injustice."'[217]

Louw insisted that he did not seek survival in justice along liberal-democratic lines. While not rejecting liberalism as such, he argued, along with the most prominent liberal thinker in South Africa, Alfred Hoernlé, that the application to South Africa of European liberalism was problematic because it had its roots in countries with a homogeneous racial or ethnic composition. By applying it uncritically to South Africa, Louw argued, liberals were hostile to the 'other right' because full democracy meant an equality reached 'over the dead body of a whole *volk*'. And if the Afrikaners became a powerless minority, 'they would be as helpless as a Jew was in Germany'.[218]

For Louw, then, the South African drama was a classic conflict between two 'rights': Afrikaner and African nationalism (he used the words 'black' and 'white' nationalism). Nevertheless, he rejected a solution which called for the abandonment of either liberalism or nationalism. Despite the 'polar tensions' between the two principles, they belonged together and constituted the texture of South African history. The stalemate between the two nationalisms could be resolved in one of two ways: either through the 'ploughing under' of the smaller groups or by the 'separate development' of the different groups.[219] Louw stated:

> For nationalism to be based on a true principle it has to be true everywhere and for everyone. . . . Accordingly, the recognition of the nationalist principle for the Afrikaner logically has to imply the recognition of all other national groups in South Africa. Hence we should not speak of ourselves as the nation of South Africa, but as one of the *volke* of South Africa.[220]

It is not difficult to see that this scheme of thought could lead to the full-blown ideology of apartheid, which held that liberal principles of freedom and justice could be accommodated by a policy of separate homelands for Africans and 'separate freedoms' for whites and Africans. Louw's essays of 1950 were one of the first publications by Afrikaner thinkers to use such concepts as 'separate development' and 'multi-nationalism', derived from the political context of Europe, which in the 1960s and 1970s would become euphemisms for apartheid. Yet Louw correctly posed the dilemma of a plural society in which the political loyalty of the large mass of the population was not to the transcendent nation or state but to their specific ethnonational or racial group.

The National Party came to power under the unifying banner of apartheid. The banner nevertheless concealed quite contradictory approaches as to what the policy meant in practice. Afrikaner business, which wanted to combine political and social segregation with an increased dependence on African labour, favoured 'practical apartheid'. By contrast, Afrikaner intellectuals, particularly those in the South African Bureau of Racial Affairs (SABRA), with whom Louw identified, argued that 'white self-determination' was neither politically secure nor morally defensible in a situation of increased reliance on African labour. These intellectuals propagated 'total separation', which envisaged the reversal of African migration from the homelands to the cities and the dynamic development of those homelands to absorb the increased population. In a report submitted in 1956, the Tomlinson Commission recommended an ambitious programme of agricultural, industrial and mining development in the homelands at a cost of £104 million for the first ten years of the scheme.[221]

The government gave the SABRA intellectuals a hearing but made it abundantly clear that it considered total separation impractical politics. As Minister of Native Affairs, Hendrik Verwoerd made little secret of his antipathy towards the Tomlinson Commission and effectively killed its proposals for homeland development. Tomlinson would later ruefully remark that for fifteen years hardly anything was done to improve conditions in the homelands.[222]

It was in the context of the debate over practical and total separation that the theme of Afrikaner survival was taken up by Henry Fagan, an Afrikaans poet who served in the United Party cabinet in the 1930s and who was the chairman of an important commission whose report, published in 1946, called for the relaxation of the curbs on Africans who wished to migrate to the cities. The pre-1948 policy of segregation, he argued, had not been an end in itself but merely a means to limit friction. That policy regulated rather than prohibited interracial contacts and ameliorated undesirable conditions.[223] By contrast, apartheid, with its aim of total separation in every sphere, including in that part of the country where whites and blacks lived intermixed, had become a goal in itself. This had blocked the channels of communication between the races and was a strange policy for a ruling group which had most to lose by a lack of mutual understanding and goodwill. He cited Hodding Carter, a Mississippi newspaper editor, who in 1959, after a visit to South Africa, concluded that no other nation in the world was so strongly divided on language, religious, racial and political grounds.[224]

Fagan believed the restrictive laws of apartheid were unnecessary to regulate racial interaction in virtually all aspects of life. Instead, it was much more prudent to allow convention to assert itself by leaving scope for 'natural, spontaneous conduct' and for the tendency for like to seek like and in this way preserve group identity.[225] Politically, more would be gained by cultivating a mental attitude 'which strives for a fair and just equilibrium between the conflicting aspirations of the various groups than in attempts to draft constitutions aimed at keeping those conflicts in check by artificial restraints'.[226]

What Fagan argued was that without a sense of community and common values having taken root between whites and blacks, it was futile to seek a solution in constitutional safeguards, as liberals hoped to do. He reminded those liberals that they would succeed only if they were able to induce the ruling group to place limitations on its own power. Fagan concluded with an observation which went to the heart of the problem:

> Without the co-operation of that [ruling group] the changes cannot be brought about. The Afrikaners, however, attach much greater value to the possession of political power than merely that of having a say in the running of the country's affairs. They regard it – rightly or wrongly – as an essential safeguard for their survival as a nation. I need hardly say that this touches the most powerful sentiment by which people can be moved. It follows that proposals containing any suggestion of the slightest threat to the political power of Afrikanerdom instantly call for resistance which may be stirred to fanatic vehemence by the urge for national self-preservation.[227]

Fagan begged the central question in his approach. He opposed the extension of the franchise until a sense of community had been fostered. But this raised an argument over which came first: did a sense of community make possible a shared franchise, or was a common franchise necessary before a sense of community could develop based on shared values? Fagan in fact proposed a return to the pre-1948 segregation era, which assumed the incorporation of an African bourgeoisie in a common society. But the African National Congress as the main movement of the oppressed had already turned against this by demanding universal franchise, and the NP was proposing a much more radical alternative to achieve long-term survival: as one of the key cabinet ministers phrased it, the total political expulsion of blacks, who would henceforth enjoy rights only in the homeland. 'The attempts to contain the immediate racial situation must continue but at the same time we must think of a broader, more incisive approach. We must look ahead a hundred years and not merely five. The danger exists that we will win all the battles and yet lose the war.'[228]

Afrikaner nationalists believed that in Verwoerd, who became Prime Minister in 1958, they had found the leader who would provide both the political will and the moral basis for a policy geared towards long-term Afrikaner survival. Verwoerd soon managed to persuade his followers that the power which his government wielded was right not only for the Afrikaners but also for all the other peoples in the country. To those whose conception of morality held that everyone should have complete equality, he conceded the right 'to throw stones'. However, anyone who did not stand for absolute equality should qualify their judgement. The question then became not simply whether the policy was moral towards blacks but also whether it was moral towards whites. Verwoerd had little doubt that Afrikaner and larger white survival should prevail over other rights: 'Every nation has the right to self-protection and self-preservation.' If that nation at the same time 'exercises that right in such a way that it uplifts the other people and protects them from disorderliness and disease and destruction, and educates and takes care of them, then it need not do it in such a way as to constitute a threat to its own survival.'[229] For Verwoerd, the state's first moral obligation was to ensure Afrikaner survival.

Verwoerd stamped out dissent in Afrikaner ranks to the rigid application of the apartheid policy. When the Cottesloe Conference was convened by the World Council of Churches in the aftermath of the Sharpeville massacre, the hope briefly flickered that the Dutch Reformed Church (DRC), by far the largest Afrikaner church, would emerge as a critic of apartheid policy. At that conference, the DRC delegation sided with the concluding statement that rejected all unjust discrimination and recognised all racial groups as part of the total population of the country. In particular it asked for a review of the migrant labour system and the appallingly low wages and poor living conditions of urban

Africans. After Verwoerd had attacked the statement, the Cape and Transvaal synods fell into line, repudiating their own delegations. Apart from a statement by the Western Cape synod in 1963 about migrant labour having become a cancer in the moral fabric of society, the church remained silent about the injustices of apartheid until 1986.[230]

Louw, who by now had returned to South Africa, took a stand with respect to a specific area of dissatisfaction with Verwoerdian policies, namely the rigid segregation of the predominantly Afrikaans-speaking coloured people. Like the Afrikaners, they formed about 10 per cent of the total population and could not in any way be considered a threat to Afrikaner survival. In an introduction to David Botha's *Die opkoms van die derde stand* (The rise of the third estate), Louw enthusiastically welcomed the book's call for the reintegration of coloured people into the social and political life of the Afrikaner community. The coloureds were in fact brown Afrikaners, Louw wrote, and the hurtful apartheid policies to which they were subjected had no base in history or morality. Louw took a less conciliatory line towards the African section of the population, urging them not to be deceived into believing that all of South Africa belonged to them.[231] He conceptualised the struggle as that of two nationalisms, each with its own territorial base. He did not consider the possibility of the various *volke* of the land voluntarily coming together in a single nation. Nor did he ask whether it was ethical to require Africans to suffer major hardship to bring about his preferred solution or whether the economy could afford the massive disruption that implementing it would necessarily entail.[232]

Although the application of apartheid was intensified in the 1960s, doubts about the survival of the Afrikaner people continued to prevail. Writing in a comparative context, Donald Horowitz remarks that apprehension about survival, swamping and subordination is a common theme in conflicts in divided societies. This manifests itself even in situations in which dominant groups are politically in a strong position. There clearly is a psychological process at work, if one takes into account the common tendency to exaggerate dangers and the extreme reactions to modest threats. Horowitz speculates that these fears about survival are actually a projection by which unacceptable impulses felt by one group are imputed to another group, which is the target of such impulses. 'If the thought is that "we wish to overcome and extinguish them", it may be expressed as "they wish to overcome and extinguish us".'²³³ There was undoubtedly an element of this, as the cry for survival under Verwoerd and his successor John Vorster continued to be heard from politicians who concentrated all their efforts on rendering blacks politically impotent.

The debate over alternative means of survival

The cornerstone of apartheid had always been the policy of separate homelands for Africans. In the apartheid scheme of thought, the homelands served three functions: they enabled Africans to enjoy 'separate freedoms', justified socio-economic discrimination against them in 'white' South Africa (more than four-fifths of the total land mass), and increased white security by deflecting and splintering Africans' political aspirations. Despite the discrimination inherent in the policy, the government hoped to win international recognition for it and defuse the external pressure on apartheid. The world community did not initially reject the policy out of hand. In a discussion with Verwoerd in 1961, the Secretary-General of the United Nations, Dag Hammarskjöld, described the requirements which had to be met if the government wanted the homelands to be considered a 'competitive alternative' by the world community:

- Sufficient and coherent territory for the homelands;
- Rapid economic growth and industrial development in these areas;
- Recognise the human rights of Africans working in the common area and remove any compulsion for them to return to the homelands; and
- Require the government to permit the homelands to proceed fairly rapidly to full independence.[234]

In the two decades following this conversation, the NP government made it only too clear that it was not interested in meeting these requirements. There was no attempt to increase the land allocated to the homelands beyond the 13 per cent which had been laid down in 1936, when the government had more limited political and ideological functions for the reserves in mind. Far from recognising the human rights of urban Africans, the Nationalist government now used the homelands as a pretext to justify the 'repatriation' of 'surplus' Africans and to deny African claims to South African citizenship and nationality.

In the 1960s and early 1970s the development of the homelands was largely neglected. Verwoerd's prohibition of investment by white entrepreneurs in the homelands constituted a severe blow to growth. Between 1960 and 1972 a total of only 85,544 jobs were created in the homelands and border areas, well below the figure of 50,000 new jobs a year which the Tomlinson Commission had considered necessary.

The government's resettlement policy further impeded development. Apart from the rapid natural population increase, between 1960 and 1980 the homelands had to accommodate a total of over 2 million Africans: 1 million removed from the farms; 600,000 from 'black spots'; and 750,000 from white cities under a policy of township relocation. The effect on the homelands was devastating. Whereas the average population density in the homelands between 1918 and 1950 was 50 to 60 persons per square mile, this had doubled to 125 persons per square mile by 1970. Between 1970 and 1980, the overall population of the homelands rose by another 57 per cent. The result of the massive inflow of people was a dramatic decline in agricultural production.[235] The homelands became overwhelmingly dependent on the earnings of migrant labour.

Thus by 1970, the separate ethnic development which Afrikaner nationalists once held out as a positive vision had become threadbare. World criticism and the diplomatic ostracism of South Africa continued to mount. In the mid-1960s, Piet Cillié, editor of *Die Burger*, could still ask how it had come about that Afrikaner nationalists, 'the first anti-colonialists of Africa', were now in the dock, charged with being colonialists and oppressors themselves. Cillié had hoped that the idea of 'separate freedoms' for the various ethnonational groups would become an 'irresistible idea . . . comparable with the principle of equality in the American Constitution'.[236] By 1970 Cillié had become despondent: 'Bantu homelands are the essential cornerstone of our [ethnic] relations policy over the longer term. They have fallen by the wayside in our focus of interests and beliefs, which in turn undermines our credibility. We must imbue our policy with idealism and urgency or else our future will become pitch dark.'[237]

From the beginning of the 1970s the NP tried to find a new legitimising ideology for its policies to replace the homelands. Willem de Klerk (brother of the politician FW) was most prominently associated with this attempt to enunciate a new legitimising universal principle. Rejecting integration, he stated that the alternative was not perpetual discrimination but 'equality in diversity'.[238] However, diversity here meant state-imposed classification of the white, coloured, Indian and black groups; and there was no evidence of a move towards equality in state spending on social services and the distribution of other resources. The positive idea of separate freedoms that Cillié wanted to promote had become fatally blurred, as the discriminatory nature of separate development was starkly revealed.

Between 1973 and 1976 white rule suffered several serious blows. In the Durban strikes of 1973, black workers for the first time flexed their muscles in a massive illegal strike. In 1974 the Portuguese buffer states of Mozambique and Angola collapsed. The Soweto uprising of 1976 signalled the beginning of broad-based black resistance. To survive in the changing political environment, the NP government developed a series of new responses. The 1977 White Paper on Defence encapsulated the belief of the security establishment that the country faced a 'total onslaught' on virtually every area of society. The Botha government, which came to power in 1978, broke with the past in openly seeking the support of the English-speaking captains of industry to strengthen the state and persuade the African working class to see the political and economic order as legitimate. The Botha government also vigorously sought to attract black allies, trying to co-opt them into consultative structures and to induce them to 'govern' their own communities and help administer the state. To facilitate this, the government reduced explicit white privilege and symbolic domination. State security and development imperatives began to take precedence over narrow ethnic concerns. The period between the mid-1970s and the end of the 1980s saw the narrowing of the racial salary gap in the civil service, the end of statutory job reservation, and a commitment to equalising spending on white and black social services.

The dramatically changing external environment and internal balance of forces injected new vigour in the ongoing debate about Afrikaner survival. Different responses can be discerned. The right wing rejected all adaptations of the apartheid order. The ethnic splinter group of the Herstigte Nasionale Party (HNP), founded in 1968, was followed by a large breakaway in 1982 when the Conservative Party (CP) was formed. Its support among Afrikaners jumped from 19 per cent in 1983 to 41 per cent in 1992. The CP objected as much to the

NP's alliance with English capital, which was traditionally caricatured as the figure of 'Hoggenheimer', as to its 'liberal' radical policies. As an editorial in the CP's mouthpiece, *Die Patriot*, phrased it: 'A party once described as the "political national front of the Afrikaner" is now visibly associating with the traditional enemy of the Afrikaner, namely Hoggenheimer, to form a relationship against fellow Afrikaners. Such a relationship can destroy the ways of the Afrikaner *volk*.'[239] Andries Treurnicht, who became leader of the Conservatives, emerged as their main ideologue. In the classic apartheid way, he argued that it was not in conflict with the will of God for a *volk* to maintain its own identity and pursue a separate destiny in its own territory.

The Afrikaner mainstream in the NP, on the other hand, accepted that major reforms had become necessary for survival, even if it meant sacrificing some of the freedoms that whites had enjoyed. Shortly after coming to power in 1978, PW Botha declared that the political challenges were such that it had become a matter of 'adapt or die'.[240] The head of the military, General Magnus Malan, referred to the 'problem of reconciling democratic principles with a total strategy' to combat the onslaught, concluding, 'I must emphasise that the overriding consideration is survival. Survival concerns every citizen in South Africa directly and indirectly.'[241]

But survival of what and by which means? Connie Mulder, who was narrowly edged out by Botha in the 1978 NP leadership contest, declared that the fight for survival knew no rules; but this sentiment was widely denounced and retrospectively associated with his downfall. If 'separate freedoms' as a motivating idea for idealistic nationalists was dead, what could replace it? Was there a moral basis to which Afrikaners could appeal for support both inside and outside the country? The hard reality was that the world backed minorities only when they expressed or embodied moral and political principles which other states felt they could not, for their own sake, allow to go under.[242] A critic argued that the West supported Israel because it symbolised idealism, but not South Africa because it embodied crass materialism. 'Afrikanerdom lacks the moral principles worth defending,' he concluded.[243]

A new motivating creed was hard to find, but the main shapers of opinion within the NP had begun to break with apartheid as a legitimising ideal. They accepted that the policy of 'separate freedoms' for whites and blacks had failed, so they turned to Afrikaner history and culture to find values on which to base a new political framework. Two veteran commentators, Schalk Pienaar and Piet Cillié, led the way in NP ranks. Pienaar wrote that the essence of Afrikaner nationalism was a successful struggle against demeaning a person in his own country. Afrikaner nationalism 'was in fatal conflict with itself' if it were to do so to other people in their own land.[244] Cillié observed:

> From our own history we know that a people worth its salt will not in the long run submit to alien government, and because we are aware of this we have not really got the heart to try it. A policy of oppression is impossible for a government of Afrikaners because it would split apart the Afrikaners themselves. Most of the elements which in the long run shape a people spiritually would revolt against such a prospect.[245]

Cillié warned that the quest for freedom lay at the heart of the problem of South Africa. If the government failed to resolve that quest, it would disastrously undermine the Afrikaners' ability to defend themselves. Hence, there was an urgent need to reconsider the basic approach to the problem. Cillié declared: 'The inexorable alternative for separate freedoms is freedom in one plural society; and if the first objective is not applicable, the other must be accepted.' If there was a need to defend South Africa militarily, it must be 'for what [it] can become, not for what it is'. It was impossible to build a united defence force on the prospect of a permanent lack of freedom for important sections of the population. He concluded: 'No common objective for all South Africa's peoples will suffice unless it includes the prospect of co-equal citizenship for all the country's children.'[246]

The framework of the debate in Afrikaner ranks began to shift significantly. The question was no longer whether apartheid was the framework but what its alternatives could be. That immediately raised the question of the most appropriate political vehicle for bringing about an alternative to apartheid. Most important, the issue arose whether the NP government would now attempt to marry the principle of 'co-equal citizenship,' of which Cillié spoke, with apartheid structures.

A contribution by Gerrit Viljoen raised serious doubts on both these scores.

Viljoen was one of the most influential voices in the Afrikaner intellectual elite in the 1970s and 1980s. A Classical scholar, he entered politics in 1979 after an academic career and served for two years as the government's main constitutional negotiator with the ANC after the ban against it was lifted early in 1990. In a book published in 1978, Viljoen set out to demolish the myth that the Afrikaners would mount a rock-solid resistance impervious to all change. There were few *volke*, he argued, who were as prepared as the Afrikaners to make drastic changes in a balanced and sober way in order to survive in changing circumstances. He warned that the road ahead pointed to a much more dangerous, risky and less protected phase of ethnic self-maintenance. In the past Afrikaners were too inclined to insist on excessive and artificial self-protection. Nevertheless, he assured his readers that despite all this, the NP was still basically concerned with nationalism: 'the maintenance and well-being of our nation and our *volk*, the survival of our identity, our cohesiveness, our sense of calling'.[247]

Viljoen now turned to what he called the 'minimal conditions' for Afrikaner survival. Here Viljoen sought to link up with Louw, who had warned, in *Liberale nasionalisme*, of the danger that members of a small *volk* could begin, to use a phrase from ancient Roman history, 'to despair of the state'. To prevent this, they must be persuaded that 'within the fold of the *volk* there was room for a complete life to be lived'. In particular, the creators of culture must feel strongly that it was important for their *volk* to continue to exist.[248] Viljoen asked: 'What unique values were the Afrikaners contributing to the history of human culture to reinforce their claim that they had a right to exist and survive?' Viljoen argued that ultimately the most profound justification (he called it the *dieper reg* – the higher right, the title of the Louw drama) of Afrikaner survival was not 'physical or economic might but the quality and appeal (*voortreflikheid*) of our intellectual and social life, the ethical values which direct it, and the interpretation and explanation of life in our arts – in short, our cultural life'.[249]

But Viljoen fatally undercut this assessment by continuing to demand a political leadership role for the Afrikaners; by insisting on strategies to maintain an Afrikaner identity; and by failing to disentangle the need for the survival of ethnic groups (that is, Afrikaners), for which some sympathy from outsiders could be expected, from that of exclusive racial groups (that is, whites), for which little sympathy was left. For instance, Viljoen argued, it was necessary to provide training and mutual help to sustain Afrikaner and white workers, once formal job reservation had disappeared. Once the racial sex laws disappeared, there was a need for 'preaching and social sanctions' to maintain the 'racial purity of our *volk*' and to counter 'miscegenation and biological mixing'.[250] Politically, Viljoen rejected integration because it would negate the 'whole Afrikaner striving to maintain their separate identity'. He still kept the option open for whites to have their 'own' land, though a smaller territory than the existing one. Finally, he was adamant about the main political feature of South Africa, saying that 'the Afrikaner is the core of our society, the hub of our politics, the dynamo of our cultural life. It was he who had to lead, take the initiative and anticipate political problems and it was he who had to tackle and solve these questions creatively.'[251] It is puzzling how Viljoen, with such a political agenda, could hope to appeal to other groups in South Africa and the outside world or to make Afrikaner culture attractive to outsiders and Afrikaners alike. His conditions for cultural and political survival seemed directly in conflict with each other.

The untenability of racial discrimination and the growing crisis of Afrikaner power prompted many Afrikaners outside as well as inside nationalist circles to reread Louw. The first existential crisis of which he warned, namely military defeat, was now only a remote possibility. Driven by the 'total onslaught' ideology, the Botha administration had armed the state to the teeth.[252] Nor was the second crisis, that of a strategically significant number of the Afrikaner political and cultural elite defecting to another cultural group, a possibility. Afrikaans culture was, in fact, flourishing. With few exceptions, Afrikaner parents sent their children to Afrikaans schools and universities; Afrikaans publishing houses brought out a great variety of fiction and nonfiction; and on state radio and television, Afrikaans enjoyed a position of parity with English with respect to programmes on the main channel.

Increasingly, the third crisis of which Louw had spoken became the main framework for the debate. Louw questioned whether a small *volk* could survive if it had become something hateful in the eyes of its best intellectuals, and he committed himself to going under rather than surviving in injustice. But this stand almost appeared to contradict the very high premium he put on ethnic survival and it did not address the question, later posed by Viljoen, of how survival in injustice could constitute a *survival* crisis, as distinct from a political crisis, for a *volk*.[253]

By the early 1980s, several Afrikaner intellectuals felt compelled to address issues raised by Louw. There was, however, a problem. Whereas Louw wrote at a time when nationalism enjoyed ideological hegemony among Afrikaners, many members of a new generation of intellectuals had broken with nationalism and now espoused individual rights and other liberal values. Could these intellectuals now participate in a debate which Louw as a nationalist had couched in predominantly nationalist terms? Louw himself was ambivalent about the issue. On occasion he declared that it was the task of *volkskritiek* to expose that which was wrong, adding that it could be the fate of a particular generation to demolish rather than to build up. More common, however, was his insistence on continuing solidarity with the *volk* and its culture, writing: 'One does not love a *volk* because it is splendid or pre-eminent; one loves it because of its miseries. One does not love it for its virtues, prowess or beauty, but because it is flawed, blind and hapless – and because it constitutes a mere possibility.'[254] Louw never considered abandoning his role of an Afrikaner intellectual critical of, but loyal to, his *volk*. Quoting Voltaire on the toleration of dissent, Louw declared that even if it were wrong, it was his duty to persuade the *volk*, so that change could come about as a result of better insights. However, he would resist with all his might change from the outside or through force.[255]

The debate over survival in justice

The Soweto uprising of 1976 and the resurgence of black political protest in the 1980s moved the debate about different strategies for survival into the mainstream of Afrikaner politics. By now almost all the most prominent Afrikaans writers and poets and many academics had become alienated from the cruder aspects of apartheid. Several writers addressed the issue of the Afrikaans language's survival, the most tangible cultural manifestation of the Afrikaner people. They argued that the very policies of government threatened Afrikaner survival by contaminating Afrikaans through its association with apartheid. Jan Rabie charged that apartheid alienated the Afrikaner youth and drove the coloured people into 'English arms or black nationalism'.[256] Other writers contended that what made Afrikaners different from a colonial people was the fact that the Afrikaans language was a multi-racial achievement developed originally by European settlers, slaves and Khoikhoi people as a lingua franca. Hence, Afrikaners and Afrikaans would have a right to survival only if they remained true to its multi-racial history and heritage.[257] A quite different note was struck by the poet Breyten Breytenbach, who was jailed in 1975 for seven years after entering the country on a clandestine mission. He emerged as the most radical, vociferous and eloquent Afrikaner critic of the establishment's survival thinking.

Breytenbach did not subscribe to the central concern of the debate about survival, namely whether Afrikaans and Afrikaners could survive after apartheid. As Walzer points out, Breytenbach, like Camus in the Algerian case, saw his people as Africans who were in Africa to stay. Unlike Camus, however, Breytenbach strongly believed that the problem of his people staying could only be solved 'within a Black socio-cultural field of reference'.[258] Afrikaners were a 'bastard people' with a 'bastard language' whose destiny was 'to decompose' in order to come together in new forms.[259] The overriding priority was not survival or securing individual rights in a post-apartheid South Africa but the realisation 'of one South African cultural identity composed of an incredibly rich variety of sources and expressions'.[260] Breytenbach excoriated the Afrikaners who had defined themselves exclusively (as white, European, Protestant) and 'allowed for greed to be rationalised as survival, developing a tribal ethos of negation, suppression and withdrawal'.[261]

Yet for all his outrage, Breytenbach did not become totally alienated. Just as Louw had demanded, Breytenbach, as a critic, shared in the shame of his people.[262] 'What exists in this country has been perpetrated in our – in my – name, in our – in my – language', he wrote in 1972. He added that 'I cannot and will not dissociate myself from this mess'.[263] In 1986 he wrote that the critic can only be effective when he speaks 'in his language, his land'.[264] His prime task was to develop a new awareness among his own people of what was being perpetrated in their name.

The stringent criticisms of Breytenbach and other Afrikaans writers were the backdrop against which the linguist Jaap Steyn returned to Louw's theme that the future of the Afrikaners would be at risk if the *volk* became something evil in the eyes of their own intelligentsia. Steyn discounted the possibility that a negative self-image could objectively be the result of insufficient achievement by Afrikaners.[265] The problem, he argued, lay with the interpreters. The great danger was no longer that Afrikaner intellectuals would neglect to object to injustice but that, in the process of correcting what was wrong, they would 'write off' the Afrikaners and 'in the process of criticising Afrikaner errors they would do it so mercilessly that the younger generation will hesitate to identify with the Afrikaans culture and people'.[266]

This was too much for André du Toit, a philosopher from the University of Stellenbosch. In a book, *Die sondes van die vaders* (The sins of the fathers), which took as its motif Louw's third threat to survival, Du Toit correctly called it absurd that Afrikaner intellectuals could be suspected of any excessive zeal in exposing the injustices of apartheid.[267] For Du Toit the problem was, rather, that the moral crisis of exclusive Afrikaner power, embroiled as it was in a system of racial domination, was becoming ever more acute; and Afrikaner youth faced the prospect of an endless military struggle without a convincing rationale.[268]

Yet Steyn had a point. If the criticism was single-mindedly focused on what was evil and hateful, why would people listen? And could such criticism not be counterproductive? Would it not lead to strengthening either the conservative claim that nothing could be gained from reform or their claim that no basis existed for a peaceful settlement short of capitulation? As Michael Walzer remarked in a general context, criticism is only heeded if the critic is seen as connected and 'one of us'.[269] To this, someone like Breytenbach might reply that the policy of apartheid did give Afrikaners a hateful stigma and that the time had come to debate the Afrikaners' survival outside the context Louw had suggested.

It was left to the Stellenbosch philosopher Johannes Degenaar, author of a book on Camus and of essays on Louw and various aspects of moral philosophy, to provide the analytical framework in which the concern for Afrikaner survival could be reconciled with the desire for a just political system. In the spirit of Louw, Degenaar attacked a chauvinistic ethnonationalism but held open the possibility of an open plural society in which individuals and ethnic groups could coexist peacefully. His most outstanding essays appeared in his book *Voortbestaan in geregtigheid* (Survival in justice), published in 1982. The opening essay, 'Mondigwording en Afrikanerskap' (Coming of age and being an Afrikaner), introduces Immanuel Kant's perspective on the Enlightenment, which he saw as a process of liberation from immaturity to one in which a person could critically review those presuppositions and structures of his which could not pass the test of morality. Degenaar rejected both the liberal model, which spoke only in individualistic terms and denied the possibility of individuals becoming mature as Afrikaners, and the nationalist model, which thought only in terms of ethnic structures and believed individuals could only become mature within the fold of the *volk*. Instead, he chose a pluralist model, which allowed for the possibility that individuals could also attain adulthood as Afrikaners.[270]

Degenaar contended that identity was not God-given but was the product of voluntary identification with a group and its values. Attaining adulthood did not mean becoming alienated from the Afrikaner group but it did represent a critical assessment of obsolete Afrikaner idioms and an opportunity to renew one's membership of the Afrikaner people creatively. That meant choosing values in the history of one's group which could pass the test of fairness and morality. It also meant thinking in moral terms about survival. It was necessary to take justice, rather than the sovereignty of the *volk*, as the yardstick for politics and to seek co-operation between whites and blacks on the basis of negotiation, not consultation.

What would a just political order look like? Degenaar did not elaborate on this but made it clear that the final test was justice: 'A creatively renewed Afrikanerhood in changed conditions . . . means choosing not mere survival, but survival in justice which was the essential condition for physical survival.'[271]

Much of the debate about survival in the 1970s and 1980s took place in a context in which white domination looked unassailable, but this world would not last. The years 1985 to 1986 constituted a political watershed. Resistance to apartheid had reached a point where the government was compelled to declare a state of emergency. Suddenly the political future of Afrikaners and Afrikaans culture looked as uncertain as Louw thought it was in 1950. Three positions with respect to Afrikaner survival now emerged. On the right, there were about a third of Afrikaners who believed that only continued domination would secure survival; a section of them entertained the idea of a much-reduced Afrikaner homeland. To the left, a position crystallised which was best articulated by Van Zyl Slabbert, who became leader of the Progressive Federal Party in 1979, ten years after he had left the University of Stellenbosch. Although his party never attracted the support of more than 5 per cent of Afrikaners, Slabbert remained an influential voice in Afrikaner intellectual circles. For Slabbert the debate about the political future of the Afrikaners and Afrikaans and survival in justice was a mere abstraction unless a settlement was negotiated with the majority. The book *South Africa's Options*, which Slabbert co-authored with David Welsh, was not particularly sanguine about the prospects for democracy in South Africa. Yet it posed the challenge to whites to break out of the condition of siege and negotiate pacts with leaders of all representative movements.[272]

The third position which emerged was the NP leadership's version of sharing power. This fell short of the demand for a genuine liberal democracy but recognised the need for a negotiated settlement. In the course of the 1980s the idea of negotiations won through among the Afrikaner and larger white elite. A survey conducted in 1989 (before the ban against the ANC was lifted) among a broad spectrum of the elite found that over 80 per cent thought that a mutually acceptable settlement between whites and blacks was possible in South Africa, that negotiations were a feasible method of resolving the conflict, that the ANC had to be one of the negotiating parties, and that negotiations did not entail bargaining only about the transfer of power.[273]

Conclusion

It is always difficult to establish the precise ways in which political ideas influence political practice. In South Africa the ideas of both Afrikaans- and English-speaking intellectuals had once served the ruling class well in constructing the policy of apartheid, which was patently geared towards promoting the interests of the Afrikaner people. It is, however, a different matter to persuade a people to give up their privileges and put the survival of their ethnonational group at risk. Nevertheless, ideas do count. In 1992 a respected analyst, John Kane-Berman, head of the liberal South African Institute of Race Relations, expressed his conviction that apartheid had started to collapse when the intellectuals supporting the NP and the Dutch Reformed Church, the main Afrikaner church, withdrew their support.[274] This concluding section will briefly look at the context in which ideas played a major role in discrediting apartheid in Afrikaner ranks and paved the way for negotiations.

Firstly, the matter has to be seen both in its universal and in its specific historical context. In his book *The End of History and the Last Man*, Francis Fukuyama offers a way of doing so. He argues that much of human behaviour can be explained as a combination of two parts: desire, which induces people to seek things outside themselves (material possessions and collective security), while reason or calculation shows them the best way to achieve them. But in addition, the *thymos* part of the soul induces human beings to seek recognition of their own worth and to invest the self with a certain value.[275] When other people slight them, they feel anger; when they do not live up to their own sense of worth, they feel shame.

In the 1950s, when more than half of the Afrikaners were still farmers and blue-collar workers, the idea of survival in justice had little chance of prevailing over apartheid, which promised massive state intervention to make them secure from black competition. By the mid-1970s, some three-quarters of Afrikaners had become a relatively secure middle class. By now, however, black resistance and world condemnation had exposed the moral indefensibility of apartheid. A growing sense of shame, mostly among Afrikaner intellectuals and some church leaders, developed about the arrogance and greed which characterised apartheid. At the same time Afrikaner politicians were confronted with the fact that their policies had failed either to produce stability or to lessen the outrage over apartheid. As the white position steadily weakened and the economy stagnated, the need for a morally defensible and politically feasible alternative became compelling.

NP politicians found it difficult to confess that apartheid was morally wrong, especially if the connotation was that apartheid was devised with malicious intent. Hence, their most common response was that apartheid was abandoned because it was not feasible to develop separate homelands for whites and Africans. Yet the charge of moral culpability is difficult to escape altogether. In a television interview, President FW de Klerk tried to address the issue by saying that once the homelands policy failed, apartheid was clearly seen to be unworkable. He added: 'If one believes a policy is unworkable, it becomes immoral to advocate it. Because then you advocate something in which you don't believe... I say it is wrong, because it is unworkable, because the emphasis shifted from creating rights to maintaining political privileges, and that is morally wrong.'[276]

Immediately after the first post-apartheid election, De Klerk was asked by an

Afrikaans newspaper how he would like to be remembered. He responded: 'I hope as a peace-maker, as someone who had the courage of his convictions to do what was right. I believe that no one's security, not even that of a section of the population, can be built on injustice. Only if we ensure justice for all shall we have peace.'[277] These statements pointed to the need of the NP leadership to find a moral basis for its policy in which the idea of survival in justice could have resonance. The demise of apartheid was, of course, a complex development in which the intellectual debate about survival in justice was only one contributing factor along with an array of political, demographic, and economic pressures.[278] Nevertheless, to ignore it would be to misunderstand the larger process.

4.

Ethnic business and economic empowerment: The Afrikaner case, 1915–1970

Asked just before his death whether he knew of any cases of an Afrikaans business being empowered by an English corporation, the entrepreneur Anton Rupert replied: 'I cannot think of any, and I am very grateful for that.'[279] Fred du Plessis, executive chairman of Sanlam, the corporation that once dominated Afrikaans business, denied that political power helped Afrikaans business to succeed. 'The Afrikaner can look back not because he was privileged to receive state grants, but because he was capable of putting himself forward and fighting for his economic position.'[280] An academic study of the Afrikaner economic advance paints a completely different picture. It attributes the Afrikaner's strong economic upsurge after 1948 mainly to the decision of the conglomerate Anglo American Corporation to sell a mining house under its control 'at a fraction of its value' to the subsidiary of an Afrikaans insurance company.[281] A recent history of the political economy stated that the National Party government gave 'massive handouts' to Afrikaner farmers, financial capitalists, small traders and workers.[282] Neither the business leaders nor the academics substantiated their claims.

This chapter is not concerned with the massive preferential treatment that whites received from government for most of the twentieth century as part of a policy, endorsed by virtually all whites, to establish a secure white dominant group. State aid specifically to Afrikaner-dominated commercial agriculture is left out of consideration, although farmers provided much of the capital for some of the Afrikaans businesses discussed here. Instead the chapter concentrates on the ethnic nature of Afrikaner entrepreneurship and on the question whether English corporations or the state tried to assist Afrikaner corporations. While

English-speakers were a minority within the white minority and were largely excluded from political power, in 1910 they dominated the economy, the bureaucracy and the professions.

A special kind of entrepreneur

Joseph Schumpeter's great insight was that entrepreneurs, driven by the gift to innovate and possessed by the dream and will to found a private kingdom, constitute the driving force of economic progress.[283] In the case of entrepreneurs belonging to an economically 'backward' group there is an additional spur: to demonstrate to their own group and the economically dominant group that they can succeed. The Afrikaner entrepreneurs not only wanted to get rich, but also desired to help their people to develop economically and promote a general sense of Afrikaner self-worth.

In his path-breaking study *Ethnic Groups in Conflict*, Donald Horowitz stressed that the struggle in multi-ethnic societies is primarily between groups over *relative* group worth and capacity. He writes: 'If the need to feel worthy is a fundamental human requirement, it is satisfied in considerable measure by belonging to groups that are in turn regarded as worthy. Like individual self-esteem, collective self-esteem is achieved largely by social recognition'.[284]

There are two routes to the empowerment of a relatively undeveloped group. In the Afrikaner case there was a general ethnic mobilisation in which the economic advancement of the group was inextricably linked to the pursuit of political power and the promotion of Dutch (and later Afrikaans) as a language. This economic mobilisation did not receive much direct state aid and did not impose serious burdens on the economically dominant group. Afrikaner entrepreneurs like MS Louw, Anton Rupert and Andreas Wassenaar took as much pride in their individual success as in the ability of their corporations to capture a larger share of the market for the Afrikaners as a group.

The other form of economic advancement is state-driven. President Thabo Mbeki of South Africa stated that the experience of the Malaysian government was of 'critical importance' to the efforts of the African National Congress-led government to promote black economic empowerment.[285] Beneficiaries of the New Economic Policy (NEP) of Malaysia, introduced in 1971, considered it 'a form of governance that helped to create a stable political culture and a thriving, open economy'.²⁸⁶ The business elite of the dominant group profited mainly through close ties with the state and large corporations. For Malay beneficiaries with state contracts there was, initially at least, not nearly the same risk of failure as for other businesses. Invariably, some of the businesses came to grief in economic downturns, causing dissension within the ruling party. For Chinese business the trade-off between political stability and economic constraints and impositions was sustainable in periods of strong growth.²⁸⁷

James Jesudason explains in detail how the leaders of a group like the Malays can enhance group capacity and group worth by expanding state enterprises and offering better jobs or limiting the enterprises and job opportunities of ethnic outsiders. The policy of ethnic preferment provides new opportunities to the politically dominant group for generating wealth, income and employment. It bolsters support for ethnic leaders, even from those who do not benefit from the policies. 'From visible evidence that some members of the community have become better off, the individual can hope that his time or his children's will come.'²⁸⁸

For Mahathir bin Mohamad, architect and driver of the NEP, group pride was at stake as much as economic advancement. In his book *The Malay Dilemma*,²⁸⁹ he defended the appointment of a small number of Malay company directors in the 1960s under the laissez-faire policy that preceded the NEP. 'The poor themselves have not gained one iota. But if these few Malays are not enriched, the poor Malays will not gain either. It is the Chinese who will continue to live in huge houses and regard the Malays as only fit to drive their cars.'

When Mahathir retired as Prime Minister after serving for more than twenty years, he noted the considerable Malay economic advancement, but also questioned whether the objective of bolstering group pride had been realised. The NEP's intention, he stated, was 'to give a head start to the Malays so that they could compete with the other races, as well as not to be too dependent on the government.' After more than thirty years of the NEP, the majority of Malay businessmen were still not able to stand independently. 'They only want government contracts, but if there are no government contracts they will fail.' Mahathir regretted that the Malays had not dispensed with 'the crutch' to free themselves from reliance on others. The main message that the Malays as 'majority race' should have understood was to work harder and depend less on handouts. 'I feel disappointed because I achieved too little of my principal task of making my race a successful race, a race that is respected.'[290] Mahathir failed to recognise that the roots of the failure lay in his policy of managing Malay advancement through the state, setting up a small elite dependent on state patronage.

A people lagging behind

Largely descended from Dutch, German and French Huguenot immigrants, the Afrikaners entered the twentieth century largely as a farming people. Wheat and wine farming in the south-west and wool farming in the east offered opportunities for capital accumulation. Most farmers, however, engaged in subsistence farming. With many fingers burnt through the collapse of some thirty district banks between 1862 and 1899, most Afrikaner capital was invested in trust companies. It was the British settlers in South Africa who seized most of the new opportunities with the freeing up of trade and industry in the nineteenth century. Along with Jews from Eastern Europe, they took over trading. It was they, rather than the Afrikaners, who first saw the potential of large-scale land speculation. During the 1830s they introduced wool farming in the eastern part of the Cape Colony, and they founded export-import firms in Port Elizabeth and Cape Town that would soon ease out the firms founded by Afrikaners. The entrepreneurs who set up sophisticated industrial and financial companies were of British origin or Eastern European Jews.

The South African War (1899–1902) dealt a crushing blow to Afrikaner economic progress in the Transvaal and the Free State. Three-quarters of the livestock in the former state and two-thirds of the livestock in the latter were destroyed. In the Cape Colony many Afrikaners suspected of sympathy with the republican cause were ruined economically. A fierce hatred of British capitalism, seen as the moving force in the destruction of the two republics, was born. An Afrikaner nationalist movement was forged out of anti-imperialist sentiments, a common commitment to preserving racial privileges, and an insistence that Dutch (and later Afrikaans) be treated as an official language, along with English, as a symbol of group worth.

The first proper census, taken in 1904, showed 556,000 Afrikaners, representing 58 per cent of the white population. These figures grew to 2,270,300 or 58.5 per cent of the white community by 1970. The number of Afrikaners living in towns and cities rose from 105,100 (18.9 per cent) in 1904 to 536,200 (47.8 per cent) in 1936 and to 1,853,260 (81.6 per cent) in 1970.[291]

Many of the Afrikaners who became urbanised in the first four decades of the twentieth century were forced off the land through war, over-stocking and undercapitalisation. They lacked skills and other resources and could barely speak English, the language of commerce and industry. An Afrikaner underclass was already evident by 1910, when the four British-controlled territories formed the Union of South Africa. In 1917 Afrikaners were estimated to have contributed only 13 per cent to the gross domestic product and only 3 per cent to the non-agricultural sector.[292] At the start of the 1930s one out of four Afrikaners was deemed to be part of the category of poor whites – white people regarded as so destitute that they could not maintain a so-called white standard of living. Educational standards were low. Out of a hundred who started school, only eight completed the twelfth or final year. Fewer than three went on to university.

Afrikaners were poorly represented in many of the white-collar occupations. In 1939 only 3 per cent of people in the professional category with the most prestige (owners of companies, directors and self-employed manufacturers) were Afrikaners. Of the white population, Afrikaners made up 3 per cent of the engineers, 4 per cent of accountants, 11 per cent of lawyers, 15 per cent of medical doctors and 21 per cent of journalists. Less than a quarter of senior civil servants spoke Afrikaans as a first language.[293] Only a quarter of apprentices in skilled trades were Afrikaners.

A 1947 study presented this portrait of the urbanised Afrikaner poor:

> His poverty, servitude and desperate search for work feeds a sense of dependency and inferiority. Feeling himself unwelcome, he presents himself poorly, he is timid, walks hat in hand and lacks the greater self-confidence of the English work-seeker. He wields no influence and no one intercedes on his behalf; his *volk* is small and subordinate to a world power that backs up the English work-seeker. He is despised and treated as an inferior by other nations.[294]

Early Afrikaner entrepreneurs

When the company Nasionale Pers was founded in 1914 (the same year as the National Party), the main objective was to publish a newspaper to oppose the government's decision to enter the war in Europe on Britain's side. Jannie de Waal, the only Nationalist MP with newspaper experience, was convinced that the paper would fail. Cape Town had a small Dutch newspaper readership and almost all the advertisers were English-speakers fiercely supportive of South Africa's participation in the war. Jannie Marais, the main financial backer, wanted a newspaper which would 'in the first place inquire about the wishes and rights of our own land and *volk*, and not the wishes and instructions of Johannesburg and elsewhere'.[295] The company's first dividend was paid out only in 1928.[296]

The establishment of the first insurance companies occurred in the aftermath of the Rebellion of 1914–1915, waged by some 11,500 northern Afrikaners against South Africa's participation in the war. Nationalists across the country launched a major fundraising drive to pay the rebels' fines and the crippling civil claims for damages. By the end of 1917 it was clear that the various Helpmekaar (Mutual aid) associations would be able to pay all fines and settle all claims. As important as the funds that were collected was the development of an enormous sense of self-empowerment and achievement. The Helpmekaar associations dramatically revealed the accumulation of considerable Afrikaner savings. Afrikaner capital started flowing to Afrikaner institutions. Between 1914 and 1922, 26 Afrikaner trust companies and boards of executors were established.[297]

WA (Willie) Hofmeyr, a Cape Town lawyer who combined his business initiatives with an ethnic commitment, played a leading role in the founding of an insurance company. He often said that Afrikaans as a language would only get due recognition once it had acquired commercial value. He was one of the founders of Nasionale Pers in 1914 and in the following year he resigned as a partner in a flourishing law firm to become organising secretary of the Cape National Party. In 1918 he became chairman of the Suid-Afrikaanse Nasionale Trust en Assuransie Maatskappy (Santam), whose offer of £200,000 worth of shares was quickly taken up. In the same year the company founded the Suid-Afrikaanse Nasionale Lewens Assuransie Maatskappy (Sanlam) with issued share capital of £25,000. By the end of the First World War, 60 per cent of life assurance policies were written by South African companies. Sanlam was the first that targeted the white Afrikaans-speaking market as its niche.

Hofmeyr and MS (Tinie) Louw, who would play a major innovative role as a senior Sanlam manager, were both well-qualified men with a sense of social responsibility for poorer Afrikaners. They challenged the prevailing consensus that English was the language of business, that government should not intervene in the labour market, and that, as *The Cape*, a Cape Town weekly, phrased it, 'making party politics a commercial business' would 'perpetuate racialism and ill-feeling'.[298] The economist Jan Sadie speaks of a conflict situation within white society between English-speakers 'who dominated socially and economically, and Afrikaners, who perceived themselves to be despised as an inferior race or out-group'.[299]

Hofmeyr and Louw resolved to build Sanlam on the basis of Afrikaner customers. In his 1922 chairman's address Hofmeyr said: 'Sanlam is a genuine Afrikaner people's institution. As Afrikaners we will naturally give preference to an Afrikaans institution.'[300] Nationalist commitment rather than entrepreneurial daring was decisive in the founding of the first Afrikaner corporations.

Louw was not an entrepreneur in the Schumpeterian sense, but a man with a pioneering vision of Sanlam's place in society. A committed nationalist, he saw himself as an innovator serving his ethnic community. 'I am committed to creating job opportunities for the Afrikaner to enable him to use his talents to secure himself in this sunny land.'[301] This corporate philosophy also made business sense. Sanlam's prospective clients were not very knowledgeable about business and finance. They were more likely to trust a Sanlam agent speaking their own language. Twenty years after its establishment, more than 90 per cent of Sanlam's policies were written in Afrikaans.

The bank Volkskas was founded in 1933 in Pretoria out of a mix of cultural and business considerations. In 1933 the Executive Council of the Afrikaner Broederbond, a secret Afrikaans cultural organisation, started a savings bank to mobilise Afrikaner capital in order to finance Afrikaner enterprises and employ the Afrikaner poor. When the government refused permission for the registration of a commercial bank, the Bond's treasurer, JJ Bosman, and some sixty Broeders founded a co-operative bank. Bosman wanted to channel the savings that the bank attracted into loans to small businesses that would employ Afrikaners and help solve the poor white problem. Using the anti-capitalist rhetoric of many northern Afrikaners, the first chief accountant declared that the bank would have crashed at an early stage 'if honour and selfish motive were the driving forces'. Volkskas became a commercial bank in 1942, but other banks fully recognised it only in 1947.[302]

Albert Wessels, a member of the second generation of Afrikaner entrepreneurs, reflected on his entry into the world of business during the mid-1930s in the following way: 'I felt obliged towards my own conscience to succeed economically in order to demonstrate to my fellow Afrikaners that we could become the equals among my English-speaking fellow citizens. The precondition was that we had to prepare ourselves and to work hard. Only once there was complete equality in the economic field could there be true co-operation among all language groups'.[303]

Anton Rupert, the most successful Afrikaner entrepreneur, also expressed himself in the classic terms of Afrikaner economic mobilisation. He declared that he did not see 'free enterprise as a means of creating wealth for its own sake'. He defined the purpose of his business as that of furthering 'our nation's progress and to help Afrikaners to gain their rightful place in industry and their future as employers and employees'. Dirk Hertzog, co-founder of Rembrandt, stated: 'Our overriding concern was to prove that, by standing together, we [the Afrikaners] could take our place in the business world with dignity and honour.'[304]

But sentiment was not enough to grow ethnic businesses. In 1939, a full three decades after Union, Afrikaners controlled a mere 1 per cent of mining business and 3 per cent of industry and construction. Well over 80 per cent of these industrial undertakings were one-man operations. In commerce, some 2,400 enterprises (mostly garages, retail shops and butchers) were in Afrikaner hands, giving them an 8 per cent share of the sector. In the financial sector the share was 5 per cent. Afrikaners owned or managed no large industrial undertaking, no major commercial enterprise, no finance house, no building society and no consumer association. Afrikaner personal income was 60 per cent of that of English-speaking whites.[305]

The lack of Afrikaner success in the corporate world raises the question why the Nationalists accepted it, despite their domination of government cabinets for more than half of the fifty years of Union. O'Dowd pointed out that South

Africa (like the US) was almost unique in that no nationalisation occurred in an economy that had originally been developed largely by foreign capital. To him the main reasons were the control over economic policy which the country gained in the Act of Union, the acquisition by South African English-speakers of a large part of British-controlled companies, and the policy of secondary industrialisation. O'Dowd writes: '[Secondary industrialisation] was a decision taken by the Pact government. The primary credit for this belongs to the Afrikaners, and it was in effect opposed by many, although not all, English-speaking South Africans.'[306]

The parastatal corporations, managed mainly by Afrikaners, became an important part of secondary industry. Conceding the almost complete absence of Afrikaner entrepreneurial achievement in the manufacturing sector, Schumann, a Stellenbosch economic historian, pointed to the Iron and Steel Industrial Corporation (Iscor) in Pretoria as proof of his claim that it was possible for 'Afrikaners, with the right kind of training, to make a success of large-scale industry'.[307] Iscor provided a training school where Afrikaner entrepreneurs, managers and scientists could acquire technical and managerial skills.

The 'economic movement'

The Depression and prolonged drought of the early 1930s focused the attention of the white political leadership on the poor white issue, which was the theme of a major research project and a conference held in 1932. The dramatic rise in the price of gold and the prolonged boom starting in 1933 changed the country's economic prospects profoundly. The projects of saving the Afrikaner poor and raising Afrikaner capital for investment purposes now became even more entangled than before.

During the centenary celebrations of the Great Trek in 1938, the Rev. JD Kestell ('Father' Kestell) of Bloemfontein called for a mighty *reddingsdaad* or 'rescue action' to save the descendants of the Voortrekkers 'living in hopeless poverty, sunken materially, morally and spiritually'. No government charity or outside help would help them; the answer lay in a collective effort by the Afrikaners. 'A people is an integrated whole – the poor and rich,' Kestell said. His call – *'n volk red homself* – a people rescues itself – became a leading theme in the ideology of the Nationalist movement.[308]

In 1939 the Broederbond's Executive Council accepted a plan for using Afrikaner savings and capital in enterprises that would 'save' the Afrikaner poor by employing them. It hoped that along this path the Afrikaners could also become 'autonomous economically'. At this time senior executives at Sanlam had concluded that it was time to escape from the narrow limits of insurance and agricultural credit to which the company was subjected. The board wanted to establish its own finance house to centralise efforts to attract Afrikaner savings for investment in promising enterprises.

Afrikaner savings by the end of the 1930s were estimated at about £100 million and the Afrikaners' purchasing power was at about the same level. Yet mobilising some of that capital for risk investment was a daunting challenge. Hendrik Verwoerd said that Afrikaners 'were almost over-organised on the cultural terrain and unorganised for economic purposes'.[309] Farmers tended to reinvest their profits in their farms, and most other Afrikaners put their savings into safe investment havens such as banks, building societies and trust companies. TE Dönges observed that Afrikaner capital was mainly invested in bonds; in his view it could have been much better invested. It was said that Afrikaners trusted their fellow Afrikaners with their political fate but not with their money.[310]

In 1939 Afrikaner economic and cultural leaders met in Bloemfontein to discuss a comprehensive plan for Afrikaner economic 'salvation'. Rejecting any element of charity, the plan was to mobilise purchasing power and capital to enable Afrikaners to become economically independent. The speakers at this Eerste Ekonomiese Volkskongres (First Economic People's Congress) read like a who's who of future Afrikaner entrepreneurs. The Volkskongres acted as the catalyst for Sanlam and the Broederbond to join hands in an attempt to bridge the acute North–South rivalry in the Afrikaner nationalist movement. What the Transvaal-based Broederbond offered was cultural entrepreneurs and what Sanlam offered was business expertise. Several Sanlam senior executives now accepted invitations to become members of the Bond.

In the opening address to the Volkskongres, LJ du Plessis, a Potchefstroom academic who played a leading role in the establishment of Volkskas, defined the goal as mobilising 'the *volk* to conquer the capitalist system and to transform it so that it fits our ethnic nature'. The message was that free enterprise was not intended primarily to create wealth for individuals for their own sake, or for a handful of individuals, but to help Afrikaners as a people to acquire a legitimate share of the economy.[311]

The economic mobilisers took the listed finance houses on the JSE as their model, but they wanted their own finance houses to marry three quite different objectives: to make a profit for their shareholders; to promote the collective advancement of Afrikaners; and to help poor Afrikaners by offering them respectable jobs. Tinie Louw's proposal to the Sanlam board for a finance house captured the spirit of Afrikaner entrepreneurship at that time. An Afrikaner finance house would have to observe sound business principles, and the profit motive would not be excluded, but his proposal added: 'While management would try to make the greatest possible profits for its shareholders, the main purpose will always be to enhance the Afrikaner position in trade and industry.'[312]

The Congress established the finance house Federale Volksbeleggings (FVB), which would be controlled by Sanlam. Afrikaners were asked to engage in conventional investment in shares in sound Afrikaans enterprises. In a secret circular to its branches across the country, the Broederbond encouraged its members to support Afrikaner enterprises.[313] In 1941 it listed ten economic duties for all 'proper' Afrikaners, among them the following:

(1) Every Afrikaner must, even if it takes great sacrifices, become a shareholder in an Afrikaans credit institution. We mention specifically Federale Volksbeleggings. [FVB's address was given.]
(2) Every Afrikaner must be a policyholder of an Afrikaans insurance company.
(3) Every Afrikaner must save and invest his savings in an Afrikaans institution. [The names of Sasbank and Volkskas were mentioned.]

By 1943 more than £2 million of new investment had gone into buying shares in Afrikaner companies, mostly in FVB. By the end of the Second World War, FVB had major investments in fishing, wood, steel, chemicals and agricultural implements. In 1946 it paid a 6 per cent dividend on its ordinary shares. In 1948 Bonuskor, an investment corporation in the Sanlam group, was the first Afrikaans company to be listed on the Johannesburg Stock Exchange.

One of FVB's first steps was to acquire a stake in a small company belonging to a young entrepreneur, Anton Rupert. In the final years of the Second World

War Rupert took to the road to sell shares to wine and tobacco farmers. He would later recount: 'I showed them a few wine labels and sold them my ideas. I sold them a dream.'[314] In 1945 Rupert's Distillers Corporation was listed – a first for a predominantly Afrikaner company. Within two decades the Rembrandt group of companies became a conglomerate on a global scale.

Afrikaans business was no monolith. The southern-based Sanlam believed Afrikaner advancement should proceed through the investment of savings in sound enterprises. It embraced private enterprise and saw nothing wrong in co-operation with English business. It looked with considerable scepticism at the establishment of Volkskas as a co-operative bank and initially did little to promote it. By contrast, the northern Afrikaners tended to prefer the co-operative system as one that did not exploit the consumer, but served the *volk*. They were descendants of people seared by the South African War and the excesses of the capitalist system.

The 1939 Volkskongres responded to this sentiment by establishing the Reddingsdaadbond (RDB) or Rescue Action Society. The idea was that Afrikaners would pay membership fees (children were asked to pay sixpence each month) in joining branches (343 were formed in the first four years). By 1946 an amount of £149,000 had been raised. Part of the fund was used for loans to small Afrikaner enterprises. Some were invested in FVB shares, some went to Afrikaner organisations and the rest were used for study loans. The RDB's most important contribution was encouraging Afrikaners to patronise Afrikaner enterprises. When war broke out, almost all the enterprises in rural towns were in the hands of South Africans of British, Jewish or Indian descent; by the end of the war Afrikaners had taken over many of these.[315]

The English-dominated private sector generally saw no need for assisting Afrikaner economic advancement. The broad-based United Party government instilled a sense of security about the prospects of the market economy. With the manufacturing sector of the 1930s and 1940s characterised by low productivity and efficiency, there was no largesse that could be redistributed.[316] Some influential voices in the English-speaking community deplored Afrikaner efforts to mobilise economically on an ethnic basis. *The Star* called it a 'politically inspired movement' and wrote that 'the sponsors of economic segregation in trade and industry cannot ultimately avoid the charge that they are fanning the flames of racial bitterness in South Africa'.[317] WH Hutt, perhaps the most prominent economist of his time, called it a 'war' against the British section of the community and part of 'the half-century-old fight against the *Uitlanders*'.[318] By contrast, JL Gray, an academic at the University of the Witwatersrand, observed that nothing could be more damaging to an understanding of the conflicts in the white community 'than the complacent belief that the Afrikaans-speaking population have no legitimate and serious economic grievances'.[319]

Taking this opposition into account, Afrikaners active in promoting economic mobilisation went out of their way to give assurances to the business world. TE Dönges, later a cabinet minister, said that Afrikaners were intent on increasing their economic share fairly and peacefully. They felt that they had no right to expect others to help them and were too proud to ask others for assistance in working out their economic salvation. Neither did they intend to embark on a boycott of English firms. However, they implored English-speakers to maintain a 'benign neutrality while the Afrikaners as a people were finding their economic feet'.[320]

The North–South divisions in Afrikaner business ranks continued to show themselves. In 1950 Tinie Louw, now Sanlam's managing director, would stress that new Afrikaner businesses 'can only evolve under the protection of an old, strong company or with the support of the most influential organisation'.[321] In effect, Afrikaners were asked to pool all their savings in Sanlam for investment purposes rather than spread such savings among Afrikaner small businesses across the country. Afrikaner nationalists in the Transvaal would bitterly resent the centralisation of Afrikaner savings in Sanlam, whose life assurance fund quadrupled between 1940 and 1949.[322]

Even in the ranks of Sanlam there were disagreements. There were those like WB Coetzer who wanted FVB to shed nationalist sentiments in embarking on mining and industrial investment, and those like CB Brink, FVB secretary, who was supportive of the idea of the northern Afrikaners to assist small Afrikaner businesses in need of capital and know-how.[323] The dominant trends favoured Coetzer's approach. The economist WH Hutt remarked in 1946 that Afrikaners struggled to make headway, not because of discrimination but because of their participation in small and medium-level businesses and because they did not have the right contacts.[324]

Winning political power

The National Party (NP) victory in the 1948 election shocked foreign investors and political leaders. Winston Churchill expressed the view of many when he voiced regret at the defeat of Jan Smuts's United Party in the following terms: 'A great world statesman has fallen and his country will undergo a period of anxiety and perhaps temporary eclipse.'[325] Apart from an abhorrence of apartheid, there were fears of a prompt South African withdrawal from the British Commonwealth, a purge of the civil service and the nationalisation of the mines, which was still a plank in the NP's platform.

The new government made it clear that it did not intend to change the country's constitutional status abruptly or without broad white support. It stressed the need for continuity, not least in maintaining a stable and professional civil service. Continuity as well as the retention of expertise in the civil service for eighty years after Union was an important reason for South Africa's economic success. The rise of Afrikaners to the upper ranks of the civil service since 1910 was exceptionally slow. Although the Union constitution of 1909 had given equal status to the two official languages, by 1931 half of the senior civil servants were unable to communicate with the public in any language but English.[326] In many state departments there was only a sprinkling of Afrikaners in the senior ranks. One of the problems was a lack of Afrikaans candidates. As late as 1939 less than a third of all white students at universities were Afrikaners.

The replacement of approximately 120,000 predominantly white civil servants between 1994 and 2001 as part of the regime change has been justified by the assertion that after the 1948 election the NP established a precedent for this by dismissing large numbers of English-speaking civil servants.[327] Shaw wrote that the NP government crippled the 'principle of an independent and professional civil service' by making political appointments to key posts.[328]

Writing in 1949, in a book that went through four editions in the next twenty years, Leo Marquard, a respected liberal commentator, painted a very different picture.[329] He noted that the Smuts government during the war years broke with the policy of a professional civil service because it could not risk appointing Afrikaner nationalists to key positions. The NP government in fact reintroduced the policy of a professional civil service. As Marquard, looking back in 1969 at the preceding two decades, noted: 'There has not been a great deal of nepotism in the public sphere.' Appointments and particularly promotions of civil servants occurred without regard to party-political affiliations, 'except when there is a fundamental policy difference'.[330] The NP government did, however, express itself clearly on the need for a fully bilingual civil service, and it also announced steps to recompense those who had been denied promotion during the war. A Grievances Commission heard evidence from some 2,875 railway employees who alleged that they had been dismissed unfairly.[331]

There were a few prominent English-speaking casualties in the change of government. The most striking case was that of W Marshall Clark, General Manager of South African Railways and Harbours; he had been promoted during the war over the heads of two more senior Afrikaner civil servants, and was asked after the election to retire on pension. Frans Erasmus, Minister of Defence, transferred Major-General Evered Poole, first in line to succeed General Sir Pierre van Ryneveld as Chief of General Staff, to an obscure post as head of South Africa's military mission in Berlin. Several other senior military officers, both English- and Afrikaans-speaking, were demoted or refused promotion. At a lower level a large number of Air Force pilots resigned on account of perceived discrimination. Van den Bos noted that Erasmus's successors 'scrupulously avoided even the slightest semblance of political favouritism in the appointments and promotions they have authorised'.[332]

In the Department of Native Affairs an Afrikaner, Werner Eiselen, was appointed Secretary for Native Affairs in 1948 over the heads of two English-speaking Under-Secretaries. But there was no purge of English-speakers. Evans notes:

> A perusal of the Public Service List from 1940–1954, which provides complete lists of all civil servants in the various departments of the state, provides no help in tracing the Afrikanerization of the [Native Affairs] Department. Although the list does break down the department's personnel on the basis of grade and rank, Afrikaner names already heavily dominated the lists for 1947 and 1948, making it difficult to see any marked changes.[333]

A study by Berridge of the 'ethnic agent in place' (English civil servants in South Africa well disposed towards the former imperial power) concludes that the vast majority of senior English-speaking servants retained their posts, despite the fact that their loyalties were to the British Commonwealth rather than the new government.[334]

Between 1936 and 1970 the civil service in general became steadily Afrikanerised (Table 4.1). Large numbers of Afrikaners entered the lower levels, while English-speakers opted in growing numbers to join the private sector, fearing discrimination.[335] On the upper levels, however, the process was slow. An analysis of the 1960 census found that the top levels of the public administration reflected the white population's composition, with 57.2 per cent being Afrikaners and 37.5 per cent English-speakers. The position was reversed in the private sector. Here only 25 per cent of Afrikaners were in the upper echelons of the job market as directors, managers and self-employed owners as against 66 per cent of English-speakers. By 1977 a quarter of English-speakers worked in the public sector, but they occupied less than 10 per cent of the top positions in the central civil service.[336]

Table 4.1: Proportion of Afrikaners employed in the public sector

	1936	1960	1970
Afrikaners as a % of white public sector	58.9%	68.2%	70.7%
Afrikaners in public sector as % of Afrikaner labour force	12.9%	13.0%	13.2%

Source: Sadie, *The Fall and Rise of the Afrikaner in the South African Economy*, p. 54.

A question of quotas

Two years after the NP had won power and eleven years after the first economic Volkskongres, another congress was held. The mood was buoyant. The Afrikaner share in mining still stood at 1 per cent. In the financial sector it had increased from 5 per cent to 6 per cent, but only 20 per cent of potential Afrikaner capital was invested in Afrikaner financial institutions.[337] However, the Afrikaner share of manufacturing and construction between 1939 and 1951 grew from 3 per cent to 6 per cent, while that in trade and commerce jumped from 8 per cent to 25 per cent.

DF Malan, the Prime Minister, addressed the Congress to spell out his government's approach to assisting Afrikaner empowerment. 'For many years the Afrikaners were virtually completely excluded from the commercial, industrial and general economic life of the country. They now want – and who could criticise them? – to get a place in the economic sun, not by pushing others out or being carried on the shoulders of others, but in their own right and relying on their own strength.'[338] This statement did not take into account the massive destruction of economic opportunities for blacks, but referred only to the two white communities. Nic Diederichs, an employee of Rembrandt at the time, remarked that, with one or two exceptions, no help was received from English-speakers. Although the Afrikaner quest to succeed in business 'was not aimed against anyone', there was an inability on the part of the English community to understand it.[339]

As an entrepreneur like Anton Rupert discovered, the NP government did not offer any special deals to Afrikaner businesses or newcomers to industry in general. The Broederbond, however, still considered quotas as a way of helping close the large income gap between the two white communities. In 1937 Hendrik Verwoerd, as editor of *Die Transvaler*, published a long article on the 'Jewish question'. Arguing that Jews held a disproportionate share of wholesale and retail trade, he called for legislation that would 'gradually ensure that each white section [Afrikaners, English-speakers of British descent and Jewish South Africans] enjoys a share of the major occupations according to its share of the white population'. Government should refuse trading licences to Jews until the Jewish share was brought into line with their proportion of the white population (it was popularly estimated at 4 per cent). Verwoerd described this as *ewewigtige verspreiding*, or balanced distribution, but added that 'this has also been called a quota system'.[340]

During the 1950s the Broederbond's Bondsraad, or national meeting attended by delegates from all Bond branches, considered similar proposals on at least two occasions. Some members argued that a quota system was a 'powerful instrument' to give young and emerging Afrikaner businesses a foothold. They asked the Broederbond to enter into discussions with cabinet ministers to 'find a basis on which Afrikaner enterprises could to a larger extent be favoured through quotas'.

But these proposals failed to win support from two prominent Afrikaner businessmen, whose companies had a record of successful entrepreneurship. At the 1956 Bondsraad meeting, Anton Rupert emphasised the essential elements for entrepreneurial success: a distinctive style of doing business, realism, enthusiasm and loyalty. Andreas Wassenaar, managing director of Sanlam, suggested that Afrikaner businessmen took stock of themselves before they complained about their economic problems.[341] There were also warnings against attempts to exploit ethnic sentiment for business purposes. CGW Schumann, the Stellenbosch professor of economics, stated: 'It can be laid down as an axiom that the undertakings which made the strongest appeal to Afrikaner sentiment were the poorest in business skills and in sincerity of aspiration.'[342]

The entry into mining

It has been said that the Afrikaners' economic upsurge can mainly be attributed to Harry Oppenheimer's selling of the mining house General Mining and Finance Corporation at a very low price to a struggling Sanlam subsidiary, Federale Mynbou. The reality was very different. The major breakthrough for Afrikaner capital occurred by way of a successful entry into the mining industry in the early 1960s. Established in 1953, Fedmyn was managed well from the start and, in the words of the *South African Mining and Engineering Journal* in its September 1964 issue, acquired a sound reputation because of its 'intrinsic merits as a virile, young mining and finance house'. By 1963 it had invested in a variety of mining interests, but steered clear of gold and diamonds. In that year it acquired a stake of 17.5 per cent in Terra Marina Diamond Corporation, which planned to obtain diamond concessions in Namaqualand and on the seabed. With a stake of 70 per cent, Sanlam was the principal shareholder.[343]

In 1963 Fedmyn decided to enter gold mining. It expressed an interest in buying a substantial share in the General Mining and Finance Corporation in which Anglo American Corporation had a 23 per cent shareholding. For Anglo American, and for Ernest Oppenheimer and his son, Harry, who were major shareholders, there were powerful reasons for making a deal with both Afrikaner nationalism and Afrikaner capital. Anglo American's management thought General Mining, while rich in assets, had lost direction and badly needed new innovative and entrepreneurial management. But the main motivation for the Oppenheimers to enter into negotiations with Fedmyn was neither their unhappiness with General Mining's poor management nor their perception that the Afrikaners' continuing absence from gold mining held a growing political risk. It was, as Harry Oppenheimer explained to Fedmyn's Willem Coetzer, to maintain the 'vital role' of De Beers Consolidated Mines in the diamond industry and, more specifically, to discourage the interest of Sanlam, Fedmyn and other Afrikaner companies in diamond mining. In talks with Coetzer he made any deal conditional on achieving an acceptable agreement on diamond interests.

A mutually beneficial deal was struck. Fedmyn undertook to strictly limit its diamond mining ventures, and any new diamond venture within the Sanlam group would have to be offered to a newly formed company that De Beers would control. Anglo allowed Fedmyn to acquire a strategic interest in General Mining. Verhoef remarks aptly: 'Fedmyn received no "hand-out", but bought every share in Genmin at market prices. AAC [Anglo American] was selling off weak-performing gold interests in return for better management for Genmin and a protection of De Beers's monopoly.'[344] Michael Spicer, a director of Anglo American, agrees.

Table 4.2: The Afrikaner share in the private business sector (in percentages), 1938–1975

Sector	1938–9	1948–9	1954–5	1963–4	1975
Agriculture	87	85	84	83	82
Mining	1	1	1	10	18
Manufacture & construction	3	6	6	10	15
Trade & commerce	8	25	26	24	16
Transport		9	14	14	15
Liquor & catering		20	30	30	35
Professions		16	20	27	38
Finance	5	6	10	21	25
Miscellaneous		27	35	36	45
Aggregate		24.8	25.4	26.9	27.5
Aggregate excluding agriculture		9.6	13.4	18.0	20.8

Source: Sadie, *The Fall and Rise of the Afrikaner in the South African Economy*, p. 28.

Table 4.3: Per capita income (in 1978 rand) of the various groups

	1946	1960	1976
Whites	389	831	3150
English	561	1050	3587
Afrikaners	266	673	2538
Asians	77	148	737
Coloureds	64	135	623
Africans	32	71	304

Source: Giliomee, 'The Afrikaner economic advance', p. 173; figures provided by SJ Terreblanche.

The deal did not represent a handout at all. All the share deals were done in strictly commercial terms. In retrospect the deal can be seen as a success all round. The one main reason was that through Sanlam there was enough centralised Afrikaner capital available to acquire General Mining entirely out of their own resources. Another reason was that there already existed a stratum of Afrikaner managers with at least ten years of experience in mining. These factors were missing in most of the high-profile post-1994 black empowerment deals.[345]

Later, Anglo American sold enough shares to General Mining to enable it to assume control. In 1974 General Mining bought control of the mining house Union Corporation to form Gencor. It was the second-largest mining house in the country with a large spread of mining and industrial interests.[346]

Table 4.2 reveals that between 1948–9 and 1954–5 the Afrikaner share of the non-agricultural private sector increased by nearly 40 per cent from 9.6 per cent to 13.4 per cent, and it would grow to 18 per cent in 1963–4.

A broad-based advance

Between 1946 and 1976 there was a broad-based increase in the per capita income of all groups in South Africa; in the case of black groups this occurred from a very low base (Table 4.3). Urbanisation and high economic growth were central to the major improvement in Afrikaners' income. Until the mid-1940s the Afrikaners as a group had the character of an impoverished labour class, with blue-collar workers and farmers or farmworkers dominant. The proportion of blue-collar workers rose from 31 per cent in 1936 to 41 per cent in 1960, and declined to 32 per cent in 1980. The proportion of Afrikaners working on farms showed a dramatic drop from 41 per cent in 1936 to 16 per cent in 1960 and to 7 per cent in 1980. Many of the Afrikaners who urbanised had left the countryside with few skills. In the cities the NP government gave greater protection to unskilled and semi-skilled white workers, who were predominantly Afrikaners. In 1957 a law was passed to reserve some semi-skilled jobs for white workers.

Table 4.4: Distribution (percentages) of Afrikaner income groups in selected years (1980 incomes)

Income category	1946	1960	1980
R0–R6,000	89.1	61.9	51.4
R6,000–R12,000	9.1	33.7	36.2
R12,000–R18,000	1.3	1.8	8.3

Source: Steenekamp, ''n Ekonomiese ontleding van sosio-politieke groepvorming', p. 193.

Table 4.5: Gini coefficients for Afrikaner income-earners for selected years

Income earners	1946	1960	1980
Total	0.464	0.441	0.446
Male	0.443	0.398	0.404

Source: Steenekamp, ''n Ekonomiese ontleding van sosio-politieke groepvorming', p. 208

Table 4.6: Income of the lowest 40% of Afrikaners compared with the top quintile for selected years

Income earners	1946	1960	1980
Total	0.241	0.277	0.274
Male	0.274	0.363	0.349

Source: Steenekamp, ''n Ekonomiese ontleding van sosio-politieke groepvorming', p. 209.

The government also assisted other sectors in which Afrikaners were dominant. Farmers benefited from favourable agricultural prices set by the marketing boards and by some new curbs on the mobility of labour. Nattrass calculated that during the second half of the 1960s state aid on average provided one-fifth of a white farmer's income.[347] Conditions and pay for white civil servants improved. By 1960 a sizeable Afrikaner middle class had developed. It took more than thirty years before a visible layer of rich Afrikaners developed, with 8 per cent earning more than R12,000 per year (Table 4.4).

Income inequality within the Afrikaner group as measured by the Gini coefficient (Table 4.5) was at about 0.45, which could be compared with 0.37 for developed countries in Western Europe during the 1970s and 0.64 for South Africa today. The income inequality among all Afrikaner income-earners, expressed in Gini coefficients, slightly improved between 1946 and 1980, as Table 4.5 shows. There was no sharp increase in income inequality among Afrikaners, as a comparison of the income of the lowest 40 per cent with the top quintile shows (Table 4.6).

The remarkable political solidarity of Afrikaners between 1948 and 1976 had much to do with the ability of the government to persuade its constituency that all classes in the ethnic group were doing well, and that no single class had hijacked the nationalist movement. This broad-based advance made it unnecessary for the government to engage in populist rhetoric or to put pressure on English firms to employ Afrikaners.

A question of state favouritism

In dealing with the relationship between large Afrikaner corporations and the government, Brian Bunting, a senior member of the South African Communist Party, remarked that there was 'abundant evidence of Nationalist favouritism for Nationalist concerns'. He pointed to the 'considerable interlocking of directorships', which saw Sanlam directors sit on state corporations, while some of the managers of parastatal companies served on the boards of Afrikaner firms. Bunting does not indicate how what he calls 'this mutual aid' was instrumental in developing Afrikaner enterprises.[348] O'Meara states that Sanlam benefited from 'government contracts and subsidies', which assisted its subsidiary Federale Volksbeleggings, but he provides no evidence.[349]

This section presents four case studies to investigate these views. It does not consider the government's promotion of white business in general, but only cases of specific (and possibly corrupt) preferment of Afrikaner businesses or of one Afrikaner business over another. It also examines the issue of whether English corporations assisted Afrikaner advancement.

Sanlam

Sanlam long remained an ethnic business at heart. Pepler Scholtz, who became managing director in 1968, remarked in an interview: 'My greatest problem in talking to English financial journalists was to convince them that Sanlam was not a subsidiary of the NP.' But he added: 'Sanlam was never solely profit-driven or solely policyholder-driven. We were an Afrikaans firm, in fact operating almost as a sectional bureaucracy that tried to strike a balance between policyholder interests and the *Afrikanersaak* or Afrikaner cause.'[350]

The fact that chief executives of state corporations sat on Sanlam's board of directors might have created the impression of an ethnic brotherhood open to insider trading. In many ways, however, it made any government patronage more difficult. Favouritism for Sanlam would almost certainly have led to an outcry from Old Mutual, its major competitor. Half of the latter's policyholders were Afrikaners. During the first thirty years of NP rule Afrikaners often held the post of managing director of Old Mutual or posts just below that rank.

There were two areas of friction between Sanlam and Old Mutual. In the ranks of senior Old Mutual managers there is still resentment expressed in interviews about what they call Sanlam's 'inside track' to civil servants. Through the Public Service Association, a body deferential to government, Sanlam negotiated a contract to write group life assurance policies for civil servants. It allowed Sanlam agents first access to government employees to sell them these schemes and all other Sanlam products.[351] Fifteen group life schemes were introduced, including schemes for teachers, members of the Defence Force and Police, and railway workers. These were all optional schemes – a civil servant could choose whether he or she wanted to join. The contracts could not be terminated without Sanlam's consent.

Marinus Daling, managing director of Sanlam, did not consider it strange that Sanlam as an Afrikaans company obtained such a contract from government. He pointed out that all over the world insurance companies develop certain niche markets according to their ethnic profile. The contracts were not money-spinners. Sanlam was forced to raise premiums and sharply reduce cover to avoid losing substantial amounts of money. This had quite a negative impact on its business and corporate image.[352] While Sanlam indeed profited very little from these group life schemes, the relevant point is that this was a clear case of preferential treatment being bestowed by government on an Afrikaner firm.

An Old Mutual manager also alleged that Sanlam used its political muscle to receive a share of the pension schemes in the independent homelands. Every time he negotiated the establishment of a pension scheme, he was forced to split the business with Sanlam. Daling responded, more plausibly than in the former case, that it was normal practice elsewhere that the risk in pension schemes was spread across two or more companies.

After the mid-1960s, with Sanlam expanding into new markets, management became anxious to dispel the impression of collusion with the government, or of any ganging up of Afrikaners against English-speakers. Even mild government favouritism would have made it difficult to penetrate the English or the black market. Bad management and poor investment decisions in the final fifteen years of the century dealt Sanlam heavy blows, and it entered the new century with a much-reduced stature.

Rembrandt

Rupert's first shareholders were primarily Afrikaner tobacco and wine farmers. At shareholder meetings during the 1940s and early 1950s, Rupert expressed himself in the classic idiom of the *volksbeweging*. 'We are entering the business world to gain a stand for our own people and to work with others, but not always for others.'[353] Rupert made it policy to keep a proper distance from government. In an interview he stated: 'I never asked any government department anything special for my company and I only once saw a cabinet minister alone and that was before 1948.'[354]

Rupert was shocked to discover after the 1948 election that the new government's support for Afrikaner business did not amount to more than lip service. The government was unwilling to change the wartime system of quotas for chemicals, rubber, paraffin and a wide range of other materials. Based on the production level of previous years, this heavily favoured the well-established firms. *Tegniek*, a trade journal started by Rupert, attacked government policy under the banner headline 'Quotas are killing us'.[355] Rupert's persistent pressure eventually led to changes in the quota system.

Rupert frequently reminded Afrikaners that as people who had experienced foreign domination, they should know that no self-respecting group or nation would work for others for ever. He proposed partnerships transcending racial or national boundaries. At the 1950 Volkskongres he argued that Afrikaner businessmen had achieved so much success that they should found a Bantu Development Corporation without private gain to help blacks start enterprises in the reserves.[356] Ten years later he asked Hendrik Verwoerd, the Prime Minister, for permission to build a cigarette factory in the Transkei. Verwoerd refused, arguing that if he approved he would also have to grant requests from other white firms, such as Anglo American Corporation, which did not have the same 'noble motives'.[357]

During the 1960s Rembrandt embarked on a policy of industrial partnerships in countries overseas where it operated, including Singapore, Indonesia, Jamaica and Malaysia. The company offered citizens half of the shares, employed local people in senior positions, and appointed a national as chairman of the board.

Volkskas

In its first three decades of NP rule, Volkskas concentrated on business with rural Afrikaners and farmers in particular. The bank's strategy was to open a branch in every rural town in the country. In 1967 Fanie Botha, a director, remarked that Volkskas had almost completely 'blanketed' the *platteland*. He warned that it had become necessary to give priority to penetrating the urban areas and in particular the industrial and commercial sectors.[358]

This was a timely warning. At a time of rapid economic growth Volkskas was largely absent in the most dynamic sectors of the economy. Pieter Morkel, chief executive of the bank in the early 1990s, remarked: 'The one field in which Volkskas traditionally was – and still is – over-exposed is in credit to farmers and co-operatives, but this is not a particularly profitable area of business and the NP government did not help to establish these links between farmers and Volkskas.'[359]

The popular myth that Volkskas was the central state's banker does not have much substance. Morkel stated: 'Most of the business of departments of central government was done through the Reserve Bank, which also did almost all the foreign transactions. State business was an insignificant part of the overall business of Volkskas.'

While Volkskas had the accounts of the government of the Transkei, Standard Bank had that of Bophuthatswana and Barclays/First National had that of KwaZulu. Of the local authorities, 34 per cent banked with Volkskas in 1994.[360] As for the accounts of provincial governments and local authorities, these were – in official bank parlance – 'high-intensity', requiring much labour power but with relatively low interest rates and service charges.[361]

Of the parastatals, Eskom did business with all banks; Armscor and Sasol mainly used Volkskas, but also banked with others. In foreign transactions they used the bank that offered the best rates. The Bantu Administration Boards used Volkskas in Afrikaans-speaking areas but other banks in Natal and the Eastern Cape. Some of the big control boards, such as the Maize and the Wheat Boards, were Volkskas clients, but for transactions related to exports, imports and the selling of surpluses, they shopped around for the best deals.[362]

Volkskas never overcame its predominantly rural and Afrikaans background. It was absorbed in a merger in 1998 under the name of ABSA.

The Afrikaans publishing companies

In the publishing business there were acute tensions between politics and business. The NP was no centralised monolith but rather a federation of provincial parties. At times tensions between the Cape NP and Transvaal NP were so acute that political leaders intervened in the rivalry between Afrikaans press groups. The issue was compounded by the fact that for the first thirty years of NP rule, cabinet ministers served as directors of the Afrikaans publishing companies in the North (Afrikaanse Pers, Voortrekkerpers and Dagbreekpers, which would merge in 1971 to form Perskor) and of Nasionale Pers in the South.

The North–South tensions in the party, which started in the 1930s, were aggravated when DF Malan, who became Prime Minister in 1948, included only three northerners in the first NP cabinet. Both JG Strijdom, the Transvaal NP leader, and Hendrik Verwoerd, who succeeded him as Prime Minister and Transvaal leader in 1958, felt a strong antipathy to what they called the 'Keeromstraat clique' (the offices of both the Cape NP and Nasionale Pers were located in Keerom Street, Cape Town). The long-standing resentment of northern Afrikaners towards Sanlam's success in attracting most Afrikaner savings for investment purposes also played a role.[363]

The main source of the conflict in newspaper publishing was the determined efforts of northern NP leaders to protect the northern Afrikaans market. For Nasionale Pers this placed an unacceptable ceiling on its growth prospects. It was more profitable than the northern companies, but it had no slice of the Transvaal newspaper market – the largest and most dynamic market in the country. Any Nasionale Pers attempt to expand into the Transvaal encountered stiff opposition from the Transvaal Nationalist leadership for both political and business reasons. Cabinet ministers were quite prepared to intervene against ethnic competitors. In 1953 Eric Louw, Minister of Economic Affairs, rejected a Nasionale Pers application for an increased quota for newsprint in order to establish a Sunday newspaper in the Transvaal.[364]

When Hendrik Verwoerd became Prime Minister, he gave notice that he would use all means to block attempts by Nasionale Pers to expand into the Transvaal. In 1965 Verwoerd hosted a meeting of the southern and northern Afrikaans publishing companies. The meeting had been prompted by the refusal by Nasionale Pers to accept a request from Dagbreekpers to print its Sunday newspaper *Dagbreek* in Cape Town. Such a step would have made it impossible for Nasionale Pers to implement its still secret plan to publish a nation-wide Sunday paper based in Johannesburg. Present were the directors of both sides, who were also cabinet ministers, and the top managers of the companies.

Verwoerd asked bluntly what Nasionale Pers's plans were for new titles in the Afrikaans newspaper market. Nasionale Pers representatives declared that they were not prepared to divulge the company's plans. They pointed out that Verwoerd was not only party leader, whose task it was to resolve inter-provincial conflicts, but also the chairman of companies with which Nasionale Pers was in competition.[365] A few days later Nasionale Pers announced its intention to publish a nation-wide Sunday paper, *Die Beeld*. Despite being boycotted unofficially by the Transvaal NP, it quickly posed a severe threat to the Sunday paper of the northern company.

In Verwoerd's term as Prime Minister, much of the state's printing business was contracted out to the northern Afrikaans publishing companies. State printing business included all official forms, receipt books, stationery paper, the official yearbook and state magazines like *Panorama*. In 1962 Dagbreekpers was helped by Jan de Klerk, a cabinet minister, to win the contract for printing the

Johannesburg telephone directory. Five other directories were later added to the Dagbreekpers business. It was, as Richard, a northern newspaper editor, called it, 'a bonanza which contributed millions to the coffers of the press'.[366] These contracts were in force for a period of ten years. In 1970 advertisements for new contracts were placed in such an obscure state publication that only Dagbreekpers put in tenders.

Apart from directories, school textbooks were the other major source of income for these companies. The NP-controlled provincial government in the Transvaal allowed only Transvaal-based companies to sell textbooks for white pupils in the province. This hurt Nasionale Pers along with others based outside the Transvaal. The plum contracts were for black school texts, which fell under the Department of Bantu Education. Marius Jooste, managing director of Perskor, used all his political connections to secure such contracts. With Verwoerd he had what an Afrikaans editor called a 'fruitful business and political partnership',[367] and he also got on well with MC Botha, Minister of Bantu Administration and Development, who was a director of two northern companies. These companies soon dominated the market for black textbooks.

There is an allusion in a novel by Richard to lucrative business deals with the public or the semi-public sector.[368] The main character, Jansen van Dalsen, is a thinly disguised version of Marius Jooste. 'Noordpers' is the collective name for the northern companies. Hendrik Verwoerd figures in his own name. This following paragraph comes from the novel:

> Printing contracts for official publications, especially journals, are coming to Noordpers. The Department of Information is planning a number of glossy journals and the chairman of the Parks Board mentions that it is planning to issue a publication with the name of *Custos*. Noordpers put in such shrewd tenders that most of the printing comes its way. From the Government Printer comes ever larger orders. The Railways and the Airways are beginning to divert the stream [to us] from [the English companies] Argus, SAAN and Caxton.[369]

When the book was about to appear, the management ordered the destruction of the entire print run. Increasingly, Perskor's business with the state meant the difference between its survival and its demise. With the Cape-based PW Botha's rise to power in 1978, Perskor went into a swift decline.

The professional management of Nasionale Pers formed a sharp contrast with the northern publishing companies, which operated in the hothouse of Transvaal Afrikaner politics. Financial conservatism, careful planning and cautious risk-taking were the watchwords, not the reckless gamble or the quick chance. During the war years Sanlam took a strategic stake in Nasionale Pers. The leaderships of Sanlam and Nasionale Pers saw themselves as partners in the same nationalist cause. David de Villiers, who was MD from 1969 to 1984, strongly denied that Nasionale Pers benefited from 'crony capitalism'. But while there was always an element of friction between government and Afrikaans business, the publishing companies also benefited from the association. They effectively lobbied against the introduction of free school textbooks.

Nasionale Pers's critics accused it of improperly offering shares to homeland officials in marketing its black school texts, but De Villiers rejected this. Nasionale Pers formed joint ventures in which 51 per cent of the shares were held by individual members of a black community and 49 per cent by a Nasionale Pers subsidiary. All the offers were public and no individual could hold more than 200 shares. No shares were given to individuals.[370]

Nasionale Pers first managed to win a slice of the printing of telephone directories after the Postmaster General, Louis Rive, had alerted it to the closing date for tenders. It put in tenders and won the contracts for the Western Cape, Eastern Cape and South West Africa. This represented approximately a tenth of the total telephone directory business. Revenue from this contract amounted to about 3 per cent of the total pre-tax profit of Nasionale Pers.[371]

The introduction of state television posed a severe threat to newspaper and book readership and advertising revenue. After negotiations between the government and the Afrikaans and English publishing companies, led by Nasionale Pers, an agreement was reached on television advertising and the introduction of pay television. All the press companies acquired an equal share in M-Net and management was placed in Nasionale Pers's hands with the consent of the other press companies. Expansion into pay television and the field of electronics saw the market capitalisation of Nasionale Pers, now called Naspers, exceed that of Sanlam by 2007. It is at present the largest media company in Africa.

The ties dissolve

A book published in 1964 to commemorate twenty-five years of progress since the Economic Volkskongres of 1939 argued that the success of Afrikaans businesses had produced mutual recognition and respect between the two white communities.[372] Afrikaans business leaders had developed a sense of self-confidence and achievement. As one said in 1968: 'We are no longer under the impression that we are other men's inferiors as far as business acumen is concerned – while we have certainly not beaten them. I think I am justified in claiming that our inferiority complex is a phenomenon that no longer plagues the new generation that is now arising.'[373]

In 1968, when Sanlam celebrated its half-centenary, Andreas Wassenaar, its MD, wrote a self-congratulatory preface to the book *Sanlam: Uit die volk gebore – Sanlam se eerste 50 jaar*.[374] 'Sanlam had become the symbol of the Afrikaner's ability to maintain himself in the business world through intelligent, honest and hard work. God grant that it stays that way.' Jan Hurter, of Volkskas, pointed to four corporations with assets of more than R300 million: Volkskas, Trust Bank, Rembrandt and Sanlam, and added: 'They were all built up by our own people, including the less affluent, who have made a giant contribution.'[375]

But while Afrikaner nationalists had learnt to capture capitalism and still used the symbolic terms of the early stages of ethnic mobilisation, the system also began to capture them. By the mid-1960s the close alliance between the ruling party and Afrikaner business had started to dissolve. This was part of a broader process set in train by the prosperity of the decade and the rise of consumer values that extended to all sections of Afrikaner society.[376] In September 1965 Hendrik Verwoerd warned that the growth of Afrikaner capitalism might later be used against the Afrikaners themselves.[377] Just before his death a year later, he wrote to the Broederbond's Executive Council and said that the greater the prosperity and the fewer the political dangers, the more difficult it would be to maintain Afrikaner unity.[378]

By the end of the 1960s Afrikaner business leaders had come to define the economic goals of the *volksbeweging* in very different terms from those of the 1940s. The goal was no longer 'independence' in each sector, or winning a share of the economic cake roughly proportional to the Afrikaner share of the white population. In 1969 Pepler Scholtz of Sanlam said that, instead of speaking of the Afrikaner 'share' of the economy, it was better to speak of the Afrikaner 'contribution' to it. He added: 'The Afrikaner is not entitled to a share only because he exists. He is only entitled to that share of business that he conquers through his own abilities and hard work.'[379] By the end of the 1960s the English business sector was much more prepared than before to recognise Afrikaner achievements in economic policy-making and in the private sector. In a 1967 supplement entitled 'The fabulous years' describing the economic 'surge' of the previous five years, the *Financial Mail* singled out the ideas, initiatives and policy decisions of twelve decision-makers in the state and semi-state sector. Nine of them were Afrikaners.[380] Commemorating the founding of Federale Volksbeleggings thirty years before, the journal published an editorial in Afrikaans on the theme of Kestell's motto *'n volk red homself*. It congratulated the group on an exceptional performance as a widely spread, diversified industrial corporation that had entered into many successful partnerships locally and abroad.[381]

Whereas building up successful enterprises had been for Afrikaner businessmen a means of gaining prestige and esteem from their fellow Afrikaners, they now tended to attach less value to recognition by their fellow ethnics and more by business leaders across the language division.[382] It is a phenomenon that tends to occur often among groups that earlier had displayed an intense hostility to capitalism but subsequently learnt to accept it as a means of group advancement.

Until the mid-1990s most business leaders were happy to celebrate the Afrikaner roots of their corporations. Among the Afrikaner people the notion of *'n volk red homself* nevertheless remained part of Afrikaner folklore. It overlooked the fact that state intervention had been essential for the rehabilitation of the Afrikaner poor in the 1930s. This included relief measures, training for the white poor, and the superior education that whites received. But the rhetoric of *'n volk red homself* also had a positive impact. It prevented Afrikaners from succumbing to the temptation of attributing poverty in their ranks to some conspiracy by employers. It also encouraged middle-class Afrikaners to accept the rehabilitation of the Afrikaner poor as their responsibility.

Conclusion

Francis Fukuyama considered the failure of the Calvinist Afrikaners to develop a thriving capitalist system until the last quarter of the century an anomaly that needed explanation.[383] Any explanation would have to point to the obstacles to accumulating capital in farming, late urbanisation, the strength of populism and socialist thinking among the northern Afrikaners, preference for safe careers in the civil service, the absence of an Afrikaner business class until late in the twentieth century, and the long-standing reluctance to utilise risk capital.

With the exception of Anton Rupert, Afrikaners did not produce an entrepreneur in the Schumpeterian mould. Afrikaner businessmen considered themselves to be part and parcel of the Afrikaners' ethnic mobilisation until the 1970s. They all benefited greatly from the massive assistance successive governments provided to white business and to whites in general. But these governments, including the NP in its first two decades in power, bestowed remarkably little ethnic patronage on them, and the English business leadership did not consider it necessary to help Afrikaner business at a discount in order to buy political favours. As a result there developed among Afrikaners a strong sense that corporate successes were a collective ethnic achievement that reflected well on both the corporation and the community from which they sprang.

5.

'Bantu Education':
Apartheid and mass black education

The greatest breakthroughs in the historical understanding of apartheid have come from scholars who work at the interface of economics, demography and politics. Outstanding among them are Charles Simkins and the late Lawrence Schlemmer. This chapter deals with 'Bantu Education', on which both these scholars worked. Although it represents one of the most controversial issues in the history of apartheid, both Simkins and Schlemmer looked at it in detached terms.[384]

Different perspectives

In 1949 a commission of inquiry into black education, under the chairmanship of Werner Eiselen, proposed a new state-controlled system. Its report ignored theories of racial inferiority, but expressed concern about the lack of a *groepsgevoel* (group feeling) among blacks. This it believed was the result of the previous government's policy, which was not geared towards the development of African culture. The report considered African cultures as both dynamic and capable of providing the basis for the modernisation of entire peoples. Instead of imitating English culture, the educational system had to inculcate pride in the *volkseie* – the history, customs, habits, character and mentality of a people. The report also evinced a strong belief in the superiority of mother-tongue education.

Among the critics of Bantu Education there were two quite different responses. On the one hand, there were politicians and activists who responded in the first decade after the system's introduction. They tended to denounce it as a destructive form of intervention, leaving the education of blacks in a worse state than before. They asserted that Hendrik Verwoerd, its political architect, deliberately starved black education of funds to make certain that black children remained poorly educated. In 1962 Albert Luthuli, president of the African National Congress, described Bantu Education as 'a huge deceit', while IB Tabata, leader of the Non-European Unity Movement, referred to the policy in the title of his booklet as 'education for barbarism'.[385]

Scholars writing about Bantu Education during the first five years after its introduction in 1954 took a quite different view. They did not suggest that the Eiselen report or the parliamentary bill that Verwoerd introduced in 1953 was based on racist assumptions. The historian Eric Walker, for instance, stated that while Verwoerd 'reminded teachers that there was no limit to the educational heights to which the pick of their pupils might one day attain, [he also said that] they must no longer teach the rank-and-file as if they were destined to go even as far as Standard VI'.[386] Gwendolen Carter, a well-regarded Africanist from the United States, wrote: 'There was much that made sense in the Nationalist arguments. It is obvious that the lack of opportunities in the South African context for Africans with advanced training makes them frustrated and bitter. Moreover, it is hard to deny the importance of basing education on the culture of the particular group.'[387] Carter referred to Verwoerd's vision of the homelands as areas where job opportunities would arise to which blacks could not aspire elsewhere.[388]

Writing much later, another set of critics also rejected segregated education but pointed out that the policy's effects were not universally negative, adding that some aspects could be considered as partly reformist. They stressed that the previous system of education provided by churches and missions was close to collapse by the early 1950s. The black labour force in the cities was unsettled, lacking housing, transport and proper wages, and youths were seen to be uncontrollable. As Jonathan Hyslop notes, Bantu Education succeeded in drawing the youth into a mass system of primary education that provided a better-quality labour force. It was, he emphasises, 'grossly inegalitarian and racist', but 'parents supported it and the attempts to boycott it failed for nearly two decades'.[389]

Davenport's widely read general history of South Africa represents an interesting case. In the 1987 edition there is no reference to the policy as one based on assumptions of black racial inferiority. However, the fifth edition of the book, which was co-edited by Christopher Saunders and published in 2000, takes a quite different line. It argues that both the Eiselen report and the Act introducing Bantu Education operated on the 'assumption of an inferior potential in African minds' and were 'explicitly designed to prepare blacks for an inferior place in society'.[390] The comment in the 2000 edition is a reflection of the fact that a new government preoccupied with the historical heritage of apartheid as a racist policy had come to power. Apartheid was no longer seen only as a wrong or misguided policy, but as evil. This view is absent in most of the academic literature published before 1990.

After 1994 blacks were formally free, but still had to compete with whites, who seemed destined to remain economically and socially dominant. Although per capita spending and class numbers were quickly equalised, black education both in the townships and in rural areas remained in the doldrums.

There have been only a few scholarly analyses attempting to present a balanced assessment of the impact of Bantu Education. In an unpublished statistical analysis completed a year before his death in 2005, the demographer Jan Sadie wrote that the 'strangest aspect of the period of turmoil accompanying "struggle education" [in the 1980s] was the steady increase in the rate of grade survival'. By this he meant the expected number of grades (formerly termed standards) likely to be completed by the average learner at the time she or he entered school. It rose from 3.3 in 1963–4 to 4.8 in 1972–3 and to 7.4 in 1993–4 – an improvement of more than 100 per cent.

Sadie continued: 'The rise in the number who reached Standard 10 out of every 1,000 starting their school career, from 10 to 489, was even more impressive.' The 1970 and 1991 censuses revealed that between these two years the percentage of the population six years and older who had attained Standards 6 and 7 had increased from 7.1 to 18 per cent and those whose level of education reached Standards 8 to 10 had grown from 2.2 to 16.4 per cent. He concluded: 'The lost generation was perhaps not quite as lost as it was claimed to be.'[391]

Charles Simkins concurs. Referring to the quantity of education provided to blacks, he noted: 'The evidence from successive censuses is clear: for all population groups, apartheid imposed no curb on the growth in the number of years of education achieved by successive birth cohorts. There is also no evidence of gender differences in attainment, apart from Indians a couple of generations ago.'[392]

There is as yet little agreement about the quality of education that was provided under Bantu Education. In 2010 a sophisticated analysis of the career of Werner Eiselen and of his report appeared, but its brief assessment of Bantu Education disappoints. It does not go much beyond summarising the partisan views of Freda Troup's book published in 1976 by the International Defence and Aid Fund.[393] I discuss Simkins's view of this important issue in the section below on mother-tongue education.

Present black perspectives

By 2012, with an ANC government completing its second decade in power, it was no longer possible to deny the crisis in black education. Instead of examining the systemic faults dispassionately, the tendency in the ranks of ANC politicians and black commentators has been to seek the roots of the failure in the system of Bantu Education. Addressing the Education Department's failure to deliver textbooks to some schools in Limpopo, President Jacob Zuma said: 'What is happening today is what Verwoerd did, where the black majority were historically not given education. We are dealing with a system that has put black people back for centuries.' According to Zuma, Verwoerd was responsible for the textbook crisis in Limpopo.[394]

Redi Tlhabi, who interviewed Zuma on Talk Radio 702, expressed outrage over the president's remark that he did not know who was to blame for the textbook scandal, but she agreed with him about Verwoerd: 'The President was right in that Verwoerd worked to create a system that was intent on stifling the black child and making sure that she or he did not thrive . . . Today, in 2012, I did not expect that the "liberation party" [the ANC] would want to further Verwoerd's goals: to keep the black child poor, uneducated and deprived.'[395]

President Zuma's comments also attracted a retort from Mamphela Ramphele, a product of Bantu Education and a former University of Cape Town Vice-Chancellor. Speaking at an education conference, she commented on the current state of black education: 'The monumental failure in South Africa was not Hendrik Verwoerd's fault but that of the current government.' She continued: 'Children under apartheid's "gutter education" were better educated than children are today.'[396]

Black politicians have not felt the need for a re-examination of their views in the light of critical comments. A journalist pointed out to Angie Motshekga, Minister of Basic Education, that while the education system in South Africa has a budget higher than most African countries, its results were poorer. The minister responded that this was due to the 'massive backlog that we inherited going back to 1948'.[397]

Senzo Mchunu, MEC for Education in KwaZulu-Natal, declared: 'One of the points we found was a problem in Maths and Science. It was Verwoerd who made the subjects difficult because he thought blacks would be a threat to him.' In Parliament, the ANC deputy chief whip Mmamoloko Kubayi stated that 'proper education has been withheld from blacks since 1948. It is the fault of apartheid that our education system is now so poor.'[398]

Outside the ranks of politicians, the views about Bantu Education are more nuanced. A recent study drew on interviews with a sample of retired teachers who were employed in the Bantu Education system. They stress the discrimination and inequities, but also mention positive aspects. Teaching principles were sound and the training teachers received equipped them appropriately for their task. In general, teachers were respected and acted as good role models.[399]

The new generation of blacks seem puzzled by this obsession with history. At the end of a conference held on 5 September 2012 in Cape Town to launch the third Carnegie inquiry into poverty, the Deputy President of the ANC, Kgalema Motlanthe, argued that the legacy of Bantu Education hampered rapid progress in the battle against poverty and inequality. There was a dramatic moment when a young black student rose to ask a simple question: 'How come the government constantly talks about Bantu Education, Bantu Education, Bantu Education? I didn't grow up under Bantu Education and I'm not sure what it has to do with me – I feel it cannot be blamed for my problems.'[400]

A senior civil servant also expressed the view that the government had to stop blaming Bantu Education for problems that black students currently experience. In presenting the financial statistics for higher education institutions for 2015, South Africa's Statistician General, Pali Lehohla, painted a bleak picture. If one looked at progression rates, he said, black students were not doing well. In the 1980s, he said, for every black graduate there were 1.2 white graduates. 'Currently, for every one black person who graduates from university, there are six white people who make it through successfully.' Lehohla remarked: 'These numbers are declaring a horror, to put it bluntly. It is totally unacceptable.' He blamed the high dropout rate largely on students' lack of sufficient funding. Yet it is difficult to imagine that black students in the 1980s were in a better financial situation than their counterparts today.[401]

Charges against Bantu Education

This chapter does not attempt a comprehensive investigation of Bantu Education but seeks to examine some of the charges against the policy made by those who regard it as a destructive form of intervention. These charges are listed below:

- Verwoerd closed down a functioning system of black education that included some good mission schools such as Lovedale, Healdtown and Adams College.
- He stunted black development by insisting on mother-tongue education.
- His policy was based on the assumption of the inferior potential of African minds.
- His policy was designed to keep blacks in the position of hewers of wood and drawers of water.[402]
- He discouraged the teaching of mathematics and science.
- The policy deliberately starved black education of funds.
- The system did not train enough black teachers, giving rise to large classes, which negatively affected the quality of teaching.

'Closing down a functioning system'

Missionary societies and churches dominated the provision of black and coloured education before the National Party (NP) came to power in 1948. In 1939 the Minister of Education in the United Party government admitted that two-thirds of black children were without any school experience whatsoever.[403] During the war years the government improved the provision of education to blacks considerably, but by 1950 less than half of black children aged 7–16 were attending school, and only 2.6 per cent of black pupils were enrolled in post-primary standards. The average black child spent only four years in school.

Among the mission schools there were a few well-performing high schools but, as Hyslop notes, the reputation of these schools 'should not obscure the fact that most mission schools were poor primary schools with large dropout rates' and that the 'mission system was breaking down at all levels'.[404] With the demand for education growing rapidly, schools had to take in far more children than they could teach effectively. The state helped by providing salaries for approved teaching posts, but overall state aid was insufficient to modernise the entire system. School buildings were dilapidated and classes overcrowded. Most schools were understaffed and there was a severe shortage of competent teachers.

After the Second World War both the United Party government and the Native Representative Council (NRC) – the official body for articulating black opinion – sensed that the system of black education was in need of a drastic overhaul. But there were some important sticking points. Most important was the question of funding. ZK Matthews, the leading black authority on education and a prominent member of the ANC, pleaded for a programme of modernisation in terms that, implicitly at least, meant apportioning resources for equal educational opportunities. But whites baulked at the expense. RFA Hoernlé, a leading liberal, observed that while a large number of the white voters did not mind 'native education', it would be suicide in most constituencies for a member of Parliament 'to advocate, let alone vote for, the proposal that whites should be taxed in order that natives could be educated'.[405]

Officials in the new Department of Bantu Education found shocking general conditions in the pre-1954 system. Some of the churches and missionary societies insisted on baptising children before admitting them to their schools. Some used this as a device to boost their membership. There was very little parental involvement and indigenous languages were only rarely used as medium of instruction. Illiteracy was rife and eradicating it became a priority for the department. Given what a director-general of the department called 'overwhelming black numbers', it was impossible to introduce compulsory school attendance. Instead the department asked parents to commit themselves to enrolling their children for at least four years.[406]

There were a few excellent schools. Among them, Lovedale Institution, founded in 1841 by Scottish Presbyterians, was generally considered the best. RWH Shepherd, who became principal in 1942, edited the *South African Outlook*, the official voice of the missionary movement. He criticised the blanket condemnation of the Eiselen report, which in his view contained many positive recommendations. He considered the introduction of public education for blacks long overdue. When the department published its first syllabus for black schools in 1955, he found much to commend, saying it was 'clearly the work of educationists and not of politicians'.[407] In September 1955 the Lovedale Governing Council announced that it had reached an agreement with the government to transfer its high school and other educational institutions to the state.

The majority of Anglican bishops decided to lease some of the church's buildings to the state to enable African teachers to keep their jobs and make it possible for black children to continue to attend school. Elphick writes that 'similar capitulations' were announced by the Methodists and Congregationalists.[408] By contrast, Catholic bishops refused to compromise. They announced that they wished to retain their schools and to support them by economising and raising private funds.

Verwoerd did not abruptly end the state subsidy to mission schools, but phased it out over four years.[409] The gradual removal of subsidies to those schools that did not fully privatise, together with a new emphasis on instruction in the mother tongue, was a bitter blow to members of the urbanised black elite, intensifying their resolve to reject Bantu Education outright.

The government allowed those schools that funded themselves to apply for permission to continue as private schools. But permission was not given automatically. Verwoerd rejected the request made by the board of Adams College in Natal to remain private.

'Based on racist assumptions'

Those who charge Verwoerd with implementing a policy with racist assumptions usually base it on a reading of his speech in Parliament in 1953 when he introduced the bill. He attacked the existing policy, which, in his words, showed the black man 'the green pastures of the European but still did not allow him to graze there'. He added: 'Education should have its roots entirely in the Native areas and in the Native environment and the Native community . . . The Bantu must be guided to serve his own community in all respects. There is no place for him in the European community above the level of certain forms of labour. Within his own community, however, all doors are open.'[410] This comment is often distorted by quoting only the first part – 'There is no place for him in the European community above certain forms of labour' – and by omitting the qualifier Verwoerd added: 'Within his own community, however, all doors are open.' Verwoerd's statement was undoubtedly the greatest blunder of his career. By one black generation after another, his words have been cited as evidence for the belief that the intention of white rule was to keep blacks in an inferior situation not only for the short term but for as long as possible.

Unlike in the 1970s, white employers in the 1950s had no problems with a mass education system that did not provide more than basic literacy. A study states: 'The overwhelming demand among urban employers was for workers with basic literacy, who could be employed as unskilled labour. In most cases "tribal labour" was preferred.'[411] Among employers there was little demand for black workers who had completed the higher school standards. The *Financial Mail* reported that 'non-white' workers took over only 36,000 'white' jobs during the 1950s.[412] Unlike in the 1970s, there was no rush among employers to break down the colour bar in the workplace.

The previous United Party government had also seen little need to train large numbers of black artisans for employment in the towns and cities. Its policy emphasised the training of whites for skilled labour in the so-called 'white areas'. Blacks could only expect to do skilled work in the reserves. In terms very similar to those Verwoerd would use later, the Secretary of the Department of Native Affairs told the De Villiers Commission on technical and vocational training in 1947 that 'the unfolding of extensive government development schemes' in the reserves would produce a large number of skilled posts.[413]

Verwoerd's formulation in 1953 affirmed what was already the situation in practice. Blacks had always been excluded from skilled or other advanced jobs in the private sector and in the central state bureaucracy. The American scholar Gwendolen Carter wrote that what was new was the creation of new opportunities for blacks in the homelands, offering them the opportunity for 'serving their own people'.[414]

Today Verwoerd is almost instinctively branded as a racist, but in *Verwoerd Speaks*, a collection of most of the speeches he gave as a politician, there is no evidence of a belief in black racial inferiority. In his lecture notes at Stellenbosch University in the late 1920s and early 1930s he dismissed the idea of biological differences among the races, adding that because there were no differences, 'this was not really a factor in the development of a higher civilisation by the Caucasian race'. He also rejected the notion of different innate abilities. He observed that what appeared to be differences in skills between Europeans and Africans were simply differences in culture as a result of historical experience.[415]

Today Verwoerd's thinking would be considered racist because he believed that biological descent, along with culture, was an immutable attribute of social identity.[416] But this view does not differ fundamentally from the consensual view held between 1930 and 1960 by most of the white intelligentsia in South Africa or, for that matter, by leading thinkers in Europe or the European colonies in Africa or Asia.

'Ensuring that blacks remain hewers of wood and drawers of water'

In the first few weeks of his term as Minister of Native Affairs, Verwoerd made an astounding proposal, which historians have surprisingly ignored. It shows that he initially did not intend to limit to the homelands the opportunity for blacks to take up skilled jobs. On 5 December 1950, six weeks after he had become minister, a meeting took place at his request with the members of the Native Representative Council (NRC). Among them were several leading ANC figures.

Stating that he expected large numbers of black people to remain in the larger cities for many years, Verwoerd announced that the government planned to give them 'the greatest possible measure of self-government' in these urban areas. All the work in the townships would have to be done by their own people, enabling blacks to pursue 'a full life of work and service'. Blacks had to be educated to become sufficiently competent in many spheres, the only qualification being that they would have to place their knowledge exclusively at the service of other black people.

Verwoerd invited the NRC members to meet him after the session for a 'comprehensive interview' about these matters and to put forward their own proposals. He also promised a prompt reply from government to their representations.[417] The NRC did not take up the offer, and it is easy to see why not. The urban black elite demanded representation at all levels of government, including provincial and central government, in common with whites. Verwoerd's proposal fell far short of that. It was made in the context of an ideology of complete segregation and Verwoerd spoke as representative of a government that NRC members viewed with grave suspicion. This moment signalled a fateful turning point in history when history failed to turn.

A new field for black politics could have been opened up if Verwoerd's offer had been accepted, particularly if it had set in motion a political process that led to talks between the government and the urban black leadership on the election of black urban councils, the formulae for the allocation of revenue, the staffing of the bureaucracy of local councils, property ownership and opportunities for black business. It would have created a whole new area for the development of black managerial and administrative capacity, something that the country was sorely lacking when whites handed over power in 1994.[418]

After his meeting with the NRC members, Verwoerd embarked on a policy that singled out the homelands as the only places where blacks could fulfil their political and professional aspirations. He tied the education system closely to the homelands system. Black high schools would not be built in urban areas, and the training of black teachers would preferably take place in the homelands.

'Intending to keep the system inferior'

Apart from opposing an increased tax burden, white politicians, particularly those of the NP, rejected increased spending on black education for fear of producing a new generation of well-educated blacks determined to overthrow white supremacy. JG Strijdom, Transvaal NP leader, warned the NP leader, DF Malan, in 1946 that it would be impossible to maintain racial discrimination if the level of black education was steadily improved. 'Our church ministers', he added, 'were far too eager to compete with other missionary societies in trying to provide the most education to blacks'. This would lead to demands for equal rights from educated people, which, if refused, would lead to 'bloody clashes and revolutions'.[419]

To put it in non-racist terms, the fear was that by expanding education to black children and allowing them to proceed to secondary school, the state ran the risk of sowing the seeds of its own destruction. An opinion survey conducted several years later showed that black children's rejection of segregation steadily increased with higher education levels. About half of children with only four years of schooling said whites could keep their own housing areas and schools, as against only a third of those in Standards 7 to 9, and a tenth of those in Standard 10.[420]

Yet for Afrikaner nationalists to deny their subordinates a proper education would undermine their self-conception as a people committed to the upliftment of the black population. Verwoerd expanded black education greatly, with the proviso that well-qualified blacks had to seek appropriate jobs in the homelands.

Verwoerd did not consider well-educated blacks a threat as long as the political and educational system directed their aspirations to their 'homelands' and to serving their own communities. He severely limited black or coloured access to the liberal white universities and established five university colleges for black and coloured students. Questioned about the wisdom of establishing university colleges for blacks, he replied: 'We shall have to negotiate frequently with [blacks] in the future over many issues, including education and politics. It would be better to negotiate with people who are well informed and educated.'[421]

Despite its flaws, Bantu Education signalled the introduction of a modern system of mass primary education for blacks, albeit one whose funding formula was heavily skewed racially. For twenty years after its introduction, the new system encountered little black opposition, with black parents failing to heed the ANC's calls for school boycotts. This opposition only surfaced in the mid-1970s after the policy had been adapted to enable large numbers of black children to advance to much higher standards than was possible in the preceding decades.[422]

'Deliberately starving Bantu Education of funds'

Strong criticism has been directed at the insufficient and discriminatory funding of black education. The common assumption is that the blame lies squarely with the policy as announced by Verwoerd. He stated in 1953 that the state's allocation to black education would be pegged at R13 million and any additional money had to come from direct taxes that blacks paid (R2 million). As a result, the gap in the ratio of white to black per capita spending on education widened from 7 to 1 in 1953, to 18 to 1 in 1969.

But pegging funding for black education was not implemented as announced by Verwoerd. The policy was adhered to only between 1957 and 1962, in which period there was an increase of only 2 per cent on spending. In the next five years, between 1962 and 1967, spending increased by nearly 50 per cent. According to

Dirk Meiring, a director-general of black education under the NP government, the Verwoerd government soon discovered that the rapid increase in the number of black pupils had made the policy quite unrealistic.[423] According to Joubert Rousseau, director-general of black education from 1975 to 1982, Verwoerd secured approval for the amount allocated to black education to be supplemented from the loan account. The loans were never paid back.[424]

Spending on school buildings for blacks, along with other capital spending, was not brought into the budget of the Education Department, as was the case in white education, but was hidden in the budget of the Department of Public Works. Especially during the first fifteen to twenty years of Bantu Education, a large part of state spending consisted of expenses related to the construction of school buildings.[425] Without taking this into account, no proper comparison of per capita spending on white and black education can be made.

The major increase in the number of black pupils should also be taken into account. The number of black children in schools increased from 800,000 in 1953 to 2,750,000 in 1970. This drastically affected the per capita spending on blacks.

It proved to be exceptionally difficult to narrow the large gap in per capita spending on white and black education. There was, firstly, a large demographic disparity between whites and blacks. In the 1950s and 1960s the average child-bearing black woman had 6.3 children compared to 3.3 in the case of white women.[426] Secondly, white teachers received much higher salaries not only because of racial discrimination but also because they were generally much better qualified.[427]

'Providing insufficient teachers'

A serious problem affecting the implementation of the policy was the inability to attract enough black teachers to meet the growing demand for education. A recent study passes this judgement on the system: 'The experience of black schooling during the 1950–70 period was one of partial modernisation, generating a higher enrolment of black pupils, without providing additional teaching resources at a comparable rate.' It adds that 'white educational opportunity . . . was consistently and considerably better than black educational opportunity'.[428]

The very unfavourable pupil–teacher ratio persisted. While the ratio in white government schools never rose above the mid-20s level, in black schools it remained in the range 50:1 to 70:1 from 1957 to 1993.[429] White teachers continued to be better qualified than their black counterparts. An interesting finding is that black matric pass rates did not respond positively to higher teacher qualifications.[430]

'Discouraging the teaching of mathematics and science'

During the 1940s quite different views emerged on whether exactly the same education had to be provided to white and black children. The leadership of the small urbanised black elite insisted on the same subjects and examinations, and on the same department to administer the education of all children. Afrikaner educators favoured providing blacks with an education that was more practically than academically oriented. Liberals were divided. Some subscribed to the view that the same education had to be provided to everyone regardless of colour; others questioned it. Leo Marquard wrote a book under the pseudonym of John Burger (1943) that strongly criticised segregation as a repressive policy. He was, however, not in favour of the same education for whites and blacks. He wrote:

> [Anyone] who has anything to do with Native education is bound to feel that the system and content of education in European schools require severe modification when applied to the mass of the Bantu. Not the least unfortunate result of the Europeanising of South Africa has been the growth of a fixed idea among Africans that the European system of education is the best possible and that any deviation from it is likely to be second-rate.[431]

Shortly before the 1948 election Marquard co-authored a book with another liberal, Julius Lewin, who was a lecturer in Native Law and Administration at the University of the Witwatersrand. They remarked that whites and blacks grew up in such different circumstances that the same syllabi could not be used in primary education. In secondary education, however, the same syllabi had to be used and the same examinations had to be written.[432]

In his 1953 speech Verwoerd also remarked that it made little sense to teach mathematics to a black child if he or she could not use it in a career. Probably taking its cue from these words, a recent study claims that, as a result, mathematics was no longer taught as 'a core subject in black schools'.[433] In fact, mathematics continued to be a school subject.[434] From 1958 to 1965 a total of only 431 black matriculants passed mathematics.[435] The number of blacks who matriculated with a school-leaving certificate remained steady. The main problem was a lack of qualified teachers in key subjects, particularly in mathematics and the natural sciences.

Liberal scholars writing in the 1960s and 1970s criticised some aspects of Bantu Education but also noted the improvement in the provision of mass education and in the general standard of literacy. A 1968 study by Muriel Horrell of the Institute of Race Relations was critical of Bantu Education, especially its use of mother-tongue instruction, but wrote approvingly of the syllabi. Those for primary classes were 'educationally sound' and an improvement on the previous syllabi, while those for the junior and senior certificates were the same as those used for white children.[436] Ken Hartshorne also states that the syllabi of some subjects were 'very much the same as those used in white provincial schools and were an improvement on those in use previously'.[437]

'Stunting black development through mother-tongue education'

Another major point of conflict between the government and the urbanised black elite was the extent to which traditional black culture had to be made part of the school syllabus. ZK Matthews argued for the 'preservation of the African heritage and for using the powers of the vernacular languages to effect social rejuvenation'.[438] Other ANC leaders, however, rejected any 'Bantuization of native education'; blacks had to be educated 'to live side by side with Europeans'.[439]

Both Verwoerd and Werner Eiselen, who headed the commission that laid the groundwork for the Bantu Education policy, believed in mother-tongue schooling as the best form of education. A professor of anthropology before he became Chief Inspector of Native Education in the Transvaal, Eiselen had a great respect for the culture of blacks and genuine concern about the preservation of Bantu languages.[440] His commission dismissed the idea that there were inherent differences between whites and blacks in intellectual ability. The commission report strongly argued that education for blacks had to be tied to 'a Bantu culture and a Bantu society'.[441]

Verwoerd received his secondary school education in the medium of English at Milton Boys School in Bulawayo before enrolling at the University of Stellenbosch. He became one of the very first students in the country to write his doctoral dissertation in Afrikaans. He received his doctoral degree in 1924, a year before Afrikaans was proclaimed an official language. Afrikaans quickly developed from a low-status language to one that could be used in all walks of life. Afrikaans-speakers, along with English-speakers, now began to experience what Neville Alexander called 'the benefits of mother-tongue education from cradle to university'.[442]

Bantu Education, as introduced by Verwoerd in 1954, entailed the provision of mother-tongue education for the first eight years of schooling. In addition, English and Afrikaans were taught as second languages. In the ninth year of school, students were expected to switch to learning through Afrikaans and English, the official languages. The department laid down the principle that it would not use African languages as a medium of instruction in the two highest school standards except if the black community requested it.

The UCT anthropologist Monica Wilson wrote in the *Oxford History of South Africa* that 'most Africans' bitterly opposed mother-tongue instruction, that 'most teachers' considered it more efficient to use English than the mother tongue, and that the system of Bantu Education caused more bitterness among 'ordinary villagers' than virtually any other law.[443] She does not provide evidence for any of these claims. Writing in the 1950s, RWH Shepherd, principal of Lovedale College, condemned the ANC's school boycott called to demonstrate opposition to the new system. He wrote that it opened the door for lawless elements 'which Congress is obviously unable to control'.[444]

An education advisory council, which the department established, polled the boards of control of black secondary schools all over the country to assess their support for different options. One does not know if parents felt it was safe to express their views freely, but the results are nevertheless interesting. The results were as follows (unfortunately the date of the poll is not given).[445]

    Afrikaans and English 64%
    Only Afrikaans 5%
    Only English 31%
    Mother tongue 1%

The scant support for mother-tongue education at secondary school level is a very strong indication of the scepticism of black parents about its value at higher levels.

In 1974 the Department of Bantu Education instructed schools in Soweto and other townships in the southern Transvaal to teach mathematics and social studies through the medium of Afrikaans in Standard 5 and upwards, starting in 1975. In the cabinet minutes there is no indication that cabinet had discussed this change in policy before the department sent out the instruction. The department's disastrous action triggered the youth uprising in Soweto in 1976.[446] It now became easy for the black resistance movement to rally against not only Afrikaans as medium of instruction but also against mother-tongue instruction after the very first years in school.

Mother-tongue education was not out of line with what many Western scholars regard as the best educational practice. Kathleen Heugh, an acknowledged authority on language use in education, remarks that developed countries teach their children in the mother tongue because they are convinced that such a policy is pedagogically much sounder. They also believe it helps people to make a greater contribution to the economy than those taught in a second or third language. Heugh observes that developing countries tend to use the colonial language of instruction because they believe – incorrectly as it happens – that it is a shortcut to a good education and job opportunities.[447]

In South Africa the result of Bantu Education between the mid-1950s and mid-1970s was positive, when measured by pass rates. Heugh writes: 'Between 1955 and 1975, there was a steady improvement in the achievement in literacy and numeracy . . . Eight years of [mother-tongue education] resourced with terminological development, text-book production, competent teacher education and competent teaching of English, resulted in a school-leaving pass rate of 83.7% for African students in 1976. This is the highest pass rate to date.'[448]

Heugh concludes that the education policy of the apartheid government consisted of two phases: the first phase, up to 1976, worked to the educational advantage of black students; the second phase, from 1976 on, to their disadvantage, with mother-tongue education being limited to three or four years.[449]

It should be stressed, however, that the matric numbers were much lower in 1976 than in later years, which saw the pass rate plummeting.[450]

In 1983 the NP government accepted the principle of equal opportunities for education, including equal standards, regardless of colour or race. The sum spent on a white pupil was still seven times that spent on a black pupil.[451] By 1990 the gap had narrowed to 5:1.[452]

Mother-tongue education in broader perspective

Charles Simkins has offered a novel approach to the conflict over Bantu Education by viewing it from the perspective of the three main ideological forces in South African society: Afrikaner nationalism, African nationalism and South African liberalism. He writes:

> It has for a long time seemed to me that there are important differences between Afrikaner nationalism and African nationalism in their attitude towards language. Afrikaner nationalism went for the high European model in language development with voluntary associations and state education regulating issues of vocabulary and 'algemene beskaafde' spoken and written use.
>
> In this, it could draw on cognate European languages, notably Dutch. It valued the development of a literature in Afrikaans and developed a pattern of school education in Afrikaans which paralleled in formal terms the English curriculum.
>
> African nationalism did not develop the same approach. In part, this was because there were nine major black languages, little civil society capacity and interest in developing them, with the formal education system playing a major role (and a suspect one, in many eyes, as a support of apartheid. It was also seen as divisive in terms of African nationalist goals, and with a rural conservatism – and with incomplete grammars and little capacity for coping with innovations in vocabulary – in relation to the languages as they were developing, especially in urban areas) in such systematisation as took place.
>
> At the same time, literary production was at best slow, and in some of the languages almost non-existent. Linguistic identity has remained at the spoken level, with nearly all black households continuing to use an African language at home. But the expectation has been that English predomi-

nantly or Afrikaans in some areas would be used in many other contexts. This has led to an ambivalent attitude towards mother tongue education. Many black parents do not want it, believing that their children get all the mother tongue they need at home and expecting school to get right on with instilling competence in English or Afrikaans.

This attitude may be counterproductive in educational terms, though it cannot be assumed to be so on the basis of experience in, say, Europe where the development of different languages is at least roughly equal. But even if it is, is it wise to force people to be free? Others are for mother tongue education, which has led the Department of [Basic] Education to allow each school to decide on its own language policy.

Now, I accept in this matter, that Afrikaner nationalism was willing to grant to others what it claimed for itself, and I think the assumption was that African languages would develop along the lines of Afrikaans in due course. But will they? The lack of teachers qualified to teach in African languages even in the foundation phase is acute, and not likely to get better for a while, since blacks able to enter higher education often have considerably more attractive career options. And teacher education for other groups sometimes contains an eight-credit module in the local African language, which is about enough for students to learn how to greet and nothing more – a pinch of incense offered to multilingualism.

I think therefore that the current situation was the case for most of the 20th century and that it will last for a long time. Even with the best will in the world, I think that Afrikaner nationalism was unable to see the asymmetries clearly, and that this in itself led to trouble, especially in the mid-70s when there was an attempt to introduce a version of parallel medium education for blacks (half in English and Afrikaans) at a time when parallel medium education had virtually disappeared for whites, partly, I imagine, because Afrikaner nationalism was not too keen on it for Afrikaans speaking pupils.

The [English–speaking] liberal critique of Bantu Education revolved around two issues: the financial one and the exclusion from the system of any cultural influence other than that of Afrikaner nationalism, in the paternal mode discussed above. Certainly, the mission schools could not have formed the basis for mass education, but they produced some very good results and they could have been allowed to continue to do so.

The closure of mission schools meant that some of the best black teachers left the system and the rest formed a more or less comfortable, more or less cynical or resigned accommodation with it, with role conflict becoming acute in the last years of apartheid. In my view, the cynicism has persisted, with less than professional performance characteristic of many teachers to this day.[453]

Conclusion

When Hendrik Verwoerd introduced Bantu Education in 1953, the state for the first time assumed chief responsibility for black education. He took special care to address two main concerns of the NP's constituency and the larger white electorate. Firstly, mass education for blacks would have a radicalising political effect. The NP's provincial leader, JG Strijdom, had warned that this could happen. This was why Verwoerd emphasised that blacks would only have the opportunity for obtaining skilled jobs in the homelands.

Secondly, Verwoerd expected that the fast-growing black population would demand an increasing share of the budget at a time when the economy was not growing particularly quickly. Verwoerd addressed this concern when he announced at the outset that the government would put a ceiling on funding by allocating a fixed sum to black education, which would be supplemented by taxes that blacks paid.

For years commentators assumed the policy was carried out as announced, and gave this as reason why a gap of 1:20 had opened up by 1970 in white to black per capita spending. But the practical implementation of the policy took a different course. By 1962 the government had discarded the idea of a ceiling on spending. Between 1962 and 1967 funding jumped by more than a third. More importantly, without telling the electorate, the costs of building schools and other capital expenses were not brought into the department's budget but that of the Department of Public Works.

Given the electoral and budget constraints, the Department of Bantu Education went far in realising its policy objectives in the foundation stage, spanning the years from 1954 to 1969. Syllabi, textbooks and other study material were prepared in nine indigenous languages. Incentives were given to teachers to improve their generally low qualifications. Afrikaans and English, the two official languages, were made compulsory subjects for the first time.[454]

In the foundation years there was also an impressive growth of black pupils from 800,000 to 2.75 million.[455] The Eiselen report set a target of doubling secondary school enrolment by 1965. This was already met in 1959, the numbers rising from 20,000 to 43,496. Between 1960 and 1966 the number of black children in secondary schools increased from 54,598 to 66,568 and the number in matric grew from 717 to 1,608.[456]

Several misconceptions about the Bantu Education policy must be noted. The use of mother-tongue education for seven or eight years was not a means of holding blacks back, as some critics assumed, but a successful way of teaching and learning. The syllabi in most subjects were the same as those for white children. Verwoerd's statement that better-educated blacks would not be able to get higher-level jobs in the so-called white areas was exceptionally harsh but it was in line with the policy followed by the previous government. There was no assumption of the inferior potential of black minds. The most important shortcomings were the lack of teachers and the large classes, which negatively affected the quality of teaching.

But it was only after the mid-1970s, when the struggle for state control entered a new phase, that the education of blacks became a major issue. It was then that NP cabinet ministers for the first time realised how deeply black activists, from one generation to another, resented Verwoerd's fateful words, expressed in 1953, that blacks could not rise above a lowly station in jobs outside the homelands.[457] Black activists aspired to a unified system of education and a common citizenship – in their eyes, the very opposite of the thrust of Bantu Education.

SECTION TWO

Attempting to share power without losing control (1980–1990)

6.

BJ Vorster and the sultan's horse

Mr John Vorster's death [on 10 September 1983] has a special element of poignancy. In the mid-1970s he assumed a degree of control over white politics that was unrivalled in our recent political history. But the great potential of his power was never fulfilled and he died a tragic figure.

Like Louis Botha, his last years as Prime Minister were characterised by political impasse and disquiet. Brought down by political scandal, he went, like JBM Hertzog, into retirement an embittered man, feeling himself betrayed by his closest political allies. Like JC Smuts, he died with much he sought to build (détente with Africa, regional stability and Afrikaner unity) either greatly impaired or in ruins.

In his nearly twenty years of high visibility in public life, Vorster left no one cold – to use the words of Jimmy Kruger, his worst political appointment. In the single interview I had with him conducted after his fall, he made a stronger impression upon me than any other South African politician. Even if one disagreed with his views, there was no way of escaping the force of his personality.

Nor could one fail to note his masterly way of building an argument and probing for weaknesses in that of his opponent. He had a unique personal approach to politics. Piet Cillié once correctly noted: 'His priority was to win over people – not people as an abstract mass but YOU.' When I argued the case for drawing the coloured, Indian and African middle class closer to the whites, he stopped me short in my tracks by gruffly remarking, 'That's what the English tried to do: they wanted to take the Cloetes and Van der Byls but they did not want to take the Vorsters, the Giliomees.'

Unlike Hendrik Verwoerd, he was not in an aloof and cerebral way concerned with proving the validity of a political dogma. Vorster's point of departure was emotional. He considered a warm-blooded loyalty to one's people, one's friends and one's colleagues as the highest political value. Apartheid, he believed, was built upon this and was thus the only recipe for stability in South Africa. He had a disdain for those on the left who he believed had turned their backs on their people and for liberals who in his view only wanted to 'skim off' the cream of other peoples. He could be as contemptuous, too, towards those who opportunistically tried to promote and exploit Afrikaner chauvinism. It was he who coined the scornful phrase 'Super Afrikaners' for elements in the Broederbond who attacked him from the political right.

What struck me most about Vorster was that he was at the same time both a very charming and a very chilling man. The charm, of course, worked in the first place for the Afrikaners. By the mid-1970s he was among Afrikaners by far the most popular leader of this century. Down-to-earth but yet unmistakably a leader, serious but a masterly deadpan joker, someone with the approach of a favourite uncle but never one to allow any liberties. He could draw on all these qualities to impose complete control over an audience, whether it be Parliament, the National Party caucus or a student meeting.

But the charm also worked for English-speaking whites, even for some liberals. It was never more apparent than when Donald Woods visited Yale University in 1977 just after he had fled South Africa. Three hundred students packed the hall to hear about the brutal South African regime and the death of Steve Biko. Woods, it is true, delivered a powerful indictment but towards the end of his speech began to recall almost fondly his encounters with Vorster and told some favourite Vorster jokes, superbly mimicking Vorster's voice. I can still see the puzzled student faces – it was hardly the way a recent exile from Russia or Iran would talk about Brezhnev or Khomeini.

The chill came through when he started to talk about the white–black power struggle. If there was any compassion for his black opponents or any sense that they were fellow South Africans, I failed to detect it. Alan Paton once wrote, 'It is one of the deep mysteries of Afrikaner Nationalist psychology that a Nationalist can observe the highest standards of behaviour towards his own kind, but can observe an entirely different standard towards others, and more especially if they are not white.'

It would be a mistake to assume that Vorster shared the explicit racism of Strijdom or the implied racism of Verwoerd. He was in fact the first Nationalist Prime Minister who unambiguously said that there were no inferior South Africans, who allowed black diplomats and sportsmen into South Africa, and who permitted (rather reluctantly) the first integrated South African sports team.

However, to Vorster, blacks were different. And they were not South Africans. If they challenged the status quo, Vorster would counter with ruthless methods. He knew what solitary confinement meant. As a leader of the paramilitary Ossewabrandwag movement he was kept in small police cells. During the early 1960s Vorster and General Van den Bergh perfected solitary confinement as an instrument to fight subversion by communists, liberals and black nationalists alike. Vorster tended to believe in 'it's them or us' and that the Afrikaner nationalists would not get any better treatment from their black nationalist opponents if they were to seize power.

In my interview with him I argued that he would be condemned by history for his failure to take stronger action over Steve Biko's death. Was it not his duty to sack Jimmy Kruger? No, he replied, one does not 'drop' a colleague in a crisis like that; loyalty comes first. Did he not feel remorse about the circumstances of Biko's death? Yes, he was sorry he had to die in such circumstances but at the same time Biko was an 'agitator' of the kind he got to know in the early sixties who would have no mercy at all for the Afrikaners.

I challenged him on the 1976 Soweto uprising. Surely that showed that the Afrikaners could not hope to continue imposing their will upon blacks. Vorster was unimpressed. Soweto 1976 was simply a 'security failure' – the police had failed to recognise that schoolchildren could be a security threat. But the police force had learnt its lesson: next time it would be ready.

We had our interview in a house just next to De Waal Drive in Cape Town. 'Just think', said Vorster, 'what would happen if I get a *klomp klonkies* together, arm them with nice big stones and tell them to let fly at the passing motor cars. Just imagine the damage we shall cause. But of course, there won't be a next time – the police will come for us.'

In one breath: Soweto 1976 and *klonkies* pelting cars in De Waal Drive.

The same quality was present when Vorster went on to tell of his negotiations with black leaders about homelands independence. Verwoerd came up with the idea that blacks would enjoy political rights only in the homelands. It was Vorster's idea to take away their South African citizenship. Like a chess player, he was prepared to wait patiently till his opponent gave the game away. Here's how he recounted the negotiations for Bophuthatswana independence:

> Mangope and I agreed about everything as far as independence was concerned. Then Mangope came up with the idea that he wanted to take only those people who were within Bophuthatswana territory. I then said to him the policy of my party is not to make territories independent but to make nations independent. I said to him that if he expected to take only some Tswanas and expect me to take the rest and give them South African citizenship, then I was not prepared to come to an independence agreement with him. On the eve of independence Mangope again came with a proposal: he was prepared to take all the Tswanas but they should be allowed to exercise a choice whether they wanted to accept his citizenship. I then said to him I was not prepared to give to blacks South African citizenship. And that was that.

So politics for Vorster was a naked struggle to safeguard and maintain the power of a people and in particular that of one's own people. He personified the tough, uncompromising side of Afrikaner power. He not only fought the black nationalists but also Albert Hertzog's *verkramptes* who undermined his policies and threatened Afrikaner unity, the source of Afrikaner power. During the seventies he assumed almost complete control of the Afrikaner nationalist movement. Sadly, the more he succeeded, the less he was prepared to use that power in grappling with the rising crisis of apartheid. Afrikaner unity had become an end in itself. Separate development was the final answer. 'Ons het klaar gepraat,' he said during the Soweto riots of 1976.

Yet John Vorster always knew that a small embattled Afrikaner people clinging to a universally condemned apartheid policy could not survive alone over the long run. For that reason he sought to attract English support, abolished the most blatant forms of racial discrimination, which became known as petty apartheid, launched his détente policy towards Africa and tried to persuade the West to reduce world pressure upon South Africa.

It was his 'opening to Africa' which aroused the greatest interest and gave him the most satisfaction in his career. The collapse of the Portuguese empire in 1974 had created a dangerous power vacuum in South Africa. Could South Africa fill the breach by becoming a vigorous regional superpower, prepared to give generous development aid and in turn being accepted by the black African states as a stabilising force?

Vorster thought so and was prepared to take considerable risks to achieve it. He believed that the conservative African states would accept South Africa provided he could deliver three things: an acceptable settlement both in Rhodesia and Namibia and a modification of apartheid. 'Give us six months and see where South Africa would stand,' he said by the end of 1974 and sparked off a frenzy of speculation.

As Robert Jaster, reputed to be Africa head of the CIA, noted in a fascinating study of South Africa's narrowing security options, Rhodesia was the major test for détente. To force the intransigent Mr Smith's arm and convince a sceptical Africa of South Africa's bona fides as an honest broker, Mr Vorster in 1975 withdrew the South African forces from Rhodesia, slowed down through-traffic to Rhodesia and had the nationalist leader, the Reverend Ndabaningi Sithole, released from jail. Given Rhodesia's and Smith's popularity in South Africa, Vorster was quite courageous in these initiatives.

According to Jaster, détente began to falter in late August 1975, in the railway carriage on the Victoria Falls bridge when Vorster and his ally, President Kaunda, had finally brought together Ian Smith with Rhodesia's top black nationalist leaders, Nkomo, Sithole, Muzorewa and Mugabe. As Jaster puts it: 'Serious dissension among the African nationalists (particularly between Nkomo and Mugabe) enabled Smith to hold out against making any concessions. Nor could South Africa apply heavy pressure on him, since the nationalists offered no credible grounds for assuming that they could provide a stable and orderly alternative to the Smith regime.' Shortly afterwards President Nyerere persuaded the other Front Line presidents that peaceful change in Rhodesia was no longer attainable and that the strategy of intensified guerrilla war should be pursued.

If détente was already dead in the spring of 1975, South Africa's invasion of

Angola during the summer buried it. The full story of Vorster's leadership in that affair still has to be told. Some highly placed sources suggest that he succumbed to military pressure in approving the invasion while his closest adviser, Van den Bergh, was overseas. However, it was Vorster who decided to withdraw after the South African forces ran into stiff Cuban opposition. The decision was prompted by important military, as well as political, considerations – the Soviets were introducing into the battle sophisticated weaponry which South Africa could not match. Here Vorster showed courage and wisdom in curtailing an operation in which South Africa had become over-extended.

After Angola, South Africa simply had to come up with some real concessions with respect to Namibia. The West (and particularly an initially hostile Carter administration) gave warning that it was unable to block sanctions against South Africa any longer. By early 1978 it looked as if Vorster had finally decided to go ahead with an internationally accepted settlement in Namibia. In my view he was the last white leader who enjoyed broad enough support to pull it off and justify it to his constituency. Perhaps he really would have settled had he not been overtaken by events in the course of 1978.

In internal policy Vorster was considerably less impressive. He moved far too slowly on the issue of coloured citizenship and could not come to terms with the existence of a large permanent black population in the cities.

Why did Vorster not do more? By 1977 he was enjoying the support of more than 80 per cent of both Afrikaners and English-speaking whites. It was Vorster whom Afrikaners had in mind when approximately 60 per cent of a sample said that they would support their leaders even if they acted in ways they did not understand or approve.

Three answers suggest themselves. Firstly, there was in his time not any consensus among Afrikaners about major changes in the apartheid policies, Vorster was not prepared to risk a party split to force the pace of change. He himself was a conservative who did not have any great enthusiasm for starting the process of integration by, for instance, building in an integrated system of industrial relations (it is fair to assume that if in power Mr Vorster would not have been enthusiastic about the Wiehahn Commission recommendations and would have toned them down) and a constitutional dispensation which would include coloureds and Indians on a basis that, to him, smacked of power-sharing.

Secondly, Vorster had an exaggerated sense of what the power and force of the state could achieve. Certainly he believed that the state was strong enough to crush any resistance. In this field he believed that the ends justified the means and he allowed the Security Police almost a free hand.

The use or condonation of questionable means ultimately led to Mr Vorster's downfall in the Information Scandal. Quite simply, Mr Vorster was persuaded by some slick operators that, by buying local and overseas newspapers and using other questionable methods, South Africa could gain a favourable reputation abroad – without having introduced major reforms. (The Erasmus Commission delivered its verdict but the jury of history is still out – was John Vorster perhaps compelled to take an unfair proportion of the rap, and was that the real cause of his anger and bitterness in retirement?)

Lastly Mr Vorster did not move because he believed that playing for time was the best stratagem. He told me a story which vividly demonstrated this aspect of his political temperament. In 1974, Mr Vorster said, he went to Mr Smith with a deal he had concluded with President Kaunda and some other states (perhaps Britain). He said to Mr Smith: 'Sanctions will be lifted, the bridge will be opened and you will get a white government for another fifteen years. My advice to you is to take it.'

'No,' replied Mr Smith, 'I want a white government for another thirty years.'

And so Mr Vorster, in trying to persuade Mr Smith, told him the fable of the sultan's horse. A sultan had sentenced two men to death. Just as they were being dragged away, he remarked that he would commute the sentence of the man that could make his horse talk. The next day one of the men was being dragged to the executioner to be beheaded. He saw the other man standing there free! He frantically shouted: 'What did you tell the sultan? I said it was impossible to make a horse talk!'

'No,' said the other man, 'I said to the sultan I can teach a horse to talk. But I need a year. And he then let me go. You know,' the free man continued with a glint in his eye, 'a lot can happen in a year – the horse can die or the sultan can die, and who knows, I might even get the damn horse to talk.'

Mr Smith was not persuaded. Did John Vorster perhaps believe that playing for time could make a dreadful, intractable problem go away? A pity, for he was a consummate politician and leader who had the power and ability to steer South Africa to safer waters.

7.

The Botha quest:
Sharing power without losing control

The scene was familiar: one of those interminable discussions about 'change' in current South African politics. Were the reforms initiated by the Botha administration sham or real? Were they fundamentally changing South African society or merely restructuring apartheid? Finally a prominent Afrikaner business leader ventured an opinion. 'We Afrikaners', he said, 'are trying to find the secret of sharing power without losing control.' The group chuckled about the obvious contradiction in terms. But the business leader was quite serious. And not without reason. Almost unwittingly he had captured in a phrase the real paradox of the reforms that have emanated from the Botha cabinet.

An article in the Spring 1982 issue of *Leadership SA* illustrates the same elusive quest. Written by Wimpie de Klerk (brother of FW) under the title 'Afrikaner Unrest: Diagnosis and prognosis', the article argues that the Afrikaner in power is also the key to stable reform. Within one generation the Afrikaner leadership has moved from exclusivist paternalism to 'the politics of consultation and joint decision-making'. Indeed FW De Klerk's own persuasive and pragmatic approach is a far cry from the authoritarian manner of Verwoerd. But at the end of the article Wimpie De Klerk undercut everything he had said about the new politics of compromise. It is the special task of the Afrikaners, he declared, 'to handle the great change in our country'. He holds out this 'exciting' perspective: 'a South Africa which with Afrikaner leadership can create a place for all its peoples, which can exercise a growing influence throughout our continent and can gain respect and acceptance in the world'. Even more important than the goals or methods of change is De Klerk's conviction that Afrikaner leadership, acting on its own, will determine South Africa's future. This leaves little place for

English-speaking captains of industry, black labour, ethnic leaders as well as coloured and Indian politicians to help shape a more just and acceptable South Africa through negotiation and joint decision-making.

So the new politics of reform and change are in a fundamental sense not so unlike the old politics of the fifties and sixties when the Afrikaners were determined to rule South Africa alone and mainly in their own interest. Political control is still to be in the hands of the dominant ethnic group, the Afrikaners, and based on an effective degree of ethnic cohesion and discipline. But while Afrikaner leadership in the past was primarily projected as aimed at Afrikaner self-preservation, it has attempted since the mid-seventies to present Afrikaner rule as being in the interests of all the peoples of South Africa.

Particularly since the coming to power of PW Botha, much attention has been given to the new willingness of Afrikaner leaders to accept that wealth, opportunities and decision-making will increasingly have to be shared among all the peoples of South Africa. But the converse of this proposition has been less noticed, though it is equally significant: only continued Afrikaner rule can ensure a stable transition of this kind. As the Minister of Constitutional Affairs, Chris Heunis, said in a speech in October 1981: 'It is in the long-term interest of South Africa that the Afrikaner should always have the privilege of the leadership role. This role of leader will be accompanied by ever greater responsibilities.' (The great task was 'to formulate and implement a new political and socio-economic dispensation for South Africa'. The Afrikaners, he said, would have to embark on it with others 'but to a large extent it will be their responsibility'.)

Indeed, a new ideology can be said to have sprung up alongside apartheid since the late seventies. This accepts economic growth, training, job creation and food production as primary goals but always premised on the maintenance of political stability, which is seen as making all these things possible. Herein lie the crucial role of Afrikaner leadership and the rationale for Afrikaner rule. Afrikaner nationalists see firm control of the state by a fairly unified Afrikanerdom as the stable 'centre' of South Africa. Afrikaner leadership is considered the only one which can both enjoy the trust of the 'core' ethnic group and successfully direct all the technocratic skills and abilities which serve the material welfare of everyone in the country. If this stable centre loses its coherence, everyone will suffer as a result of the inevitable loss of stability and efficiency.

This, baldly sketched, is the theory of Afrikaner equilibrium which inspires the National Party (NP) leadership. And although some of these Afrikaner claims are clearly exaggerated, it is true that the relative degree of political stability South Africa has enjoyed is also due to the fact that control is in the hands of a single ethnic group which must take direct responsibility for ensuring internal peace. The level of violence in South Africa is far less than that in Northern Ireland, not to speak of Lebanon, where control is far more diffuse. And owing to the intervention of outside parties and political irresponsibility, violence in these countries is far more common. But in South Africa, too, it has become clear, particularly since the mid-seventies, that there are definite limits to the extent to which exclusive ethnic and white domination can be maintained while ensuring economic growth and political stability.

When PW Botha became Prime Minister in 1978 he set out on the risky adventure of transforming the old style of Afrikaner domination into the new style of Afrikaner technocratic leadership. The goal was nothing less than the expansion of the Afrikaner base by partially incorporating old ethnic racial antagonists while still keeping his primary base, the Afrikaners, intact. The new strategy aimed first of all at a rapprochement between the Afrikaner state and the English-dominated private sector in the common pursuit of an economic growth rate that could meet the material aspirations of both black and white. Secondly, it sought to prevent increasing racial polarisation by beginning to forge a bourgeois alliance between the whites and the coloured and black elites – the third of the Asian population, the quarter of the coloureds, and the 5 to 10 per cent of the Africans who could be considered middle class. The idea was to 'co-opt' appropriate leaders of these groups into the system of administration as a stabilising force. Thirdly, the challenge was to undertake these initiatives and still retain the Afrikaners' trust – the cement of ethnic cohesion. This was PW Botha's quest: to 'share' power in a symbolic rather than a real way, while still keeping effective control over both the South African system and Afrikaner politics.

PW Botha's first and most dramatic breakthrough was to end the old antagonism between the Afrikaner government and the world of English big business. In the area of purely economic matters a degree of consensus has developed between government and big business that few would have dared predict twenty or even ten years ago. Perhaps most important was the government's acceptance of the need to curb state expenditure as a precondition for promoting growth through the private sector. The proportion of public spending in GDP was cut from 27 per cent in the mid-1970s to 23 per cent – an achievement equalled by few other member countries of the International Monetary Fund.

The government has also stopped boosting the relatively weak manufacturing sector through expanding its subsidies and special protection. It has accepted the mining and finance houses as the real dynamos of the economy and has allowed them to assume control of a very large part of the manufacturing sector. Finally the government invited the business sector at the Carlton and Good Hope conferences to contribute the resources and know-how of free enterprise to the development of the economically depressed black rural areas.

All this led to feverish speculation that a new coalition of political and economic managers was being formed that could sweep away the apartheid order through a common commitment to growth and free enterprise. But this enthusiasm soon began to wane as the suspicion grew that the government wanted to employ its new association with big business for entrenching apartheid. Harry Oppenheimer voiced the common mood of the private sector when he stated: 'When the government says it wants to rely on private enterprise, it is really thinking of using private funds and know-how to carry out its policy. This is not what I understand by private enterprise.'

Indeed, it became clear that there was a crucial disagreement between government and the business sector on the role of free enterprise. The government wanted free enterprise to operate within the apartheid structures; however, business regarded the abolition of the essential features of apartheid – influx control, group areas, separate amenities, and so on – as a precondition for the free enterprise system to operate effectively. By the beginning of 1982 it was obvious that Afrikaner leadership and big business had failed to forge a firm alliance based on a common conception of a new dispensation for South Africa.

The Botha quest has, secondly, entailed an attempt to co-opt coloured and black collaborators to help administer their segregated ethnic communities and serve as a buffer between middle-class white South Africa and the huge impoverished proletariat. This does not mean any diminution of control, for the important thing about formal co-optation is that what is shared is responsibility for power rather than power itself. The future strategy of the Afrikaner leadership is a three-part co-optation exercise:

- the co-opting of coloured and Indian elites into the 'white' political system (short-term objective),
- the co-opting of independent homeland governments into a confederation of South Africa (medium-term objective),
- the co-opting of a black urban petty bourgeoisie (small-scale businessmen, traders, teachers and civil servants) who could be entrusted with the administration of the townships and hopefully even influx control (long-term objective).

It is this co-optation strategy which Wimpie de Klerk describes as 'the politics of consultation and joint decision-making'. Time and again commentators stress the extent to which the Botha government is already engaged in 'negotiating' with the coloured and black elites, which it seeks to woo. However, the inappropriateness of this term becomes clear when reference is made to James Anderson's classic distinction between three distinct leadership styles: command, persuasion and negotiation.

Under both Verwoerd and Vorster the government simply resorted to the command style in implementing its racial policy. In this case the dominant actor is so confident of being in firm control that decisions are simply dictated and little thought is given to the reaction of the subordinates. To his credit, PW Botha as Prime Minister sensed that rising world opinion against apartheid and the internal political situation have made the command style no longer appropriate. His administration accordingly has shifted towards the persuasion style. What South Africa has witnessed since 1979 is an attempt by the government to persuade those coloured and black leaders thrown up by the apartheid system either to accept the proposed South Africa confederation or, in the case of the coloureds and Indians, to participate along segregated lines in the new constitutional dispensation.

The essential characteristic of persuasion is that the subordinate group is endowed with some resources which the ruling group wants and tries to obtain without, however, sacrificing its own position in any significant way. The only resource the various black, coloured and Indian leaders possess in the current political game in South Africa is rejection of participation in government schemes and denial of legitimacy to government policy. The government has been trying to persuade them to accept its offers without, however, being prepared to give up its own position. Both the proposed confederation and new constitutional dispensation are based squarely on the apartheid order. In effect the government has presented coloureds and Indians, on the one hand, and homeland leaders, on the other, with set constitutional programmes worked out beforehand rather than with proposals that were open to bargaining.

The government has of course tried to package its style of persuasion as negotiation. However, negotiation in the true sense of the word involves give and take and a spirit of compromise in order to reach a mutually acceptable position. This the Afrikaner leadership does not yet consider because it still considers itself strong enough to do without it. If it is prepared to engage in constitutional change, it still insists that all initiatives be the prerogative of the Afrikaner leadership. Moreover, it has not yet moved along the road to power-sharing. The new constitution is carefully structured in such a way as to prevent or circumvent any attempt by the coloured or Indian Houses to get a hand on the levers of power. Their only real power is a negative one: to withdraw en bloc from the system and thereby cause embarrassment to the government. But this has been forestalled by putting in place fall-back positions and fail-safe mechanisms at every point.

But even if all exercises in co-optation and persuasion were successful, the third aim of the Botha quest demanded that he also keep his Afrikaner base intact. Effectively this meant rallying both the middle- and lower-middle-class Afrikaners behind the NP – after the labour reforms of 1979–80 there was little hope of retaining Afrikaner working-class support. It was at this point that Botha ran into the deepest trouble: the NP's Afrikaner base began to erode alarmingly. While some 85 per cent of Afrikaners supported the NP in the 1977 general election, this dropped to 66 per cent in 1981 and 55 per cent in the 1983 by-elections.

It is important to realise that this is not purely an ideological revolt against the policy of 'sharing' power but there are also potent material reasons behind the Afrikaner split. The mobilisation of Afrikaner unity over the past fifty years has been based on catering to a wide range of Afrikaner interests. Under the Nationalist government the Afrikaner business class, professionals, civil servants and workers all prospered. This produced dramatic results: while only 27.5 per cent of the Afrikaners were in white collar jobs in 1936, the proportion had shot up to 65.2 per cent by 1977.

But apartheid, the basis of Afrikaner unity and advance, also had costs. These costs, together with the flaws of the capitalist system as it operates in the South African context, began to hit home with a vengeance in the mid-seventies when growth in the Western economies came to a virtual halt. Political as well as business leaders woke up to a critical shortage of skilled labour, low worker productivity, hopelessly inadequate black education, a consumer market limited by the partial incorporation of blacks, curbs on exports, the collapse of subsistence farming in the homelands, mass black unemployment or underemployment, and a persistent double-digit inflation rate. And to this had to be added an increasingly disaffected black working class.

To counter some of these ills, the Afrikaner leadership and the business class were forced to promote black advancement and to withdraw some of the traditional protections, subsidies and inflated wages and salaries granted to lower-class whites. Consequently, lower-class whites suffered a drop in living standards of approximately 20 per cent in the late seventies. Subsequent pay increases have somewhat made up for this, but it is safe to estimate that the real income of white workers and lower-class civil servants is currently between 10 and 20 per cent lower than that of 1974. Poorer farmers are also facing critical times. Taking 1970 as the base, the average prices of farming costs had risen by 269 per cent in 1981 as against a rise of only 195 per cent in the prices of agricultural products. Subsidies and tax concessions enable the large farmers to prosper economically but they barely help to keep the poorer ones afloat. The abandonment by whites in the last decade of some four thousand farms in the Transvaal has been the result mainly of bankruptcy.

It is thus misguided to think that the right-wing advance can be attributed solely to rank prejudice and ignorance. To an important extent it is a lower-class white revolt against sudden economic insecurity, made especially unpalatable by the new relationship between the Afrikaner government and English big business and the narrowing economic gap between whites and blacks. It is difficult to see the NP gaining more than 60 per cent of the Afrikaner vote again.

Thus Botha's strategy of 'sharing' power without losing control has run into trouble on two fronts. By trying to position himself between reform and Afrikaner unity, Botha has been forced to sacrifice a considerable portion of both. After nearly five years Botha's half-hearted enterprise has produced mixed results. He has gained the qualified backing of a business class which is prepared to applaud any reformist moves but is unwilling to give real political and ideological support to Afrikaner technocratic rule. Botha has also persuaded black and coloured politicians to enter the political framework imposed by the NP to play the game of co-optation. However, they clearly lack positive identification with the system.

It is against this background that the proposed new constitution will have to be judged. Whatever its defects, the 1983 constitution represents a new start in our political history even if only because of all the hopes and expectations it will create. The Afrikaner leadership clearly wishes that it will give fresh impetus to the strategy of 'sharing' power without losing control, by co-opting non-Afrikaner citizens to the system of rule. In this whole process the President – the Afrikaner *hoofleier* – will have to play the decisive role.

Can this strategy work? To evaluate this properly, it is vitally important that the nature of both the Afrikaner leadership and the NP be correctly assessed. As to the first question, it is important to grasp that despite appearances the Afrikaner leadership is a collective one in which the political, economic and cultural Afrikaner elites develop consensus on central issues before any major advance in policy or action. The Afrikaner *hoofleier*, whether he be Prime Minister or President, is expected to embody the will of the Afrikaner people and the ethnic consensus. It is this role that Vorster played almost to perfection in the mid-seventies. In the first two years of his administration Botha started out boldly on a course which moved beyond the limits of the ethnic consensus. The symbolic signals he sent (the Carlton meeting and his visit to Soweto) and the rhetoric ('apartheid was a recipe for permanent conflict') were new and dramatic but unnerving for large segments of his ethnic constituency. Increasingly the collective leadership began to reassert itself. When Botha began to hold back on reform, he not only sacrificed momentum but also failed to recoup his losses. Botha can never lead a unified Afrikanerdom again – ethnic trust once forsaken cannot be restored.

In this perspective the prospect of a strong executive President under the new constitution appears crucial. The first point that has to be made is that the current political strains within Afrikanerdom will be enormously aggravated by a reformist President determined to push through those reforms considered desirable by the business sector and the coloured and Indian elites. Secondly, the new constitution will bring a vital element of uncertainty into the Afrikaner political game if it is viewed purely in abstract terms. Indeed, the constitution makes it impossible to remove the President without the approval of all three Houses. Although unlikely, it is possible to see a reformist President winning such a measure of support from the coloured and Indian Houses that the white House will be unable to remove him – in the case of a conservative President, this scenario is impossible to conceive.

For both these reasons it seems inevitable that the President will be firmly bound to the NP caucus. There will be great pressure on particularly a reformist President that he does nothing which will further upset the Afrikaner equilibrium. He will have to give firm assurances to the NP that he will not act at all against the principle of Afrikaner collective leadership and the prevailing ethnic consensus about reform. As long as the President does not have a separate base through direct election by voters, but is effectively chosen by the NP caucus, his freedom of action is severely constrained. He certainly does not appear to have the scope to construct viable alliances across racial and ethnic lines.

But is it not likely that the NP will increasingly become a middle-class rather than an ethnic party? And will this not give the President the desired freedom of action to push through reforms?

In view of the loss of the Afrikaner far right, the NP will of course intensify its efforts to attract English support. However, the Afrikaner leadership will not be prepared to pay much for this support, for instance by reforming social apartheid (the Immorality Act, Group Areas, and so on). It has no intention of changing the fundamentally ethnic nature of the NP. It would welcome English electoral support but not strong English infiltration of the organisational and leadership structures of the party to the point where it becomes something like the United Party of the 1930s. (Although some 25 per cent of English-speakers currently support the NP in elections, only 3 per cent of the NP members of Parliament are English.) There is a historical lesson firmly embedded in the political thinking of Afrikaner leaders today. This points to the experiences of Generals Hertzog and Smuts, who became increasingly dependent on English support and ended up by having only the minority backing of Afrikaners. To this is added the strong conviction that South Africa is not governable with only minority Afrikaner support. In this view a middle-class coalition of Afrikaners and non-Afrikaners, of whites and non-whites, will be unable to ensure stability if confronted by a vengeful, insecure Afrikaner right wing.

Yet it should be obvious that South Africa will become even more ungovernable if it has to depend only upon an Afrikaner ethnic base, which itself is showing signs of growing strain. By the year 2000 whites will constitute only 12 per cent of the population and Afrikaners only 6 or 7 per cent. In this period the economy will become predominantly based on skilled black labourers, who will have acquired a strategic leverage for use in political bargaining. The present constitution makes no provision for blacks, and power is shared with coloureds and Indians only in a symbolic and advisory capacity. It is difficult to avoid the conclusion that the alliances the government will be able to construct across racial lines will turn out to be fragile when the black challenge begins to build up.

There are two great dangers on the South African political horizon. The one is that political stagnation and economic stagnation will reinforce each other. A sluggish economy will mean that new groups cannot be given new resources (thus keeping conflict to a minimum) but will have to be paid off with a portion of the existing resources. The high hopes for a steady 5 per cent economic growth rate in the eighties have already dissipated. A similar redistribution of resources at the cost of whites, as happened in the seventies, will give a major boost to the Conservative Party, further checking reform initiatives. A low economic growth rate would at the same time mean that the benefits which non-white collaborating elites acquire for their communities will remain small and disputable. They could suffer a steady loss of credibility, limiting their capacity to act as mediators.

So for the politics of co-optation to be successful in its own terms, a dynamic economy is vital. However, short of a new mineral Eldorado, the only remedy for the South African economy is to start curing its fundamental ills such as inferior, segregated coloured and black education, low worker productivity, and restrictions on the flow of black labour. And it now appears as if the government needs a much broader base than at present for bold actions to be launched in these fields and for both local and international business to acquire the necessary confidence to invest on a large scale.

The other danger is that of the Afrikaner political base disintegrating before a viable middle-class coalition is built to take its place. Confronted with a rising white right-wing threat and growing black unrest, the government will be sorely tempted to defend its shrinking political base by expanding executive powers through further erosion of the rule of law and the parliamentary process, and by curbing the flow of information, expending ever more resources on military and security purposes, tightening influx control and intervening in the economy. Yet democracy and viable middle-class alliances depend on exactly the opposite. They rest on constraints on politicians, a relatively free and independent private sector, strong and responsible trade unions, freedom to enter the job market, autonomous cultural institutions such as universities and churches, and a free press acting as an early warning system about conflicts building up. Above all, they need bridges across racial groups formed by people from different classes and ethnic groups identifying with the same institutions, symbols and leaders.

Wimpie de Klerk is right in according a key role to Afrikaner leadership in shaping a more just South Africa. As Harvard's Samuel Huntington declared: 'New politics may only be made possible by old leadership.' But for Afrikaner leadership to assume a dynamic role it will have to grasp some fundamental truths. Firstly, the surest way to lose control is not by the sharing of power but by the failure to do so, thus setting up sole control of the state as the supreme, winner-takes-all prize. Secondly, for the sharing of power to be a stabilising mechanism it will have to proceed from a position of strength, not granted under pressure. Thirdly, viable coalitions would have to be built with leaders whose very political identity is decreed from above, as will be the case in the new constitutional dispensation. Even collaborators who have been co-opted want to be part of a ruling bourgeoisie, not a segregated one. Lastly, incremental change is only possible if there is a consensus of values. Our apartheid order makes such consensus impossible.

How can a multi-racial, middle-class reform coalition come about? A real start can be made if the President is popularly elected, instead of by the NP caucus. With an independent electoral base the President will be able to construct new cross-racial alliances in a bold and imaginative way and begin to draw blacks into the political system. This will infuse the new constitutional system with a vitality and legitimacy that nothing presently on the table offers. It will of course introduce an element of risk to the Afrikaner leadership, but with an enhanced commitment to free enterprise that leadership should realise that a calculated risk is often a prerequisite for great gains.

Undoubtedly a great deal of idealism and sincerity underlies the statement of someone like Wimpie de Klerk when he speaks of a South Africa in which the Afrikaner leadership 'can create a place for all its peoples'. But the problem with this is that it will be seen exactly as that – an Afrikaner creation imposed from above and not something brought about by negotiation, firm alliances and growing consensus among all the middle-class peoples of South Africa. And to the extent that this is true, the prospects for economic growth and political stability will not improve.

Sharing power without losing control is a holding action, not a breakthrough.

8.

The Botha quest:
Changing everything, except the way we think

Einstein is reputed to have said: 'The power set free from the atom has changed everything, except our ways of thought.' He proved to be right. Although nuclear arms have changed the whole nature of war fundamentally, politicians and generals continue to think about war, victory and defeat in the same old ways. In a book edited by Gwyn Prins, *Defended to Death: A Study of the Nuclear Arms Race* (1983), a group of Cambridge scholars remarks: 'The noble old meanings of words about war are used without thought, and this has the effect of making nuclear war seem normal.'

On a quite different level there is the danger of something similar becoming true in the case of South Africa's new constitutional dispensation. White South Africa has just thrown overboard a tried and tested constitution operative for more than seventy years. In exchange a new political system has been introduced in which consensus government will supposedly replace the old confrontational style, one in which common values rather than conflicting interests will hopefully prevail. Yet there is little indication that the basic thinking of white South Africa has changed in ways which can in any real sense be called fundamental. In fact, the new constitution may do little more than persuade whites that part of our society has been normalised.

White South Africa is in every respect a typical middle-class society. It sees its wealth and standard of living as its just reward and not as something gained at the expense of blacks. The great majority of whites are aware of and somewhat guilt-ridden about the political flaws of our system. But this is surpassed by the middle-class survival ethic. This ethic firmly rejects any political formula that will remove the ability of the government to act swiftly and ruthlessly in defence of white political interests or, to be more specific, white middle-class interests. For the Afrikaners there is a vital additional consideration. They do not only want to maintain these class interests but are determined to remain the dominant ethnic group of the country, the one on which the all-powerful executive arm of government rests. Afrikaner nationalism is the driving force of the government, apartheid merely its instrument.

White greed and Afrikaner arrogance? Perhaps, but the matter of whites clinging to power is not irrational, at least not from a short-term perspective. It is quite possible that a black majority government in South Africa will guarantee the personal safety of whites and that it may even administer the country fairly efficiently. But there should be no illusion about the cost to various segments of the white middle class: half the white civil servants may lose their jobs; and white farmers will sacrifice most of their subsidies and, in the border areas, control over their land while the government starts to aid peasant production. At the same time, white industrialists will have to invent novel ways to handle a tough, confident and politically mobilised black workforce. And this is talking only about the medium-term job and income prospects.

For all these and other reasons whites consider their political power as a commodity that must be preserved with the greatest skill and caution. The constitution of 1983 has changed little in this way of thinking. For the government the constitutional debate, starting with the election of 1977 and culminating in the referendum campaign of 1983, was a massive exercise in persuading voters that its proposals were the best possible formula for sharing power without losing control. The National Party (NP) ran a brilliant campaign with respect to the white electorate.

It also ran an abysmal campaign as far as the coloured, Indian and African non-electorate was concerned. In retrospect it is now clear that the two-thirds majority in the referendum of November 1983 was far too large and that it gave rise to a dangerous credibility problem. Indeed, the more the NP convinced whites that the new constitution was the best possible safeguard for their interests, the more the coloured and Indian non-electorate became persuaded that it would gain little or nothing from participating in it. While over 60 per cent of coloured and Indian people polled in 1982 were prepared to accept the new dispensation (there was then still the possibility of a single chamber instead of three), this has dropped to a bare 17 per cent of registrable voters of both these groups.

The same kind of political asymmetry is evident if we look at the construction of the new dispensation in class terms. When whites say 'let us draw the coloured and Indian people nearer to us', they have the middle class of both these communities in mind. After all, one of the main reasons for whites becoming amenable to political reform is the rise of a coloured and Indian middle class. Taking occupants of white collar jobs as a rough yardstick, the percentage of middle-class people in the coloured community rose from 12 per cent in 1970 to over 20 per cent in 1983, while that of Indians went up from 38 per cent to over 50 per cent in the same period.

But it is exactly the coloured and the Indian middle classes who spurned the opportunity to participate in the elections. In a real sense the government left its constitutional reform too late. In the 1970s the top strata of the coloured and Indian populations made major socio-economic advances: they began to receive equal salaries with their white counterparts in the civil service and private sector; they were promoted to jobs previously barred to them; and they became home-owners, often with the same coveted housing subsidy that whites received.

What the new coloured and Indian middle class was demanding by 1980 was an open society in which it – like any other middle class – could choose where to live and vote for the political party that represented its class rather than its racial category. But this is exactly what the new constitution with its imposed group areas and political ethnicities does not offer. As a result, the boycott in places where the most advanced sections of the Indian and coloured communities live – Durban and Cape Town – was stunningly effective.

The figures for Cape Town are particularly telling. Only 5 per cent of eligible voters in the metropolitan region went to the polls. And the number of those who did vote was considerably lower than the figures for the old Coloured Representative Council (CRC). Whereas in the 1975 CRC election some 44,270 coloured people in Cape Town voted, only 25,110 did so on 22 August 1984 in spite of the growth of the coloured population in the city. The middle class stayed away en masse.

Ironically, the new dispensation attracted the 'wrong' classes from the government's perspective. They are those in the middle levels of the working class, mostly semi-skilled or newly skilled artisans, low- and middle-level civil servants, petty traders and (in the case of the coloured population) agricultural labourers. They form a category of people which generally have unrealistic economic expectations of the constitution – the racial equalisation of wages and salaries in the private as well as the public sector, subsidised housing and transport at a time when the government is withdrawing such subsidies, and better public facilities and services in the townships, which the government wants to be financially self-sufficient.

The government will obviously try its best to enhance the legitimacy of the system by making educational norms and standards the same for each population group and by equalising welfare expenditure on the different population groups. But given the fact that the government hardly dares leave Africans out of the process, the expectation of dramatic gains for the coloured and Indian people is unfounded.

The University of Cape Town economist Charles Simkins in a recent study came to this conclusion: 'It is calculated that in 1976 welfare expenditures per capita stood at R187 for whites, R74 for coloured people, R82 for Asians and R22 for blacks, with an average expenditure of R56... If the equalisation of per capita expenditure were achieved by 2000, everyone could enjoy the same level of services as coloureds and Asians had enjoyed a quarter of a century earlier, given the realisation of the most probable projections.' The people who will notice anything will be the whites – even in the case of a high welfare budget and high economic growth, their standards will drop by nearly a third.

Thus, some observations about the newly established dispensation stand out. Firstly, it drew support from the lower and the less qualified income groups, people who have socio-economic expectations that the government is unable to meet. Secondly, it did not increase the legitimacy of the South African political system if measured by participation in the elections. This point emerges clearly in the calculation of the Progressive Federal Party research officer Nic Olivier. To take the coloured elections first: for the Republic as a whole, the percentage poll (i.e. for registered voters) was much higher in the Coloured Representative Council elections in 1975 than in 1981. Percentage-wise, the Labour Party lost support. In 1975 it polled 29 per cent of all registered voters and 17 per cent of all eligible voters; this dropped to 24 per cent and 15 per cent respectively by August 1984. In the elections of 1984 for Indians the poll was even lower – 24 per cent of registered voters compared with the 33 per cent of the coloured election, and 16 per cent of registrable voters compared with the 17 per cent for coloureds.

Thirdly, there is no conclusive evidence of a definite shift in the white ways of thought. The new dispensation is in fact far from the dramatic breakthrough in white political attitudes it is often claimed to be. In a poll conducted by a West German team under Professor Theo Hanf some 75 per cent of a white sample agreed with the statement that 'we can make many concessions to non-whites as long as whites have the main say in politics'. And in 1977 the same team found that 55 per cent of a white sample agreed with the statement that 'we should consider strengthening our position by accepting coloureds as equal citizens'. The intense referendum campaign, together with the overall socio-economic advance of white society, pushed the support up by 10 per cent by 1983.

Another aspect of white thinking that has not changed is the inability to read the coloured and black people's minds and to anticipate their political responses to white 'solutions'. Whites genuinely believe that the new constitutional dispensation is testimony to a radically new white attitude to the coloured and Indian population. There is no reason to depict white South Africa as cynical or duplicitous. Apartheid has created a no man's land between peoples, such that it is almost impossible for whites to recognise the political pain of others. Whites seem doomed to be perennially startled by the political responses of the subjugated. The great Afrikaans poet Breyten Breytenbach once observed: 'The first thing to point out is that apartheid works. It may not function administratively, its justifications and claims are absurd. And it certainly has not succeeded in dehumanising – entirely – the Africans, the coloureds or the Indians. *But it has effectively managed to isolate the white man.* He is becoming conditioned by his lack of contact with the people of the country, his lack of contact with the South African inside himself . . . His windows are painted white to keep the night in.'

Had this constitution, based on group areas and separate ethnic elections, been introduced twelve years ago, the majority of the coloured and Indian people might well have accepted it. By August 1984 the situation had changed. The promise of a new political dispensation providing for common political symbols, a formally equal citizenship and a measure of political integration had taken on a different aspect. To use the words of C Vann Woodward, the great historian of American race relations: 'So long as integration had been truculently withheld, it had seemed infinitely more desirable than when it was grudgingly proffered at prices that seemed too high.'

Obviously the majority parties in the three Houses of Parliament would concentrate their minds on finding ways to invest the new dispensation with credibility and legitimacy. But given their meagre popular base, the coloured and Indian Houses face a Herculean task in persuading sophisticated middle-class people of Cape Town and Durban that they are making any appreciable difference to their living conditions. The real gains will be made beyond these cities in the *dorpies* where coloured and Indian people will walk taller and where the social distance between the communities will become smaller. Those whites who grew up in a small town will agree that this is a gain not to be despised.

On balance, the new dispensation does not seem to have brought South Africa appreciably nearer to the ideal of peaceful accommodation. Or so it seems at a first glance. Indeed, a future historian writing a century from now will be most perplexed by three features of the contemporary South African political scene. Firstly, he will be amazed that white South Africa could have risked so much to gain so little. Ever since 1976 it was clear that political stability in South Africa required an expanded political base. The 1984 political incorporation of coloured people and Indians does not in any meaningful way strengthen the political base. Coloureds and Indians had not threatened stability when they were completely excluded politically. As marginal groups, they had no desire to side openly with the two contending sides; as relatively small groups, the growth of the middle-class strata in their communities was quite impressive and politically stabilising. And yet to incorporate these two groups in a new constitutional dispensation, white South Africa was prepared to insult Africans on a breathtaking scale. They were excluded from not only political institutions but the very constitution itself.

Secondly, the historian will be at a loss to explain how South Africa could allow an acute contradiction between 'ex-corporating' blacks as political citizens by denationalising them, and incorporating them as industrial citizens by granting them the right to form trade unions and engage in collective bargaining. Thirdly, the historian will wonder how whites hoped to contain the tensions flowing from these contradictions while the survival struggle among blacks was becoming ever more acute. The constitution was proposed and implemented at a time when blacks had suffered a real decline in living standards. And influx control was tightened at a time when the homelands were unable to support more than 10 per cent of their inhabitants and when a massive drought made it all the more urgent that blacks move to the cities in search of work.

Again, the root of the trouble lies in the way whites think. Studies conducted in the first half of 1984 by two Johannesburg academics prove the point. The one undertaken by Professor Deon Geldenhuys of the Political Science Department at RAU found that 77 per cent of a sample of whites think that blacks have no good reason to take arms up against whites. The other, conducted by JJ van Wyk, established that 73 per cent of a sample of the black elite thought that blacks *do* have good reason to take up arms.

From one perspective, then, the government seems misguided in its constitutional reforms and the white electorate quite out of touch with black political aspirations. According to this view, the constitution of 1983 has brought precious few positive results in exchange for the huge amounts of time, money and emotion that whites expended on bringing about the new dispensation.

But this may be a superficial reading. If matters had been so clear-cut, genuinely reformist whites (between a quarter and a third of the white electorate) would not have been so bitterly divided about the constitution.

A serious case can be made for the view that those who supported the constitution on the ground that it was a step in the right direction were both wrong and right. They were wrong in their assumption that this would diminish the disaffection of middle-class coloureds and Indians, but right in their view that it was at least a start, and one which need not be false.

Quite simply, the constitution was necessary not for the coloured people or the Indians, but for whites. Whites had to be shown that the basic racial ground rules and symbols could change without the world collapsing and that the white right-wing bogey is a myth. Secondly, it was a necessary start for the kind of political dispensation towards which South Africa seems to be clearly heading:

a federation in which the South African 'state' (whites, coloureds and perhaps Indians) will be grouped together with various black formations – ethnic, class and regional.

Can this be accomplished peacefully? What can be done to give the process momentum? Perhaps one should start by saying what should not be done. Any attempt to co-opt the black urban insiders as a separate group would be extreme folly. The recent riots in the Vaal Triangle have shown how intense the hatred is of any insiders who seem to profit from the apartheid system.

In making the right start, some necessary steps must be taken. Firstly, the citizenship issue must be resolved. A federal citizenship, higher than South African citizenship, must be introduced which any South African can claim. Secondly, influx control must be abolished. This can be presented as a dramatic gesture of conciliation and it will enable blacks to build up stable political parties. Thirdly, blacks must be allowed to elect their representatives freely. Fourthly, forums must be created where negotiations, even if only about local government, can take place.

All this can be done, but with one qualification: the NP cannot do it alone. Given the alienation the constitution has produced among blacks, any initiative will only have credibility if it is supported by most vigorous opponents of the present constitution. And here the names of leaders like Dr Van Zyl Slabbert, Chief Gatsha Buthelezi and Dr Allan Boesak come to mind as future brokers.

On this second reading, then, the constitution has produced some results: it has educated the whites and has made black political rights the top item on the agenda. The government now has a stronger base from which to address blacks, and credible brokers have been identified.

The greatest obstacle to getting negotiations started with blacks is the old ways of white thinking. Chief among them is the belief that political dispensations can be handed down by whites and gratefully accepted by non-whites. The coloured people and Indians have already shown whites how wrong they were. Only by not making the same mistake with respect to blacks and by getting proper negotiations under way can the constitution of 1983 be rescued.

9.

'Great expectations':
President PW Botha's Rubicon speech of 1985

President PW Botha's speech on 15 August 1985 to the National Party (NP) of Natal was the turning point at which white rule in South Africa failed to turn. Botha was expected to use the speech, broadcast to a huge international audience, to turn around the South African crisis that had worsened after the outbreak of uprisings in the townships in September 1984. Spurning the expectations of bold reforms, Botha projected himself as the uncompromising leader of a white minority determined to fight to the end for its survival. The speech triggered a massive outflow of capital and intensified sanctions against South Africa. A line in Botha's speech, 'Today we have crossed the Rubicon', promptly became the object of scorn and ridicule.

Today it is still a major question why Botha refused to give a speech that the world would have considered as a true crossing of the Rubicon. A journalist recently speculated that Botha's courage deserted him at the last moment,[458] while two historians attribute Botha's Rubicon speech to the 'evolutionary regression' of his character.[459] FW de Klerk,[460] Botha's successor, and Andreas van Wyk, Director-General of Constitutional Development and Planning at the time of the speech,[461] both believe that he was irked by the high expectations raised by RF (Pik) Botha, Minister of Foreign Affairs, in a visit to Europe a week before the speech. Robin Renwick, British Ambassador to South Africa, maintains that the security chiefs had persuaded the President to enforce the status quo with strict security measures.[462] Anton Rupert speculated that a critical intervention was a threat by De Klerk, Transvaal NP leader at the time, to withdraw his party from the NP's parliamentary caucus.[463]

This chapter reviews the existing explanations for Botha's stand and adds another two. One is that Pik Botha, in briefing American, British and German diplomats on the pending speech, presented a package of reforms that the cabinet had recommended to the President as a fait accompli in order to force his hand. Another interpretation is that President Botha had accepted the package, but decided to spread its announcement over four NP provincial congresses. The alternative interpretation is that Botha was shocked by the groundswell of sanctions his speech had triggered and then announced the entire package in an attempt to salvage the situation.

A feared leader

PW Botha, who became Prime Minister in 1978, was strongly influenced by the Westminster-style of politics that characterised South Africa's political system from 1910 to the end of the 1980s. Politics were a matter of the winner-takes-all, demolishing the opposition rather than building alliances and consensus. A pragmatist rather than a reformer, Botha saw his challenge as strengthening the Afrikaner-dominated state through a slow but steady process of deracialisation. He was determined to make Afrikaner control more broadly based rather than introduce a liberal democracy.

Botha's political ideology consisted of three main elements. The first was that racial and ethnic groups formed the building blocks of the political and social system, and that there could be no interracial democratic competition.[464] Another core belief was that Afrikaner leadership alone could bring about orderly change. He knew full well that the Afrikaners would lose most by ceding control over the state. Hence the government had to retain their trust in every move it made. He told two biographers: 'We must not yield our leadership. You can only lead when you make it possible for people to trust you.'[465]

Having started his career as a party organiser, he kept a close watch on the swings in the white electorate and among Afrikaner voters in particular. He was acutely aware that reform was eroding his Afrikaner base. The proportion of Afrikaners supporting the NP dropped from 85 per cent in the 1977 election to the low 60s in the early 1980s. In the early 1990s it would drop to approximately 50 per cent.

Thirdly, Botha believed that the Soviet Union, using surrogates in the Third World in its rivalry with the United States, caused most conflicts in the world.

He even suspected it of pursuing a master plan for bringing South Africa, with all its mineral riches, under Soviet control. In his view it was not apartheid that in the first place was causing the conflict in South Africa, but communists who had infiltrated black political organisations and the African National Congress (ANC) in particular.[466] In 1977, when he was Minister of Defence, his department published a White Paper spelling out the belief that South Africa faced a 'total onslaught' in virtually every area of society. He turned the State Security Council (SSC) into the main body of government where security issues were discussed.

Within his first three years in office Botha imposed his authority over the party and the government. Ambassador Renwick noted that Botha was 'prone to furious rages' and that 'his ministers were terrified of him'. Through eruptions of his fierce temper, he intimidated any challenger.[467] In 1982 or 1983 Botha apparently suffered a stroke, after which his outbursts of temper became worse. This stroke was probably a precursor of the one he suffered in 1989. In the earlier stroke he was rushed to hospital in secret following the rupture of a cerebral blood vessel. Neurologists who studied the scan after this episode remark that such a lesion is often accompanied by a lessening of the inhibition of such traits as outbursts of temper. Another symptom that may occur is a suppression of some sensory stimuli, as, for instance, in the left visual field. This was reported in Botha, who failed to notice stimuli in the peripheral visual field on his left side.[468]

Yet Botha continued to do his work effectively.[469] He came well prepared to any meeting, but did not exert power like Hendrik Verwoerd through intellectual domination or like John Vorster, who always sought consensus at the expense of bold moves. His power was more direct and personal; he was a straight talker, tough, brutal, overpowering and, at times, thuggish, vindictive and petty. He was far from convinced of the need for fundamental political reform that would bring the black community into a common system. He opposed not only some of the proposals for reforms, but also being sucked by stealth into reforms he rejected. According to Magnus Malan, he would crush any person who was not open with him but tried to bypass him.[470]

Jannie Roux, Director-General in his office and Cabinet Secretary, sums up Botha's hold on power succinctly: 'He was not afraid of taking decisions and he disliked long discussions in cabinet. He looked people straight in the eyes and told them just what he thought. He had no secret agenda and never pulled any punches.'[471] After a visit to the country in 1983, Pérez de Cuéllar, UN Secretary-General, remarked: 'Two world leaders have made a big impression on me: China's Deng Xiao-ping and South Africa's PW Botha. They understand power.'[472]

Botha was fully aware of the fact that the NP's support was ominously on the wane, with the government unable to suppress the revolt in the black townships that had broken out in September 1984. Between September 1984 and mid-1985 the image of government had deteriorated rather than improved in a ratio of roughly 40 to 25 per cent.[473] The electorate showed strong opposition to the political incorporation of blacks. A 1987 poll revealed that only a quarter of Afrikaners and a third of English-speakers agreed with the idea of a fourth chamber for blacks. A mere 3 per cent of Afrikaners and 11 per cent of English-speakers wanted a single mixed Parliament with the majority in control.[474]

By the mid-1980s the military leadership had little doubt that South Africa faced a revolutionary challenge. In August 1985 the SSC discussed a document stating that the United Democratic Front (UDF) and its affiliates were directly and indirectly promoting the goals of the ANC and the South African Communist Party. They were trying to create 'free zones' and 'no-go areas' and make the country ungovernable. At a meeting of the SSC, held on 18 July 1985, twelve principles were listed for countering 'the revolutionary onslaught'. They included the need for government to retain the political initiative, to improve the life of the population and to reimpose its authority. Principle number 8 reads: 'A government's goal should not only be to exterminate insurrectionists but also to eradicate their influence over the people.'[475]

A bold reformer in many ways, Botha was at his wits' end in confronting the issue of black rights. On more than one occasion he challenged his cabinet: 'Is there anyone among you who believes we can overcome this crisis without having to fight?'[476] No one dared to reply. But if Botha was willing to fight, he did not know how to fight, except through repression. Only two alternatives existed to his government drifting ever further into a state of indecision and vacillation. The one was to reunite Afrikanerdom and prepare for a prolonged state of siege; the other was to try to split the ANC. The one was as difficult as the other. The Conservative Party (CP) was itself split between a faction prepared to embark on a struggle to the bitter end and those wishing to negotiate a deal with blacks that left whites a substantial degree of 'self-determination'. All that united the CP was its undying hatred of Botha, who had precipitated the NP split in 1982 by forcing out Andries Treurnicht, who became the CP leader.[477]

Fighting the ANC had become considerably more difficult after the organisation in the late 1970s adopted the North Vietnamese model of avoiding direct military conflict in favour of mass popular campaigns and struggles. The leadership of the ANC in exile was still determined to pursue a strategy of weakening the state until it was forced to negotiate for the transfer of power. Enjoying large-scale support from the Soviet Union, it had little interest in negotiations before that point had arrived. 'The government could have negotiated with the ANC in the mid-1980s if it really wanted to do so', Magnus Malan recounts, 'but the ANC could not. Why would it take the chance?'[478]

In retrospect it is clear that if the ANC had rejected a government offer to enter into open-ended negotiations in 1985 or 1986, it would have found it much more difficult to attain the moral high ground in the Western world as it did a few years later. But this is conjecture. The only conceivable circumstance in which the ANC would split was a government offer to negotiate without the condition that it forswore violence. Botha could never bring himself to make such an offer.

The security forces did not favour negotiations with the ANC. Johan van der Merwe, who was head of the security police in the mid-1980s, recounts: 'Electorally the NP would have committed suicide to start negotiations with the ANC.'[479] The memory of the ANC bomb in Church Street, Pretoria, in 1983, which killed 18 people, was still fresh. At its Kabwe conference, held in June 1985, the ANC decided to attack soft as well as hard targets and to make the country ungovernable. The Cold War was still a reality. Ronald Reagan and Mikhail Gorbachev had not yet met at Reykjavik for path-breaking talks and the Berlin Wall had not yet fallen. The presence of a large number of Cuban troops in Angola, the dominance of communists in ANC decision-making structures, and the increasing use of ANC symbols in the mass protests of the mid-1980s all created a situation where the government would have found it very difficult to justify to its constituency negotiations with the ANC. It was only towards the end of the decade, when the popular uprising had largely been crushed, that NP leaders came to consider it as an option.

The Machiavellians of Pretoria

PW Botha was much more of a modernising technocrat than John Vorster, his predecessor. He made Chris Heunis Minister of Constitutional Development and Planning and allowed him to appoint experts from the universities to facilitate reform. In the first phase Heunis made extensive use of Professor Ben Vosloo, Professor of Political Science and Public Administration at the University of Stellenbosch, to help conceptualise the Tricameral Parliament. He also recruited to his staff Ig Rautenbach and Rassie Malherbe, law professors from the Rand Afrikaans University, and Willie Breytenbach, a political scientist in Botha's office.

In the second phase, starting at the end of 1984, Heunis appointed a prominent legal scholar, Andreas van Wyk, as Director-General of his department. Joh van Tonder, a contemporary of De Klerk as a student at Potchefstroom and later Professor of Political Science, became Chief Director of Constitutional Planning, and Fanie Cloete, an ex-student of Vosloo and Van Wyk and an academic authority on public administration, Director of Constitutional Planning.

In the place of bureaucrats there were now scholars who had studied the leading advisers of rulers and governments since the late Renaissance in Europe on how to reform in the face of stiff resistance. Given Botha's reluctance to accommodate blacks in a single political system, the reformists in the Department of Constitutional Development and Planning followed what Cloete called a strategy based on the ideas of Niccolò Machiavelli (1469–1527). Machiavelli had grappled with the task of building a state in northern Italy strong enough to impose its authority on a hopelessly divided society. This is a challenge that countless regimes have faced in history. For instance, during the 1960s Brazilian elites, living under the dictatorship of President Getúlio Vargas, declared that they wanted the government 'to make the revolution before the people do'.[480]

In his study *The Prince*, Machiavelli warned that a precarious moment arrived when a ruler embarked on reform with the common good in mind. He risked making enemies of 'all those who prospered under the old order', while gaining only lukewarm support 'from those who would prosper under the new'.[481] To succeed, he must first concentrate all power in himself. He may be compelled to use violence and other 'reprehensible actions', but 'their effects' may justify such steps. It is the ruler who uses violence 'to spoil things' that is blameworthy, not the man who uses it to mend them.

Thus for Machiavelli the key question is not whether the prince's actions meet the standards of Christian morality; it is whether he takes appropriate action in cases where he was 'compelled [necessitato] to act without mercy, without humanity, and without religion'.[482] He warns against the prince lending his ear to different advisers with different agendas. The ideal was for him to listen to a single, astute adviser.

For the Pretoria reformists the two main contemporary academic authorities were Samuel Huntington, a Harvard political scientist, and Arend Lijphart, a Dutch political scientist based at the University of California, San Diego. Although some label him an 'ultra-Machiavellian',[483] Huntington uses as his main example in his study of reform the Fabian Society of London during the 1880s and 1890s. The Fabians desired to build representative democracy and reformist socialism through gradual, piecemeal, evolutionary change.[484]

For Huntington there are two possible reform strategies. One is for the reformer to make known all his goals at an early stage and then try to achieve most of them (he calls this the *blitzkrieg* approach). The alternative is the Fabian strategy, which he describes as 'the foot in the door approach of concealing aims, separating the reforms from each other, and pushing for only one change at a time'.[485]

As a guest of the Department of Foreign Affairs, Huntington visited South Africa in 1981 and addressed a conference where Chris Heunis also spoke. Here he warned that at some point in the following decade or two a combination of challenges would make it very difficult for the white minority to hold on to power. 'Revolutionary violence does not have to be successful to be effective. It simply has to cause sufficient trouble to cause divisions among the dominant group over the ways to deal with it.'[486]

To avert a situation where a government loses the initiative, Huntington proposed combining the *blitzkrieg* and the Fabian approaches. Power must be concentrated in the hands of the government, which at all times has to retain the initiative. The reform package has to be broken up into distinct elements, which then have to be introduced separately. New allies must be sought for each stage of the reform process, culminating in a grand reform coalition of the NP leadership, moderate blacks, business leaders and key managers in the civil service and semi-state corporations. Most of the work of winning support for reforms had to take place in secret.

Applying this technique to South Africa was not without major problems. Both President Botha and Heunis were Cape-based politicians who had a fairly good knowledge of and even an emotional tie with the coloured community. However, neither knew black people well nor had any idea of the increasing hold the ANC and its internal ally, the UDF, had acquired over the better-educated blacks, coloured people and Indians.

Botha also had to face the fact that he was accountable to his party, which insisted that the removal of blacks from the political system was the surest way to secure white political survival. He lacked the free hand of a Reza Pahlavi, the Shah of Iran, or the military-based dictators of Latin America. Heunis and his advisers and Pik Botha and his senior staff were all ready to apply the approaches of Machiavelli and Huntington, but PW Botha listened not only to them but also to the 'securocrats', particularly Magnus Malan, the Minister of Defence, Pieter van der Westhuizen, chief of the SSC's secretariat, and to Niël Barnard, head of the National Intelligence Service. Also influential was Jack Viviers, a journalist who had been seconded from the Nasionale Pers group to Botha's office as his chief communications adviser.

In the absence of commonly agreed principles or priorities, Heunis and his advisers fell back on delicately steering and prodding the debate to the point where the President could buy into their proposals. The situation calls to mind Huntington's observation: 'The problem for the reformer is not to overwhelm a single opponent [in this case, Botha] with an exhaustive set of demands but to minimize his opposition by an apparently very limited set of demands.'[487] Alternatively, the proponents of substantial reform had to secure agreement for some abstract principles, hoping the President and the conservative faction of the cabinet would not discover their concrete implications until it was too late.

Heunis considered himself a political leader who, as he called it, 'shifted boundaries', by using ambiguous wording for ambivalent proposals. '"Got that one past them," [Heunis] once chortled after a speech by Pres. Botha had announced a fairly significant shift in policy in such a way as to have escaped the attention of the Conservative Party.'[488]

The former academics in his department backed Heunis to the hilt. Fanie Cloete formulated the strategy as follows: 'We had to get the politicians to make piecemeal concessions on principles in order to achieve greater openness or flexibility and afterwards to provide concrete details and to make sure that the new principles were irreversible. This process, however, slowed down as the decision on the key principle, namely power-sharing with blacks, approached.'[489]

Their best case for far-reaching reform was to develop the argument, backed by hard data, that the white power base was inexorably weakening. The white proportion of the population was steadily shrinking, the economy was stagnating, and international pressure was growing. Joh van Tonder recounts: 'We showered them with data. We got experts from other departments and from the business sector. We even coached them what to say.' The name of the game was incrementalism – engineering a common political system step by step, preferably by forcing the conservatives to swallow the implications of abstract principles they had already accepted or the rhetoric they had used without grasping the practical implications. PW Botha once complained: 'I only later realised what some of the things you have made me say actually mean.'[490]

Botha's support was based on three pillars: the NP constituency across South Africa, the NP of the Cape Province, of which he was long the leader, and the military. The messages he received from these sources of support were not always consistent. By mid-1985 he had not yet made up his mind between intensified repression and reform. It was indeed an open question whether major political reform was advisable in the unstable environment of the mid-1980s. Many townships were out of control and the trade unions were beginning to challenge the political order. Had Botha read Machiavelli, he could have quoted back at the reformists a passage in *The Discourses*: '[The prince] will find that a small section of the populace desire to be free in order to obtain authority over others, but that the vast bulk of those who demand freedom, desire but to live in security.'[491]

In similar vein Botha told Parliament: 'There is clear evidence that the vast majority of the [black urban] areas support the government's action to maintain order and are themselves beginning to oppose the elements of crime and violence that are thwarting efforts to improve the quality of life and participation in political processes.'[492] General Malan and senior military officers believed that improving living conditions in the townships and black schools would go a long way towards persuading blacks not to press for a government dominated by the majority.

If Machiavelli and Huntington suggested a method for bringing about reform by stealth and cunning, Arend Lijphart proposed a constitutional formula. Since the early 1970s scholars working on South African politics had been advocating 'moving away from the Westminster model', by which was meant a simple form of majority rule where the winner takes all. As an alternative, Lijphart proposed consociationalism, a term that he later replaced with power-sharing. He used it in his book *Power-sharing in South Africa*, published in 1985 just when the debate within government about bringing whites and blacks into a common system had started. The key idea was limiting the largest party's power. Mechanisms included a grand coalition in which parties are represented in proportion to their vote, concurrent majorities and federalism. His essential power-sharing requirement was the existence of groups or parties formed on the principle of free association. In fairness to Lijphart, it must be said that all the existing and subsequent constitutional plans of the South African government in the 1980s violated this principle.

In 1978 the opposition Progressive Federal Party (PFP) accepted a new set of constitutional proposals. It favoured a genuine consociational approach, providing for the free association of people and communities, and a power-sharing cabinet with its head appointing members proportional to the strength of the relevant parties.[493] The PFP leader, Van Zyl Slabbert, in a book co-authored with David Welsh, emphasised power-sharing 'among groups' as an alternative to 'simple majoritarianism', which, it argued, had failed to produce a democratic outcome in any deeply divided society.[494] All parties with a minimum of 10 or 15 per cent of the vote would be entitled to representation in cabinet and there would also be a minority veto.

'Power-sharing' in a Tricameral Parliament

Between 1977 and 1982 the government took a crucial step away from apartheid by conceding that there could only be one sovereign Parliament in which people other than whites could also be represented. The original idea of three separate Parliaments was replaced by that of a single Parliament for whites, coloured people and Indians. The Tricameral Parliament, introduced in 1984, gave representatives of whites, coloured people and Indians, each in their own chamber, jurisdiction to administer their 'own affairs'. 'General affairs' would be discussed in joint committees of the three Houses and joint sessions of Parliament. Consensus was the goal, but the deadlock-breaking proposals all favoured the white ruling party. There was to be common debate about 'general affairs' and bills could be delayed, but there was no way in which the majority white party could be outvoted in the joint sessions.

The government and its supporters in the Afrikaans press called this the 'politics of consultation and joint decision-making', but it is more appropriate to call it 'sharing power without losing control'. Like President Botha, Heunis saw firm control of the state by a fairly unified Afrikanerdom as the stable centre of South Africa. An Afrikaner leadership was seen as the only one that could both enjoy the trust of the 'core ethnic group' and successfully direct all the technocratic skills and abilities to serve the material welfare of everyone in the country.[495]

There was a marked ambivalence in the way the government attempted to sell the new Parliament. To the more *verligte* voters it stated that including coloureds and Indians in a common system was simply 'a step in the right direction', leading to the incorporation of blacks as well. In campaigning for a yes vote in the 1983 referendum on the constitution, Botha called it 'a new basis for national unity upon which reform along evolutionary lines in a stable environment could take place'.[496]

But to its more conservative supporters the NP leadership projected the Tricameral Parliament as an effective way of shoring up white power. It maintained that blacks would be accommodated separately through the homelands system and a new system of black local authorities. The NP's chief information officer wrote to Andries Treurnicht, leader of the right-wing faction of the party which rejected the plan: 'I would like to know your view of the idea that we at any price have got to associate the coloureds, as a bloc of 2.5 million, with the whites in order to broaden our own power base, and not surrender them to the "black-power" situation.'[497]

To give the plan a measure of respectability the NP had to compromise on its core principle of 'white self-determination'. As NP leader, Botha warned from the start that a white power monopoly was outdated, but he advocated the division, not the sharing, of power. In a well-publicised speech in Upington in July 1979 he said: 'I reject mixed political parties and power-sharing because it is Prog policy.'[498] When Alex Boraine, a member of the PFP (or Progs for short), asked him two years later if he believed in power-sharing, he told him not to talk nonsense.[499]

Now, with the NP having accepted a single Parliament for whites, coloured people and Indians, Botha could no longer duck the question whether the Tricameral Parliament entailed power-sharing. When Parliament opened in January 1982, tensions between the followers of Botha and the right wing under Treurnicht reached fever pitch.

On 22 February Botha summoned a special cabinet meeting. After an extensive debate he stated that the government accepted power-sharing, but that this should not conjure up 'too many ghosts'. The government used the term quite differently from the PFP, the official opposition. While the PFP did so in the context of a unitary state and a liberal democracy, the NP refused to emasculate 'white self-determination'.[500] But the genie was out of the bottle. This was the first time an NP leader had used the term power-sharing.[501]

Treurnicht had remained quiet in the special cabinet meeting, but in the NP caucus meeting of 24 February he threw down the gauntlet by denouncing Botha's acceptance of power-sharing as 'collaboration with Prog policy'. Suddenly open revolt loomed large. Fanie Botha, a senior cabinet minister, moved a motion of confidence in Botha as chief leader and his right to formulate policy. When Treurnicht and 21 other members walked out, one of them, JH (Koos) van der Merwe, told journalists waiting outside: 'I have done with the Prog PW Botha.'[502] The Conservative Party, which would soon be formed under Treurnicht's leadership, would attract close to half of Afrikaner support over the next ten years.

To rub salt in the NP's wounds, John Vorster, the previous Prime Minister, said in a statement that he could not fault Treurnicht's rejection of power-sharing and his actions. Significantly, it was speculation that he would announce power-sharing with blacks in his 'Rubicon speech', held four and a half years later, that would ignite Botha's notoriously short fuse, prompting him to abort the original plan for the speech. He would not repeat the mortal sin in the eyes of Nationalists of splitting the party and the *volk*.

What Botha and Heunis failed to realise was that the government was paying a heavy price for bringing coloureds and Indians into the system: it had virtually no credibility among blacks when it tried to incorporate them. Heunis, the same man who would in 1985 try to open negotiations with blacks, gave a categorical assurance in 1982 that blacks would not be part of a new dispensation. 'If blacks were to become part, the protection of minorities would disappear . . . This is an issue that is non-negotiable.'[503]

The Tricameral Parliament sent a powerful negative message to blacks: they remained foreigners in their own country. They had to be satisfied with voting for governments in their homelands and accept a new system of black local authorities. To add to the combustible elements, the black local authorities, elected in 1984 on polls with a low voter turnout, were almost designed to precipitate an explosion. They would enjoy almost all the powers of their white counterparts, but were left without a viable revenue base. Few township residents owned property, with the result that the revenue that could be raised from rates was extremely limited. Many residents had indeed stopped paying housing rents and charges for water and electricity. Undeterred, the new councils sharply increased the charges for rent and electricity.

In September 1984 riots broke out in the black townships of the Vaal Triangle, south-east of Johannesburg. The UDF, which was closely linked to the ANC, spearheaded the protests. They quickly spread to other parts of the country and would continue unabated for the next nine months. On 20 July 1985 the government declared a state of emergency in 38 of the country's 254 magisterial districts. Two days later the ANC leader, Oliver Tambo, issued a call for the masses to make South Africa ungovernable. Abroad, the proclamation of a state of emergency was seen as 'the last attempt by a politically doomed and morally bankrupt regime to stave off the retribution that waited'.[504]

The noose of international censure and sanctions tightened. Credit ratings dropped sharply. Several European countries recalled their ambassadors from South Africa. Increasingly, investors and foreign governments felt that only radical reforms would stave off the crisis.

The Special Cabinet Committee (SCC)

In 1983 the government established a Special Cabinet Committee (SCC) to investigate closer co-operation between the South African government and the governments of the independent and non-independent homelands. For the handful of cabinet ministers serving on it, the SCC would become the key forum for debating black political rights. FW de Klerk considered his membership of the SCC to be as important as his membership of the cabinet or his leadership of the Transvaal NP.[505]

All the cabinet divisions were reflected here. On the one side there were the reformists (Chris Heunis, Pik Botha, and Barend du Plessis, Minister of Finance) and on the other side the conservatives, who were sceptical about proposals for power-sharing (De Klerk, Louis le Grange, Minister of Police, and Gerrit Viljoen, Minister of Education and Training). What was even more important was that every contender for the presidency once PW Botha left office was a member of the committee. To a large extent the future leadership race was to be decided here.

Chris Heunis, the chairman, spoke with words pouring out in a torrent, often leaving his listeners suspended in bewilderment while trying to catch his argument. De Klerk described him as someone 'whose brain worked faster than his tongue'.[506] The academics who worked for him found him accessible and often more than a match for them in debate. Andreas van Wyk describes him as the most *verligte* as well as one of the most intelligent members of the cabinet. 'Intellectually and emotionally he was far more convinced of the need for change than the theatrical Pik Botha, the vacillating Kobie Coetsee and the still reserved FW de Klerk.'[507] But Heunis as a reformer was hamstrung by his strong emotional dependence on his political mentor and leader, PW Botha, who dominated the relationship between the two. Botha was reluctant to walk the road of political rights for blacks, but until the Rubicon speech Heunis believed that he could take Botha along.[508]

Pik Botha was undoubtedly the most consistent reformist voice in government from the mid-1970s. He had been a career diplomat from 1953 to 1970, when he became Minister of Foreign Affairs. He knew better than any of his colleagues how dangerously in conflict with world opinion the South African government was. The government's star performer on television, he was confident of winning over the electorate to far-reaching reforms. One poll after the other showed him to be the whites' popular choice to succeed PW Botha. While Pik Botha indeed identified genuinely with Afrikaner history, his decision to remain an NP member was purely strategic. In many ways he remained the diplomat, not the foreign minister. 'I am not the South African government,' he told a startled American diplomat in 1981.[509] Chris Heunis was fond of referring to him as the *foreign* minister.[510]

The third key member of the SCC was De Klerk. With his seat in Vereeniging far from safe, he knew that any brash move could mean defeat and the possible end of his career. As someone with his eyes firmly on the NP leadership, he positioned himself carefully in the middle of the conservative and *verligte* wings of the party. Unlike Heunis, who pushed for the extension of general affairs in the Tricameral Parliament, he pleaded for extending the principle of 'own affairs' as far as possible.[511] He rejected a fourth chamber for blacks, pointing out that the NP only accepted the Tricameral Parliament because the numbers favoured the whites.

According to Fanie Cloete and Joh van Tonder, who both sat in on SCC meetings, De Klerk wanted a 'constellation of states', where representatives of the independent and non-independent homelands would meet with the NP government to take decisions without any votes being taken. Cloete states: 'FW de Klerk was one of the most consistent, rational, goal-oriented politicians I have ever met. But the framework was a very conservative value system. His core values were order, discipline, own affairs and communal self-interest.' The principle that ethnic groups should enjoy 'self-determination' trumped all others.[512] Van Tonder agrees: 'By 1985 and 1986 De Klerk was still sticking firmly to the fundamental NP policy position of separate nations with separate statehoods.'[513]

But there was also another reason why De Klerk disagreed with Heunis. He intensely disliked reform by stealth and the obfuscation it entailed. He would later remark that he and Gerrit Viljoen were often the only SCC members who grasped what Heunis was driving at. De Klerk insisted that the reform proposals should be presented in unambiguous terms and that their logical consequences be thought through and clearly spelt out. Later, Stoffel van der Merwe, a *verligte* cabinet member, remarked that once De Klerk had made clear the implications, 'everyone shied away from their proposals'. He was then considered a 'spoiler'.[514] Yet De Klerk's strategy was also the classic one used by conservatives or what Huntington calls 'stand-patters'. By forcing the reformists to spell out their intentions, they could stop reform in its tracks.

When President Botha opened Parliament on 25 January 1985, the former academics in the Department of Constitutional Development and Planning wrote the passages in his speech dealing with political reform. The speech carefully balanced the reaffirmation of existing government policy with proposals for reform. Structures had to be created for black communities outside the homelands through which they could themselves decide on their own affairs up to the highest level. The same bodies could co-operate with the South African government and homeland structures on matters of common interest. A 'national council' of representatives of the government and non-independent homelands and of other black communities would be established to advise on matters of common concern.

Although lip service was still paid to the idea of independence for the 'self-governing' homelands, the new constitutional goal was to balance co-operation by all groups on matters of common concern with 'self-determination' for each population group on their 'own affairs'. The question of black citizenship would be reviewed. Also significant was the granting of full property rights to blacks in areas where they qualified for leasehold rights.[515]

In the first few months of 1985 Heunis proceeded along two tracks. The one was on confederal lines, which was the only option to which PW Botha was committed. He proposed to homeland leaders that they and government leaders work together on common issues. He hoped to widen the net to include those African leaders operating outside government structures.[516] Black leaders inside the system showed little interest. Mangosuthu Buthelezi, the one with the most credibility, had been rebuffed when the government paid scant attention to the Buthelezi Commission, which in 1981 had proposed a power-sharing government for an integrated KwaZulu-Natal province. Buthelezi, who had no interest in a confederation, now demanded a statement of intent before any negotiations began. Black leaders increasingly insisted that Nelson Mandela and other ANC leaders had to be released before talks could begin.

Realising the futility of the confederal option, Heunis and his officials also tried to develop a more integrated system. In March 1985 he and his senior officials met at Warmbad in Transvaal and formulated a package of proposals. At the end of July Heunis submitted the package to the SCC, which approved it.[517]

A month earlier Heunis had reported to the President that he could not make progress in getting black leaders to participate in the constitutional forum. Botha now offered to hold a meeting of the extended cabinet to discuss ways in which the government's position could be made more attractive. This meeting took place on 2 August in Pretoria in a building called the Old Sterrewag (Old Observatory), which served as a conference facility for Military Intelligence. The intention was that Botha would announce the decisions taken here to the congress of the Natal NP in Durban, which he was to open on 15 August.

According to Daan Prinsloo, Botha's biographer who worked closely with him on the book and ordered his papers after his retirement, the parameters laid down by the President were quite clear: 'own affairs' had to stay, 'one man one vote' had to be rejected, and the black communities had to be accommodated in a different way from coloured people and Indians.[518]

That meant a confederal model consisting of the Tricameral Parliament, the homelands and perhaps some black city-states as subsidiaries. At the head would be a confederal cabinet to which homeland leaders could be appointed. Botha firmly rejected the idea of elected black representatives for multi-racial bodies. The furthest he would go was the appointment in 1986 of blacks, coloureds and Indians on the executive council of bodies in local and provincial government.[519] Dawie de Villiers, a cabinet minister, stated: 'Botha often said the government could enter into negotiations with blacks, but his bottom line was clear: there will be no surrender of power.'[520]

What happened at the Sterrewag on 2 August is still shrouded in mystery. Those interviewed for this chapter agree that it was a low-key meeting with little participation from the floor. It was clearly more a party political meeting than a cabinet meeting. Some even describe it as a team-building exercise. Since it was well known that Botha disliked extended discussions in cabinet, ministers who had to present a controversial reform initiative often cleared it with him before a cabinet meeting. Heunis clearly had followed this route and received Botha's nod. With the package having been cleared by the SCC, none of the members challenged Heunis's presentation. Botha said little.

Immediately after the meeting the President wrote identical letters to Chancellor Kohl of Germany and Prime Minister Thatcher of Britain to tell them that breakthrough proposals had been made to him at Sterrewag, to which he was giving serious consideration.[521] Seven months later, when divisions were paralysing his cabinet, he looked back to the discussion at Sterrewag. According to the cabinet minutes, he said that the big problem was the accommodation of the black community and he also stressed that he was not in favour of one man, one vote in a unitary or federal state. He continued: 'The [SCC] had made all sorts of inputs into his [Durban] speech, which had created confusion.' He almost plaintively asked: 'I thought on August 2 [at the Sterrewag] that we had clarity, but I do not think we have it anymore. Because you want me to say we stand for a unitary South Africa, you allow me to say it, you write it in my speeches, and I accept it, but what do we mean by that?'[522]

Three accounts by Sterrewag participants exist. The first is a recorded interview with Chris Heunis by his son some twenty years after the event. According to Heunis, the main decision was to include blacks in the cabinet, in anticipation of the outcome of negotiations over the constitutional accommodation of blacks.[523] Asked whether that meant the unbanning of the ANC and the release of Mandela, he replied: 'Not at that stage, but it would inevitably lead to that. Once you admit that they have to be included in cabinet, you also admit they are part of the South African citizenry and have the right to be part of government.'[524] The proposals by Heunis also included the possibility of allowing the independent homelands to request their reincorporation into South Africa, but his department did not consider that a priority.[525]

De Klerk gives the narrowest interpretation of the decisions made at the Sterrewag. According to him, the meeting took certain decisions to enable Heunis to embark on a new initiative in negotiations with blacks. They were that the six non-independent homelands would 'not necessarily' be expected to progress to independence; blacks outside the independent homelands would become South African citizens; and negotiations would take place with them on how they would be accommodated in a new constitution, including getting a say in decision-making at all levels of government where their interests were involved. Black representation on the President's Council would be considered. De Klerk describes the Sterrewag decisions as the end of the whole ideology of grand apartheid and as an initiative that had the potential of persuading the world that real change was under way.[526]

If De Klerk's interpretation was the most restrictive, that of Pik Botha could be considered as maximalist. At meetings a few days later with representatives of Western leaders, he stated that at Sterrewag some far-reaching 'recommendations' were made to President Botha for his consideration. They included the political involvement of blacks at the highest level, citizenship for all South Africans, the concept of a single territory for the whole of South Africa, and negotiations with 'responsible' black leaders based on an open agenda. According to Botha, the meeting's resolutions constituted a single stream of sweeping change.[527]

A report in the *Sunday Times* of 11 August, clearly based on an informed source, reiterated the Foreign Minister's interpretation. It stated that the following was decided: South Africa would become a single constitutional unit again, the cabinet would be expanded to include black leaders, who initially would be the homeland leaders, negotiations would take place with the true black leaders, and influx control would be abolished.[528] This maximalist approach stressed the reintegration of South Africa into a single unit, which would symbolically signal the end of apartheid, while the minimalist approach of De Klerk still tried to keep some blacks out.

In the speech President Botha would give at the Natal congress two weeks later, he announced only some of the proposals. However, if his speeches at all four provincial congresses held in August and September are taken into account, he accepted (or would come to accept) virtually the entire package proposed by Heunis. Before discussing the Rubicon speech, it is necessary to look briefly at Botha's speeches at the other three provincial congresses, which took place after the Natal congress. Here Botha proposed substantial reforms of NP policy. They were the reincorporation of the homelands; negotiations, which included the issue of Nelson Mandela's release and the unbanning of the ANC; and the expansion of the cabinet to include black leaders.

As regards the first of the three issues, it is clear that Pik Botha, the minister who dealt with the independent homelands, was almost on his own in pushing hard for their reincorporation. He had become exasperated with the financial profligacy of their governments. That of Transkei had threatened to plunder the Transkei government pension fund if the South African government curbed overspending, and Lennox Sebe of the Ciskei had bought a snowplough for the local airport after a visit to Germany. Early in 1985 Botha asked the legal advisers of his department to prepare the necessary legislation to make it possible for the independent homelands to apply for reincorporation. He visited the leaders of the independent homelands and advised them that a policy change was in the pipeline in terms of which they would be allowed to apply for their reincorporation into the constitutional framework of South Africa. Making their citizens once again South African citizens would remove one of the major grievances arising from apartheid policy.[529]

By trying to force this issue, Botha incurred the displeasure of Heunis's department, which did not consider it a priority.[530] Yet Botha used the Free State congress to announce that his government was prepared to restore South African citizenship to all those blacks resident in 'white South Africa' who had lost it on account of the granting of independence to some homelands. At the Cape NP congress he went further. He stated that his government was committed to an undivided South Africa based on the principles of one state, a common citizenship and universal franchise for all, but within structures that South Africans themselves would choose.[531]

Secondly, there was the issue of negotiations with credible black leaders on the matter of black representation in cabinet. Van Zyl Slabbert, leader of the official opposition, remembers an exchange early in August at a meeting of a special parliamentary committee under the chairmanship of Heunis. Here Slabbert said: 'The government talks of negotiations, but are you going to talk with genuinely representative leaders or are you going to choose the leaders with whom you wish to negotiate', to which Heunis replied: 'We shall get to that.' On his way to the meeting Slabbert ran into Pik Botha, who said: 'Big things are coming. You must help us.'[532]

Pik Botha was also busy with the issue of the release of Nelson Mandela. Early in 1985 President Botha had made an offer to free Mandela should he renounce violence, but Mandela rejected this. Sensing that Mandela held what he called a 'veto power' on both his release and future all-party negotiations, Pik Botha tried to get Mandela to forswear violence 'if only by implication'. He hit on the idea of getting the leaders of the independent homelands and Buthelezi to give an assurance to the President that Mandela would not resort to violence and would respect the law. Pik Botha later wrote: 'Ek onthou dat die idee PW geval het'[533] (I remember that PW liked the idea). But this is stretching it a bit. The brutal way in which PW Botha rejected the demand for Mandela's unconditional release in his Rubicon speech leads one to conclude that the Foreign Minister had assumed too much. It is also unlikely that Mandela would have approved of this plan.

At the Transvaal congress Botha committed himself to talks with the ANC provided it forswore violence and detached itself from the South African Communist Party. 'If the ANC makes such an announcement, they could come back to South Africa tomorrow. We shall not act against them. We shall negotiate with them.'[534]

The most important issue for Heunis was that of black representation in cabinet. This was the so-called power-sharing part, which both Heunis and Pik Botha realised had to be carefully handled in view of the storm which use of the term had caused in 1982. In an interview with his son Jan, who was a constitutional adviser to the government in the 1980s, Heunis called the inclusion of blacks in cabinet the key element missing from the Rubicon speech, adding that the President later announced it at the Cape congress.[535] Here Botha said that all groups and communities within the geographical boundaries of South Africa would receive political representation at the highest level of government, but without one group dominating the other. On this occasion Botha also rejected apartheid if it meant the domination of one group over another, the exclusion of any group from decision-making, and discrimination on the basis of race.

Taking into account the announcements at all the provincial congresses, the *Sunday Times* report of 11 August, which spoke of the establishment of a single constitutional unit and the appointment of black leaders to cabinet as a first step towards real negotiations, was not far off the mark. Hence there was good reason for reformists like Heunis and Pik Botha to be very satisfied with the outcome of the Sterrewag meeting. Dave Steward, a senior Foreign Affairs official who would accompany his minister on the trip to Europe a week later, recounts that after the meeting there was great excitement. There was a general feeling that at last the government had managed to extricate itself from the political deadlock in which it was caught. It was his impression that there was general acceptance of the idea that whites and blacks would share a common constitutional destiny, and that white and black leaders would jointly make decisions on matters of common concern, while leaving it to the different communities to decide on their own affairs. There was also consensus that white and black leaders would soon meet to negotiate a system that would give constitutional expression to this idea.[536]

Carl von Hirschberg, Deputy Director-General of the Department of Foreign Affairs, recounts: 'When I met Pik in his office after the Sterrewag meeting, he was bursting with enthusiasm. He could hardly contain himself. It was his account of the policy changes agreed to at the meeting that I used in the draft I prepared as an input for PW Botha's Durban speech. It is my clear impression that PW had agreed to these changes, so I was not particularly concerned that he might reject them.'[537]

Von Hirschberg was not part of the Foreign Minister's inner circle. His colleagues regarded him as essentially a level-headed person who would not work on something based on a misinterpretation or wishful thinking. He remarked recently: 'I called for transcripts of all four speeches of the President at the end of the provincial congresses and analysed them with a fine-tooth comb. Sentences, even phrases lending themselves to more positive interpretation, I highlighted and extensively redrafted. I was surprised at the end of the process how much positive material the speeches had hidden in them. I used this material liberally in drafting replies to the letters that poured into the Presidency from Heads of Government like Thatcher, Kohl, Mitterrand, Reagan and others. These were all referred to the Foreign Minister, who submitted replies for the President's signature. It is interesting that the President never once altered a single word in the replies. With each wave of responses and replies, we were able to extend the boundaries of Government policy.'[538]

He also said: 'With the benefit of hindsight, it is a great pity that the proposed changes were so sensationalised before the Durban speech. PW Botha was an enigma if ever there was one. He was indeed a reformer – vide the positive elements hidden in his four speeches; and his acceptance of the drafts we sent to him in reply to the letters from Heads of Government. They all contained some extension of Government policy.'[539]

President Botha had indeed moved far, or had been nudged to move far. Opening Parliament in January 1985, he had accepted the permanence only of those blacks settled in the 'white areas'; at the Cape congress early in September, he had come to accept one citizenship in a single South Africa with a universal franchise. Peter Sullivan, a senior political reporter, wrote after the latter event of the President's 'great courage'.[540] On the face of it, the Machiavellians in Pretoria had made enormous progress.

The key question is: why did the President not announce the full package in his Rubicon speech? There are opposite views on this. One is that Botha cared and understood little about the outside world and acted purely from a party political perspective in spreading the announcement over the four congresses. Doing so would avoid creating the impression that he was favouring one provincial party over the other. Also, a message spread out over two months would limit the shock to his more conservative supporters.[541]

The other possibility is that Botha did not realise at Sterrewag where the reformers were leading him. Magnus Malan recounts people in his circle saying that it would take at least five years for the NP government to persuade the electorate to accept the Sterrewag recommendations.[542] Botha ripped the heart out of the inputs of Heunis and Pik Botha, not realising the enormous damage the speech would do, given the expectations that had built up. He would announce the rest of the Heunis package at the other congresses in order to salvage the situation. But the damage had been done, and neither he nor his government would get any credit for what were in fact bold moves.[543]

From Sterrewag to Vienna

To inform the leaders of South Africa's main trading partners of the imminent new policy direction that the President would announce, Pik Botha flew to Europe. On 8 and 9 August he met separately with emissaries of the British, US and German leaders. He made it clear in a subsequent report to PW Botha that, while he had mentioned the Sterrewag recommendations, he also emphasised that the President was still considering them.

In Vienna he met with Robert McFarlane of the US National Security Council, Chester Crocker, US Assistant Secretary of State for Africa, and Herman Nickel, who would soon become US Ambassador to South Africa. He stated that the recommendations included 'the political involvement of blacks at the highest level, citizenship for all South Africans and the concept of a single territory for the whole of South Africa'.[544] The Foreign Minister also explained the government's position with respect to the release of Nelson Mandela and the factors complicating this. (Three days after the meeting he denied that he had said that Mandela would be released unconditionally.)

Speaking in San Francisco the day after the Rubicon speech, Crocker stated that Botha's message 'contained the stated hope of drawing black leaders into negotiations about the sharing of political power'.[545] However, in his memoirs, published seven years later, Crocker left an unflattering account of Botha's briefing in Vienna: 'Pik Botha was at his Thespian best, walking out on limbs far beyond the zone of safety to persuade us that his president was on the verge of momentous announcements. We learned of plans for bold reform steps, new formulas on constitutional moves, and further thinking relative to the release of Mandela.'[546]

In Vienna Botha also met Ewen Fergusson, a senior official from the British Foreign Office and special representative of Prime Minister Margaret Thatcher. Here he spoke of proposals for 'co-responsibility for decisions on the highest level that affect the entire country, one citizenship, and one undivided South African territory'. He added that because of 'sensitivities in South Africa', terms like 'power-sharing' or 'a unitary state' had to be avoided. There would be no constitutional blueprint in Botha's speech, only guidelines that had to be worked out further by leaders. After the Vienna meetings Botha travelled to Frankfurt to meet representatives of Chancellor Kohl.

Dave Steward, the senior Foreign Affairs official who accompanied Botha on the visit, recounts that while Botha spoke of 'big plans', he did not go beyond presenting them as 'strong recommendations'. He stressed that the final decision was the President's prerogative.[547] Werner Scholtz, a South African diplomat who attended the briefings, recounts: 'Pik Botha spoke with great enthusiasm and several times said: "Gentlemen, we are crossing the Rubicon." Pik Botha presented the proposals as virtually the final draft of the president's speech. The representatives of the Western powers believed Pik Botha because they thought he spoke with his president's full blessing and had cleared everything. It simply was inconceivable that he would try to sell reform proposals that were still half-baked recommendations as important policy shifts.'[548] Neil van Heerden, a senior Foreign Affairs official who briefed regional African leaders in advance, sums it up as follows: 'Pik Botha would definitely try to extract the maximum political and diplomatic advantage from the Sterrewag recommendations, but he would certainly not lie or deliberately mislead.'[549] But Botha's speech was such a communications disaster that the US officials felt they had been misled.

After the disaster of the Rubicon speech, much of the discussion revolved around the question whether Pik Botha had 'over-promised' in these meetings. De Klerk mentions that it is not clear what angered PW Botha most: the fervid media speculation after the Sterrewag meeting or 'too much enthusiasm' from Pik Botha in selling the decisions abroad.[550] Botha had received permission from his President to inform representatives of Western leaders in Vienna and Frankfurt of the important speech they could expect. By then the President already had received the Foreign Affairs input for his speech, which spoke of common decision-making at all levels in a single constitutional unit and a formula for bringing about Mandela's release. The Foreign Minister was clearly hopeful (but not certain) that these points would be included in the President's speech. The emissaries of the Western leaders whom Pik Botha met in Europe in all probability interpreted his briefing as a clear sign that the South African government was poised to announce the end of apartheid and to set the stage for all-party negotiations.[551]

When Pik Botha flew to Europe, he did not know whether his President had accepted the input from his department for the speech he was to give at the Natal congress. He was undoubtedly encouraged by the fact that the President had kept quiet at Sterrewag and was prepared to consider the far-reaching recommendations made to him. He had reason to be confident that Western governments would give strong backing to these policy initiatives if he presented the decisions and recommendations as part of a single package.

President Botha, on the other hand, probably thought that he had clearly spelt out the framework in which he would consider any political reform: the appointment of some homeland leaders to the cabinet in a confederal form of government; the continued exclusion of the independent homelands from the constitutional framework of South Africa; and the rejection of elections based on a common electoral roll.[552] To those whom Pik Botha briefed in Vienna and Frankfurt, this would not signify much more than a warmed-up version of apartheid. Clearly the apparent unanimity at the Sterrewag meeting obscured major disagreements.

Why did Pik Botha put such a positive spin on a speech that his President had not yet made? An important reason could be that the Foreign Minister felt that urgent steps were needed to prevent an imminent escalation of sanctions. Given South Africa's poor credibility, his intention was simply to make sure that Western governments understood how bold the moves actually were, thus preventing them from being dismissed as mere 'steps in the right direction'.

There is also another possibility. Pik Botha knew that the President had not yet made up his mind and that there was still a strong body of conservatives who would have hesitated to speak up at the Sterrewag meeting. They would rather mobilise opposition to the recommendations in private meetings with, or in messages to, the President before the Natal congress. According to this perspective, the Foreign Minister used his meetings on 8 and 9 August in Europe not only to stave off further sanctions, but also to put pressure on the President to accept the recommendations as he interpreted them.

The orthodoxy among NP insiders today is that the President abruptly changed his mind when news reached him that Pik Botha 'over-promised' in briefing emissaries of the main Western leaders. Ters Ehlers, the President's private secretary and aide-de-camp, who worked closely with him during these days, disputes this. He is adamant that the President did not once mention his Foreign Minister in giving the reasons for deciding to make his 'own speech', as he called it.[553]

Drafting a fateful speech

After the Sterrewag meeting President Botha requested Chris Heunis, Pik Botha and Barend du Plessis to submit inputs for his speech on behalf of their departments. For the Department of Constitutional Development and Planning it was particularly important that a picture be conveyed of a government that had abandoned old-style white arrogance and that it was intent on searching for solutions through negotiations in good faith with recognised black leaders.[554] The department's input committed the government to restoring the citizenship of all blacks, including those living in the independent homelands. It would negotiate with black leaders about black participation at all levels of decision-making, including the highest level, where their interests were affected. Government pledged to recognise black human dignity, eradicate all forms of discrimination, find democratic solutions and create equal opportunities.[555]

Heunis was scheduled to give a speech in Stellenbosch on the day after the President's speech, but he cancelled it at the last minute. This draft speech is the best indication of the spirit in which his department wanted the President's speech to be given. It expressed the desire of government to negotiate with black leaders on the question of black participation in the decision-making processes. Conflicting aspirations and demands had to be reconciled and there should be no non-negotiable positions. There should be a search for common interests and a desire to remedy the legitimate grievances of blacks.

Pik Botha, together with two of his senior officials, Carl von Hirschberg and Marc Burger, worked on the Foreign Affairs input for the speech. Written with a rhetorical flair rare in official documents, the input tried to assuage white fears, meet black demands and satisfy foreign expectations. It started out with the assumption that it was the South African enemies that had rejected peaceful negotiation because it would lead to 'joint responsibility for peace and progress'. The challenge to South Africa was 'to build a better future out of [differences in] cultures, values, and languages, which are demonstrably real in our heterogeneous society'.

The government intended to do so in two ways. Firstly, by 'negotiation between leaders . . . in which there will be give and take'. Secondly, by starting the negotiations from the basis that 'we are all human beings, created by the same God' and that all were endowed with the 'inalienable human rights of life, liberty, and the pursuit of human happiness'. It also gave the assurance to the government's supporters that it would never surrender to outside demands. 'South African problems will be solved by South Africans and not by foreigners.' The solution was to be found in 'co-operation and co-responsibility' by means of a system that acknowledged the 'right of each and every one to share in the decisions which shape his destiny'. It rejected a numbers-based approach with a 'winner-takes-all' outcome. Instead it proposed a system based on 'population groups'. These groups would have to take responsibility for decision-making at all levels of government in matters of common concern without the domination of one group over another.

The government and the 'black leadership' would negotiate the structures for this group-based approach. The government would not 'prescribe who the leaders of the black people are'. It would consider Nelson Mandela's release if it received satisfactory indications from respected black leaders or from himself that he would conduct himself in a law-abiding manner.

On the issue of a common South African citizenship for all, it stated that the government respected the independence of the 'independent national states'. However, if these governments should decide in the interests of their people 'to negotiate with the South African government on the conferment of South African citizenship on their citizens', they would be welcome to do so.

The input also addressed the vexed issue of the political violence that was then sweeping the urban areas. It implicitly acknowledged the role of apartheid by emphasising the government's commitment to addressing legitimate grievances and abolishing all discrimination on the basis of colour or race. 'Any reduction of violence will be matched by action on the part of the Government to lift the State of Emergency.'

The input ends with a ringing declaration. 'The implementation of the principles I have stated can have far-reaching effects on us all. I believe that we are today crossing the Rubicon. There can be no turning back. We now have a manifesto for the future of our country ...'[556]

Apart from the reference to Mandela, the inputs from Foreign Affairs and Constitutional Development did not differ much. Between the meeting in Vienna and the speech on 15 August, media speculation both in South Africa and abroad reached a frenzy. *Time* magazine described it as the 'most important announcement since the Dutch settlers arrived in South Africa 300 years ago'. *Newsweek* wrote that 'promised reforms may be the best, if not the last, chance for eventual harmony among the races of South Africa'. A few days before the Natal congress, Gerrit Viljoen, the minister responsible for black affairs, told an audience of Afrikaner women that 'the future position of whites would be radically different from the present and that the country's youth would have to be prepared for drastic changes'.[557] He was probably referring to future prospects in a general way, but his words simply increased the excitement. Even *Die Burger*, which rarely deviated from the Botha line, wrote of major changes that were likely to be announced until it received word of Botha's furious state of mind. It promptly published a cartoon depicting 'anti-South African forces' pumping up expectations.[558]

On 10 August Botha decided to deviate from the original intention to put across a strong and consistent reformist message. In retirement, Botha told a journalist that Pik Botha had deliberately inflated international expectations in order to embarrass him. 'That was his game, that's why he does not come here.'[559]

But there is no evidence for this. Prinsloo's biography of Botha states that a report by a senior journalist, Tos Wentzel, in the *Weekend Argus* of 10 August provided 'the catalyst' for Botha's decision to discard most of the initial inputs. The journalist later revealed that his anonymous source was an academic who had just left Heunis's department to take up a university post. Wentzel wrote that the President would announce far-reaching changes in his speech and speculated that 'the government was trying to find a power-sharing formula with blacks without stating this too openly for fear of a right-wing revolt'.[560] (He subsequently told Prinsloo that he protected his source by referring to the Foreign Minister's 'over-selling' in Vienna.)

Botha said something similar to Ters Ehlers: 'I am not going to let people like Chet Crocker prescribe to me the kind of speech I must make.'[561] Botha had never forgiven the United States for not coming to South Africa's assistance in Angola in 1975, as some CIA agents apparently promised it would do. On a personal level he disliked Crocker keenly. Clearly, Botha had soon come to regret not speaking out at Sterrewag, when the far-reaching recommendations were discussed. The words 'Prog speech' or 'a Crocker type of speech' must not be taken literally. These were the terms in which Botha indicated his refusal to cross the Sterrewag bridge of black political accommodation.

To this must be added the frenzy of press speculation that threatened to discredit any reform initiative. In the first part of the speech Botha would give, he warned about the deleterious consequences of this kind of politics. (Ironically, Pik Botha strongly emphasised the importance of the reforms to prevent them from being dismissed as mere tinkering with the apartheid system.)

There also was a real threat that the speculation could jeopardise future negotiations. Botha had just received a letter from Margaret Thatcher, his strongest supporter among Western leaders, in which she suggested: 'We should exchange our ideas as far in advance of your announcement as possible and preferably without attracting attention.'[562] It is also possible that Heunis had conveyed to him his unhappiness about all the loose talk about power-sharing, since that could undercut his strategy for negotiations. At that stage Heunis was only concerned about making his opening move, namely inviting homeland leaders to serve in the cabinet.[563]

Finally, there was the factor of Botha's character and his style of leadership.

He was alarmed to learn that as he was still busy contemplating his response to the recommendations of the Sterrewag meeting, the press had already announced his decisions. 'Power-sharing' touched a particularly raw nerve, because it was the very same word that had caused the NP to split in 1982 on the much less weighty issue of coloured and Indian participation.[564] Botha's entire career was directed at preventing blacks from gaining first a foothold in, and then control over, government.

The stakes for the country were incredibly high, but Botha was not the kind of leader who could be pressured into a course of action about which he had doubts. It is possible that he felt trapped by the snares that the Machiavellians had prepared and now decided to cut loose and reassert his authority and control. He never understood how vulnerable to foreign pressure his government and the country's economy had become. He decided to lash out, regardless of the consequences, and to re-establish his dominance in policy-making.

In the late afternoon of Saturday the 10th, Botha told Heunis he was not prepared to give the 'Prog speech' that he had prepared for him. Heunis said that it was not a Prog speech, but a draft reflecting the Sterrewag decisions.[565]

On 13 August there was an indication that the reformers' plans were going awry. The President corrected Stephen Solarz, a visiting US congressman who, on the basis of an interview with Pik Botha, stated that South Africa was now committed to a unitary state: 'No, no, he could not have said it because it is not so. Not a unitary state.' (Solarz probably misunderstood Pik Botha, who probably referred to the independent homelands being reintegrated into South Africa.)

On 14 August Botha summoned some cabinet members to a meeting where he read a speech in which Daan Prinsloo, an official in his office, had consolidated the inputs of Pik Botha, Heunis and Barend du Plessis and some introductory comments that PW Botha had drafted in the light of growing international expectations. A devastated Heunis felt that his department's proposal had been gutted. To cap it all, he felt humiliated by being forced to listen to the amended speech. He later told his son: 'We sat there like a bunch of little children, listening to him reading his speech to us. No one protested, in fact everyone nodded in agreement.'[566]

The speech Botha gave on 15 August was screened live to a world audience of more than two hundred million. Instead of a heroic leader renouncing apartheid and reaching out to blacks, they saw 'an old president's twisted, hectoring image', making it difficult to listen to what he said.[567] 'Don't push us too far', he warned at one point with a wagging finger, confirming the stereotype of the ugly, irredeemable Afrikaner.

As regards the speech itself, Botha announced reforms that at other times would have been recognised as major policy shifts. Influx control was on its way out. Independence for some black peoples was part of the solution, but those who refused it 'will remain part of the South African nation, are South African citizens and should be accommodated within political institutions within the boundaries of the RSA'. Structures would be established where all South African communities would attain the goal of 'co-responsibility and participation'.[568]

This, in effect, meant the collapse of one of the core ideas of apartheid: the government now considered at least some blacks as full members of the citizenry, enjoying 'legitimate rights'. At the same time, Botha ruled out almost everything that listeners to the broadcast in Western Europe or the US would have understood as democracy. He rejected both majority rule and 'one man, one vote' and turned down even a compromise solution such as a black chamber in Parliament. That left precious few alternatives. To listeners not versed in NP reform rhetoric, it was a major mystery how Botha could call the speech a crossing of the Rubicon and a 'manifesto for a new South Africa'.

Dave Steward, who would become President FW de Klerk's main communications adviser, sums it up well: 'PW Botha showed an absolute lack of understanding of modern political communication. Instead of addressing his real audience of hundreds of millions of TV viewers in the West, he addressed the NP faithful. Instead of language that his real audience could understand, he used the rough and tumble idiom of South African political meetings. Instead of a short, well-rehearsed statement containing the message he wanted to convey, he delivered a long, rambling speech.'[569]

There were two particularly disastrous parts. The one was a rejection of the plea for the unconditional release of Nelson Mandela. He denounced Mandela and his comrades in arms who had tried to overthrow the state in the early 1960s and made it appear as if they were solely motivated by communist convictions. There was no reference to legitimate grievances and he presented no evidence that Mandela was indeed a communist.[570]

The other very negative part was the rejection of a statement of intent, on which Buthelezi, the major internal black leader, insisted as a prerequisite for negotiations. He sought an assurance that the negotiations would be about 'power-sharing' and not about structures where blacks would merely be consulted. Quite incomprehensibly, Botha linked the demand to what he termed a 'wish to destroy orderly government'.[571] Refusing to free Mandela unconditionally or to make a statement of intent, Botha drove Buthelezi and the ANC leaders into each other's arms in jointly rejecting negotiations with his government.

Pik Botha was forced to pick up the pieces. He called it 'a speech with which I definitely could live',[572] and told a press conference that President Botha considered it 'one of the most historical occasions', adding: 'I agree.'[573] Years later he remembered the press conference as 'one of the most difficult tasks of his life'. 'I tried to persuade the media that the [reformist] elements on which we all waited were hidden under all the aggression and *kragdadigheid* (forcefulness)'.[574]

The foreign press immediately fingered the Foreign Minister as the man who had created false expectations. The *Los Angeles Times* reported that in his meetings ten days earlier with British, German and American diplomats he led them to believe that his President would announce important steps such as 'dismantling apartheid, abolishing rural tribal homelands, freeing imprisoned black nationalist leader Nelson Mandela and lifting the month-old state of emergency'. In addition, there would be other major concessions in the speech: 'the acceptance of millions of urban blacks as permanent city dwellers and the possibility of South African citizenship to residents of the non-independent homelands'.[575]

Oliver Tambo, president of the ANC, almost certainly enjoyed one of his best days in office. His response, issued in Lusaka, spoke of 'a ruling group who could not help show itself for what it is – a clique of diehard racists, hidebound reactionaries and bloodthirsty, fascist braggarts who will heed nobody but themselves'. He continued by saying that rather than release and talk to 'the genuine leaders of our people', Botha promised to negotiate with his 'salaried employees'. The time had come for the Western world to 'abandon all pretence that it has any say in influencing South Africa other than through the imposition of sanctions. South Africa has crossed her Rubicon.'[576]

Even before the Rubicon, South Africa was in deep financial trouble. The country was always strongly dependent on foreign investment for growth. But a decline in investor confidence in gold and growing political uncertainty resulted in a serious weakening of confidence. Between 1980 and 1985 direct foreign investment in South Africa as a proportion of total foreign liabilities slumped from 46 per cent to 25 per cent, while the percentage share of portfolio investment declined from 19 per cent to 13 per cent. By contrast, the share of short-term loans surged ahead from 18 per cent of the total to 39 per cent.[577] Patty Waldmeir, a correspondent of the London *Financial Times*, remarked that in the perception of foreign investors, 'South Africa was unstable and small, unstable countries, unlike large ones, do not borrow money'.[578] It was because South Africa had become so vulnerable that the Rubicon speech was such an unmitigated disaster.

The Western reaction was swift and severe. Chase Manhattan, one of South Africa's main short-term lenders, had already decided on 31 July to stop rolling over loans to South African lenders, but did not announce this. It was, as an executive of Chase remarked later, not the bank's intention to facilitate change in South Africa. 'We felt that the risk attached to political unrest and economic stability had become too high for our investors.'[579] After the Rubicon speech Chase Manhattan announced that it would no longer roll over loans to South Africa, and other banks followed suit quickly. With two-thirds of its foreign debt short-term, South Africa was forced to default and declare a unilateral moratorium on foreign debt. These debts were later rescheduled, but South Africa's continuing ability to raise foreign loans had received a mortal blow.

The rand fell sharply, capital fled the country and markets were forced to close. South Africa faced an escalation of sanctions. In late August 1985 the US Congress passed the Comprehensive Anti-Apartheid Act, which banned new investment and loans, withdrew landing rights for aeroplanes, and severely curbed imports of coal, uranium, iron and steel. The European Community and the Commonwealth also imposed a variety of milder sanctions. South African whites were never more isolated. Gerhard de Kock, Governor of the Reserve Bank, would remark half in jest that the speech cost the country billions of rands – at a rate of a few million rand per word.[580] But even a well-packaged, eloquent speech in place of the Rubicon speech would not have dispelled the serious doubts about the country's growth prospects.

Although the reforms announced in the NP's four provincial congresses amounted to a major policy shift, the government's political credibility had received an almost fatal blow in Durban. The British Ambassador, Robin Renwick, described it as a turning point.[581] The Rubicon speech signalled the day when the Botha government unmistakably lost both the initiative and its credibility. In terms of security it could still hold the ring, but politically, economically and diplomatically it would not recover.

What would have happened if Botha had made a speech that the international community interpreted as a decisive step to abandon apartheid and negotiate a democratic dispensation with credible black leaders? Everything depended on the concrete steps that would follow. In retrospect it is clear that the best course for the government was not to pursue a national deal, but a series of regional power-sharing deals along the lines proposed in 1981 by the Buthelezi Commission for KwaZulu-Natal. Such multi-racial governments with considerable autonomy had the potential of becoming counterweights to the ANC. The government's failure to make a courageous political move meant that increasingly it would have only one option left: to try to strike a deal with the ANC. And because it continued to fritter away time and opportunities, the outside world, including the West, would soon insist that the only equitable solution in South Africa was one that the ANC endorsed.

Conclusion

A recent article analysing successful governance reforms singles out three variables as of critical importance. They are a strong and consistent commitment among the politicians at the helm, a high level of technical capacity and some degree of isolation from societal interests, and the opportunity to use incremental approaches with cumulative benefits.[582] As far as the first variable was concerned, the NP leaders, with the exception of Pik Botha and Chris Heunis, were not committed to substantial reform. The NP was beholden to a constituency that had not been persuaded of the need for substantial reform. As for the second variable, there was a reasonable technical capacity, particularly in the Department of Foreign Affairs and the Department of Constitutional Development and Planning, but President Botha made his decisions mainly with an eye to white party politics. Accordingly, the officials of these departments had to use a strategy of incremental reform in which the acceptance of broad, non-racial principles was the crucial first step.

A very bold leader who had made up his mind could have embarked on a new road after the Sterrewag meeting. PW Botha, however, was profoundly sceptical about incorporating blacks into the political system. To complicate the matter even further, he was being asked to approve a momentous change at a time of large-scale disturbances. He had failed to speak up at the meeting of his cabinet two weeks before the Rubicon meeting where far-reaching recommendations were made, and probably was taken aback by the frenzy of media speculation. Feeling trapped, he offered to people in his inner circle two unconvincing reasons (a report in the *Cape Argus* and a refusal to satisfy Chester Crocker) for not wanting to give a speech that reflected the spirit of the Sterrewag meeting. In his Rubicon speech which he gave in Durban, he resorted to the style he was familiar with: the confrontational and abrasive one suitable for an NP congress but repulsive to Western audiences. In the end, Botha's Rubicon speech was a disaster in that it failed to meet the high expectations. FW de Klerk learnt the lessons of the Rubicon debacle well when he took the world by almost complete surprise in making his famous speech of 2 February 1990.

10.

Breyten's outrage

Shortly after being released from jail in 1982, Breyten Breytenbach published two nonfiction books, *The True Confessions of an Albino Terrorist* (1984) and *End Papers* (1986). While *True Confessions* is an emotional and moving account of his prison years, *End Papers* brings together detached, even clinical commentary on politics, culture and literature during the previous two decades. In 1987 Breytenbach, Frederik van Zyl Slabbert and Alex Boraine organised a conference in Dakar, Senegal, between a group of predominantly Afrikaners and a delegation from the African National Congress (ANC) in exile. Breytenbach participated in the debate and also, later, in an exchange of notes with the author of this chapter, elaborated on his views. The chapter focuses on Breytenbach's political commentary and analyses between 1984 and 1987.

Confronting fundamental options

An important part of Breytenbach's *True Confessions of an Albino Terrorist* is a dissection of the relationship between him as detainee and his interrogators. The spell in prison intensified his hatred of apartheid, the National Party (NP) government and the officials who interrogated him. Prison became an allegory for apartheid, perverting all human relationships.[583]

After Breytenbach's release from jail in 1982 he was more convinced than ever that no significant reform could be expected from the government. 'The structure must be shattered by violence... The land shall belong to no one. Not even to the deads [sic]'.[584] Apartheid had cut the Afrikaners off from the people in their own country and had led them to betray their identity. 'Apartheid is a mutation of power and greed. No religion can justify it, except that warped doctrine the Afrikaners have fashioned from their desert faith. Their god is a cruel, white interrogator.'[585]

On several occasions Breytenbach refused to call himself an Afrikaner, not to win the favour of his international audience, but because he wanted 'his own people to repeat the repudiation; he wants them to become Afrikaners according to a new understanding of the name'.[586] He strove for a system in which Afrikaners would enjoy political rights along with other Africans. Replacing a minority dictatorship by a majority dictatorship would be unacceptable. At the same time, however, he rejected constitutional devices or safeguards that would tie down a future black government. As he phrased it, a resolution of South Africa's political crisis would have to occur within a 'black socio-cultural field of references'.[587] Whites would have to learn to trust a black government. As he once playfully phrased it, a white would have to 'trust his black nanny to carry him, and to trust her not to drop him'.[588]

The question was: could the ANC, as it was constituted in the 1980s, be trusted as a government? On this question Breytenbach remained ambivalent. He wrote: 'I have for many years given my allegiance and support to the ANC, which is the political formation representing the majority of Africans.'[589] However, he was profoundly pessimistic about the possibility of a victorious ANC ushering in a genuine democracy. He pointed out that the South African Communist Party (SACP) dominated the ANC organisationally, militarily, financially and ideologically. While the ANC stood for the liberation of the African people, the SACP saw the overthrow of apartheid as only a first step, to be followed by a socialist transformation of the kind seen in the Eastern European countries.[590]

Breytenbach was convinced that it would be the exiles that would dominate the ANC were a swift transfer of power to occur. He thought it unlikely that the ANC would transform itself into a free, democratic organisation. The present totalitarian state could be replaced by one that was totalitarian in a different way, 'more hegemonic but minus the racism'. Breytenbach wrote: 'I must warn you the system by which we're trying to replace the present one will grind us down, me and you, inexorably.'[591]

The question is how Breytenbach could contemplate a possibly violent transfer of power only for the white totalitarian state to be replaced by a black one. The short answer is that for him the destruction of apartheid was the first priority.

Walzer sums up his main message well: 'He won't paint pretty pictures of a liberal or democratic future . . . the old must be dismantled in any case. There was no other way.'[592]

But there are also other reasons for his radical position. In *True Confessions* he is not only denouncing apartheid and the people administering a pernicious system; he is also lashing out against his enemies, including the ANC and the SACP.[593] His relationship with the ANC leadership was always brittle. In the early 1970s he and a few white radical activists formed a non-communist organisation, Okhela, that wanted to work not only with ANC cadres inside South Africa, but also with trade union leaders (who were shunned by the communist-dominated exiled unions at that stage) and Steve Biko, leader of the Black Consciousness Movement. The ANC leadership in exile neither sanctioned Okhela nor did they trust Breytenbach.

When he embarked on a clandestine visit to South Africa in 1975 to promote the aims of Okhela, a senior ANC office-bearer betrayed him to the South African security police. Breytenbach commented bitterly on being left in the lurch while in jail: 'Not only did the ANC withhold assistance from my dependants, not only did they disavow me, but the London clique of bitter exiles intervened to stop any manifestation of international or local support for my cause. They blackballed and maligned me, abetted by well-meaning "old friends" inside the country. Even Amnesty International was prevailed upon not to adopt me as a prisoner of conscience.'[594] Breytenbach never pretended to be a disciplined cadre of any movement or organisation. The ANC in exile took and pocketed his denunciation of the regime, but was never prepared to intercede on his behalf.

'A condition of flux'

When he walked out of jail in 1982, Breytenbach encountered a changed country. In a long analysis written for a French publication in September 1984, he stressed that apartheid could no longer be regarded as unmitigated repression. 'All of a sudden', he wrote, 'things seem to be in a condition of flux.' He warned, however, that the government tightly controlled policy changes with the aim of containing and even exploiting confrontation. Urban blacks would be given more security and enough political autonomy to justify being grouped as representative entities in a larger confederal set-up. Suffering as a result of diplomatic setbacks, the ANC faced internal upheaval and might be amenable to talks. 'All of the above', he concluded, 'will reinforce the power of those now ruling South Africa, and it will be self-indulgent blindness to pretend otherwise.'[595]

The sudden explosions of black rage in 1960, 1976 and 1984, each followed by floundering efforts on the part of the state to restore order, prompted many commentators to radically revise their assessment of the capacity of government to respond effectively to mass uprisings. The spectre of a protracted civil war concentrated their minds. Instead of emphasising the power of government, they now tended to dismiss the possibility of the white government resuming the initiative or offering a platform for negotiations. The same would happen after September 1984 when a violent uprising broke out in the Vaal Triangle and soon spread to most parts of the country. Breytenbach's assessment of the stability of the system changed markedly.

In April 1985, with 250 people killed in the violent protests that had erupted nine months earlier, Breytenbach wrote an article that appeared in abridged form in the *Los Angeles Times* and *International Herald Tribune*. He concluded that the nature of the conflict had changed substantially. Despite the revolt, whites refused to compromise on what they saw as the core condition of their survival: a 'white minority power monopoly'; on this they would brook no negotiation. But blacks were no longer pleading for participation. 'The white state is rejected . . . The civil war in South Africa has started.'[596]

In a paper delivered early in 1985 on the ethics of resistance, he stated unambiguously that the state had to carry the responsibility for the violence that was threatening to spill out of control. The state was unique in its introduction of massive state violence against its citizens. 'It has the capacity to wreak havoc in Africa.'[597]

In 1986 Breytenbach returned to South Africa for a first visit after his release from jail. Accepting the Rapport Prize, he warned of the danger that apartheid could only be 'smothered in blood'.[598] However, where he earlier tended to dismiss any possibility of significant change emanating from the Afrikaner intelligentsia, he now challenged them to take their future in their own hands: whites could still avert a revolution and the Afrikaners could still break out of their isolation.[599] In addressing students in Stellenbosch, Breytenbach pointed out that it was not necessary to renounce their *Afrikanerskap* to become South Africans.

They could claim their place in a future order if they participated in a struggle whose aim was to undermine and subvert the place they now occupied. However, failure to participate in the struggle would weaken Afrikaners' claims in a post-apartheid order.[600]

Breytenbach was now no longer the angry prophet, excoriating his people, but a valued interlocutor, appealing to their better instincts. Among Afrikaners the profound ambivalence towards Breytenbach deepened. Even in jail he was never cast out. As JM Coetzee remarks: 'The terrorist in Breytenbach could be incarcerated and punished, while the poet in him could be left free.'[601] It was the unique way in which he expressed a feeling for the land, and a love for the language, that gripped people's attention.[602] For successive generations of Afrikaner students, he remained a charismatic figure, projecting idealism and integrity.

Organising the Dakar conference

While Breytenbach was in jail, Van Zyl Slabbert, as leader of the official opposition in Parliament, tried on several occasions to persuade State President Botha to release him earlier. After his release a close friendship developed between them, although their views still differed. As late as November 1985 Slabbert had not yet given up on the government initiating a movement towards substantial change. In a private interview with Botha, he said that the idea of an all-powerful ANC was a myth. Botha 'could pull the teeth of the whole ANC story'. It was, in Slabbert's words, 'not on' for the ANC leadership to insist that the government must 'negotiate the transfer of power out of [their] own hands to whatever majority'. He also agreed with Botha that a white person had a right to maintain 'his cultural rights, his way of life, his language', and 'to have his children educated in his own way'. He pointed out that there were few, if any, historical precedents for the peaceful transfer of power from a minority to a majority. Black liberation was impossible without white security.[603]

Botha failed to discern the intention of Slabbert's initiative, which was an attempt to get the government's backing for the idea of a convention in which the major black and white leaders would seek a compromise. The President made the far-fetched claim that more than half of the black population supported him and were satisfied with the rights the apartheid system had yielded to them. This frustrating interview with Botha prompted Slabbert to make an abrupt change of course: from a loyal critic, using Parliament as his base, to a critical ally of the liberation movement. Early in 1986 he resigned from Parliament, calling the institution irrelevant.

Slabbert thought that a civil war could be averted by starting talks with the ANC. In 1985 Thabo Mbeki had told him and other members of his party's executive that the armed struggle was the only way forward for the ANC. Privately, however, he said to Slabbert that 'talking is better than killing' and that negotiations could be explored.[604] With increasing urgency, Slabbert spread the message to white voters that no resolution of the country's crisis was possible without the ANC.

Shortly after leaving Parliament, Slabbert and Alex Boraine, a PFP member of Parliament who had resigned with him, founded the Institute for a Democratic Alternative for South Africa (Idasa). At a meeting in New York shortly afterwards, Slabbert met Thabo Mbeki. He told him not to underestimate the importance of growing numbers of Afrikaners, particularly academics, who had broken with Afrikaner nationalism and apartheid. Here the idea emerged of a meeting between a group of mainly Afrikaans-speaking South Africans and some leading members of the ANC.[605]

A few months later Slabbert and Breytenbach met on the island of Gorée off the coast of Dakar, Senegal. They decided that Dakar was a suitable venue. Slabbert and Boraine went fundraising in the United States, and found George Soros, a well-known international financier, willing to donate a substantial sum, although he feared that South Africa was doomed and the conference futile. In the meantime Breytenbach used his contacts with Danielle Mitterrand, the French President's wife and head of the France Libertés foundation, to smooth entry into Senegal. She enjoyed a good relationship with Abdou Diouf, the Senegalese President.

On 3 June 1987, just more than a year after the proclamation of a national state of emergency by the South African government, the press broke the news of an imminent meeting in Dakar between an ANC delegation of 11 senior members (more than half went on to become cabinet members), led by Thabo Mbeki, and a group of 59 people invited by Idasa. Breytenbach stated that his love for the land and its people prompted him to help organise the meeting. 'As long as people talk, there is no time for shooting.'[606] The Idasa group consisted of people who were personally invited by Slabbert or Boraine and who did not represent any institution. Half were white Afrikaans-speaking academics, teachers, journalists, artists, directors, writers and professionals. The group also included several coloured Afrikaans-speakers, ten English-speaking businessmen and academics, and three German political scientists working on South Africa.

The only known record of the Dakar conference, held from 9 to 12 July, is an ANC document of 80 pages, written by Tony Trew and some anonymous ANC members.[607] A few members of the Idasa group published their impressions in the journals *Die Suid-Afrikaan* and *Frontline* and in newspapers. There is also a film of the Dakar meeting, produced by Kathy Boraine and Hennie Serfontein.

During the conference Breytenbach and Slabbert rarely spoke in public, apart from at press briefings. Their views were well known, and it is also possible that, as the organisers, they did not want to play too prominent a role. As could be expected, the topic of violence dominated the discussion. Other topics included the quest for a democratic alternative, the ANC's commitment to an equitable non-racial future, economic policy in a post-apartheid society, and cultural and language rights, with a particular emphasis on the future position of Afrikaans.

Violence and a negotiated settlement

As the ANC conference account makes clear, its delegation was imbued with the notion that on all issues, including that of violence, the organisation occupied the moral high ground. The ANC had been in the vanguard of a long peaceful struggle for rights and liberty against apartheid. It had turned to violence in the early 1960s, but only when its non-violent protests fell on deaf ears. The ANC delegates stated that the organisation in principle refused to engage in mass violence and, if civilians died, this was unintentional. It was committed to observing the Geneva Protocols and the guiding principle of the 'proportionality of means'.[608]

The ANC delegates took a deterministic view of the struggle. They believed their organisation had seized the strategic advantage and that 'victory was certain'. They envisaged negotiations at a 'two-sided table' as an imminent prospect. On the one side would be the representatives of the state and all other 'racist' forces (which would include Inkatha and other 'reactionary' organisations) and, on the other side, the forces for liberation and popular democracy under the

ANC's leadership. Among the latter would be representatives of trade unions, churches and selected 'progressive [white] liberals'.[609]

André du Toit gave the keynote speech on the subject of violence.[610] To him the state's violence and the ANC's armed struggle had both become historical realities. He took issue with the notion of two clearly defined sides waging a battle, preferring instead to speak of a proliferation of internecine conflicts, and warning that indiscriminate violence and terror on the part of the insurgents could damage the political cause of resistance. He warned the ANC: 'Revolution is not around the corner – the heady assessments of recent years are gone.' The state would never win legitimacy by using large-scale coercion, but there were also distinct limits to the ANC challenge to state power.[611] In the Dakar declaration, endorsed by all participants, deep concern was expressed about the proliferation of uncontrolled violence.[612]

The conference's emphasis on uncontrolled violence was misplaced. Reports would later indicate that most of the violence emanated from the two major contenders for power, the government and the ANC. The government was intent on using force to eliminate the ANC as a factor, and although the cabinet tried to avert its gaze, state agencies deliberately targeted ANC activists to 'eliminate' or 'remove' them from society. While both the ANC and its internal ally, the United Democratic Front, lacked the capacity to control what was happening on the ground, their general strategy was to use violence against black policemen, councillors or informers, described as agents or collaborators, and against political opponents interested in negotiating with the government, particularly Inkatha (coloured and Indian 'collaborators' were not targeted at all). Violence was the ANC's veto against any black effort to bypass it. The Idasa group ignored the possibility that the ANC was trying violently to establish its hegemony over black South Africans.[613]

The prospects for a negotiated settlement were next on the agenda. All the conference participants endorsed such a settlement. The government's demand that the ANC first had to forswear violence was generally seen as the main obstacle in this regard. Thabo Mbeki explained that accepting this demand would put the ANC in a no-win situation: 'It is too easy for one's opponents to set off bombs exactly to demonstrate that you are not in control of your forces.'[614] The political stalemate could be unlocked by the unconditional release of Nelson

Mandela. 'The cessation of conflict is not and has never been a necessary condition for negotiations to take place.'[615]

While this was true, it evaded some issues. Escalating violence also had a dynamic of its own and could fatally damage the prospects for a negotiated settlement. As Slabbert pointed out, 'the strategy of armed struggle had direct consequences for other democratic strategies'.[616] Bombs going off could stifle a willingness to talk. At the end of the conference the participants unanimously endorsed the goal of a negotiated settlement leading to a non-racial democracy. They generally saw the government's insistence that the ANC should unilaterally forswear violence as the main obstacle to such negotiations.

What were the prospects for a negotiated political settlement if the issue of suspending violence could be overcome? One of the major problems was that no one at the conference really knew how much support the ANC actually enjoyed. Opinion polls commissioned by the government in the second half of the 1980s showed consistently that the ANC attracted the support of more than 85 per cent of blacks (and more than 60 per cent of the electorate), while the NP managed to muster the support of some 20 per cent of blacks.[617] For fear of scaring its supporters, the government did not publish these polls.

Lawrence Schlemmer, an academic in the Idasa delegation with long polling experience, stated in an address to the conference that the ANC enjoyed majority support among the population. It could thus afford electoral competition. Arguing that national unity was only possible within diversity, he urged the movement to accept decentralised power, regionalism and federalism.

Pallo Jordan, ANC head of research, rejected any form of decentralised power. There had to be unity and 'unity could only be demonstrated through unity in action'. He argued that all groups existing in South Africa had been 'created, sustained and nurtured by state policy. The cleavages can be unmade precisely because they were manufactured [by apartheid].' The emergence of a new nation had to be based on a rejection of the divisions on which apartheid was based. He warned that the future government would adopt a policy of 'liberatory intolerance' towards organisations based on race or ethnicity.[618] This was an ideological interpretation as sweeping as apartheid.

The other ANC delegates were also not prepared to make any significant concessions to minorities. They did not think a Bill of Rights was necessary to assuage their fears and were of the view that the Freedom Charter offered enough guarantees for them. They also dismissed pleas for power-sharing, federalism or the decentralisation of power. They claimed that any or all of these mechanisms to curb the power of the majority could serve to buttress existing privilege. The ANC had begun only two years before to admit members of racial minorities to its executive. Nevertheless, some of the Idasa delegates insisted that the ANC's record of fighting against racial exclusivists, such as the Pan Africanist Congress, spoke for itself.

Dominating the discussion was the assumption that the ANC's commitment to non-racialism made minority or group rights superfluous. The debate reminded one of a comment by Staniland: 'Nationalism could speak unto nationalism; liberalism often seems just to be talking to itself.'[619] Not only the ANC delegates but also some of the members of the Idasa group insisted that the ANC, far from being a nationalist movement, was genuinely non-racial, even liberal in character. Hanf, a German political scientist who attended the conference, later expressed a view that was quite common at the conference: ANC thinking reflected not so much nationalism per se as 'the universalism of Christian as well as Marxist thought . . . rooted in the concept of the brotherhood of all men'. All South Africans 'were brothers in the eyes of the ANC', which desired 'equality and fraternity' and 'rejected all forms of group thinking'. The 'power of this non-racial ethic' was 'extraordinary' and 'heroic'. It was for this reason 'that any form of communalism was anathema to them'.[620]

The ANC's plea that its commitment to a non-racial democracy be accepted without minority safeguards was ultimately based on a moral argument. Ranking apartheid with the evils of the slave trade and the Holocaust as an ultimate crime against humanity, it depicted the ANC's struggle as one that would liberate not only blacks but whites as well. Guarantees to minorities would demean the liberation struggle and the freedom that it would bring for all.

In his writings before the conference, Breytenbach at times tried to assuage fears of white marginalisation in a future political order by arguing that black society was composed of different political groups, which ruled out 'a unitary black majority'. Whites should not be afraid of majority rule. Negotiations could prevent the tyranny of an absolute majority and the marginalisation of minorities.[621]

But the question was: what would happen if the ANC won with an overwhelming majority in the first election, making it unnecessary to form a coalition government? Some scholars working in the field strongly warned against the disastrous consequences of untrammelled majority rule operating under the guise of a liberal democracy. They pointed out that the latter system worked only in a homogeneous society, where political beliefs and material interests rather than racial identity determined voters' choices.[622] Kedourie warned that the 'worst effects of the tyranny of the majority are seen when the tyranny of the majority is introduced in countries divided by religion or language or race'.

These scholars suggested an alternative form of democracy, called consociationalism or power-sharing between groups, always on the condition that the groups should not be defined and imposed by the government (as in apartheid) but be voluntarily formed. In a book entitled *Political Domination in Africa*, Sklar warned that democratic movements that disregarded consociational precepts 'did so at their own peril'.[623] However, the ANC delegates scoffed at this model, preferring instead what they called an 'ordinary democracy'.

In the discussion on a post-apartheid economy, Leon Louw, an office-bearer of the Free Market Foundation, entered a plea for massive decentralisation and privatisation, to which the ANC delegates replied with a strong insistence on state intervention to 'democratise' the economy. Some expressed the view that the system ultimately had to culminate in socialism. Appealing to the Freedom Charter, they demanded the nationalisation of the mining and banking sectors, the redistribution of the land, and collectivised agriculture. The new South Africa would have to guarantee 'the masses of the people freedom from hunger, disease, ignorance, homelessness and poverty'. Schlemmer warned that all-or-nothing strategies could actually strengthen the regime.[624] The few businessmen who attended the Dakar conference took note of the ANC's radical economic policy. The business community in South Africa would soon embark on initiatives to win the movement over to market-oriented policies.

The Idasa delegates were silent about the fact that communism and communist activists exercised an extraordinary influence on the ANC in exile. Breytenbach was the only participant who expressed a word of caution. Referring to communism, he said that 'in supporting the struggle we are supporting a move towards a system which we have seen in neighbouring countries not to be successful'.[625] He had pulled no punches in his *True Confessions* about the extraordinary strategic leverage of communists in the movement. At the conference none of the internal South Africans quoted Breytenbach's view. Tending to dismiss the propaganda of the South African government too readily, they missed the opportunity to delve deeper into an important issue.

Remarkably, the conference did not discuss the rapid decline of democracy in Africa and the steady deterioration in state capacity in independent African states by the 1980s. All-powerful dominant parties strutted the stage and tolerated little opposition. They rigged elections, emasculated the courts, cowed the press and stifled the universities. Leaders made themselves exceedingly rich.[626] There was a tendency at the Dakar conference to assume that the ANC was too smart to fall into this trap. As Du Pisani, an Afrikaner political scientist, remarked in his notes: 'The organisation draws upon all the most recent developments in international law.'[627]

The position of Afrikaans

In his account Alex Boraine noted: 'Hermann Giliomee, Lawrie Schlemmer and others kept raising the issue of the future of the Afrikaans language.'[628] In his view Pallo Jordan put these people in their place when he replied in fluent Afrikaans that they should not worry only about Afrikaans but about Xhosa and Zulu as well. Jordan said something along the same lines: 'The future of Afrikaans is assured – if for no other reason than that it is the language of many black people.'[629] Boraine continued: 'They had not been reassured about the position of Afrikaans in a democratic society; indeed to this day Giliomee remains obsessed with Afrikaners and their language.'

African nationalist movements in other parts of Africa wasted no time in elevating the colonial language, whether English, French or Portuguese, to the position of the only effective public language, but the conference took no note of this. The ANC delegates would not concede that a minority language enjoyed a legitimate claim to enforceable language rights. Du Pisani described their stance: 'The ANC is prepared to give assurances on cultural rights to Afrikaners.' Paraphrasing the common view expressed by ANC delegates (but using an exclamation mark to distance himself), he stated: 'The best assurance for the continued existence for Afrikaans is the fact that the ANC cadres talk Afrikaans!'[630]

Few members of the Idasa group questioned the ANC assurances that it would not marginalise minorities. There was no reference to other countries in Africa where nationalist movements, soon after coming to power, ruthlessly displaced members of minorities from civil service jobs or expelled them from the country in the name of Africanisation. Schlemmer later described the mutation of the ANC's non-racialism. 'It starts off from the position of non-racism and it then qualifies this with a commitment to closing racial gaps in order to achieve a legitimate basis for non-racialism, and from there it proposes a range of race-based affirmative action and empowerment policies to give effect to this.'

The ANC delegates gave little indication of how they thought that the ANC could impose its ideas about democracy and socialism. It was pointed out to them that the state had succeeded to a large extent in reimposing its authority by using emergency powers. A member of the internal group recorded his sense of bafflement. 'Listening to the ANC was like reading Revelations 21. They had an apocalyptic vision of a great moment of Change, where all democratic forces would be on the one side of the negotiating table under the leadership of the ANC, with the government on the other side, working out the hand-over of power. It was not even a round-table concept, but a two-sided table.'[631]

In this context I posed the question: if there was only a scant prospect of the ANC toppling the state, was it not advisable to seek a compromise solution? I argued as follows: 'The conflict is not between democracy and racism, but between Afrikaner and African nationalism. There is a need to fuse the two. The way forward is bi-communalism. Non-racialism cannot be established by the elimination of Afrikaner nationalism. There are fears that the Afrikaner minority will be in the position of the Jews under Nazism.'[632]

I accepted that Afrikaner nationalism and African nationalism were quite different in nature – African nationalism was territorially based, tolerant and integrative, while Afrikaner nationalism, based on ethnicity, tended to reify differences in descent and culture in order to prevent a common nation being forged – but the fact was that neither could prevail over the other and neither could exploit the full potential of South Africa without the other. In this context I cited NP van Wyk Louw's words about the tragic situation in which the respective 'rights' of two nations stood implacably opposed to each other and in which a solution that allowed the one to triumph over the other itself became unjust.

I argued that, if this was accepted, both Afrikaner and African nationalism had to be accorded some legitimacy. Negotiations and a future government would be based mainly on a coalition of the two 'nations', 'blocs' or 'groups'.[633] I had failed to recognise that Afrikaner nationalism had steadily become eroded during the 1980s and was at war with itself. The National Party could win only half the Afrikaner vote in the 1992 referendum and would disintegrate over the next ten years.

My comments sparked a heated response, with Jordan in particular strongly rejecting the view. Breytenbach also disputed the view that a parallel could be drawn between 'the exclusivist ideology of Afrikaner nationalism and the integrative movement for national liberation'.[634] In written comments he and I exchanged just after the conference, he deplored any attempt to depict the ANC as a nationalist movement that used non-racialism as an opportunistic tactic to attract allies from outside the black community.

In these notes, which were later published, Breytenbach expressed himself as follows:

> It is not true that the ANC only 'pretends' to be non-racist while its driving force actually is a black nationalism ... We have no right to suspect them of operating under false pretences ... It was to be tragically blind to talk of a struggle between two nationalisms ... I don't think that the road to nation-building goes through any form of entrenchment of 'group rights' or 'blocs'. Those 'flowers' are lethal [*doodsblomme*]. At the very least it attempts to take apartheid out of the cancer in order to retain the cancer.

Commenting on the exchange, Pallo Jordan extolled the ANC non-racial tradition that 'had been drilled into the average ANC member so that it was almost second nature'.[635] He dismissed NP van Wyk Louw's notion of Afrikaner and African 'rights' that stood implacably opposed to each other. Such views granted to Afrikaner nationalism an 'unwarranted legitimacy to a political doctrine that is *radically evil*' (his italics). He added that Louw's liberal credentials notwithstanding, on this score he was 'an abject apologist for tyranny and oppression'. In a future South Africa, the Afrikaners, like minorities elsewhere, had to rely on democratic institutions and practices to protect them against discrimination and oppression.

Jordan's view foreshadowed that of the ANC in the negotiations that started in 1990 and its implementation of a policy of transformation. It appealed simply to 'a non-racial democracy', but used policy to make structures in all walks of life 'racially representative', 'representative of the population composition'. While using democratic language, the ANC in fact practised what Taylor called a form of 'democratic exclusion' that recognises a single political identity and imperiously excludes other identities.[636] In his introduction to the book *The Liberal Dilemma in South Africa*, Van den Berghe puts the issue well:

> If your constituency has the good fortune to contain a demographic majority, racism can easily be disguised as democracy. The ideological sleight of hand, of course, is that an ascriptive racially-defined majority is a far cry from a majority made up of a shifting coalition on the basis of a commonality of beliefs and interests. 'Majority rule' in Africa can thus easily become a veneer for racial domination.[637]

The Dakar conference demonstrated in potent symbolic terms that the ANC had become part of the mainstream debate about South Africa's future and the government could no longer silence it. For the English press (with the notable exception of *The Citizen*) the *Dakar-gangers* engaged in a potent act of dissent. The Afrikaans press, and *Die Burger* in particular, denounced the conference, arguing that it was an attempt by Slabbert to embarrass the government, expose Parliament's lack of legitimacy and boost the ANC as an extra-parliamentary movement.

As Chris Louw points out, the extraordinary efforts on the part of the Afrikaans press to denounce the conference contained an implicit acknowledgement that negotiations between the government and the ANC were indeed on the agenda.[638] The problem was that the government had become bogged down by indecision. All the Afrikaans press could do was to discredit the Idasa group as useful idiots. In Parliament members of the Conservative Party pointed out that several university lecturers, who were state employees, were among the participants in the conference. Although the ANC was a banned organisation, the state took no action against these lecturers, who, on their return, openly discussed the ANC's policy objectives and strategies.[639]

Conclusion

In his essay on Breytenbach as part of his study of the major social critics of the twentieth century, Michael Walzer noted that 'poetry is probably easier than social criticism, for the poet listens with his inner ear, while the critic depends on an actual dialogue'.[640] Except for his brief 1973 visit, Breytenbach's exposure to other social critics in South Africa was limited. *True Confessions* recounts his 'dialogue' with interrogators and fellow prisoners under harrowing conditions. *End Papers*, written in exile, was an attempt far from the scene to make sense of the first signs of apartheid breaking up.

The Dakar conference for the first time subjected Breytenbach, like all the other participants, to wide-ranging debates and dialogue with white and black South Africans over the country's future. Like Slabbert, he played the role of interlocutor encouraging dialogue, believing in what JM Coetzee called 'the potential for a complete turnaround in the history of South Africa'.[641] However, when Breytenbach returned to South Africa in 1991 such a hope was quickly dispelled. He would write bitterly of the ANC's betrayal of the revolution. He had not fought for a new hegemony with 'the same mechanisms, the same sadness'.[642] But, then, he had always stressed that, as a poet, he spoke only for himself and 'with the right to imagine a future beyond the dreams of politicians'.

11.

The elusive search for peace

What is it that imparts to places such as South Africa, Northern Ireland and Israel the same melancholy quality? Why do they fail to get at the root of their unhappy internal conflicts? Is finding peace, in the words of Harvard political scientist Samuel Huntington, a question of applying the right reform recipe, 'a small amount of luck and a large amount of political talent'? Or will the bi-communal conflict in these countries remain intractable and immune to compromise – what Albert Camus described as a fatal embrace? Writing of the civil war in his native Algeria, he said: 'It is as if two insane people crazed with wrath, had decided to turn into a fatal embrace the forced marriage from which they cannot free themselves. Forced to live together and incapable of uniting, they decide at last to die together.'

Northern Ireland, Israel and South Africa are unhappy because they lack the one thing nations in Western Europe or North America take for granted – a state representing a unified people, living securely under laws considered legitimate by all, or almost all. Whites and blacks in South Africa, Jews and Palestinians in Israel, and Protestants and Catholics in Ulster all live under essentially the same political system: two communities or nations locked together by the domination of one over the other. It is a matter that goes beyond ordinary politics. As Donald Horowitz points out in *Ethnic Groups in Conflict* (1985), a relationship of ethnic domination crucially affects one's sense of personal worth, which is one of the central motives of human behaviour. In divided societies like South Africa, Israel and Northern Ireland most people's self-esteem is determined by that of their communal group – whether it enjoys the status of a dominant group or whether it has to suffer the indignity of subjugation. The longer the struggle continues, the more 'communal group worth' becomes a focal concern of both the individual and the group.

It is a particular characteristic of divided societies that 'exit' from the group is extremely difficult, as is evident in terms such as 'Catholic atheists' and 'black men with white hearts'. Membership of the group is determined by birth. And because the groups in Northern Ireland, Israel and South Africa live separately, go to separate schools and play sport separately, they quickly develop stereotypes and phobias, including the belief that the other group is intent on ploughing them under or even exterminating them. The warning by the Secretary-General of Inkatha, Oscar Dhlomo, that sanctions could precipitate the accession to power of another Hitler reflects the fear of a horrific outcome should groups in a divided society be driven to the wall.

Some observers still believe the conflict in Israel and Northern Ireland is over religion and that in South Africa it is over race and the privileges of race. This is an error, though an understandable one, since it is tempting (but wrong) to interpret all conflicts in terms of their outward manifestations. In fact, racial or cultural distinctiveness is ultimately significant only to the extent that it contributes to the sense of uniqueness of groups. Race and religion are merely badges of communal identity which determine political allegiance for all except a few.

It is of course this badge that also determines life chances. The conflict in South Africa, like those in Israel and Northern Ireland, is fuelled by the head start the dominant group enjoys. It is a start due to its superior access to virtually all the resources of the state – economic, educational, political, administrative and social. While members of the dominant section attribute their prosperity and success to their own hard work and ingenuity, the subjugation of the dominated group as a nation is at the root of all the inequalities and inadequacies they suffer.

The situation does not improve as the elites among the subordinates begin to achieve a middle-class way of life. For them the remaining forms of discrimination and status inequalities become quite intolerable. This explains why the conflict in South Africa or Northern Ireland has intensified despite the fact that racism or sectarianism is much less overt than a mere ten years ago. We have the paradox, typical of communal conflicts, that, while the dominant group has become more 'liberal' in its racial attitudes and keener to accept mixing or reject discrimination, well-educated subordinates have been getting steadily angrier and more bitter about their condition.

But unequal access is only part of the conflict. To see only this aspect is to conclude incorrectly that peace can be found by remedying the unequal access. In fact, unequal access is simply a manifestation of a larger conflict in societies such as Northern Ireland, Israel and South Africa. This is the conflict over national identity and security. It is a conflict which is rooted in the ethnonational domination by one group of the land and the state: as a result it controls national institutions such as Parliament and the army, and monopolises national symbols and values. It is a national sovereignty which a group will not yield without bitter struggle. The Jerusalem historian Meron Benvenisti powerfully expresses the dominant group perspective: 'If the issues at stake are thought to be of the greatest importance, if they involve one's most cherished cultural, national, and material values and rewards, if one considers them inalienable rights and is ready to struggle for them, then one perceives oneself at war even while pursuing one's civilian life.' The other side of the coin is the subordinate group's refusal to settle for gradualism and piecemeal reforms because this leaves the issue of their national status, freedom and sovereignty unresolved. Thus their leadership seeks not redress within the system, but the very destruction of the system itself.

It is for this reason that centrist parties hoping to bridge the communal gap, such as the Progressive Federal Party in South Africa, the Alliance in Northern Ireland, and groupings such as Peace Now in Israel are doomed to failure and despair. On security issues they are invariably outflanked by ethnic parties. Ethnonationalism – and here Afrikaner nationalism represents a salient case – enjoys a great advantage as a form of political mobilisation: it combines profound emotional attachment to the ethnic group or nation with a strategy to promote the interests both of the individual and of the ethnic group as a whole. In short, ethnic mobilisation comes to provide for the dominant group the only credible mechanism for controlling its political and social environment.

It is this need to control the environment that has been largely neglected in the debate over an alternative political system for South Africa. An exception is the scholar Paul Sites, who, in his *Control: The Basis of Social Order*, challenges the traditional view of socialisation. His work argues that the basis of the social order is not individual adaptation to a social order resting on at least some shared values. It is rather individuals seeking to control their environment in order to gratify their need for a national identity and for security. They will employ mechanisms ranging from outright coercion to manipulation of political procedures to maintain the group that enables them to control their environment.

National identity becomes particularly important when a polarised situation turns into open strife. In the Israeli case, which involves frequent wars, a study by a group of psychiatrists found that Israeli behaviour displays an attachment to the nation so profound as to be virtually inseparable from the individual self. In the case of the Palestinians there has been a similar tendency to see the nation as part of the extended self. Personal and national identity have been merged: the nation and the homeland have become part of the extended self. As a group of American psychiatrists who studied the conflict in Israel phrased it: to lose one's homeland 'is to risk the fragmentation of the self, an eventuality which people will resist with their very lives'.

The Afrikaners have used the National Party over forty years to secure power and control their environment. Afrikaner nationalists may be less explicit about it than in the past but they still appropriate South Africa as their homeland and the state as a *boereplaas* (Afrikaner farm). In a recent study of Stellenbosch University, arguably the most outward-going of Afrikaner universities, Jannie Gagiano found that Afrikaner students accord a high degree of legitimacy to the Afrikaner-controlled state. He remarks:

> The Afrikaner community has appropriated the state as their 'own', like one would establish ownership of a farm, and it is well known that a farmer worth his salt has the sole authority over his domain. Thus it is very common for an Afrikaner to speak of 'our' minister of this or that, 'our' defence force, 'our' police force and so on, but much more rare for his other countrymen to do so. This sense of 'ownership' helps to legitimise minority rule and demands for loyalty to the state and its institutions.

This mindset expresses itself in what can be called a high repression potential. A recent survey showed Afrikaner students at the University of Stellenbosch to be highly critical of any parties or institutions to the left of government and very supportive of oppressive action by the state against opponents striving to replace the ruling group within their own. More than half the sample of students approved of the detention of people participating in peaceful demonstrations and three-quarters approved of the police shooting demonstrators who damage property or throw stones and other missiles at them.

Proponents of increasing pressure against South Africa or Israel act in the belief that pressure would help to bring an intransigent ruling group to the conference table where a transfer of power could be negotiated. Pressure, moderately applied, can achieve limited success, as Dr Chester Crocker, the architect of the Reagan administration's policy of constructive engagement, well understood. However, pressure which directly challenges a group's control can greatly exacerbate a conflict situation. Paul Sites makes a point too easily overlooked:

> If a group's existence is threatened and if control tactics consistent with its values and purposes are not sufficient to maintain the group's existence over time, control tactics inconsistent with its values and purposes will be used in an attempt to ensure survival. If a group is forced to use control tactics inconsistent with its values over a long period of time, the values and purposes of the group will change in order to bring about a consistency.

Not much store should be put upon rationality when dominant groups are driven to the wall. Theodor Hanf, a German analyst of ethnic conflicts, with intimate knowledge of both South Africa and Lebanon, observes that it is by no means certain that economic considerations would govern the behaviour of a dominant group if it felt – whether rightly or wrongly is immaterial to the consequences – that its existence was threatened. A scorched-earth policy is hardly economically rational but it is one often practised in civil wars between ethnic and religious groups.

Whereas in the past most bi-national conflicts were quickly and bloodily resolved, a new pattern of conflict seems to have emerged in the last two decades in divided societies. One now witnesses low-key violence leading neither to full system breakdown nor to renewed full control by the formerly dominant group. These societies become locked in a 'neither peace nor war' stalemate.

There are several reasons for the stalemate in Northern Ireland, South Africa and Israel. The first is the impossibility of revolution due to the vastly superior resources a modern state commands compared with the instruments of violence available to rebellious subordinates. Petrol bombs are no match for machine guns, armoured cars and, above all, loyal security forces. Without these forces transferring their allegiance to those who challenge the state, no revolution has succeeded in the twentieth century. Such a shift of loyalties is unthinkable in the three societies under discussion.

But if revolution is impossible, there is also no way in which the state can curb the vastly enhanced expectations of services which subordinates want the state to supply. Their demand for immediate and massive state intervention to root out discrimination and end all ethnic disparities keeps discontent simmering. So does their deep resentment of unrepresentative technocratic bureaucracies and their unsatisfied urge for community or so-called people's control. The 'civic' or the 'community' becomes their main reference group rather than the church or professional affiliations, as was the case in the past. Not surprisingly, the revolutionaries strive to transform civic and other local organisations into radical movements that can confront the state again and again in the hope that its will collapses.

There is also a third reason why South Africa, Northern Ireland and Israel cannot restore full stability. The state in all three societies is fighting with one hand tied behind its back. The tie is a common commitment to Judaeo-Christian principles and a fierce desire to remain part of the Western family of nations. Government spokesmen in both South Africa and Israel have repeatedly warned the discontented populace that the state 'has not begun to unleash the full military might at its disposal', or words to that effect. Short of the state's existence actually being threatened, this is an idle warning. As in the case of the American and Russian nuclear arsenals, the lethal weaponry of the Israeli or South African security forces is useless for dealing with secondary threats, which public disturbances represent. Bursts from machine guns rather than rubber bullets would immediately quell an uprising, but they come with a price no Western-oriented government is prepared to pay.

This price involves not only economic losses suffered as a result of trade and investment sanctions. Something more is at stake. If the security forces start killing demonstrators randomly, they jeopardise a state's most precious asset – the cohesion of the ruling elite. As Huntington observes: 'Revolutionary violence does not have to be successful to be effective. It simply has to create sufficient trouble to cause divisions among the dominant group over ways to deal with it.' If ruling group consensus collapses, the state's ability to coerce becomes fatally compromised. Government concern in this respect was shown in the speed with which South Africa responded to the public outcry over the shooting of Africans in Langa, Uitenhage, in 1985 or the Israeli reaction to the killings of Palestinians in Sabra and Shatila outside Beirut in 1982. Commissions of inquiry excoriating the security forces are considered small risks compared with the danger of the ruling group becoming paralysed by guilt.

That there is no complete peace in South Africa or Israel has as much to do with the self-imposed constraints the ruling elite accepts as with anything else. As Hanf remarks, the methods to preserve ethnic group domination in South Africa are ruthless by the standards of liberal democracy but they are nothing compared with the brutality of Oriental and African despots drawn from ethnic minorities. He gives a chilling account of how the Alawite regime in Syria dealt with uprisings by a group of fundamentalist Sunni Muslims.

> In 1981 demonstrations in Hama, the fourth largest city in Syria, spilled over in revolt. The government subjected Hama to artillery bombardment and hundreds of hostages were shot. A year later there was another uprising in Hama. When it appeared that the army was unable to put it down, the government did not hesitate to use the airforce. The whole city centre of Hama was literally erased by bombs and napalm. The number of dead is estimated at 30,000 and 40,000 ... The world learnt of the atrocities of Hama only long after the event, for hardly any journalist dared to report them, with good cause. About 40 Arab and some western journalists have met with violent deaths after filing critical reports about Syria.

Any large-scale massacre perpetrated by the South African security forces would produce a pervasive sense of self-doubt among the ruling elite. When such feelings get the upper hand, the days of a repressive regime are numbered.

It is the quest for a more durable peace that prompts repressive regimes in divided societies to embark on reform. But reform is a course fraught with danger. This has never been better formulated than by Alexis de Tocqueville: 'Experience teaches us that, generally speaking, the most perilous moment for a bad government is one when it seeks to mend its ways . . . Patiently endured so long as it seemed beyond redress, a grievance comes to appear intolerable once the possibility of removing it crosses men's minds.'

When Ulster's 'progressive' Terence O'Neill in the late 1960s, and the Afrikaners' *'verligte'* PW Botha in the late 1970s, set out to reform their regimes, they had very similar objectives in mind. Uppermost in their minds was the desire to achieve a less coercive stability that would encourage both local and foreign investors. Both leaders raised hopelessly unrealistic expectations; both societies suffered violence and turmoil; and both economies experienced severe setbacks. The negative outcome surpassed the worst fears of those who propagated reform.

It is important to understand why reform has produced less rather than greater peace. Both O'Neill and Botha knew that they could not offer the subordinated groups political equality without destroying their own party base. To cite Michael MacDonald's compelling study *Children of Wrath: Political Violence in Northern Ireland*, O'Neill chose the next best options: he offered Catholics symbolic, not substantive, citizenship and made symbolic gestures (visits to Catholic schools, meetings with Catholic Irish dignitaries, and conciliatory speeches) that were intended to appease Catholics without upsetting the Protestant masses.

O'Neill fell between two stools. The subordinate Catholic population demanded less symbolism and more substance. In particular, they wanted a body of enforceable civil rights and less Catholic unemployment. While upper-class Protestants went along, the most vulnerable part of O'Neill's Protestant coalition, the working class, sniffed betrayal. They insisted on symbolic demonstrations of Protestant supremacy. Out of the demonstrations and counter-demonstrations developed the spiral of violence that shattered Ulster's peace. O'Neill's party split and the opportunity for reform was lost. The debate is now between those who argue that only the cataclysm of Britain's withdrawal will, after the inevitable bloodshed, bring peace, and those who contend that the only reasonable option is to seek a solution which slowly converges towards peace, each round of trouble being a little less active than the last, each showing some advance towards understanding,

Botha's quest for a more durable peace has been described as an attempt at 'sharing power without losing control'. Botha also made ringing speeches about 'adapt or die', he met black dignitaries, and visited townships and the homelands. He came to personify the new willingness of Afrikaner leaders to accept that wealth, opportunities and decision-making will increasingly have to be shared among all the peoples of South Africa. But the converse of this proposition has been less noticed: only continued Afrikaner control of the state could ensure a stable reform process. 'It is in the long-term interest of South Africa', constitutional engineer Chris Heunis said in 1981, 'that the Afrikaner should always have the privilege of the leadership role.'

The gap between this ruling-class pretence and the brutal reality did not in the first place upset the desperately poor, who constitute half of the black, a third of the coloured and a quarter of the Indian communities. It was, above all, the middle class in the black communities, excluded from white schools and residential areas, who considered the inflated reform rhetoric a personal affront.

Reform also shattered the fragile peace for another reason. As the Botha government extended a form of implicit citizenship, it began to expect from the subordinates a reciprocal acceptance of increasing obligations. It required them to exercise their symbolic vote or, if they refused, to refrain from intimidating those who did want to vote. It wanted them to respect the councillors elected and comply with their decisions to increase rents and service levies.

In a real sense, South Africa's 'unrest' and Ulster's 'troubles' are due to the fact that reforming regimes make larger demands on the subordinate community in terms of requiting or claiming its consent than does an unapologetically sectarian or racist regime. But instead of gratefully taking up their places in the reformed structures, the subordinates consider reform as either cosmetic or a sign of weakness and make civil rights and nationalist demands which the regime is incapable of conceding. In both South Africa and Ulster, the repression that followed resistance triggered new waves of violence.

Israel did not make the same mistake. Its leaders have always been explicit that Israel is a Jewish national state in which Arabs would enjoy no national but only cultural and some civil rights. But while O'Neill and Botha underestimated the perils of reform, Israel failed to calculate the dangers of its continued occupation of the West Bank. It was one thing to deny the Israeli Arabs, forming 16 per cent of the population within the Green Line, a national identity. It was quite another to do this while also suppressing an autonomous Palestinian identity in the occupied territories. Before the West Bank blew up, there were signs that Israeli Arabs were increasingly prepared to advance through the prevailing system, which is relatively free of overt discrimination. The Palestinian intifada (uprising) of December 1987, however, put Jewish–Arab communal relations throughout greater Israel on the agenda. The solidarity strikes of Israeli Arabs have served notice that the bi-national character of Israel cannot much longer be denied, and that merely crushing the uprising will not produce peace. Israel is now confronted with an impossible situation: its identity needs rule out integration, while its security needs make a Palestinian state impossible. The pre-intifada situation is better (or less bad) than any alternative. It is all Israel's political system can handle.

The intifada once again demonstrates that groups with nationalist grievances can thwart the will of powerful states and armies. Military forces become strangely impotent if they are used not for the purpose of war but for crushing rebellious civilians. Hebrew University's Shlomo Avineri made this telling comment: 'An army can beat an army, but an army cannot beat a people.' Historians have known this for a long time, but it is apparently not grasped by military men and politicians who are good at calculating guns, airplanes, tanks and missiles. As Avineri observes: 'What cannot be counted – like a people's will – just does not appear in their quantified map of the world.'

Before one can speak of any accommodation in strife-torn South Africa, Israel and Northern Ireland, we must face up to some rarely acknowledged hard facts, if only to realise how difficult the search for peace is. The first is that, while many people on opposing sides want peace, few of their leaders are prepared to pay the price. Leaders, generally speaking, have fewer problems with violence than they have with peace. We may criticise them for shortsightedness as long as we remember that ultimately it is the leaders, not their critics, who are held accountable for peace efforts that end in disaster. It is also leaders, rather than their critics, who know that communities can live with horror for a very long time without undergoing the revulsion that would lead both sides to sanity and peace.

Another hard fact is that no unanimity exists over interpreting the conflict and, much less, over ways out of the conflict. The 'interpretation problem' exists firstly among the nationalists in both camps, who deny that they are confronted by nationalists. In communal conflicts the competing national entities typically refuse to accord their national adversary the dignity of a respected foe, much less accept them as a negotiating partner. The reason is simple: once they accept the nationalist credentials of the other side they dilute, and thus jeopardise, their claim to sovereign authority over their homeland.

Accordingly, the discourse between the NP and ANC leadership has been restricted to attempts to demonise each other. President Botha has sought to portray the ANC as a despicable band of terrorists led and inspired by communists, waging war on the peace-loving people of South Africa. And Mr Oliver Tambo projects the Pretoria regime as a fascist gang of reactionary racists which suppresses the hopes and aspirations of all the progressive people of South Africa.

Both, of course, are wrong. It is precisely the failure to grasp the depth of the nationalist commitment of the other side that is responsible for the political stalemate in South Africa. On the one hand, the government's attempts to co-opt black leaders in a white-controlled system have been a major affront to all black nationalists, who deeply resent the underlying assumption that they could be bought off through patronage and slightly improved material conditions. On the other hand, the ANC believes that whites are merely clinging to their privileges and that upper-class whites, at least, can be persuaded to think their property and other survival interests will be better protected by an ANC government.

There is also an interpretation problem among those in the liberal or the radical camp who argue that the nationalist dimension in the conflict is exaggerated or simply a smokescreen for privilege. They tend to argue that the sole responsibility for the conflict lies with the dominant group, which refuses to abandon its position of power and privilege. They also contend that the dominant group does not have any set of separable interests, and that its failure to merge in a common society is largely due to shortsighted leaders who exploit ethnic and national sentiments and interests for their own narrow political gain. Not surprisingly, this analysis soon leads to a dogmatic insistence on a so-called non-racial or non-sectarian society and the rejection of all group politics – as if the historical reasons why people have formed national groups are somehow fallacious or spurious.

In divided societies it is always safer to propagate the politics of class ('rational interest') rather than the politics of ethnicity or nationalism ('blood' ties). However, if ethnic or national divisions remain deep and strongly felt (as they are in South Africa), is it not counterproductive (if the quest is peace) to insist that the entire group basis of society and of politics be swept aside? It is especially dangerous to reject the concept of a middle ground, cultivated by those who hope that shared economic interests will over time become the basis of action and who in the interim are prepared to tolerate, and even use, group affiliations in building a relatively better order. It is, above all, the middle ground in divided societies which can win support from the two main camps for interim forms of accommodation, in that it recognises the need of both groups for identity and security and their right to a decent existence, and allows both a fair measure of political and social dignity.

The debate over South Africa's constitutional options has had an unreal quality. Invariably, proposals are made for constitutional formulae without first asking two obvious questions: What is negotiable? And can a framework be established which would enable the parties to work towards accommodation? On the issue of negotiability, leading thinkers in the field of conflict resolution have broken with the notions that conflict is only about interests, and that individuals can be socialised into the correct behaviour (including voting behaviour). There is a growing realisation that the major concern in divided societies is over needs and values such as national security and national identity, which are extremely difficult, if at all possible, to negotiate. The new approach to conflict resolution is, in the words of John Burton, not to insist on negotiations that should 'solve' the problem but rather to facilitate an evolutionary process towards a greater fulfilment of social needs, and to enable parties to move deliberately from point A to point B. 'In this way', Burton concludes, 'change can be more than the mere substitution of one ruling elite for another who will also pursue sectional interests at the expense of human needs.'

This applies fully to the South African situation. What is not negotiable at this stage from the Afrikaner (and larger white) point of view is a transfer of power. Furthermore, the issue of national sovereignty cannot be fudged, which is what the hollow reformist rhetoric tried to do. Over the short to medium term, Afrikaner political leaders will insist on taking final decisions authoritatively and conclusively – after, of course, hearing representations from all sides.

What is negotiable is an extension of civil rights to blacks. Also negotiable is a dualist approach that progressively acknowledges both white and black rights and claims by means of a dual set of national symbols that increasingly express both the European and African character of the state. A dualist tradition is not unknown to South Africa. On the whole, the Union of South Africa (1910–61) successfully reconciled two different traditions – an Afrikaner one leaning towards nationalism and republicanism, and an English one leaning towards the British empire and individualism. The challenge once again is to build a transcending tradition – an inclusive South Africanism – that can keep the state together.

The development of dualism would depend on whether a framework could be established in which the adversaries could work towards a common good. This in turn depends on whether the conflicting parties are able to understand that convergence towards peace would be slow but that progress could be made if each side had an ever-stronger grasp of what peaceful accommodation required.

A framework for co-operation would have to include the following elements:

The mutual acceptance of the limits of power

Accepting the limits of power means on the one hand that those challenging the state should realise that a revolution, or even a substantial weakening of the state, is very unlikely. A victory for the 'progressive' extra-parliamentary opposition is not somehow preordained. On the other hand, it is equally necessary for the state to accept its inability to restore full stability and confidence or to impose workable political 'solutions'. The economy can only recover if the government can succeed in carrying society with it rather than always fighting against it.

Both sides should realise that, while they are able to frustrate and in the long run destroy their adversary, this can only be achieved at the expense of the economy, whose weakening is in the interest of neither. South Africa's wealth lies in the continued functioning of a sophisticated economy which offers both entrepreneurs and workers a due reward. To sacrifice the economy for the single-minded pursuit (or defence) of power is to bequeath a wilderness to the next generation,

The acceptance of a dual tradition in South African political life and a realisation that a settlement which excluded one side was unworkable

The Afrikaner nationalist tradition stresses 'multi-nationalism' with Afrikaner dominance of the state and insists on political representation through state-defined groups. The African nationalist variant pursues a territorial form of nationalism, insists on individual political representation, and wants to impart to the state an African character. While Afrikaner and African nationalist claims on the state cannot be resolved at the moment, a start can be made by reaching compromises on the issue of representation.

The great majority of whites will for the foreseeable future insist on representation of whites by whites as the main element of so-called white group rights. On the other hand, even cabinet ministers in private interviews no longer demand that the other statutory groups can only be represented through their own group structures. Increasingly, whites are prepared to negotiate a different form of participation for the 'open' category of people who refuse participation through a statutory group.

Black attitudes on this are ambiguous. Obviously most blacks strongly oppose white self-representation if it is part of an overall system of apartheid with imposed structures of group representation. However, should representatives of communities that are not white be allowed to decide on their own form of representation within a common legislative body, resistance to white self-representation would considerably decrease. The Buthelezi Commission survey indicated a considerable willingness among blacks to accept group representation provided it is achieved along lines other than political apartheid.

Thus the white demand for white self-representation and the black one for individual representation may well be reconcilable if membership of the group is voluntarily chosen and if the system is not a cover for naked national dominance.

There is theoretically no reason to demand that all segments of the polity should be identified by the electoral process. Abstract arguments whether whites have the right to claim separate representation are clearly only of academic interest if whites consider themselves a community (as they in fact do) and if an agreement could be reached with black representatives about a common political system and the forms of representation.

The shelving (for the time being) of the concept of majority consent

Approaches to conflict-ridden divided societies have focused on ways of fashioning a new majority through the electoral process. The hope is that the legitimacy imparted by elections would give such an authority to the new government that it would be able to stabilise society. However, as we have argued, the essence of a divided society is the dual sets of national loyalty and accountability which the different communities have developed over time. As a result, there cannot be a question of securing a majority in the sense in which the term is used in liberal democracies in the West.

The fact is that a fully representative government assumes the existence of a nation state, which does not exist at this moment in South Africa. Another fact is that the electorate has been unwilling to risk its security by entering into an open competitive system. It is shortsighted to brand this unwillingness as racism. Pierre van den Berghe, an analyst of plural societies, who counts among the fiercest critics of apartheid, points out that majority rule can easily become a liberal veneer for racial domination. He concludes: 'If your constituency has the good fortune to contain a demographic majority, racism can easily be disguised as democracy. The ideological sleight of hand is that an ascriptive, racially defined majority is a far cry from a majority made up of shifting coalitions of individuals on the basis of commonality of beliefs and interest.'

The compromises and concessions within such a framework for co-operation would be particularly painful for those sections in the extra-parliamentary movement which in the heady days of 1985–6 thought that victory was not far off. Any willingness to compromise in this quarter would depend to a large extent on the perception taking root that the government is indeed serious about reaching an accommodation. The main symbolic gesture the government can make is to concede what the extra-parliamentary movement has always insisted upon – that the government and its policies left movements such as the ANC and PAC little option but to embark on a course of violence in 1960. Once the government admits this, the door would open for an offer of amnesty to exiles abroad and the unbanning of the ANC and PAC. Once this deadlock is broken, the debate can begin about future peaceful options.

In the meantime, the most important requirement for finding a more stable peace in divided societies is a lateral shift in thinking. What South Africa cannot afford is a 'walls of Jericho' tradition in which the same rhetorical demands and defences are shouted at walls that refuse to crumble. Political stalemates such as those in South Africa, Northern Ireland and Israel are not necessarily a negative state of affairs. At the very least they provide an opportunity for fresh thinking. And only new ideas and novel initiatives will yield success in our elusive search for peace.

SECTION THREE

Losing power (1989–1999)

12.

Surrender without defeat: Afrikaners and the South African 'miracle'

During the final months of the 1980s one of the last developments that pundits would have predicted for South Africa was that the ruling Afrikaner group would give up power more or less voluntarily, to be replaced by a stable, inclusive democracy. Over the longer run the more common prediction for the country was that of a low-level insurgency ending in a full-scale civil war and a racial conflagration. In the short to medium term most serious analysts anticipated power shifting from the existing Afrikaner monopoly to an Afrikaner-led, multi-racial oligarchy ruling as coercively as the apartheid regime. In 1988, Ken Owen, a respected liberal editor, commented on the white–black struggle: 'Barring massive external intervention I would put my money on any alliance dominated by Afrikaners. They have the capacity to devastate the region *and yet to survive.*'[643]

The political supremacy enjoyed by Afrikaners as the 1990s broke was vast in proportion to their numbers. They formed just over half of the white group but represented only 8 per cent of a total population of 40 million. Outwardly there was no indication that they were prepared to abandon power or its spoils. The National Party as the instrument of Afrikaner ethnic mobilisation and of apartheid was then in its forty-second year of power, enjoying a safe majority in a parliament from which the black majority was excluded. Afrikaners were in a predominant position in the cabinet and controlled the top levels of the central state bureaucracy, the state television and radio corporation, and the senior levels of the security forces. The Afrikaner advance into the private sector, which was still dominated by white English-speakers, was progressing rapidly. In the late 1970s Afrikaner capital controlled less than 10 per cent of the companies listed on the Johannesburg Stock Exchange, but this figure increased to 20 per cent by 1990. Managerial positions in the parastatal sector remained largely an Afrikaner preserve.

The NP government was far more responsive to Afrikaner lobbying than to representations from English big business or institutions commanding the support of blacks, who constituted 70 per cent of the population. A study conducted in the mid-1980s fittingly described the South African state as a *boereplaas* – literally, an Afrikaner farm. Afrikaner students were alone in speaking approvingly and proprietorially of 'our' government and 'our' army.[644] This army was considered to be more than a match for anything that any African state or liberation organisation could offer. By conscripting all white males, the state could count on loyal foot soldiers, particularly among Afrikaners. Asked in 1989, a few months before the African National Congress (ANC) was unbanned, how they would respond to a government controlled by that movement, 44 per cent of Afrikaner students (as opposed to 10 per cent of English-speaking white students) said they would resist physically, while a further 32 per cent indicated that they would emigrate.[645] Cabinet ministers gave no indication that they entertained the idea of giving up power. A typical statement at the time was that of the most reformist of all ministers, RF (Pik) Botha, who said in 1978 that power-sharing with blacks would not be accepted, 'not now, not tomorrow, not in a hundred years'.[646] Even worse for him was the statement 'one man, one vote within one political entity'. This meant 'destruction,' a 'sort of suicide', which no nation in the world would be prepared to commit.

This Afrikaner state was challenged on several fronts, but nothing suggested its imminent demise. The state was being isolated by way of a dense mesh of sanctions; financial sanctions, taking the form of a refusal to roll over bank loans, made it all but impossible to attract new foreign investment or overcome the burden of a serious problem of balancing payments. Nevertheless, trade sanctions were being circumvented, albeit at a cost, as new markets outside Europe and the United States opened up. The economy was projected to continue to grow at a rate of 2 to 3 per cent per year. While with brief exceptions the urban centres and white residential suburbs remained calm, the state was severely shaken by a series of civil protests bordering on insurrection in the segregated black townships, leading first to the partial imposition of a state of emergency in 1985 and then to a nationwide one in 1986. The draconian emergency measures failed to stamp out all resistance, but by and large stability had returned by the late 1980s. In 1989 the leadership of the banned ANC, which spearheaded the struggle for black liberation, felt compelled to acknowledge to its cadres that it lacked the capacity to escalate the armed struggle in any significant way. Two years earlier Mangosuthu Buthelezi, the main black leader operating within the apartheid structures, had commented scathingly on the absence of any visible signs of the liberation struggle: 'After 25 years of endeavour every bridge in the country is still intact. Every system of electricity and water supply is intact and there is not a single factory out of production because of revolutionary activity. The classical circumstances in which an armed struggle wins the day . . . are just not present in South Africa.'[647]

The ANC-led resistance also took the form of a mass-based popular revolt consisting of rent and service charge boycotts, political strikes and stay-aways, marches and demonstrations. These forms of mass action, which took place during the 1980s and after the unbanning of the ANC in February 1990, were far more successful in weakening regime morale than the guerrilla struggle. But well-placed observers and leaders of the ANC struggle recognised that these actions would not defeat the regime. Chester Crocker, US Assistant Secretary of State in the 1980s, declared in a study published in 1992 that the resistance 'had no hope of forcing the government to capitulate, but the government could no longer hope to regain the legitimacy it had lost in the 1980s'.[648] This was confirmed by the ANC's chief strategist, Joe Slavo, who at a critical stage in the negotiations wrote in the ANC mouthpiece *Mayibuye*: 'The enemy is not defeated.'[649] In November 1996 Nelson Mandela spoke critically of 'superficial' black journalists who 'assume that we have defeated the whites on a battlefield and that the whites are now lying on the floor helpless and begging for mercy and that we can impose conditions on them'.[650]

Yet by the end of 1996, less than ten years after Buthelezi's comment, the Afrikaners had lost all formal political power. The ANC held 62 per cent of the parliamentary seats as opposed to 20 per cent for the NP, the largest opposition party in a parliament that operated in the classic Westminster mode of majoritarianism. Having had its demand for a constitutionally entrenched, power-sharing cabinet rejected, the NP had withdrawn from the Government of

National Unity in which the negotiating parties had agreed to participate for an interim period of five years, ending in 1999. At the senior levels of the bureaucracy and the state television and radio corporation, Afrikaner incumbents were rapidly replaced by ANC supporters, mostly blacks or Indians. While still headed by Afrikaners, the police and defence force showed every sign of being loyal to the new government and the constitution. A new economic advance was taking place, one spearheaded by two black companies financially backed by the largest Afrikaner conglomerate, Sanlam. The black share of companies on the Johannesburg Stock Exchange looked set to soon match or even surpass that of the Afrikaner share.[651]

Orthodoxy and revision

These developments startled the world and prompted Nelson Mandela to refer to South Africa's transition as a 'small miracle.' The London *Financial Times* commented that the regime change was one of the most extraordinary political transformations of the twentieth century, where 'the people have defied the logic of their past and broken all the rules of social theory'.[652] One of the most common theoretical assumptions was that a ruling ethnic minority with a deep attachment to a 'homeland' could neither be forced to give up power nor would it willingly do so. During the apartheid years these two propositions were recurring themes in the political writings of Alan Paton, novelist, foremost liberal, and lifelong student of the Afrikaner mind. Paton was convinced that if attempts were made to force the Afrikaner to accept majority rule in a unitary state, he 'would rather be destroyed than yield'. Yet Paton also believed that the Afrikaners could turn away from domination and choose what he termed 'the common society' within a federal state. His latest biographer neatly captures the essence of his convictions on this issue. '[Change] would come about only when the Afrikaner leaders came to the realisation that it must. He did not imagine that they would be forced from power by blacks, or that Liberals by some electoral ju-jitsu might take their place. The initiative, he believed, would remain with the Afrikaner until the Afrikaner chose to give it up.'[653]

When the Afrikaners did give up power in the first half of the 1990s, analysts tried hard to explain the unanticipated development. One explanation, succumbing to what Bergson called 'the illusion of retrospective determinism' (i.e. what actually happened had to happen), deems it to have been inevitable. In this vein a recent study of the NP concludes that the combination of external and internal pressures made it 'virtually impossible' for the apartheid government to maintain its existing practices by late 1989.[654] A much stronger case can, however, be made for the view that under President PW Botha, who resigned for health reasons in 1989, or under several possible successors other than FW de Klerk, the NP could and would have dominated the country into the next century, introducing new but quite unworkable policies designed to keep Afrikaner control. The question is: why did the Afrikaner leadership not pursue this course?

Some analysts embrace the explanations of what Walker Connor in a famous critique called the 'nation-building school', which he contends generalises on the basis of First World polities. Connor took issue with this school's central assumption that the well-spring of ethnic discord is not identity needs but economic demands, making it possible for ethnonational groups to be bought off if their material interests are guaranteed.[655] Among analysts studying the Afrikaners' surrender of power there is no shortage of those who believe that consumerism saved South Africa. One commentator wrote: '[We] avoided a civil war [because] many whites were presented with a choice between their political power and their consumer goods – and quickly chose the latter.'[656] In a similar vein a sociological analysis states: 'It yet has to be proven anywhere that a BMW-owning bureaucratic bourgeoisie with swimming pools and servants readily sacrifices the good life for psychologically gratifying ethnic affinities.'[657] This ignores the fact that perhaps 90 per cent of Afrikaners were not in this class and that more than four-fifths of Afrikaners in polls taken in the 1980s indicated that they believed that the income and living standards of whites under black majority rule would suffer. In August 1992, when it began to be clear that the ANC would dominate the next government, two-thirds of whites were 'not at all convinced' that their pensions or savings were safe under a new government, as against only 12 per cent who were.[658] If the NP's constituency, as distinct from its negotiators, was so alarmed about its material prospects, the question that needs to be answered is not whether we are dealing with an effete bourgeoisie but why whites allowed their representatives to put their future at risk.

A third explanation explores the possibility that the Afrikaner surrender was the result not so much of rampant consumerism but of an ideological collapse.

According to this view, there was an inherent weakness in the NP's 'culture of domination' and a singular lack of moral authority when confronted by a confident ANC leadership extolling human rights and non-racialism – positions all backed by the Western world, which the Afrikaners took as their frame of reference.[659] Again the question is: if it was inherently so weak, why did apartheid, as one of the world's most hated systems, last so long? Why were Botha and others prepared to prolong it well beyond 1994?

Finally, one can note a fourth explanation. This argues that the NP simply miscalculated in the negotiations and constitution-making process, which stretched from February 1990 to December 1996. Whereas De Klerk at one stage had openly expressed his conviction that the NP would 'have its hands on the tiller for many years to come',[660] he was reduced at the end of the process to a position of haggling over the perks that would go with the job of being the official Leader of the Opposition in a one-party dominant system.

This chapter will align itself more closely with the latter two explanations but will discuss the themes and questions within the broader context of Afrikaner mobilisation and its ideology of ethnic survival. The essential argument is that, just as apartheid was based on the idea that it could ensure Afrikaner ethnic survival, the regime change of 1994 was brought about not so much by middle-class interests superseding the emotional identification in Afrikaner thinking but by the belief that apartheid could no longer be sustained by a shrinking white minority. Once the apartheid idea had collapsed, there was no alternative ideology that could justify Afrikaner or white supremacy or even significant minority protection as distinct from individual rights.

Confronting the ethnic survival crises

Early in the 1970s a sociologist and pollster in South Africa observed that, because of popular myths and perceptions, significant proportions of whites in South Africa were oriented towards survival rather than domination and that the latter was an inevitable consequence of the former. He added that any analysis had to contend with what he called 'gut-level fears and anxieties'.[661] The most prominent theme in Afrikaners' political thinking during the apartheid era was an obsession with the way in which the Afrikaners as a small nation could contend with different survival crises. Afrikaner nationalists commonly believed that survival in a hostile environment could only be secured if they kept the power that they had won in 1948. As an Afrikaner opponent of the NP leaders observed in 1959: 'They regard it [political power] as an essential safeguard for their survival as a nation.' Any threat to it 'instantly calls for resistance which may be stirred to fanatic vehemence by the urge for national self-preservation'.[662]

At the most basic level there were Afrikaner fears about physical survival, which must be seen against the backdrop of settler history, dating back to 1652, when a small Afrikaner population lived among great numbers of indigenous peoples in a vast territory. These fears and anxieties were not idiosyncratic. Explaining the unwillingness of Afrikaners to cede or share power, the historian Lewis Gann wrote in 1959 that in societies in Africa, Eastern Europe and Russia there was no underlying harmony on which a democracy could be built – only minorities with conflicting ideals, interests, fears and grave anxieties. For dominant minorities, matters like national identity and political self-determination are not mere abstractions, but a matter of life and death: they know that they can expect rough treatment once they become subject to a nationally distinct majority. As Gann observes: 'This will especially be true if the minorities appear to be possessed of more than their fair share of economic wealth; then they are likely to be liquidated altogether.'[663] A thought very much along these lines was once expressed by the most respected Afrikaner poet and essayist, NP van Wyk Louw. He wrote that if the Afrikaners lost power and became a mere expatriate minority they would be 'as helpless as the Jews in Germany'.[664]

The Mau Mau uprising in Kenya, the mass evacuation of French settlers from Algeria, and the chaotic Belgian retreat from the Congo were all deeply unsettling to whites in South Africa. Afrikaans newspapers provided full and often lurid accounts of these traumatic events. Fear of an equally violent catastrophe lay close to the core of Afrikaner thought, giving rise to a series of draconian security laws. Liberals like Paton or Helen Suzman rightly criticised these laws but made little effort to come to grips with the descent into disorder and despotism in many other African countries and the realistic fear that these developments could be replicated at the tip of the continent. Despite the fact that not only the state but also many private white citizens armed themselves, the fear did not subside. By 1987 four-fifths of Afrikaners stated in a national poll that under black majority rule the physical safety of whites would be threatened and white women would be molested.[665] In 1990, two months after negotiations started, 49 per cent of whites agreed with the statement that there was reason to fear for their own safety and that of their family in the future; 43 per cent felt otherwise.[666]

Although fears about physical survival were not always openly expressed, concerns over white material survival were always prominent in the public debate. As a result of their late urbanisation Afrikaners struggled to make headway in the urban economy. When the NP came to power in 1948 about two-thirds of the Afrikaners consisted of blue collar and other manual workers or struggling farmers who soon afterwards had to leave their land. Both classes needed state support to maintain themselves as part of the white dominant group. Apartheid was at heart an attempt to turn the white poor into a state-subsidised petty bourgeoisie, properly housed and clothed, protected from black competition, and socialised in white supremacist behaviour. This was not achieved overnight, and white South Africa retained a predominantly working-class character for quite some time. Blue collar and other manual workers formed 50 per cent of the employed white population in 1971 and 44 per cent in 1983.[667] By this latter date, the government could proceed with more confidence in the field of industrial desegregation. In the meantime, however, increasing numbers of Afrikaners found employment in the state sector. By 1968, twice as many Afrikaners were in public sector jobs than before 1948. Ten years later more than a third of Afrikaners were employed in this sector as compared to only a quarter of other whites. A great concentration of white middle-class workers in the state sector developed. By 1990, 46 per cent of all white middle-class employment outside the primary sectors was in the state sector.

It is sometimes argued that South Africa's democratisation in the 1990s was made possible by the success of both apartheid and capitalism in turning the white electorate into an independent middle class with a diminishing need for the state. This perspective must be questioned. White state employees would inevitably be threatened by any shift to black majority rule. Furthermore, the distribution of wealth within white society had become quite unequal, with the top quintile controlling four-fifths of the wealth at the end of the 1970s. While the incomes of the top three quintiles in the white group had stagnated between

1975 and 1991, those of the lowest two had declined by a staggering 40 per cent in the same period. These figures hardly present us with the profile of a white community as independently wealthy and able to prosper in the face of a hostile or indifferent black regime.[668]

If political domination advanced white material interests, its longer-term effect on Afrikaner cultural survival was more ambiguous. To paraphrase Milan Kundera on the Czech struggle, the fact that Afrikaner people as a distinctive ethnic group have survived during the past century has less to do with political cunning or armed force than with the huge intellectual effort that went into a small nation developing Afrikaans as a 'high-culture' language, to use Ernest Gellner's term.[669] Afrikaans originated in the first two centuries of settlement as a Dutch-based vernacular spoken by settlers, slaves and indigenous peoples. Turning away from both Dutch and English to build up Afrikaans constituted a choice, a project or, to use Pascal's term, a wager. Originally branded a 'kitchen language', Afrikaans was deliberately turned into what was called a white man's or civilised language. Furthermore – and this was ultimately of paramount importance – the white Afrikaner nation came to see its distinctive identity as expressed by that language. In 1925 Afrikaans became an official language, and the Afrikaner nationalist movement thereafter concentrated much of its efforts on ensuring that Afrikaans assumed an equal role alongside English as the medium of public discourse. A surprisingly vibrant literature soon developed, and Afrikaans took its place in science, technology and the marketplace. In nationalist thinking, the people's very existence was manifested in the 'living language' of Afrikaans.

After the NP came to power in 1948, it enforced the principle of mother-tongue education at the school level, while five universities catered to Afrikaners at the tertiary level. The government constantly emphasised the constitutional provision that Afrikaans and English be treated on an equal footing, but it used this provision flexibly in the schools. The fear gradually developed that the future of Afrikaans was in jeopardy if the subordinate population spurned it. When the government embarked on a massive extension in the provision of education to blacks in the early 1970s, it also attempted to impose the equality principle in black schools in townships around Johannesburg and other towns in the Transvaal province. It stipulated that all black pupils in these areas had to take Afrikaans as a subject and be taught mathematics and social science with Afrikaans as the only language of instruction. This was the fateful precipitant that caused the so-called Soweto Riots of 1976, by far the most serious black uprising at that point against apartheid.

By now Afrikaans had become widely identified as the language of the oppressor – the medium used when policemen arrested blacks or when officials instructed blacks to show their pass, which was the most effective check on black urbanisation. Black resistance was expressed in a rejection of Afrikaans and Afrikaners. The more apartheid in its own terms 'succeeded' by getting blacks to accept 'self-government' in their own 'homelands', the more Afrikaans as a language failed. One after the other 'homeland' government chose English and an indigenous language as its official languages. The future of Afrikaans was threatened from two sides. Its close association with domination was like an albatross round its neck. At the same time, however, there was every prospect that a black government would elevate English to the status of sole official language, spelling the end of Afrikaans and Afrikaans culture – and, with it, the demise of the Afrikaner people.[670] The demographic picture was ominous. The best possible Afrikaner ally was the coloured people, a predominantly Afrikaans-speaking group almost as large as the white Afrikaners. Apartheid had alienated their elite, who were now turning to English. Whereas 18 per cent of South African people spoke Afrikaans as their mother tongue in 1970, only 15 per cent was projected to do so in 2000.

There was, lastly, also a question about the ethical quality of survival. Prominent intellectuals pursued the chimera of a just solution, or less ambitiously counselled against a patently unjust one, to the country's racial problem. The most eloquent and lasting contribution was an essay by NP van Wyk Louw, which analysed the different survival crises that conceivably confronted a small people like the Afrikaners. These included military defeat, mass immigration, and absorption by an Anglo-Saxon or Bantu-speaking (African) nation. For intellectuals, however, the greatest of these crises would occur 'when a large number of our people come to believe that we need not live together in *justice* [Louw's emphasis] with other ethnic groups; when they come to believe that mere survival is the chief issue, not a just existence'. Succumbing to this 'final temptation' could have grave consequences since it could lead to a critical number of intellectuals withdrawing their allegiance (something Louw never did). Louw posed the question: 'Is it possible for a small people to survive for long if it becomes hateful or even evil in the eyes of the best people in – or outside – its ranks?' He believed that it was possible for his people one day to emerge from the 'dark night of the soul' and say, 'I would rather go down than survive in injustice'.[671]

A socio-political order and a justificatory framework were needed to deal with the threats and challenges on all the different levels – political, physical, material, cultural and ethical. Afrikaner nationalists believed they had found the answer in apartheid. This was not only an ideology but also an ethnic survival system that fostered and concealed Afrikaner domination. It comprised two parts: an ethnonationalism as the base and apartheid as a body of operating principles. The nationalist part of the system was an assemblage of loosely formulated beliefs, values and fears. On one level there was a special claim to the land based on the spurious assumption that the greatest part of the land was empty when the settlement was founded at the Cape in the mid-seventeenth century. On another level the claim was made that Afrikaner political power and cultural identity rested on a covenant or contract with an all-knowing God.[672] This was soon extended to an argument stressing the centrality of nations in God's creation and their God-given separate destinies.

A nationalist ideology, however, rarely has clear and coherent ideas about a proper political and social order. Apartheid developed as an action-related system of ideas taking the Afrikaner historical experience as its point of departure and projecting that onto other peoples in the country. Just as the Afrikaners had thrown off British cultural hegemony, so the black people, according to the ideology, had to realise their own separate ethnic identity and build up their own ethnic power base. Apartheid, however, was not the rationale or the end of the system of rule. Already in the late 1960s John Vorster, who had become Prime Minister in 1966, said that apartheid was merely the means by which an Afrikaner identity could be retained, maintained and kept 'immortal' within a white sovereign state. He added: 'If there were better means to achieve the same end they had to be found.'[673] This was an approach to which all his successors subscribed.

Until the final decade of its rule the NP leadership continued to believe that, conceptually, apartheid was an ethically justifiable system that enabled all the 'nations' in South Africa to survive. However, it became increasingly difficult to reconcile the contradiction between the ideal and the harsh reality, consisting as it did of black 'homelands' that were not economically viable, the annual arrest of hundreds of thousands of pass-law offenders seeking work in the cities, the prosecution of those who transgressed the racial sex laws, and so on. Whereas the apartheid system in the 1950s and 1960s almost unthinkingly exploited an uneducated, poorly trained labour force, of whom a large complement were migrants, the realisation dawned in the early 1970s that this super-exploitation was bad not only for economic growth but for future white security. In 1971 a cabinet minister warned about the huge racial wage gap, declaring that 'such gigantic differences in living standards . . . would lead to murder and violence'.

After a wave of industrial strikes by extremely poorly paid black workers in 1973, Prime Minister John Vorster exhorted employers to treat blacks not 'as labour units, but as human beings with souls'. The government took the lead by narrowing the racial wage gap in the public sector, but vast inequities remained. The Soweto uprising imparted a greater urgency, particularly after PW Botha came to power in 1978. He told party followers: 'We are moving into a changing world. We must adapt, otherwise we shall die.' He also urged them to learn the lessons of their own history: 'the moment you start oppressing people . . . they fight back. We must acknowledge people's rights and . . . make ourselves free by giving to others in a spirit of justice what we demand for ourselves.'[674]

At the same time, the leadership gave the assurance that white security remained of paramount importance. The government claimed that the country was confronted with a 'total onslaught', which assailed the entire socio-political order. According to government spokesmen, the overriding consideration was 'survival'. But there was no real moral basis for the appeal of the Afrikaner and the larger white minority for support in their struggle. The harsh reality was that the world backed minorities only when they expressed moral and political principles that the outside world felt should not be suppressed. To the outside world, the white minority embodied, above all, crass materialism. While smarting under this global, and particularly Western, condemnation, the NP had no intention of giving up power as it entered the 1980s. However, fatal systemic weaknesses persuaded a new leadership to find a different solution to the crisis.[675]

The undermining of a system

While obnoxious to the world, the system of Afrikaner domination was quite stable at the beginning of the 1980s, resting as it did on three pillars: vastly superior state power, white unity, and black political fragmentation. Over the next decade this system disintegrated until it finally was abolished in the mid-1990s. The system was undermined on the one hand by long-term demographic and economic trends and on the other hand by swelling black resistance. This produced such ideological and political disarray in Afrikaner leadership ranks that they decided to risk the unbanning of the liberation movements, followed by negotiations for a power-sharing system. The lack of any strategic vision on the leadership's part, coupled with tough bargaining by the ANC negotiators, produced the outcome very few had expected and many feared: largely untrammelled majority rule in a unitary state.

The changing demographic equation, and more specifically the rapidly shrinking white minority, distinguishes the South African conflict most strikingly from all other ethnic conflicts. Seen against the broad sweep of South Africa's history, one of a handful of really important facts is that until the mid-twentieth century the proportion of whites relative to the total population was always sufficient to occupy all the strategic positions in the political, economic and administrative systems in the country. Unlike, say, the colonisers in the north-eastern parts of colonial Brazil, whites in South Africa never needed to establish a free, semi-skilled mulatto class to occupy the intermediate positions in the system of domination. By the middle of the twentieth century, however, a vital change had begun to make itself felt. Between 1910 and 1960 whites constituted 20 per cent of the total population, but by 1960 the white demographic base began to shrink. By 1985 the white segment had fallen to 15 per cent, and it is projected to fall to 11 per cent by 2010. An acute shortage of white manpower began to develop in both the public and private sectors. This shortage increasingly forced employers in the private sector to breach the industrial colour bar to meet the need for skilled and semi-skilled manpower. The state had overreached itself in both its spending and administrative capacities in trying to control blacks. The mammoth Department of Bantu Administration and Development found itself incapable of stemming the flow of blacks to the cities. 'Voting with their feet', urbanising blacks brought about a 'silent revolution'. While blacks accounted for only half of all city dwellers in the mid-1980s, they were projected to outnumber all other groups by three to one by 2000. Blacks became homeowners and entrepreneurs and started to dominate vital segments of consumer spending.[676]

South Africa's economy began to stagnate in the mid-1970s after fifty years of impressive growth of about 5 per cent per year. Between 1975 and 1991 the annual rate of growth fell to only 1.6 per cent, well below the 3 per cent annual population increase.[677] Real per capita income in the period slumped by about 25 per cent. Some of the decline in the growth rate was due to factors over which the state had little control, such as the rise in energy prices after 1973 and the weaker market for South African commodities. Behind the country's economic woes, however, there also lay a long story of economic mismanagement. Ironically, the economic malaise sprang mostly from the determination to make white South Africa economically self-sufficient and capable of repulsing any threat to its political autonomy. South Africa could afford to do so since its economy was largely built around gold, which was assured of a market, albeit at a fixed price until the early 1970s. There was, however, a serious downside. Firstly, gold is a finite and declining resource. As the mining industry was forced to increase wages in the early 1970s, its share of the Western world's gold production began to decline steadily. Secondly, the white demand for security, coupled with the luxury of having gold as a major export earner, produced a quite uncompetitive manufacturing sector. The drive towards import-substitution dates back to the 1920s, when the government started to build high tariff walls and established the Iron and Steel Corporation. Little effort went into becoming efficient enough to export. By the early 1990s manufacturing exports per capita were lower than any upper-middle-income country except Brazil.

The state also introduced other policies designed to make the ruling group invulnerable. After the Second World War massive plants to extract oil from coal were built as part of a plan to raise the country's oil production to a half of its domestic requirements. State aid to agriculture by 1970 provided on average one-fifth of a white farmer's income. To prevent black migration to the cities, the state put numerous obstacles in the way of black employment, with the result that production became increasingly capital-intensive and labour-saving – this in a country with abundant sources of labour. To placate white workers, the training of blacks for more skilled work was made a low priority. Labour productivity stopped growing in 1980 and capital productivity declined by over 30 per cent between 1970 and 1991. Employment in the private sector dropped by 47,000 jobs during the 1980s. By 1990 fewer than 10 out of 100 new entrants could find work in the job market of the formal sector of the economy. Between a quarter and a third of the economically active black labour force could not find regular employment. This greatly aggravated the incidence of both political violence and crime.

The economy had already started to shed black labour in the early 1970s. Realising the security threat this posed, the government made two fateful decisions in order to promote economic growth. The first was to expand greatly the provision of black education and, with that, the productivity of black labour. In 1960 there were only 717 blacks in the most senior classes in school. By the mid-1980s there were just over 50,000 black and 50,000 white university matriculants, but by 2000 it is predicted that seven out of ten matriculants will be black. By the end of the 1980s the urban black population was far better educated and trained – and much more radicalised – than before. Surveys consistently showed that the higher the level of education of blacks, the more acute their political discontent and the more pressing their demands. It was schoolchildren and students with little hope of finding acceptable jobs who spearheaded the successful ANC-led efforts of the 1980s to disrupt the black educational system and make the black townships ungovernable.

The other fateful decision was made in 1979 when the government scrapped statutory job reservation and all other impediments to the advancement and training of black workers. It also allowed black trade unions to participate in the statutory industrial relations system. Blacks now enjoyed effective industrial civil rights without any meaningful political rights. The government's expectation that the black trade union movement would not become politicised quickly proved to be quite misguided. In fact, it became the best organised part of the liberation movement, arranging strikes and 'rolling mass action' at critical points to back up black demands and weaken the will of NP negotiators in the early 1990s. In an effort by employers to buy off militant black workers, wage increases were granted, but they were unaccompanied by any commensurate improvement in productivity. The labour market became ever more rigid, worsening the unemployment crisis. Confronted with such a hostile environment, investors took fright. Gross fixed investment plummeted from 26 per cent of GDP in 1983 to 16 per cent in 1991 – a level at which it was impossible for the economy to grow, since a 14 per cent level was needed simply to replace the capital equipment that was wearing out. At the same time, government spending rose sharply from 15 to 21 per cent. This was partly the result of an effort to mollify white civil servants but also in order to provide services to the rapidly growing black population and to narrow racial pay differentials. To fund this increased spending, the government heavily taxed the middle- and upper-income sectors and borrowed so much that its debt rose from 5 to 19 per cent of the budget between 1975 and 1992.

The NP government realised that the country needed a more legitimate political framework in order to attract new investments. Taking the first step in the aftermath of the Soweto uprising, it started a process that led in 1984 to the incorporation of the coloured and Indian groups, forming 8 and 3 per cent of the population respectively, into a new tricameral parliamentary system. Although the 'other two' chambers had little power, the new Parliament irrevocably undermined the symbolism of white supremacy. Unexpectedly it also materially contributed to the destruction of two of the three pillars of the Afrikaners' power: their own unity and black political fragmentation.

Afrikaner political unity was finally shattered when the Conservative Party (CP) was founded in 1982 after 18 parliamentary representatives of the NP had broken away over the issue of 'power-sharing' with coloureds and Indians. It managed to win over 40 to 50 per cent of Afrikaners in the next ten years. Although there were class dimensions to the split, with the CP based more strongly on lower-income Afrikaners than the NP, the real line of division concerned different ways of securing Afrikaner political survival. The split ended the life of the NP as a purely ethnic party. Government policy was no longer the tortuous outcome of several battles fought on different sites in the nationalist movement. The party had become a catch-all (white) party, with the votes of English-speakers constituting more than 42 per cent of its support in the 1987 election. The political leadership increasingly assumed a vanguard role. There was a major reduction of accountability as the NP parliamentary caucus became marginalised, with NP leaders strengthening technocratic forms of decision-making.

No longer constrained in the same way by the checks on power that a nationalist movement traditionally imposes on its leadership, NP leaders began to resemble free-floating political entrepreneurs, guided less by loyalty to the ethnic cause than by calculations about their place in the future centres of power. FW de Klerk and his future chief negotiator, Roelf Meyer, who as ethnic politicians had previously opposed reforms of the apartheid order (De Klerk did so until 1987), would as negotiators be more willing to retreat in the face of ANC demands than their NP colleagues, who earlier had been considered much more liberal.

The South African state had turned into a multi-racial state that relied on racially mixed security forces to impose order and on black homeland leaders like Chief Gatsha Buthelezi to counter the ANC-led movement to isolate South Africa economically and internationally. The NP now rested on a broader base, but it had lost almost all ideological cohesion. In two polls, one undertaken in 1977 and the other in 1992, Afrikaners were asked to rate what they considered to be the most important policy of their party. The responses were largely identical: at 27 per cent in both polls white security was the highest priority, while language and culture rated seventh in 1977 at 1 per cent. Fifteen years later it was eighth at 3 per cent. One could argue that language and culture were so well protected that there was little reason to be worried, but the result still is remarkable testimony to the waning of specifically Afrikaans cultural concerns during the apartheid era.[678] The dream of an exclusive white land had vanished as streams of impoverished blacks flowed to the outskirts of the cities and trickled into the white suburbs, raising fears about a collapse of 'First World' standards. White voters were persuaded that the old order of black exclusion from power had finally come to an end. They were prepared to accept blacks in government provided a new political order guaranteed security, predictable politicians, competent bureaucrats, a strong economy and secure property rights. Afrikaners and the larger white community still strongly insisted on what Walker Connor calls the freedom from domination by non-members, which in practical terms meant separate white political representation and a white veto. In Africa, however, that constituted white privilege, and that was what the ANC's struggle was about.

Such had been the outrage of blacks over their exclusion from the Tricameral Parliament that another pillar of white power, namely the lack of black unity, had disappeared. All government efforts failed to attract moderate black leaders with demonstrable support into talks about drafting a new constitution. For the first time in a century sufficient black unity existed in the greatest part of the country to prevent the government from using black moderates as a shield in a form of indirect rule. The uprising of 1984–6 all but eliminated the credibility of black councillors elected in the 1980s to run the black townships, none of which had a proper revenue base. Reluctant to devolve any power to the Natal region for fear of losing control, the government by the mid-1980s had alienated Chief Buthelezi, the only internal leader with a mass base. Except in rural Natal, where Buthelezi held sway, the ANC or its proxies were able to prevent any black movement not under its control from becoming a significant force. The state re-established a large degree of control by the end of 1986, but it had become clear that popular resistance could not be crushed altogether. At the end of the 1980s the security forces had begun to give up on winning the hearts-and-minds battle. Mike Louw, who was a senior officer in the National Intelligence Service (he became its head in 1992), remembers the situation in the late 1980s as follows: 'Nowhere was the situation out of hand, but it was clear that politically and morally we were losing. Everywhere in the black townships we encountered intimidation and a strong political consciousness. The political system had become obsolete and a long, bloody struggle lay ahead. It had become clear that the sooner we negotiated a new system the better.'[679]

In a perceptive article on South Africa, published in 1981, Samuel Huntington made the point that revolutionary violence does not have to be successful to be effective. It simply has to create sufficient strife and concern in the dominant group about ways to deal with it. Once the leadership is no longer able to apply its instruments of coercion ruthlessly, a crucial pillar of the system of domination disintegrates.[680] This was what started to happen by the second half of the 1980s. The government's inability to find a moderate black leadership with whom to negotiate produced a deadlock in government. An account of the meeting of a special cabinet committee held in March 1986 shows how fundamental the differences in the power elite were. President Botha remarked that he did not favour one man, one vote in a unitary or federal state, adding: 'I thought . . . we had clarity, but I do not think we have it anymore, because you want me to say we stand for a unitary South Africa. You allow me to say it, you write it in my speeches and I accept it, but what do we mean by that?' FW de Klerk commented that he could live with a rotating presidency, but 'somewhere there must be somebody who had enough power in his hands, somewhere in a good government there must be a PW Botha who had the power and authority to ensure that things went right in the country'.[681] As will be seen, De Klerk's hope that there would be white representation in a mixed cabinet, underpinned by some institutionalised form of power, became his main negotiating goal in the early 1990s.

The Afrikaner elite recognised that remaining in an impasse was also dangerous. In mid-1986 the Afrikaner Broederbond, the secret communication channel between the government and the elite, issued a circular to that effect, entitled 'Political Values for the Survival of the Afrikaner'. It declared that 'the greatest risk that we are taking today is not taking any risks'. The abolition of statutory discrimination had become a 'prerequisite for survival' while black exclusion from politics 'had become a threat to survival'. It concluded that the State President did not have to be white and that ultimately the future of the Afrikaners depended on their will to survive and their faith and energy.[682] Also in 1986, the Dutch Reformed Church, by far the largest of the Afrikaner churches, finally abandoned its support for apartheid as a system, having long justified it theologically. It decided to follow the New rather than the Old Testament, pointing out that the idea of race plays no part whatsoever in the New Testament while the idea of the diversity of peoples is always presented biblically within the context of unity. The church also abandoned some other cherished ideas: that it was one with the Afrikaner people, that it was the moral conscience of the *volk* and state, and that the Scriptures presented a particular model for race relations. For the first time it specifically stated that racism was a sin. Implicitly this meant that the vaunting of any group over others was racism and hence a sin. Afrikaners could no longer think of themselves as a chosen people; the idea of the covenant was dead.[683]

Towards democratic uncertainty

While ethnic groups only relinquish power in exceptional circumstances, they almost always seek allies. This is particularly true of the Afrikaners, a small and basically insecure group. The apartheid system, which appropriated a monopoly of power, was something of an anomaly in Afrikaner history. The more than three centuries of settlement in South Africa are studded with totally unexpected Afrikaner alliances or proposed alliances with unlikely partners, ranging from African chiefs and imperialists to socialists. When the government confronted the deep impasse in the white–black power struggle at the end of the 1980s, it knew its constituency would welcome any major black partner that could assist it in dealing with the intractable problems of massive black poverty, unemployment and crime. The dominant political question had now become not whether to take a black party into government – to that, all except the right wing agreed – but whether the ANC constituted such a partner.

A more important question, however, was whether this black–white cooperation should occur in a democratic context. Some analysts argued in the mid-1980s that the introduction of universal franchise had become possible because little cultural distance characterised white–black relations. The two largely shared the Christian religion and had become economically interdependent.[684] Roelf Meyer, the chief NP negotiator in the latter half of the negotiations, endorsed this view when visiting Belfast in mid-1996 with his ANC counterpart, Cyril Ramaphosa. Meyer indicated that he believed it wrong to compare the South African experience with that of Northern Ireland because 'we [in South Africa] basically had no fundamental differences to resolve'. He continued: 'It was almost as simple as a matter of colour or race that separated us. We had to remove the problem to reach out to each other, and to discover each other as human beings.'[685]

Meyer's reference to the 'simple matter' of race and colour that separated whites and blacks can be seen as a collapse of both the ideology of apartheid and of Afrikaner ethnonationalism and the historical and political claims and status associations attached to it. His statement can be read as testimony to the unqualified ideological victory of the anti-apartheid movement worldwide and of modernisation theory, which postulates the eradication of ethnic and racial differences within a common society. There was one problem: this view was not shared by the constituency that Meyer and his party represented. In successive polls in the final years of the 1980s, only a third of whites agreed that whites and Africans had enough common values to create a future democratic government. After the ANC's unbanning, the figure increased and reached 59 per cent in mid-1992, but after a series of attacks on whites it dropped again to a third by the end of 1992. Once questions became more specific, dramatic differences were revealed. In a 1992 poll the following statement was made: 'South Africa is an African country where others have to take second place.' Of blacks 56 per cent agreed with this statement as against only 5 per cent of whites. In a 1986 poll only 3 per cent of Afrikaners (and 8 per cent of English-speakers) were prepared to accept a unitary state with one parliament and one vote for every person.[686]

In such a context the government was increasingly attracted to the paradigm of consociationalism or power-sharing as an alternative to the Westminster form of majority rule. It had billed the Tricameral Parliament (incorrectly) as power-sharing, and its constituency considered this non-threatening. Why not try it with blacks? In discussions between 1971 and 1990 with NP politicians, Arend Lijphart, the internationally renowned proponent of consociationalism, argued that they were making a big mistake if they thought that their choice was between a broad sharing of power and exclusive white (and Afrikaner) power. He told them their only real choice was between sharing power and losing power.[687] In the end they accepted this argument, strongly believing that negotiations did not entail bargaining over only the transfer of power.

There were several factors that facilitated the pursuit of a power-sharing settlement with the ANC. Firstly there was Nelson Mandela, then still in jail and engaged in informal, secret talks with government officials. Almost without exception, NP leaders considered him a 'godsend', a man whose stature and integrity they immediately recognised. He was no moderate in NP terms but he consistently argued that majority rule, which he considered non-negotiable, had to be balanced by guarantees that ensured that white domination would not be replaced by black domination.

Secondly, De Klerk was a democrat and civilian politician. He viewed with distaste the sidelining of the cabinet under the state of emergency, which saw the State Security Council, comprising politicians and security officials, making the most important decisions. When De Klerk assumed control in 1989 he was assured of conservative backing in the party caucus, but the reformists were suspicious of him. Polls showed that the NP's support among white voters was being seriously eroded on both the left and the right while it remained paralysed about its future direction. De Klerk had no wish for security officials to be further involved in political decisions. That meant he had only one option for shoring up his base: he had to seek a political solution, which meant that he had to move to the left. Since the party fought the election in 1989 on the premise that the poll constituted the last one from which blacks were excluded, he had no more than five years to find that solution.

Thirdly, whites had enjoyed the franchise in South Africa for nearly 150 years, and there was little prospect of them supporting a solution in which they had to sacrifice their democratic rights. An important comparative article has recently argued that the consolidation of a democracy in Africa occurred in settler societies because there had been a tradition of electoral competition, unlike patrimonial regimes where competition previously had been outlawed.[688] Of course the settlers long blocked the extension of democracy or used a partial extension to thwart popular democracy. When the NP in the early 1980s incorporated coloured people and Indians in the democratic process, its chief propagandist privately presented it as '[broadening] our own power base and thus avoid turning them [coloureds] over to a black power situation'.[689] It was only when the NP leadership in the late 1980s was confronted with a stark choice between extending democracy to blacks and a costly battle of attrition that the democratic tradition of whites became an important variable. Having made the choice for democracy, the leadership could claim that black enfranchisement was not a break with or denial of history but actually in line with the political tradition of whites and their interests. Gerrit Viljoen, initially the government's chief negotiator, defended a negotiated democracy as indispensable for the survival of whites as a shrinking minority. He said in early 1990: '[We] who want change want it exactly because we realize that our survival depends on orderly change . . . The whole approach of government is to shift the emphasis from race to the quality of government and the broadening of democracy in spite of the risks.'[690]

The fall of the Berlin Wall two months after De Klerk became State President presented the NP with a large window of opportunity. De Klerk now told his constituency that without Soviet backing, the ANC was no longer a threat. With the entire world moving away from the socialist experiment, the ANC would be forced to respect private property and follow other investment-friendly policies. De Klerk began to use to great effect the argument that time would not be on the side of whites, and Afrikaners in particular. He argued that the settlement Ian Smith and white Rhodesians were forced to accept constituted a classic case of negotiations that had been delayed too long. Two months after his 2 February 1990 speech, he declared to a meeting held in the offices of *Die Burger*: 'We have not waited until the position of power dominance turned against us before we decided to negotiate a peaceful settlement. The initiative is in our hands. We have the means to ensure that the process develops peacefully and in an orderly way.'[691] In the period that followed, De Klerk and his senior ministers consistently spelt out that whites had a choice between being driven back into a corner or staging an outflanking movement that could yield a strategic position in a new, legitimate political system.

The NP entered the negotiations in 1990 from a position of strength and with a reasonably confident assumption that it could engineer a constitution that would severely restrict the power of the majority and thus diminish democratic uncertainty. Its negotiating proposals made provision for a rotating presidency as the kingpin of an intricate scheme that would carefully limit the power of the majority and that of the minority (or minorities). The NP ended the negotiations in 1996, having failed to secure any of its major political and cultural objectives. Instead of non-elected negotiating parties drawing up the constitution over a prolonged period of time (as the NP proposed), an elected constituent assembly did so (as was the ANC's position). Instead of a power-sharing cabinet and rotating presidency within a federal system (NP), there would be a largely unitary state and majority decision-making in both the executive and legislative branches. These branches would effectively be fused and dominated by the largest party in the typical Westminster style (ANC). Drawing more than 80 per cent of the black vote in the 1994 election, the ANC was assured of remaining the dominant party for quite some time. Economically the NP got its way when the ANC accepted the market system and property rights, but in cultural affairs it had little reason for satisfaction. The recognition of eleven languages looked like a barely concealed formula for making English the sole official language, and the ANC refused to grant either mother-tongue education or single-medium schools unconditionally. The cultural autonomy of Afrikaans schools and universities was heavily qualified by the insistence that English streams be introduced in these institutions to provide greater access to blacks.

We are left with two main questions. Why did the NP concede so much in the negotiations, ending up not with power-sharing but with majority rule? Why did its white constituency accept majority rule, which more than 90 per cent had firmly rejected in polls taken in the late 1980s?

The following explanations seem plausible. Firstly, apartheid had used or debased all the available capital that normally goes with the demands that ethnonational minorities make to ensure their survival. In the negotiations the NP was unable to argue convincingly that the Afrikaners or the larger white group as a whole constituted a minority rather than a former dominant group. It was impossible to demand that the NP as a white party be given a veto and at the same time pretend that it had made a decisive break with apartheid, which, by its own admission, had failed. The NP could make no territorial or federal claims since Afrikaners lived dispersed all over the country and since neither they nor the larger white group commanded a majority in any region. The formal acceptance of 'Western standards' across racial lines made it impossible for the NP to argue that there were unique cultural values that had to be specially protected.

As a result of all this, the NP decided to pursue a non-racial position and make the party the expression of values and interests. Apart from its traditional middle-class white base, the NP also attracted lower-income coloured people, middle-class Indians, and a small section of conservative blacks across the class spectrum. It also claimed to be the representative of the specific interests of business, civil servants and the security forces. All this strengthened the ANC's argument that the country's politics were about interests and not race, making an 'ordinary' (Mandela's word) liberal democracy feasible. To counter this, the NP had to make the obvious point that comparative evidence showed that in deeply divided societies there is normally no significant floating vote, which usually gives liberal democracies their vitality. Instead, race and ethnic affinities decisively determine voters' preferences. Hence, power-sharing was necessary to avoid the alienation of minorities and to provide a safe basis for investment. But the NP was unable to stand up to the ANC position that race and ethnicity had been tainted by apartheid and that no formal recognition should be given to these identities.

Secondly, the ANC retreat from nationalisation as a main plank of its platform made it more difficult for the NP to claim that its presence in government was indispensable for the protection of free enterprise. The NP had come to the free market position very late in the day, and the very state of the economy testified to its violation of some cardinal principles of neo-liberal economic management. There was a huge debt, the civil service was bloated, tariff walls were high, and corruption and white collar crime were rife. Apart from De Klerk and one or two others, the top echelons of the NP were far from impressive as politicians outside their traditional Afrikaner context. It was difficult to make the argument that the NP added much value to the governing process or that its administrative talents were indispensable.

Thirdly, the end of the Cold War weakened the NP position. There was now no reason for the West to back a conservative government. Mandela's stature and the ANC's long struggle for black liberation made it seem the natural successor of the NP. The US government started leaning towards the view that as long as the ANC subscribed to a market system, its political demands could be considered reasonable. At a critical point in the negotiations the US Assistant Secretary of State for African Affairs declared that all sides had to recognise 'the right of the majority to govern'. No side could insist on 'overly complex arrangements intended to guarantee a share of power to particular groups which will frustrate effective government. Minorities have the right to safeguards; they cannot expect a veto.'[692] The ANC itself could not have formulated it better.

Finally – and there is no other word for it – De Klerk lacked the necessary toughness to face down the ANC on critical points to ensure that his bottom-line demands were met. His great strength as a debater was also his weakness: he believed that he could persuade everyone of the reasonableness of his case or that some legalistic formula could always be found to paper over irreconcilable differences. When the ANC broke off negotiations in mid-1992 to embark on two months of rolling mass action, he was unable to sit this out. He believed that any security clampdown would destroy the chance of the remaining international sanctions being lifted soon. He also thought that there was a risk of an economic meltdown if there was a refusal to resume negotiations on the part of the ANC leadership, who had endured long periods in jail or had lived on low salaries in exile and who might be prepared to continue to do so to clinch victory. Only by sitting out the difficult period between July and September

1992 could De Klerk test the ANC leadership's resolve. However, as a man who in white politics was known as essentially a peacemaker and a centrist, he lacked the will to do so. In the end De Klerk set no conditions for a resumption of the negotiations and met almost all the ANC demands. The ANC had seized the upper hand. With increasing confidence Mandela rejected De Klerk's demands for formal power-sharing in the cabinet, treating them as attempts to cling to the vestiges of white power. All De Klerk could get was Mandela's verbal assurance that he needed him and that he had a role to play. That, however, was subordinate to Mandela's insistence on having the power to make the final decisions. The final deal was so far from the NP's original demands that when the cabinet met to ratify it, an outraged minister shouted at De Klerk: 'What have you done?! You have given South Africa away!!'[693]

The NP was now squarely confronted with majority rule, precisely what it had promised its constituency it would prevent. De Klerk still hoped to retain more than marginal influence by a good NP performance in the election. When the NP received 20 per cent of the vote instead of the 30 to 35 per cent De Klerk had expected, the hope of influence based on electoral strength was dashed. The other hope was that the NP would exert influence by acting as the gatekeeper to three powerful sectors: the business community, civil servants and the security forces. But all three had given up on the NP as it began to backtrack in the negotiations and as the ANC moved swiftly to give them assurances. Civil servants were promised their jobs or satisfactory retirement packages; the security forces were promised amnesty instead of a repeat of the Nuremberg trials; and the business community was assured that the new government considered private-sector investment as a top priority. Business quickly decided that a dominant party that comes to power through an election, tolerates an opposition, and respects civil rights constituted a sound platform for stability.

The puzzle remains: why did whites not revolt against the deal or overthrow De Klerk, given their resistance to majority rule? As the scion of a political family and former conservative, De Klerk enjoyed an extraordinary measure of trust. No member of the caucus could ever believe that he would betray that trust or his people. Every time resistance surfaced in caucus he argued that, short of security action, no alternatives existed. He could assure all the members of his caucus, of whom a great majority were professional politicians, that there was an excellent chance that they would continue their political careers in the new structures. He dealt with the white electorate by holding an all-white referendum asking only for an endorsement of the negotiations well before serious negotiations started. As details of the unthinkable emerged, whites were gripped by a mood of resignation. The dismantling of the apartheid system had started in the early 1970s, and every time the electorate had quickly adjusted to the new situation. This time, it was true, the matter was far more serious, but after almost seventy years of depending on an interventionist state, no white class – whether it be business, workers or civil servants – had retained the capacity to organise separately to challenge the political leadership.

The military formed a possible source of resistance. However, it was small (fewer than 70,000 full-time soldiers, of whom only half were white) and had a long tradition of subservience to the political leadership. Moreover, De Klerk, probably sensing trouble, refused ANC demands for a multi-party aggregation of the security forces and carried out a small purge of officers suspected of backing or instigating 'third force' activities. General Constand Viljoen, a widely respected former head of the Defence Force, at one stage threatened to mobilise right-wing forces of resistance and seize sufficient land to carve out a future Afrikaner *volkstaat*. The undisciplined conduct of right-wing paramilitary organisations made effective action impossible. Viljoen and his movement were drawn into the election by a promise that the new government would consider a *volkstaat* and would appoint a *volkstaat* council consisting of right-wingers to research and deliberate on such a plan.

Election day was peaceful. Afrikaners were split almost down the middle between the right-wing parties and the NP. Ironically, the NP's electoral support base was much more non-racial than the ANC's. It drew half its votes from people who were not white, while only 6 per cent of the ANC's support was not black. But the most important fact was that power had passed to blacks. Afrikaners with cultural concerns now had to fend for themselves under a new dominant party that did not have much patience for subnational identities or anything but an increasingly English-based, individualistic culture.

Conclusion

It would be tempting, though wrong, to consider what happened to the Afrikaners as evidence for the assumption that the emotional power of ethnicity is exaggerated and that material interests are decisive when the chips are down.[694] The situation was exceptional in South Africa in that the small, shrinking Afrikaner minority was facing severe economic and political problems and was hopelessly over-extended in the country's political and administrative systems. It had to make tough decisions about its future political survival as a group. De Klerk made his decisions in the spirit of Edmund Burke's dictum that leaders have to take their followers not where they want to be but where they ought to be. He knew that a shrinking white minority clinging to a monopoly of power offered no guarantee for the survival of his people. He was also confident that he could convince the ANC that an effective ANC–NP coalition was the best platform for realising the economic potential of South Africa. De Klerk was able to persuade his party, his constituency and the security forces to give up exclusive power and accept a new vision.

Where De Klerk failed was in his management of the negotiating process and in his strategy towards realising his goal of power-sharing or of achieving an effective coalition government. He never signalled to the ANC in any serious way that this was his bottom line, nor did he try to understand the ANC's real agenda behind the bland assurances the movement's negotiators offered him that the ANC would continue to consult and work with him and his party. The ANC succeeded in getting what its spokespeople called an 'ordinary' system of majority rule by flatly refusing to have the principle of power-sharing written into the constitution. It did approve, however, of a vaguely worded provision for a Government of National Unity in the interim constitution to assuage white voters' fears. Once the ANC had settled in the seat of power, it was confident that the NP had no real power to constrain it. It rejected the inclusion of any sort of government of national unity in the final constitution, which came into force on 4 February 1997. Three weeks earlier De Klerk stated:

> The decision to surrender the right to national sovereignty is certainly one of the most painful that any leader can ever be asked to take. Most nations are prepared to risk total war and catastrophe rather than to surrender this

right. Yet this was the decision that we had to take. We had to accept the necessity of giving up the ideal on which we have been nurtured and the dream for which so many generations of our forefathers had struggled and for which so many of our people had died.[695]

The Afrikaner leadership handed over power because it had miscalculated, believing that it was indispensable to the ANC.

Whites did not mount much resistance once the prospect of majority rule began to take shape. Part of the reason was that the process remained shrouded in ambiguity for quite some time. But there were also deep-seated reasons. There was little that people in a modern state could do to roll back the process, and this is particularly true if they are as outnumbered as whites in South Africa were. Moreover, whites had become convinced of the failure of apartheid in the 1980s and saw no easy alternative. The electoral link between the NP and the white constituency had effectively been removed in 1989, well before the start of negotiations. Constitutionally there was no course of action available to resist De Klerk. All that those who were prepared to take up arms could do was to embark on random terrorism; alternatively, they could contemplate establishing by force an ethnic state in one of the regions. But for most whites this held little attraction.

Had someone other than De Klerk been elected as leader in 1989 a prolonged stalemate could have ensued, or South Africa might have witnessed a different leader pursuing a different strategy with a different outcome. If the particular events that did unfold demonstrate anything, it is that leaders do make a difference, particularly if they have the ability to take the party and their people with them into uncharted territory. What makes De Klerk different from a Gorbachev is that he is still the leader of his party and has managed to retain a following and a considerable degree of respect despite failing in his high-risk gamble. It says much for De Klerk, but even more about the Afrikaner people – their pragmatism, their fatalism, and perhaps also their resilience.

13.

Admit defeat and seek an independent cultural space

The defeat of the Moors in Grenada in 1492 spelt the end of seven hundred years of the occupation of a large part of Spain by the Moors. After the final battle the mother of Boabdil, the commander of their troops, came upon him where he sat crying. Her words to him were: 'It is fitting that you are crying like a child over something that you failed to defend like a man.'

A week ago,* FW de Klerk, National Party leader, for the first time admitted that during the constitutional negotiations the Afrikaners were compelled to relinquish their self-determination.[696] Earlier the NP had held up the fig leaf of power-sharing. There is now very little reason to beat around the bush. The truth is that the NP has suffered a shattering defeat with respect to both power-sharing and cultural self-determination.

In the final constitution that is now operative there is no effective guarantee for single-medium schools or mother-tongue instruction. There are no ways in which the status of Afrikaans as an official language can be enforced. There is nothing that can prevent the SABC from further scaling down Afrikaans.

Clearly this was not inevitable, as is made clear in Patti Waldmeir's fascinating new book, *Anatomy of a Miracle: The End of Apartheid and the Birth of the New South Africa*, which will appear next month in the United States. In interviews she had conducted, ANC leaders admitted that at critical stages of the negotiations that were conducted between December 1992 and August 1993, they were prepared to make concessions. The NP, however, never asked for any.

Reading the manuscript of this book, one gets the idea that a tough negotiating

---

* First published in *Rapport*, 2 February 1997.

position could on critical points have forced the ANC to yield somewhat. As long as it could win the prize of centralised political power, the ANC would in all probability have been prepared to grant to Afrikaans-speakers as a group some cultural space and also give Afrikaans a greater measure of official recognition. The condition was, of course, that the group would not be defined in racial terms.

The NP leaders failed pitifully with respect to securing minority rights, especially language rights and control over schools. This failure must largely be attributed to poor strategic planning and the absence on the part of the NP of any non-negotiable principles, with the possible exception of private property.

To find a proper place in the new constitutional order it is imperative that Afrikaans-speaking people start openly admitting their stunning cultural defeat. Recently a perceptive historian pointed out what should follow as a necessary second step. This is to grasp that in the past, as at present, there were always conflicting definitions of who and what constituted an Afrikaner.

It all revolves around a single question: how should the Afrikaners as a small and vulnerable community respond to defeat? During the final phases of the Anglo-Boer War, a fifth of the republican Afrikaners in the field were fighting on the side of the British forces because they believed that persevering with war would end in a senseless massacre. They were prepared to accept the conflicting assurances of the British victors, who insisted that any form of ethnic consciousness be renounced for the sake of national reconciliation. The middle class in particular was embarrassed by the often clumsy efforts to secure a place in public life for Afrikaans and security for the Afrikaner poor who were unable to compete.

Today the shape of things is not fundamentally different. During the past decade or two the Afrikaner middle class has sold out the poorer Afrikaners. The middle class itself is divided as a result of its conflicting definition of what constitutes Afrikaner identity. In one camp there are what I would call the pluralists. They accept that a person can have an array of identities – professional, religious, class or cultural. They realise also that any identification has to arise from an association that is voluntary, and that the decision to opt for a particular social identity is not morally more acceptable than embracing a different form of identity.

In this respect pluralists fundamentally part ways with apartheid. At the same time pluralists believe that the embrace of one's own culture provides an acceptable sense of belonging and that culture-based schools and universities constitute a legitimate minority demand.

In South Africa those Afrikaners who have reflected on the best available strategy realise that it is vital to make the Afrikaners as a group inclusive and to enrich their culture in such a way that it attracts others. A culture that is open-minded wrestles with its past and accepts responsibility for the injustice and oppression that have been perpetrated in its name. At the same time it guards against becoming paralysed by slanted historical interpretations of its past that give no credit to what it has built up.

Pluralists are not afraid of conflicts that may arise as a result of their demand for cultural space. The experience of other societies shows that their cultures are enhanced when they face other cultures confident of their own power and conscious of their own worth. Conflict, on the other hand, arises when one culture tries to swamp another culture and language.

I call the Afrikaners in the opposing camp 'corporatists'. For them our society consists of three large corporations – organised labour, business and the state. For them there are only individual and corporate interests. In order to promote 'social harmony' they want to encourage the growth of a state-orchestrated national language, culture and identity. For them minority languages and cultures should retreat to the private sphere.

Corporatists are prepared to grant to minorities a small formal niche in public life (almost like the apartheid order, which wanted to 'grant' certain things to people who were not white). This is the mindset also of the South African Broadcasting Corporation with its miserly allocation of time to the minority languages and its 'We are one' philosophy. It is at the heart of the policy of the Education Department, which believes the right to mother-tongue education is subordinate to the right of access to schools.

The corporatists suffer from the illusion that these things will reduce conflict. It is this kind of thinking that leads some Afrikaners – according to a recent opinion survey, as much as a third of the community – to accept English as the only official language. As one would expect, it is the best educated people who are inclined to share this sentiment. Their tendency to regard this view as a 'natural response' makes one think of the wise words of the famous American economist Joan Nelson: 'One's ideology is like one's breath: One cannot smell it.'

The funny thing is that in a typically nasty way they try to ostracise the pluralists with epithets like apologists for neo-apartheid, anti's and right-wingers. They are ignorant of the extent to which corporatists elsewhere in the postmodernist world are regarded as oppressive, culturally sterile and right-wing. To crown it all, they are blissfully unaware of the fact that their own breath stinks.

14.

Nelson Mandela and the last Afrikaner leaders

During the period of National Party (NP) rule, Afrikaner nationalists bluntly refused to yield power because they believed that their survival as a nation depended on it.[697] Some foreign correspondents shared the view that Afrikaners were determined to cling to power indefinitely. One of them was Allen Drury, a Pulitzer Prize-winning American novelist and commentator, who wrote in the mid-1960s that the white community, which had established one of the world's most sophisticated and viable states, could not understand why they were expected to give it up. He added: 'They will not do so.'[698] This chapter discusses some of the neglected features of the apartheid era and in particular the informal efforts on the part of both NP and ANC leaders to avert a violent showdown. It discusses and offers a new interpretation of why the De Klerk government decided to cede power.

Academic perspectives

During the 1960s academics based outside South Africa tended to expect a violent revolution in the country. The most prominent scholar propounding this view was Pierre van den Berghe. In 1965 he wrote that 'the likelihood of revolution seems high. Mounting internal strains and external pressures doom white supremacy and racial segregation within the near future.'[699] RW Johnson's *How Long Will South Africa Survive?* predicted that while the apartheid regime would survive the eighties, at some point later it would have to give in.[700]

But whether whites would give up power and under what conditions they would do so remained a matter of dispute. In 1971 Heribert Adam argued that the regime was a modernising racial oligarchy capable of devising ever more sophisticated means to exploit black labour and deflect assaults on white power. He did, however, anticipate that interests would increasingly diverge in the white power bloc and that apartheid would be terminated once the dominant white classes considered it too expensive.[701] Other analysts put the emphasis on military pressure coupled with Western sanctions. In his 1977 analysis of how long South Africa would survive, Johnson expected that the ANC's military wing, Umkhonto we Sizwe (MK), operating from bases in neighbouring countries, would cause sufficient trouble on both sides of the South African border for Western powers to intervene and force the abandonment of white rule. Revisiting the theme in 2015, Johnson admitted that he had been wrong. MK, he concluded, was essentially 'impotent' and Western sanctions were always more important.[702]

Sanctions were part of a general economic crisis, comprising runaway government spending on consumption, falling fixed investment and growing external debt. A popular version maintains that the lack of international investment funds led to 'the collapse of white rule'.[703] A more sober perspective is needed. The economy was indeed stagnating as a result of sanctions, but there was no real fiscal crisis. Derek Keys, managing director of General Mining Corporation, who went on to serve as the last NP Minister of Finance, stated in 2010: 'From a financial point of view, South Africa did not have to negotiate in 1990, but conditions were tightening . . . [The] situation was serious but it is not as if we had fallen off the precipice. The economy could go on.' Barend du Plessis, Keys's predecessor as Finance Minister, had made the same assessment that a government determined to cling to power could carry on for many years.[704]

The ANC's switch in the early 1980s to what was called a 'people's war', combining mass protests, consumer action and strikes with sabotage and occasional armed attacks, was much more effective than the strategy of guerrilla warfare of the 1960s and 1970s had been.[705] But by the end of the 1980s the government had weathered the storm. The US Central Intelligence Agency (CIA) reported in January 1989 that no fundamental changes were imminent. It stated that the government 'has weathered more than four years of unprecedented domestic and international pressure'. According to the report, its aim was to delay fundamental change as long as possible, believing the security forces could guarantee continued white prosperity until well into the next century. Nelson Mandela was unlikely to be released unless the government was certain it could contain any black mobilisation. The report added that the ANC leadership realised that majority rule was not round the corner.[706]

Two important factors have been largely neglected in scholarly assessments. The first is the grave error made by the apartheid planners in the early 1950s in expecting the black population to increase to about 20 million by the year 2000, and the government's failure to adjust its policy after the error was discovered in the late 1960s.[707] During the apartheid period there was a fourfold increase of the black population, from just over 8 million to over 31 million. During this time the white population grew from 2.5 million to a mere 4.5 million. The South African case calls to mind Auguste Comte's famous dictum: demography is destiny.

Another factor is the resilience and determination of the white leadership to hold on to power. Conventional analyses of revolution often highlight the defection of a strategic stratum such as the intellectuals, the military or the clergy. In the Afrikaners' case, none of these strata had turned against the government.[708] The key shift happened at the top of the political power structure between June and December 1992 when a small number of people in FW de Klerk's inner circle decided no longer to insist on power-sharing. More than thirty years before it happened, the historian Arnold Toynbee highlighted the will to dominate as a key factor in a remarkably prescient essay.

Toynbee's perspective

In 1959 the journal *Optima* carried an article by the historian Arnold Toynbee. His reputation has diminished sharply in recent times, but in the first fifteen years after the end of the Second World War he was among the most cited historians in the world. In his twelve-volume work, *A Study of History*, he argued that the critically important factor in the rise and fall of civilisations in world history had been the success, or failure, of creative minorities and perceptive leaders in responding to challenges.

The article was written against the background of the rapid decolonisation of Africa by the European colonial powers, which had started two years before. He pointed out the contrast between the empires founded by the Spanish and the Portuguese on the continent of South America and those built up by the British and the Dutch in Africa. The Spanish, for instance, also exploited the native peoples, but the division between first-class and second-class citizens was less overtly racist in that it allowed for some people of mixed ancestry to gain entry into the elite. Barriers to prevent access to the top were not racial, and hence were not impermeable. The result was continued Spanish predominance even after independence. So, too, people of European descent (or predominantly European descent) in the former Portuguese colony of Brazil continued to play a dominant role in many sectors.

In stark contrast to this stood the colonies that the Dutch and the British had founded in Africa (and, one could add, the British in North America). Political upward mobility for subordinate races was exceptionally difficult and intermarriage virtually ruled out. Toynbee pointedly observed that in the South Africa of the 1950s there was no easy way of entry into the dominant caste for an able and adaptable black person.

Looking ahead to changes in the balance of power, Toynbee stressed that a cultural struggle would be more drawn out and more morally complex than a clear-cut military struggle. But, he wrote, 'the dénouement may be more tragic'. Sooner or later, Toynbee stated, ruling minorities had to accept the status of 'an unprivileged minority' living under a majority whom they consider culturally inferior. The alternative was to hold on to their present supremacy by sheer force against a rising tide of revolt.

Toynbee warned that holding on against the tide was fatal for a minority. He warned: 'Even if its belief in its own cultural superiority was justified, numbers would tell in the long run, considering that culture is contagious, and that an ascendancy based on cultural superiority is therefore a wasting asset.' He expressed sympathy with the dilemma of minorities: voluntary abdication in favour of a majority whom one feels to be one's inferior 'was a very hard alternative for human pride to accept'.[709]

The next sections of this chapter revisit the apartheid period from the perspective of leaders on both sides of the divide in order to establish how they saw the opportunities available to them. One can only gain a proper understanding of apartheid and of the nature of the settlement in 1994 by placing the main historical actors at a point in time when different courses still seemed open.

Looking ahead in 1948

Within the camp of the victorious Afrikaner nationalists there were contrasting perspectives on the unexpected NP victory in the 1948 election. Eben Dönges, Minister of the Interior, who would introduce most of the apartheid laws, told a foreign journalist that for him and his colleagues the policy of apartheid was there to protect the present and next two generations against the dangers posed by the growing black and coloured population.[710] By contrast, NP leader DF Malan said after the 1948 election: 'Today South Africa belongs to us once more. South Africa is our own for the first time since Union, and may God grant that it always remained our own.'[711] By that he meant the Afrikaner nationalists' own.

Among leaders of the African National Congress (ANC), the oldest and most prestigious black organisation, there were mixed feelings about the 1948 election result. Albert Luthuli, a future winner of the Nobel Prize for Peace, said that with blacks little more than spectators of the political game, it was irrelevant which white party won. Oliver Tambo and Nelson Mandela, future ANC leaders, disagreed. Mandela recounts that Tambo said: 'I like this. Now we know exactly who our enemies are and where we stand.'[712]

In 1950 Hendrik Verwoerd, an ex-professor of sociology, became Minister of Native Affairs in the NP government and he went on to serve as Prime Minister from 1958 to 1966. He made it his business to tell blacks exactly where they stood. Shortly after becoming a cabinet minister, Verwoerd met with ex-members of the Native Representative Council, who had suspended the sitting of this body. Among them were some ANC stalwarts. He ruled out direct representation of blacks in Parliament or in the provincial councils, but offered them what he called the greatest measure of self-government in the urban black townships. Verwoerd stated that in order to provide services for the townships, blacks would have to be educated and trained to be sufficiently competent in many spheres.[713]

This was the only occasion on which such an offer was made, and it was in conflict with the NP's 1948 policy platform. The black leaders attending the meeting rejected the proposal, insisting on representation at all levels of government. This was a possible turning point at which South Africa failed to turn. Black city councils could have been employed in the same way that black trade unions in the 1980s used their legalised status effectively in a manner the government had never anticipated.

Verwoerd then embarked on a rigid policy of restricting black political rights to the eight black reserves, later depicted in apartheid ideology as national homelands. These reserves in total made up 13 per cent of the land mass of South Africa. Until 1990 it remained policy to link even settled urban blacks to their various homelands. The policy boiled down to restricting political rights for the rapidly expanding black population to the fragmented and overcrowded reserves.

Nelson Mandela, already an outstanding leader in the early 1950s, helped to steer the ANC into an activist but non-violent form of politics, which included boycotts, stay-at-homes, passive resistance and protest demonstrations. The state finally crushed the movement by charging 156 of the leaders, Mandela included, with treason. The trial, which started in 1956, dragged on for five years before all the accused were acquitted.

At the same time the cunning of history was at work. In the courts there was no segregation of the accused. The 156 accused in this case were all seated alphabetically and had frequent opportunities for talking during breaks. Mandela had long been suspicious of some of the white communists, but just before the Treason Trial he had become friends with Ruth First and Michael Harmel. He nevertheless wanted the ANC to remain an exclusively black organisation. Most members of the Communist Party were whites before the party was banned. Afterwards whites predominated on the executive, but the national chairman was an Indian and the secretary-general was black. During the Treason Trial Mandela mixed with white communists almost on a daily basis. He would remain loyal to his communist allies for the rest of his career. During the early 1960s he would briefly serve on the central committee of the party.[714]

Appealing to government

From the beginning of his career Mandela admired British political institutions, in particular the British Parliament. He saw those institutions as the cornerstone of a new political order in a free South Africa. In 1960 Mandela, on trial for treason, proposed that the black population be allowed to elect 60 representatives to the South African Parliament, which was slightly less than a third of the total number of seats at that time. He also suggested that the measure could be reviewed after every five years.[715]

This was the kind of measure Toynbee probably had in mind for whites if they wished to avoid a situation in the future where the ruling elite would be forced to capitulate without power and without honour. But apart from the fact that the white electorate was quite unprepared for it, there was another problem. In the dominant white group there was a division between the Afrikaners, forming 55 per cent of the electorate, and the English community, economically and culturally dominant, who made up the rest.

The 'winner-takes-all' electoral system, which today is still used in both Britain and the United States, is unsuitable for a deeply divided society like South Africa. It does not reward moderation but encourages the largest ethnic group to mobilise separately and to become increasingly radical in defending its power. In South Africa there was not only a sharp division between white and black but also between the two white communities. Implementing Mandela's proposal of 60 black parliamentary representatives would almost certainly have set up a black–English alliance that would have meant the political death knell for the Afrikaners.

The killing of 69 black South Africans by the police at Sharpeville on 21 March 1960, followed by black protests in several cities and a capital flight, triggered the first serious crisis for white rule. In April 1960 the government banned the ANC and other organisations and imprisoned numerous activists. It called a referendum for a republic in which only whites, forming only a fifth of the population, would participate. After a yes vote was delivered, the government decided to proclaim the republic on 31 May 1961.

On 20 April 1961 Mandela wrote to Verwoerd on behalf of several black organisations, stating that the NP government, representing only a minority, was not entitled to take such a decision without obtaining the express consent of the African people. Blacks feared the proposed republic under a government which, in Mandela's words, was 'already notorious the world over for its obnoxious policies'. The danger existed, he wrote, that the government would now 'make even more savage attacks on the rights and living conditions of the African people'. This situation 'could be averted only by the calling of a sovereign national convention representative of all South Africans, to draw up a new non-racial and democratic Constitution'.

Three weeks after the republic had been proclaimed, Mandela again wrote to Verwoerd. He stated that no constitution or form of government could be decided without the participation of black people, who formed an absolute majority of the population. He demanded a national convention of elected representatives of all adults. The body should have sovereign powers to determine, in any way the majority would decide, a non-racial democratic constitution.[716]

Verwoerd's office failed to reply to Mandela's two letters. When he stood trial later, Mandela pressed Verwoerd's secretary to admit that the failure to reply to his letters would be considered 'scandalous' in 'any civilised country'. The secretary replied that the letters had remained unanswered because the tone was aggressive and discourteous. Mandela later acknowledged that 'there may have been something in this'.[717] But the demand for the calling of a national convention was also problematic from a white point of view. A majority would be able to write the constitution.

In the course of 1960 Mandela, along with some other leading figures in the resistance, decided to form Umkhonto we Sizwe (MK) to wage an armed struggle against the state. They had to face the fact that Albert Luthuli, the incumbent ANC president, was firmly opposed to such a militant course. There was a meeting between Mandela and Luthuli to resolve the issue. In his published autobiography Mandela acknowledges that the outcome of his clash with Luthuli was very messy since the latter retained his commitment to non-violence. According to Mandela, Luthuli agreed that 'the military body should be a separate and independent organ, linked to the ANC and under the overall control of the ANC, but fundamentally autonomous'. Mandela goes on to state that he enlisted some white Communist Party members. The party had already decided to embark on violence and a few members had executed acts of sabotage.[718]

The question whether it was the ANC or the SACP which made the decision to start the armed struggle, and of Mandela's role, remained dormant until Mandela's death on 5 December 2013. Then the whole issue blew up. The South African Communist Party issued a statement in which it declared that Mandela had once been a member of the party's central committee. Around the same time, two important works by professional historians appeared. The one was by the late British historian Stephen Ellis, holder of the Desmond Tutu chair at the University of Amsterdam.[719] The other was by two Russian historians, Irina Filatova and Apollon Davidson.[720]

According to Ellis, the SACP conference that resolved to take up arms took place in a white suburb of Johannesburg. Of the 25 delegates in attendance, eight or nine were black Africans.[721] Filatova and Davidson write that Mandela was present as a member of the SACP's central committee. They add: 'The fact that the armed struggle was originally a decision by the SACP, not the ANC, is confirmed by documents from the Moscow archives.'

The controversy intensified when the Mandela Foundation released the 627-page original manuscript of Mandela's account of his life, which had been smuggled out of prison.[722] It now appears that some very interesting passages were expurgated from the manuscript when producing the published version of Mandela's autobiography, *A Long Walk to Freedom* (1994).

There is now little doubt that Mandela was indeed a member of the SACP executive during the period 1960–2 when MK was formed. During his tour through Africa in 1962, just before his imprisonment, he discovered that several leaders of African states he met rejected communism. When he returned to South Africa, Mandela projected himself as a nationalist. Joe Slovo, SACP leader, complained: 'We sent Nelson off to Africa as a Communist and he came back an African nationalist.'[723]

From the early 1960s to the early 1990s both the ANC and the SACP depended heavily on Soviet Union support. In 1965–6 the ANC received $560,000 and the SACP $112,000 from this source.[724] On Robben Island Mandela never gave an indication of any communist leanings. A fellow inmate, Neville Alexander, who frequently debated issues with him, was convinced that Mandela did not subscribe to the so-called National Democratic Revolution, the key SACP doctrine. This sets out the party's plan to establish a socialist society under ANC rule through a two-stage revolution. In Alexander's view, the ANC's predominantly bourgeois leadership had no intention other than serving the interests of the capitalist class.[725]

The unexpurgated prison manuscript was completed and smuggled out of prison in the mid-1970s. At that point Mandela had distanced himself from some of the SACP members on Robben Island. The differences were partly personal, especially with Govan Mbeki, a hard-line Stalinist. But there were also differences about strategy, particularly on how to deal with the Bantustans.

The overall impression one gets from the manuscript is that Mandela was no liberal democrat. He endorses dialectical materialism and considers anti-communism a sickness, contracted from attendance at missionary schools or listening to government propaganda. He argues that force could be used in the struggle against the NP government, even if the black majority were against it.

From the early 1960s the state's security agencies received intelligence that the SACP had succeeded in infiltrating the ANC and that Mandela was a member of its executive from 1960 to 1962. The question is: how did this knowledge affect the treatment of ANC- or SACP-aligned prisoners? Mandela himself commented on this in his unexpurgated memoirs:

> In comparison with the wave of detentions since 1963 that in 1960 was like a picnic. To the best of my knowledge and belief no individuals were then isolated, forced to give information, beaten up, tortured, crippled and killed as has been happening since 1963. Speaking comparatively, the security police still had a number of men who carried out their duties according to the law and who resisted the temptation of abusing their powers. Apart from keeping us in confinement, withholding newspapers so as to prevent us from knowing what was happening outside, the atmosphere was generally free of the brutalities and acute tensions that characterize the subsequent detentions.[726]

Piet Swanepoel, a senior security policeman to whom Mandela refers favourably in this context, recently stated that knowledge of the communist influence on the ANC triggered a 'greater harshness' on the part of the security officers when dealing with prisoners and detainees.[727] Torture of detainees and deaths in detention became common.

Considering Mandela's release

The second Prime Minister during Mandela's term in prison was John Vorster, who served from 1966 to 1978. Like other NP leaders, Vorster believed that Mandela was a communist and that the ANC, as well as the SACP, was a proxy of the Soviet Union. Initially the Vorster government enjoyed so much latitude that little thought was given to substantial reform or to the release of Mandela and some of his colleagues from prison. The economy was booming. During the 1960s it grew at an average rate of 5.9 per cent per year.

From the mid-1970s the tide turned against the white regimes in southern Africa. The economy became bogged down by the sudden jump in oil prices together with a slump in commodity prices and growing demands from a much more assertive black workforce.

The collapse of the dictatorship of Portugal in 1974 was the start of a rapid withdrawal of Portugal from its southern African colonies. Soviet-aligned regimes came to power in Mozambique and Angola. A South African attempt to intervene in Angola misfired badly. The Soviet government airlifted some 30,000 Cuban troops to that country. US Secretary of State Henry Kissinger warned Vorster that owing to opposition in the American Congress, the Ford administration would not be able to counter further Soviet intervention in southern Africa.

In June 1976 a major uprising erupted in Soweto, near Johannesburg, and quickly spread to townships across the country. The troubles starkly exposed the political isolation of the white community. The situation was so serious that on 8 August 1976 the Vorster cabinet had on its agenda the issue of the release of Nelson Mandela, who had been in prison for twelve years by that time.[728] There is no record of any decision.

What would have happened had Mandela indeed been released in 1976? Neville Alexander records that in 1971 he and Mandela debated using the apartheid structures, flawed as they were.[729] Two years before the Soweto uprising, in 1974, Mandela had written a secret memorandum, entitled 'Clear the Obstacles and Confront the Enemy', which was smuggled out. In this document Mandela confronted the fact that the government of Transkei, which was the putative homeland of most Xhosa people, had opted to take apartheid-style independence in 1976. In terms of a 1971 law, Mandela, who was born in the Transkei, would lose his South African citizenship. Undeterred, Mandela wrote in his 1974 memorandum that the ANC faced an entirely new development: the independence of the Transkei, which was sure to be followed by that of other Bantustans. Mandela wrote: 'The Transkei will have an independent legislature, judiciary and executive and may control its foreign relations', and then added:

> For the first time since conquest the people will run their own affairs. Now Africans will be able to be judges, magistrates, attorneys-general, inspectors of education, postmasters, army and police officers, and they will occupy other top positions in the civil service. Would it not be far better to consider independence as an accomplished fact and then call upon the people in these so-called free territories to help in the fight for a democratic South Africa?[730]

Mandela would never have recognised the independence of Transkei in the way in which the government conceived it. However, if he had proceeded to use the structures of an independent Transkei to fight apartheid and promote liberation, the existing strains in the ANC might well have become too great to contain. A major split might well have occurred in the movement, putting South Africa on a quite different course from the one it took between 1976 and 1990.

PW Botha's offers to Mandela

In 1978 Vorster resigned. He was succeeded by PW Botha, who had transformed the South African military into a formidable force. Botha believed South Africa was facing a so-called total onslaught, the aim of which was to subvert and ultimately overthrow white rule. In this an important role would be played by the ANC, which Botha also considered a Soviet proxy.

Botha firmly believed that Mandela was still a communist.[731] He had, however, become receptive to the advice of National Intelligence that Mandela was the main icon of the world-wide anti-apartheid struggle and that it was counterproductive to keep him in prison.

In 1985 Botha offered to release Mandela provided he unconditionally forswore violence as a political instrument. This was the sixth such offer since he was imprisoned. As before, Mandela refused. He did not believe that the ANC was capable of overthrowing the state, but he was quite certain that eventually the government would be compelled to negotiate for the simple reason that blacks formed a growing demographic majority. As Toynbee had predicted twenty-five years earlier, he thought that the government would only with great reluctance embark on negotiations. He resolved to do anything possible to prod the government on this way.

One way of making it easier for the government to negotiate a democracy was to reduce the total number of blacks that could vote. By the early 1980s there were already 8 million out of approximately 22 million blacks who were considered citizens of so-called independent states and, as such, deemed by the government to be disenfranchised. Early in 1986 Mandela told the journalist Benjamin Pogrund that he was prepared to consider recognising the independence of the Bantustans. As Pogrund states, this was 'an unusual and significant view contrary to that of the ANC in exile'. When Pogrund asked whether he could report this view to a cabinet member, Mandela said yes.[732] One does not know what strategic objective Mandela had in mind when he communicated this very controversial view to Pogrund. He always rejected the Bantustan policy and would never consider endorsing it in exchange for his freedom. At the same time, he was prepared to work with anti-apartheid homeland leaders.

Initially Mandela seemed flexible on a controversial issue like minority rights. Like the Bantustan option, it was abhorred by the ANC in exile, which would not budge from the first-past-the-post electoral system coupled with the rule of winner takes all. Yet, even after his release Mandela said he was flexible on all the fundamental issues, including minority rights.[733]

A major uprising

A major uprising broke out in South Africa in 1984, and the turmoil did not subside until the government proclaimed a nation-wide state of emergency in 1986. Thousands were detained without trial. In his ill-fated 'Rubicon speech', held on 16 August 1985, Botha rejected the unconditional release of Nelson Mandela, who had become the focus of the worldwide campaign against apartheid. He made it appear as if Mandela and his comrades had been motivated solely by communist convictions in the early 1960s. There was no reference to grievances that were widely considered legitimate, and he presented no evidence that Mandela was indeed a communist. More than anything, this speech and the rejection of the demand for Mandela's release destroyed the government's credibility as an agent of substantial reform.

President Botha had to accept that the state was no longer able to force blacks to participate in the institutions the government had unilaterally created. It had become necessary to talk to the leadership of the ANC. The government's secret polls showed that the movement enjoyed the support of at least 60 per cent of the population.

Mandela knew from the early 1960s that overthrowing white rule by means of insurrection was impossible and that only in negotiations could whites be persuaded to cede power and live under a democratic system in which their rights were guaranteed. To prepare himself for such negotiations, he learnt Afrikaans in prison and studied Afrikaner history. He told his Afrikaner interlocutors in prison that he saw distinct similarities between the Afrikaner struggle for freedom in the very first years of the twentieth century and the black struggle for freedom.

The electorate, however, was far from ready to embark on a radical change. A large proportion rejected the conventional form of majority rule on which the ANC insisted. A poll conducted in 1988 among whites in the Witwatersrand area, the biggest urban conglomeration, listed five political preferences for a new constitution. Only 11 per cent of white English-speakers as against 3 per cent of Afrikaners endorsed the option of 'a single mixed parliament with the majority in control'.[734]

In 1988 Botha instructed Niël Barnard, head of the National Intelligence Service (NIS), assisted by three other senior civil servants, to discuss the possibility of a negotiated settlement with Mandela. Forty-eight such meetings took place. Barnard reported back to Botha after each session. When Barnard's team raised the issue of Mandela's alleged sympathy for communism and his refusal to break with the Communist Party, Mandela replied that while in his youth he had found aspects of communism attractive, he was not a communist. Yet he refused to break with the SACP, the ANC's main ally: 'If I desert them now, who have been in the struggle with me all these years, what sort of ally would I be to you or to the government?' He answered his own question: '[People] would say that Mandela is a man who turns the way the wind blows; he is not to be trusted.'[735] It was a shrewd answer that was difficult to counter.[736]

The officials also explored other issues. Was the ANC genuinely interested in a peaceful settlement? Mandela made it clear that majority rule was non-negotiable, but added that the new system had to be balanced and had to ensure white domination would not be replaced by black domination. 'Minorities have a legitimate interest in security,' he said.[737]

Mandela kept pressing for a meeting with the President, and Botha finally agreed. Prior to the meeting Mandela wrote to Botha that one of the key points in future negotiations would be 'the [ANC] demand for majority rule in a unitary state and the concern of white South Africa over this demand, as well as the insistence on structural guarantees that majority rule will not mean the domination of the white minority by blacks'. He continued: 'The most crucial task which will face the government and the ANC will be to reconcile these two positions. Such reconciliation will be achieved only if both parties are willing to compromise.'[738]

On 5 July 1989 the meeting between Botha and Mandela took place in the President's office. Botha had suffered a stroke a few months earlier. By all accounts he was no longer the same man as before. By meeting Mandela, Botha clearly wanted to signal to his cabinet that he was still in charge. In his autobiography Mandela wrote about his meeting with Botha: 'He completely disarmed me. He was unfailingly courteous, deferential and friendly.' When I interviewed Mandela early in 1992, he told me that a stranger would not have been able to tell who the prisoner was and who the president. 'We met as equals,' he recounted.[739]

Mandela told me, as well as several other people, that one of the greatest disappointments in his life was having to negotiate with De Klerk rather than Botha. After 1994 Mandela continued to speak highly of Botha while frequently criticising De Klerk, sometimes unfairly. The main reason was that Mandela and De Klerk were competitors for electoral support and the international limelight. Another reason was the difference in age. Mandela and Botha were of the same age while De Klerk was nearly twenty years younger. Having been Minister of Defence before he became leader, Botha embodied the military's toughness and discipline. De Klerk, by contrast, could easily be mistaken for a professor of law, which he nearly became, or a modern-day bureaucrat.

We shall never know all that was said at the meeting between Botha and Mandela because Barnard gave orders that the tapes of the meeting had to be destroyed. Botha was furious when he discovered this, but it was clearly the sensible thing to do because Mandela had not been informed that the meeting was being taped. Barnard's account of the meeting, based on his notes, showed that the meeting was very cordial and that no substantial issue was discussed, except the release of one of Mandela's fellow prisoners.[740]

Botha did not discard his original views about the nature of the insurrection that Mandela had plotted way back in 1960. Interviewed in 1995, he said that Mandela 'was led into this affair by the communists and international forces'. He seemed to suggest Mandela was manipulated by these forces. He told the interviewer that he had warned Mandela against the dangers of international Marxism and communism.[741] It would be unwise to describe Botha's musings as those of an anachronistic Cold War warrior. An informed observer like Barnard has stated recently: 'Mandela totally underestimated the influence of the SACP.'[742]

Giving up power

In August 1989 the National Party won the general election and De Klerk was elected President. Two months later, on 9 November 1989, the Berlin Wall fell. De Klerk later wrote that he immediately considered it a golden opportunity to negotiate what he thought would be a balanced settlement with the ANC. He calculated that without the substantial Soviet support which the ANC had enjoyed since the early 1960s, it would find itself off balance for a long while and would be compelled to modify significantly its demand for majority rule.

When he first met Mandela in December 1989, De Klerk observed that the inclusion of group rights in a new constitution would ease the concern of minorities over majority rule. But with Mandela a free man, it was a new ball game. Mandela told De Klerk that the ANC had not fought apartheid for seventy-five years to accept a disguised form of it.[743] Mandela knew that both power-sharing and group rights were anathema to the ANC in exile, and he would not concede group rights easily.

When De Klerk set out to negotiate, he did not intend to drop his insistence on group rights. Robin Renwick, British ambassador to South Africa, who often met De Klerk, described his discussions with De Klerk in the form of a diary. In an entry dated 26 October 1989, he stated: 'As De Klerk was continuing to talk about the need to protect group rights, I suggested to Gerrit Viljoen and others that this terminology should be changed to emphasise minority rights. De Klerk told me that he was not in the business of "reforming himself out of power". What he was thinking of at this time was power-sharing, not a transfer of power.'[744]

On 11 December 1989 Renwick wrote: 'Mandela met De Klerk at the Tuynhuis. Mandela said that the National Party concept of "group rights" was seen by his people as a way to preserve apartheid. De Klerk's response was: "We shall have to change it then."'[745] Renwick's entry for 19 March 1990 reads: 'In the future constitution, he [De Klerk] considered the key to be the protection of minority rights. [The] protection of individual rights would not of itself protect minorities. He talked about some form of power-sharing, and was, he said, in a hurry in his search for a solution. The ship he had launched would never be turned around, but he insisted he was not about to commit suicide.'[746]

During the negotiations, protests again flared up and the country was soon in an acute state of instability, resulting in a higher death toll than in the 1980s. In assuming the dual role of presiding over the transition and leading the National Party in the negotiations, De Klerk had put himself in a very difficult position. During the 1980s he resented the way in which he and some other ministers had been sidelined in discussions about the state's response to the uprising. He told Barnard, chief of the NIS: 'I intend to restore civilian government in its full glory.' He acted as if it could be done immediately and did away with the core parts of the National Security Management System, which President Botha had used to restore order.

De Klerk did not rely on the assessments and advice of the heads of the security services and intelligence agencies. Barnard believes that De Klerk thought 'he had enough political acumen to handle everything personally, which was a great error of judgement'. In 2007 Major-General Chris Thirion, former Deputy Head of Military Intelligence, wrote in an open letter to De Klerk: 'If I think of De Klerk, I think of a president who did not trust his security forces.'[747]

Mandela persisted in alleging that government forces were responsible for most of the violence, but was rarely in a position to give concrete evidence. By examining court records, Anthea Jeffery has been able to call into question many of the allegations made by ANC spokesmen or press reports at the time.[748] The subject of the extent of the involvement of members of the security forces will probably remain highly contested for many years to come. Nevertheless there is some consensus that the ANC and Inkatha were together responsible for most of the over 20,000 deaths that occurred in the violence between 1984 and 1994.

A complex proposal

In September 1991 the NP federal congress accepted a complex proposal for power-sharing on different levels as the negotiating position of the party. For the national legislature the NP proposed a bicameral system, with the First House elected by universal franchise on the basis of proportional representation. The Second House would give representation to nine regions, each of which would be allocated an equal number of seats to be filled by regional elections. Each party that won a specified minimum number of votes in a regional election would be given an equal number of seats. The Second House would vote on matters affecting regions and minorities. A weighted majority would be used in voting in place of a conventional majority vote.

At the executive level the NP proposed a presidency consisting of the leaders of the three biggest parties and a rotating chairmanship. Decisions, including the appointment of the cabinet, would be by consensus. The cabinet would be a collegial one, also operating on the basis of consensus. De Klerk described these proposals as an attempt to prevent power from being vested solely in the hands of a single individual, political party or group – and as a rejection of domination of any kind.

The government called a referendum, which was held on 17 March 1992. The voters were only asked to endorse the negotiating process, but NP speakers and NP-supporting newspapers insisted that a yes vote meant support for the sharing of power. Izak de Villiers, editor of *Rapport*, called for a yes vote on the grounds of the 'undeniable fact' that the government 'insisted on power-sharing and would never accept giving up power'.[749] In a full-page advertisement in *Die Burger* the day before the referendum, the NP exhorted voters to vote yes if they rejected the ANC's demand for majority rule. On 17 March 1992 two-thirds of white voters voted yes.

Colin Eglin, who represented the Democratic Party at the negotiations, later observed that De Klerk had been 'very naughty' in claiming he kept to the undertakings he had given. In the referendum, he said, De Klerk referred to the party's September 1991 proposals 'and put them out saying I am not asking for a blank cheque, I am asking for this'.[750]

Opinion surveys taken in the six months after the referendum made it clear that, in the formulation of the pollster and analyst Lawrence Schlemmer, 'whites were essentially voting yes because they feared the consequences of a no vote on the economy, but their commitment was to negotiations, and very little more'. They 'were essentially voting to give [De Klerk] a mandate because of the very high trust they have in De Klerk not to sell them out'.[751]

In May 1992 the ANC walked out of the negotiations and embarked on three months of extensive mass action. When Mandela met De Klerk during the last week of September 1992, he secured virtually all the ANC's objectives. The two leaders agreed that the final constitution would be drafted by a body elected on the basis of universal franchise, which the ANC was sure to dominate.

Apart from the requirement to recognise certain basic human rights, there were some other minor checks. One was the need to adhere to some vaguely phrased constitutional principles; the other was the replacement of parliamentary sovereignty with constitutional sovereignty.

De Klerk tried to get Mandela to agree to a system of shared decision-making in the proposed government of national unity, which would serve for five years, but the issue remained unresolved until 17 November 1993. In a last-ditch effort to reach agreement, De Klerk and Mandela met on the eve of the final session of negotiations for an interim government. Also present were the chief negotiators, Roelf Meyer and Cyril Ramaphosa.

Mandela insisted on simple majority rule, which meant that a majority (50 per cent) would be sufficient to break any logjam. Mac Maharaj claims that the ANC negotiators were prepared as a fall-back to accept a 60 per cent vote should De Klerk reject this stance, but Mandela insisted that a simple majority was sufficient. He did not know, he said, how he could run a cabinet in any other way. De Klerk accepted this and communicated it to the cabinet the next morning as a foregone conclusion.[752] Jan Heunis, the government's chief legal adviser, recalls his shock when he learnt that the NP had agreed to majority rule. He knew that its leadership had no mandate for this. The mandate, he writes, was for a consensus-seeking model with built-in vetoes.[753]

There was also the matter of the NP's promise to white voters. In the 1989 election the NP leadership had promised that it would seek voters' endorsement for any deal that deviated radically from the NP's 1989 election platform. This platform promised to bring about an inclusive democracy in which 'groups' would be recognised as the basic components of the system. There would be power-sharing among them with no one group dominating another, and self-determination for each group in its own affairs.

De Klerk also promised a particular kind of referendum. In March 1990 he pledged: 'After the completion of the negotiations the constitutional proposals would be tested in a constitutional manner among the electorate. And only with their support would a constitutional dispensation be introduced.'[754] Izak de Villiers, *Rapport* editor, writes in his memoirs that it was assumed that a second referendum of white voters would be called to seek their endorsement once agreement about a constitution had been reached. He tells of his dismay when three weeks after the March 1992 referendum 'a senior minister' told him: 'Izak, we don't want to have a second referendum.'[755]

Thus majority rule was introduced without the voters' approval and without the voters knowing the form of the future constitution. In striking contrast, a referendum was held in Northern Ireland in 1998 only after the new constitution had been negotiated. Whether Mandela would have agreed if De Klerk had insisted on such a procedure at the very start of negotiations is difficult to say. It reflects badly on the press that it failed to highlight this aspect of the negotiations.

A right-wing challenge

The security forces were baffled by De Klerk's moves but, steeped in the tradition of military subordination to the authority of an elected government, they did not resist the political leadership. The major unknown factor was the ex-Chief of the Defence Force, General Constand Viljoen, who was convinced that the ANC was still pursuing a revolutionary agenda. He believed that De Klerk had caved in to their demands.

Viljoen planned to disrupt the elections, have De Klerk removed as leader and restart the negotiations. Some believed that he could raise fifty thousand men mainly from the reserve army but also from some Defence Force units. In a briefing, General George Meiring, Chief of the Defence Force, warned the government and the ANC of the ghastly consequences of Viljoen's opposing the election.[756]

To dissuade Viljoen, for whom he said he had 'the highest regard', Meiring held several meetings with him. At one of them Viljoen said: 'You and I and our men can take this country in an afternoon', to which Meiring replied: 'Yes, that is so, but what do we do the morning after the coup?' The white–black demographic balance, the internal and foreign pressures, and all the intractable problems would still be there.[757]

Although De Klerk and Viljoen shared a conservative political outlook for most of their careers, they strongly opposed each other during the negotiations. De Klerk rejected Viljoen's demand for a *volkstaat* (ethnic state) for Afrikaners within the boundaries of the South African state, while Viljoen believed De Klerk had sold out.

It was Mandela who grasped the need to engage Viljoen and make a symbolic concession to him and his right-wing followers. This would take the form of an article in the constitution granting self-determination to cultural groups. Viljoen formed a party, the Freedom Front, which won close to half a million votes in the first election. When Parliament met for the first time in a free South Africa, Mandela broke ranks in the procession to greet Viljoen and tell him how glad he was that they had found each other. Recently Viljoen told his biographer that he was sad that Mandela did not serve more than one term, and that if he had done so, Afrikaners might have been better off today.[758]

Power and regime change

History is in many ways an account and interpretation of power – how it is won and lost. Yet a good grasp of the basic qualities of power remains elusive.[759] Leo Tolstoy remarked in the final chapter of his novel *War and Peace*: 'The new history is like a deaf man replying to questions which nobody puts to him.' The 'primary question', Tolstoy went on, is: 'What is the power that moves the destinies of peoples?' He doubted whether this power, 'which different historians understand in different ways', was in fact 'so completely familiar to everyone'.

History should be an antidote to the belief that superior political or military power determines the outcome of conflicts. In an article that appeared in the 21 November 2013 issue of the *New York Review of Books*, Freeman Dyson, a renowned physicist, tells the story of a study in the early 1970s about how to end the war that the United States was fighting in Vietnam. The study was commissioned by the RAND Corporation, whose experts considered themselves the brains of the US military establishment.

Working separately, two groups, one consisting of two economists and the other of several historians, reached completely different conclusions. The economists concluded that in a struggle to put down an insurgency what matters is not a sympathetic understanding of their struggle, 'but rather a better understanding of what costs and benefits the individual or the group is concerned with and how they are calculated'. To paraphrase: if the costs of an uprising become too high for the insurgents, they will back down. As a result, the oppressive regime will prevail.[760]

The group of historians who worked on the RAND Corporation's project came up with a completely different answer. They looked at numerous cases of insurgency and asymmetrical wars, particularly the French colonial wars in Algeria and Vietnam, and the British colonial wars in Africa and Malaysia. In a six-volume study they concluded that most of the wars lasted five to seven years and ended when one side lost the willpower to keep on fighting. This was a major insight, but it was lost to the world. To this day, the US Army has suppressed the historians' report.[761]

By the end of the 1980s the South African government was not desperate to start negotiations. It was rather the fall of the Berlin Wall that provided the incentive for De Klerk to attempt to get an agreement with the ANC while its main source of financial support, the Soviet Union, was in retreat. The business elite was concerned about the situation in the country, but its call for regime change was faint. Soldiers and policemen remained loyal and willing to continue to defend the state, though among army conscripts considerable unease about defending an unjust system had developed by the late 1980s. Nevertheless, in a poll conducted in the late 1980s less than a third of English-speaking students and less than a tenth of Afrikaner students declared themselves prepared to accept a prospective ANC government.[762]

Chris Heunis, Botha's Minister for Constitutional Affairs until 1989, offered this sober assessment: sanctions had made it necessary for the government to negotiate, but 'there was no need to negotiate only about the hand-over of power'.[763] Niël Barnard, the only person who saw both Botha and Mandela on a regular basis in the late eighties, believes that Botha would not have accepted majority rule, but would have said to Mandela: 'Let's govern together for ten years and let's see how it goes.' He thinks there was a good chance that Mandela would have accepted the idea.[764] There was no sign, however, that the electorate favoured radical change.

Until the final years of the 1980s De Klerk supported the idea of retaining the pillars of apartheid. After his election as NP leader early in 1989, he singled out morality as his main motivation for ending apartheid and for seeking a settlement. In an interview I had with him two months after his momentous speech on 2 February, he said that hanging on to power would be immoral.[765] In a television programme broadcast in 2002, he agreed with Frederik van Zyl Slabbert, ex-leader of the liberal opposition, that he could have been in power for at least ten more years. His main problem with that was that it would have been 'devoid of morality'.[766] PW Botha did not share this view of morality, and it is extremely doubtful that a clear majority of the white electorate would have given De Klerk and his party a yes vote in the referendum of March 1992 if it had known that majority rule would be the outcome of the negotiations.

Why did the Afrikaner community nonetheless go along with the deal struck between the ANC and the government in September 1992? One answer would be that after the white referendum, the tie between the government and its traditional electorate was cut. There was nothing any white group of voters could do to stop the process.

But there may also be a deeper reason. In his doctoral dissertation, completed in 1999, the political analyst and pollster Lawrence Schlemmer looked at the polls of the preceding thirty years. He concluded that Afrikaners, much more than white English-speakers, had begun to stress their religious identification in preference to a class or ethnic identification. To be living an upright moral life had come to be seen as more important than serving the Afrikaner community.[767]

The Western world's moral sanctions, much more than economic sanctions, had sapped the Afrikaners' will to cling to power. Sooner or later, Toynbee argued, ruling minorities have no choice but to accept the status of 'an unprivileged minority' among a majority whom they once considered culturally inferior.

The Communist Party, which fought both apartheid and capitalism, has been one of the greatest beneficiaries of the regime change. The SACP currently enjoys more influence in cabinet than it did under President Mbeki, but the present quality of leadership is far inferior to what it was under Joe Slovo. In addition, it has become financially dependent on the trade union federation

Cosatu. RW Johnson calls the SACP leadership 'a predatory elite which rules and despoils South Africa'.[768]

The Institute of Race Relations, the oldest liberal think tank in South Africa, found that 40 per cent of the cabinet are members of the SACP. No cabinet member questioned its report. In March 2015 the executive director of the Institute published a column under the title 'So word SA tree vir tree na sosialisme gelei' (How South Africa is being led step by step to socialism).[769]

Support for socialism in ANC ranks is not strange. Black South Africans were the last substantial community in the world to receive their freedom, the Soviet Union was for long the only ANC backer, and communists were the ANC's only allies in South Africa when the struggle against white supremacy entered a new phase in the early 1960s.

At present the ANC government is in a serious bind. An influential economist sums up the situation well: 'The government is in a cleft between trying to pursue market-friendly policies on the one hand and appeasing socialist and left-wing elements on the other, who see the private sector as the enemy.'[770]

Conclusion

For more than fifty years, from his speeches in the dock in the Treason Trial (1956–61), through his letters to Hendrik Verwoerd (1961) to his presidency (1994–9), Mandela cast a huge shadow over white politics. He never wavered in his conviction that the majority had the right to rule and would insist on it if their adversary refused to yield. Yet he also knew that white fears of black majority rule were great. To break the logjam, Mandela toyed with the idea of using the homeland structures to fight the Bantustan policy. This certainly would have met with strong opposition from elements within the ANC in exile. With the benefit of hindsight it is clear that Afrikaner leaders were foolish to waste these opportunities, partly because they believed Mandela was still a communist. During the all-party negotiations (1991–3) Mandela compromised by dropping the ANC demand for nationalisation, but he remained firm on majority rule.

The NP under De Klerk started the negotiations well, but abandoned most of their political demands in September 1992 in the hope of securing a stable coalition with the ANC. Some observers argue that the negotiated settlement boils down to blacks winning political power and whites retaining their property, but, as recent developments show, retaining property rights in the absence of political power will be no easy task. Mandela served only one term as president. It is possible that in a second term he could have helped to consolidate a liberal democracy by curbing both the communist elements and the ultra-nationalists in his party. But he came too late and went too soon.

SECTION FOUR

An elite abandons its people (1994–2018)

15.

Stellenbosch University turns against itself: A reply to Professor Wim de Villiers's dismissive attitude to the university's history

The future of Afrikaans as a medium of instruction at university level is to be decided shortly[†] when the Constitutional Court hears arguments about the dispute over the language policy of Stellenbosch University (SU), in which English enjoys a dominant position. If the ruling goes against Afrikaans, only one of 37 campuses in the country, namely the Potchefstroom campus of North West University, will provide students with the opportunity to complete their undergraduate studies in the medium of Afrikaans.

By coincidence the centenary edition of *Matieland*, the SU magazine for alumni, has just appeared. It contains a message from the Vice-Chancellor, Professor Wim de Villiers, under the heading 'Saam vorentoe' (Forward together). One would expect of him to offer a balanced reflection of what SU had accomplished during its first century. However, there are only a couple of cursory remarks, mainly with a negative drift.

De Villiers writes: 'Maties began as a "volksuniversiteit" (a university for the Afrikaner people). That was the "idea" that Stellenbosch stood for at the time – upliftment through higher education, but only for some, not for all. Clearly this idea was way too narrow. But this does not mean we are against Afrikaans. Afrikaans is one of our languages of instruction . . .'

Here the Vice-Chancellor is treading on thin ice. He is violating the most important principle when one deals with history, namely to judge every action within the framework of the time during which it took place.

The Union constitution of 1909 made provision for the effective equality

---

[†] First published in *Rapport*, 16 September 2018.

of two official languages. Initially, however, this granted rights only on paper. Within the economically dominant English community there was the strong expectation that English would soon supplant Dutch (and later Afrikaans) as the public language. As an observer expressed it at the time: 'English methods and the English language are bound increasingly to win their way and permeate the whole structure of society.'

The financial means of the new South African state were so meagre that it could only establish one independent university, and even this single university would require substantial support from the private sector. The Botha government embarked on a plan to transform the South African College in Cape Town into the University of Cape Town (UCT). In the spirit of the constitution's stipulation that the two official languages should enjoy equal status, FS Malan, the Minister of Education, wanted both English and Dutch as languages of instruction at the envisaged university. However, the mining magnates who were willing to provide huge sponsorship were strongly opposed to the use of Dutch. They wanted UCT to attract high-quality English-speaking academics from foreign shores.

It was in these circumstances that the idea of Stellenbosch University was born. Jannie Marais, a Stellenbosch farmer who had made a fortune on the diamond mines, donated a substantial sum for the founding of a university at Stellenbosch on condition that at least half the lectures were given in Dutch or Afrikaans.

To come back to the Vice-Chancellor's message to alumni in 2018. One wonders what he means when he writes that the development of SU as a university that would serve predominantly the Afrikaner community was 'too narrow-minded'. Surely it is naive to think Afrikaans could have developed as a language if it had to compete on equal terms with English right from the start at SU. In 1915 only 15 per cent of Afrikaans children progressed further than Standard 5, and only 4 per cent were fluent in English.

In 1915 Langenhoven wrote this satirical poem about Afrikaners pleading for the 'peaceful coexistence' of the two official languages at SU.

Friends, let's make peace and keep the peace / let the lion and the lamb graze together / the lamb on the grass and the lion on the lamb / you can be the lion and I will be the lamb / soon I will become part of the lion / to the credit of the lamb . . . and the pleasure of the lion.

The Vice-Chancellor gives the assurance that neither he nor the university is against Afrikaans, and then continues: 'Afrikaans is one of our languages of instruction – but on the basis of sound pedagogical principles, not fomented by ideology or ethnic identity.'

The Vice-Chancellor is clearly unaware of the consensus in the literature about language maintenance: a sectional or national language cannot maintain itself against a world language, such as English, without speakers of the former language regarding it as an important part of their social identity. In the book *Language Endangerment and Language Maintenance* (2002) Stephen Wurm defines the iron law of language preservation as follows: 'One of the most important factors for the maintenance and reinvigoration of a threatened language is the attitude of speakers towards their own language and the importance they attach to it as a major symbol of their identity.'

One does not know what the Vice-Chancellor means by the words that SU should not be driven by any 'ideology'. One cannot help thinking of the dictum formulated by the American economist Joan Nelson, 'One's ideology is like one's breath; one can't smell it.'

Is there any university without an ideology? Is the Vice-Chancellor trying to say that a university like UCT has not been driven by any ideology? In the volume commemorating the SU centenary, Professor Bill Nasson, a celebrated historian with ties to both SU and UCT, writes that UCT was never really driven by a demand for racial integration, but rather by an 'anti-Nationalist feeling' which enabled it to position itself with the 'besieged anti-apartheid front'.

What astonishes me most about the Vice-Chancellor's review of SU's first century is that not a single word is uttered of what can be seen as its greatest accomplishments during its first century, namely its resistance against British imperial ideology and the establishment of an indigenous intellectual tradition.

In 1918, when SU opened its doors, JFW Grosskopf wrote that the university must keep abreast of humanity's intellectual heritage and traditions. At the same time it should guard against idolising that which was international at the cost of what was uniquely South African.

One of the most notable contributions by Stellenbosch University was its key role in developing Afrikaans as a literary and intellectual medium of communication. The German scholar Heinz Kloss expressed this achievement as follows: 'In the whole world Afrikaans is the only non-European/non-Asian language to have acquired full university status, and that is used in all branches of life and in the world of scholarship.'

Not only was universal knowledge domesticated in the Afrikaans universities but they also incorporated some vital aspects of the cultural heritage of the continent of Europe in their syllabi. One thinks here especially of Roman-Dutch law and of the Dutch and German tradition of history writing based on primary sources, and the striving to discover *'wie es eigentlich gewesen'* (how things actually were). Invariably, history written in Afrikaans stresses cultural as well as economic forces.

In 2017 Mahmood Mamdani, one of Africa's most highly rated intellectuals, said that universities elsewhere in Africa did not represent any specific intellectual tradition. The only exceptions were the Afrikaans universities, which transformed Afrikaans into the vehicle of a domestic intellectual tradition. He deplored the fact that the South African government did not attempt to emulate the achievement of Afrikaans but kept on stressing education through the medium of English.

In 2015 the Children's Institute at UCT reported that the under-achievement of black children at school is such that by the end of secondary school they are at least five years behind their 'privileged' counterparts.[771] In 2016 South Africa's Statistician General, Pali Lehohla, expressed 'horror' about the failure rates of blacks. They had been taught in their second language, while whites had generally received mother-tongue instruction.

Stellenbosch and other Afrikaans universities transformed racially far too late but they were never institutions that welcomed only Afrikaners. In the mid-1970s the Afrikaans universities were more successful in attracting English students than the English universities were in attracting Afrikaans students.

The Stellenbosch Vice-Chancellor speaks about a university which 'wants to continue in the provision of the great need for instruction in Afrikaans', but significantly does not mention a single figure to quantify the current offering of Afrikaans courses at the university. My information is that in the Social Science Faculty the departments of History, Sociology, Political Science and Social Anthropology use virtually no Afrikaans. In the Law Faculty Afrikaans is for all practical purposes absent.

Back in 2016, when it had become clear where the university was heading with its language policy, Professor Marius de Waal of the Law Faculty said in Senate: 'It is very clear what the English student can expect in the context of this formulation. The question is, what can the Afrikaans students expect? Students who want teaching in Afrikaans. What are their rights, what are their expectations? The cynical or literal interpretation would mean that a few words, a few token words in the course of a lecture, would be in compliance with this formulation.' This is precisely the policy the Law Faculty follows today, but the Vice-Chancellor keeps on talking about how much value SU attaches to Afrikaans. In his *Matieland* article he speaks about 'the great need for tuition in Afrikaans' and declares that this need is the reason why the university continues to meet the demand for tuition in Afrikaans. Unfortunately the words have no meaning.

In his article the Vice-Chancellor offers an explanation for SU's virtual abandonment of Afrikaans as a language of tuition. He states that instead of a '*volksuniversiteit*', SU wants to become a 'world-class university'. The rush to climb in the world rankings is indeed one of the important reasons why the university has anglicised so rapidly. This attempt seems to have been futile. The international Centre for World University Rankings, which assigns rankings to a thousand universities, shows that SU dropped from 330th (third in South Africa) in 2017 to 448th (fifth in South Africa) in 2018. Philip Altbach and Ellen Hazelkorn have sounded a warning in this regard: the ranking system perverts the true function of the university, namely to transfer the knowledge and skills graduates will need in the communities they will one day serve.[772]

The Afrikaans-speaking community in the Western Cape, which makes up more than half of the people in the province, requires a university where they can be trained in the language with which they can one day serve this community. This applies especially to the training of teachers and legal practitioners.

When SU reviewed its language policy in 2017 the Federation of Governing Bodies of South African Schools, which, together with the South African Teachers

Union, is the most representative body in Afrikaans education, submitted a memorandum. It declared: 'Our members are unanimously in favour of retaining Afrikaans as a fully-fledged language of instruction at US [University of Stellenbosch]. This means that the use of Afrikaans must in no way be diminished at US. The US should continually promote and develop tertiary education in Afrikaans.' The Stellenbosch management and the University Council ignored this appeal, thereby drawing a line through a century-old relationship.

It is especially the coloured Afrikaans-speaking community that has been left in the lurch by the SU's failure to provide Afrikaans tuition. In 2013 the Council for Higher Education conducted a study to determine the success rate of different population groups that enrolled for a bachelor's degree in the period 1970–2010. The percentage of white and Indian students who received bachelor's degrees climbed from 18 to 29 per cent. The figure for black students dropped from 11 to 9 per cent, and the figure for coloured students dropped from 10 per cent in 1970 to a disastrous 6 per cent in 2010. During the past fifteen years the number of coloured Afrikaans undergraduate students at SU has remained stagnant in the range of 1,300 to 1,400. Black numbers rose slowly from about 1,000 in 2010 to 2,336 in 2017 in a total undergraduate student body of just below 20,000. The home language of three-quarters of them is not English.

By contrast, the number of coloured English-speaking students multiplied five times from 512 to 2,588, while that of white English-speaking students doubled from 2,384 to 5,458. From this it should be clear that the great beneficiaries of SU's language policy are the white and coloured English-speakers.

In 2016 the movement Gelyke Kanse/Equal Opportunities took SU to the Cape High Court for violating its own language policy of 2014, which accorded equal status to Afrikaans and English as languages of tuition. In the court proceedings SU admitted that a fifth of its lecturers could not teach in Afrikaans and that the university violated its own language policy in 268 modules.

My proposal is that SU implement both an Afrikaans-medium and an English-medium stream. It has been calculated that this will cost 4 per cent of the university's budget. Whether SU will easily follow this route is doubtful. In recent times SU has become known for simply following the easiest path when it comes to the matter of language.

In 2005, when the *taalstryd* (language struggle) erupted at SU, Koos Bekker,

MD of Naspers and a University Council member, made a telling remark in an article that was published in *Die Burger*. If SU becomes anglicised, he said, it would signal that the university has chosen the road of *papbroekigheid* (spinelessness). I have fully subscribed to that sentiment all along.

16.

The rise and decline of Afrikaans as a public language and the possible demise of the Afrikaners

The rise of Afrikaans as a public language within the course of the first seventy-five years of the twentieth century is a truly remarkable phenomenon. The German linguist Heinz Kloss observed: 'Unless we consider Arabic an African tongue . . . Afrikaans is the only non-European/non-Asiatic language to have gained full university status and that came to be used in all branches of life and learning.'[773] During the twentieth century only Hebrew and Afrikaans, of all the world's small speech communities, managed to achieve this level of development. Two large speech communities, Bahasa (Malay and Indonesian), achieved the same feat.

In 1994 the sociologist and pollster Lawrence Schlemmer concluded that Afrikaans, though spoken as a first language by only six million people, forming 15 per cent of the population, was the strongest language in South Africa in the way it was used formally and informally.[774] As remarkable as the rise of Afrikaans has been its sudden decline as a language of instruction at universities and schools and as a language of record in the courts since 1994. This final chapter discusses these themes.

The rise of Afrikaans

By the end of the nineteenth century the Afrikaans literary output was still limited and its status as a public language very low. The Anglo-Boer War (1899–1902) was the major turning point in the rise of Afrikaans. The war shattered the relations between the two white communities. When the constitution for the new state, the Union of South Africa, was drafted, the delegates agreed that for economic growth and stability the greatest priority was to foster reconciliation between the two white communities. The choice as the symbol of reconciliation fell on granting effective equal status as official languages to English and Dutch (Afrikaans would replace Dutch in 1925). It included the right to receive education in the mother tongue in public schools and universities.

Within a decade or two Afrikaans became the symbol of Afrikaner identity. In a comparative context Wurm has described the importance of this development well: 'One of the most important factors for the maintenance and reinvigoration of a threatened language is the attitude of speakers towards their own language and the importance they attach to it as a major symbol of their identity.'[775]

Comparative studies show that the constituency-based system of representation, which South Africa took over from Britain, favours the largest ethnic group in an electorate. It was almost inevitable that the Afrikaners, making up more than half the voters, would try to forge a sense of unity on the basis of an ethnic nationalism. Unity was achieved by appealing to white Afrikaans-speakers and by segregating the coloured community. It ensured the victory of the National Party (NP) in 1948, but in a longer-term perspective the political alienation of a large part of this community has represented the greatest loss that Afrikaans and the Afrikaans-speaking community have suffered.

At university level Afrikaans became an instrument of decolonisation by either creating its own intellectual tradition or emphasising a part of the common European heritage other than the English one. In 1918, when Victoria College became the University of Stellenbosch (SU), JFW Grosskopf argued that every university in the world should strive to remain in touch with the common intellectual heritage of mankind. At the same time it should guard against elevating the national and the universal as the highest good. Grosskopf warned in terms that are as applicable in 2018 as they were in 1918: very often 'internationalism' served as a mere cloak for advancing the interests of empires and great powers. He argued that a university like Stellenbosch, existing in a multi-ethnic society, should rather reinterpret the 'national idiosyncrasies' without taking the metropole as the ultimate reference point. This was particularly true of the disciplines of philosophy, history, law, literature and linguistics.[776]

In the nineteenth century, with Britain extending its sway over the subcontinent, Dutch- and Afrikaans-speaking intelligentsia tried to develop a distinctive approach to the challenges of becoming indigenous in Africa while upholding some key Western values.[777] When James Bryce, a renowned British constitutional scholar, visited the Republic of the Orange Free State, he said: 'In the Orange Free State I discovered, in 1895, the kind of commonwealth which the fond fancy of the philosophers of the last century painted . . . an ideal commonwealth', with a constitution 'the pure and original product of African conditions'.[778] He stated that this republic came closest to the ideal 'of free and independent persons uniting in an absolutely new social compact for mutual help and defence, and thereby creating a government whose authority has had and can have no origin save in the consent of the governed'.[779]

Soon after the establishment of the Union of South Africa, CFJ (Tobie) Muller, a young Stellenbosch philosopher, published a thought-provoking essay *Die geloofbelydenis van 'n nasionalis* (A nationalist's confession of faith). It made a nationalist appeal, but also warned against the pitfalls of nationalism. The Afrikaners, he wrote, had developed their nationalism in the 'school of misery', and the line of distinction between them and the English-speakers was 'drawn in blood'. But, he continued, the Afrikaners must not allow their nationalism to degenerate into a hatred of other nations. It was also not good enough simply to be different from the English-speakers. To be legitimate, nationalism had to have a moral purpose. Nationalism was the best counter to a 'jingo-imperialism' in South Africa that aimed at dissolving different peoples into an insipid, bland, English-speaking 'uniformity' that drew on Britain as its source of strength.

Over the next eighty years several influential Afrikaans philosophers, most notably Johannes Degenaar and André du Toit of Stellenbosch, made important contributions to developing a local philosophical tradition and searching for a liberal solution suited to South Africa. As a recent study noted, this thinking represented a remarkable *tussen-bewussyn* (in-between consciousness) emanating from thinkers rooted in a community that stands between Europe and Africa.[780]

Early in the 1920s Stellenbosch University's *Annale* became one of the first scientific journals to accept contributions in Afrikaans. Afrikaner academics eagerly accepted the challenge of offering alternative approaches to those emanating from Britain. In law they stressed the importance of Roman-Dutch law, initially irritating their English colleagues who wanted to focus only on English law. In 1937 the *Tydskrif vir Romeins-Hollandse Reg* (Journal for Roman-Dutch Law) appeared for the first time. On its editorial board sat both Afrikaner and Dutch academics.

The journal offered legal academics the opportunity to publish articles in Afrikaans on Roman-Dutch law. With growing numbers of Afrikaner lawyers appointed to the bench, the influence of Roman-Dutch law on South African jurisprudence steadily increased. The work of the Stellenbosch legal scholar JC de Wet constituted a breakthrough. He published path-breaking works especially on the law of contracts (1947) and criminal law (1949). He refused to have his works translated into English as a way of forcing English jurists to learn Afrikaans.

The most outstanding Afrikaner historian was PJ van der Merwe, who between 1937 and 1944 published a trilogy on the *trekboere*, who pioneered European expansion into the interior between 1700 and 1900. He and other Afrikaner historians were strongly influenced by the German historian Leopold von Ranke, whose dictum of establishing *wie es eigenlich gewesen* acted almost as hallowed formula for writing 'objective' history.

While liberal and Marxist historians emphasised material interests (individuals in the case of liberals; class in the case of Marxists), Afrikaner historians rejected the notion that any action undertaken in the name of culture or nationhood was simply a cover for middle-class actors in advancing their material interests. Instead, they stressed that concerns with culture constituted a crucial element of nationhood. What a scholar of Eastern and Central European history has written is true of the twentieth-century Afrikaners: 'A culture is the sum total of the subjective perceptions of a community; the rules by which it orders its life, its sense of a common past and shared future, and its socially constructed picture of the world.'[781]

During the 1930s the Afrikaans contributions to the discipline of history began to make great strides. Historians, of whom several were trained in the Netherlands and Germany, rejected the chauvinistic form of history called *volksgeskiedenis* and started to write what was called 'scientific objective history' in which great emphasis was placed on the study of primary sources. In the discipline of history the most prestigious journal was the *Archives Yearbook for South African History*, founded in 1938, which published the most outstanding master's and doctoral dissertations on aspects of South African history. Senior academics, both Afrikaans- and English-speaking, served on the editorial board. As can be seen in Table 16.1, Afrikaans more than held its own.

Table 16.1: Dissertations in Archives Yearbook (by language)

	Afrikaans	English
1938 to 1949	22	14
1950 to 1959	30	14
1960 to 1969	24	16
1970 to 1979	10	4
1980 to 1989	17	5
1990 to 1997	6	6
Afrikaans total = 109		English total = 59

The rise of Afrikaans as a language of advanced research in the arts and humanities was soon extended to the natural sciences and medicine. In 1980 Afrikaans was the 32nd most frequently used language in the articles indexed by *Chemical Abstracts* (more than those in Hindi, Armenian and Arabic) and 25th in *Index Medicus*.[782]

The era between 1925 and 1975 can be described as the era of the Afrikaner *volksbeweging*, or the national movement. Its message was that Afrikaans had the potential of expressing itself in every sphere of life, including academic books and articles. University lecturers were generally expected to use Afrikaans in their contribution to scholarship or in exchanges in public. This was particularly true in the fields of the arts, humanities and law.

Despite coming under threat during the 1990s, Afrikaans remains the dominant literary language in South Africa, judged solely by the number of locally produced books. The following figure gives the literary production profile of the late 1990s. Of the approximately 5,000 books of poetry, drama and fiction published in South Africa, some 60 per cent were written in Afrikaans. English followed at 33 per cent while 7 per cent of titles were in one of the other (black) African languages. Books written in Afrikaans, as the great poet and essayist NP van Wyk Louw said, must speak to the best of minds and the deepest of longings of people and give them something they can obtain in no other language.

At present the Afrikaans novel is probably stronger than ever before with outstanding works by Karel Schoeman, Etienne van Heerden, Ingrid Winterbach and Eben Venter appearing during the past two decades. In poetry there are the striking contributions of Breyten Breytenbach, Antjie Krog and Marlene van

Niekerk. In 2017 Breytenbach received the Zbigniew Herbert International Literary Award in Warsaw, which honours outstanding artistic, intellectual and literary achievements on the world stage.

Table 16.2: Literary production during the 1990s

Language	Poetry	Drama	Fiction	Total
Afrikaans	283	53	2464	2800
English	302	127	545	974
Multilingual	34	20	109	163
African languages	342	283	635	1260

Source: Francis Galloway, 'Statistical trends in South African book publishing in the 1990s', *Alternation*, 9, 1 (2002), p. 221.

Despite demographic pressure Afrikaans held its own in the first two decades of the new century. According to research by the SABC in 2015, the 6.8 million people whose first language is Afrikaans are responsible for 35 per cent of the country's purchasing power. The 1.2 million listeners to the radio station RSG compares well with the main English-medium stations, and RSG generates the most income for the SABC. The lack of any comprehensive Afrikaans offering on state television prompted Naspers to start an Afrikaans pay channel in 1999. It is now the most profitable channel on DStv.

As in other countries, the circulation of Afrikaans newspapers has dropped sharply. Afrikaans readers nevertheless continue to buy Afrikaans newspapers. Three-quarters of Afrikaners read only Afrikaans papers.

Afrikaans theatre suffered a major blow when the government abolished the state-financed arts councils. The gap was filled by the private business sector, which has sponsored arts festivals in several towns. The most successful are the arts or word festivals that annually take place in towns like Oudtshoorn, Stellenbosch and Potchefstroom, The attraction of these festivals lies in the fact that they strongly and consciously address a particular culture and community. One of the latest additions is the Suidoosterfees directed primarily at the coloured Afrikaans community.

It is sometimes argued that Afrikaans culture is so vibrant that it would be able to survive the loss of universities that teach in Afrikaans. This is a serious mistake. The flourishing state of Afrikaans is the result of previous investment in the language. Without investment in the production of a new generation of Afrikaans-speakers in Afrikaans schools and universities, the language will inevitably decline and perish.

A critique of neo-colonialism in African universities

The primary nationalism in South Africa's history was the British nationalism that dominated the political system, the economy, culture and social manners. Afrikaner nationalists reacted to it by stressing their own culture; Africans did so by emphasising their race.[783] The African National Congress (ANC) since its founding in 1912 has embraced English in its public communications. This view changed briefly during the 1950s when it tried to draw the different communities of South Africa together in a common struggle against apartheid. The Freedom Charter of 1955 adopted a more subtle approach that recognised the plurality of nations and cultures.

When the movement was banned in 1960, several thousand Africans went into exile to states north of South Africa where they found that local educated elites embraced the colonial language (English, French or Portuguese) as the official language and as the main medium of instruction in schools and universities. The exiled ANC did not take to heart the criticism of this policy offered by a few African intellectuals. One was Kwesi Kwaa Prah, born in Ghana, who spent most of his career teaching sociology in southern Africa. He wrote in 1995 that Western colonialism had set itself the task of replacing the tongue of African people with the language of the colonial power. It had created an elite that was nominally African but in reality was mesmerised by and beholden to Western culture.

Professor Emmanuel Ayandele, one of the most outstanding Nigerian academics and university chancellors, remarked that while African universities tried to give their curricula an African cast, they remained for the most part centres for the diffusion of Western culture. 'Culturally they are amorphous, a class of Africans with an English, French or American veneer.'

Two African academics strongly criticised the local black political elite for its insistence on English tuition from the early school years to postgraduate studies. In their critique they highlighted the contrast offered by the Afrikaans universities.

The Yoruba novelist Kole Omotoso posed this question: 'If the Afrikaners needed a new language that could make the Western influence on the one hand and their African experience, on the other, intelligible, why would Africans think they could contain the same experience in the language of Europe alone without domesticating that thought in African languages?'[784]

In 2017 Mahmood Mamdani, a Ugandan academic whose book *Citizen and Subject* is widely acclaimed, gave the prestigious TB Davie Memorial Lecture on academic freedom at the University of Cape Town. Students who had put the 'decolonisation of the curriculum' on the agenda keenly expected Mamdani's endorsement of their campaign. They were in for a surprise. Mamdani said that universities elsewhere in Africa represent no specific academic tradition. Afrikaans was the only exception by transforming itself into a language that was the bearer of a particular intellectual tradition. He deplored the fact that the ANC government made no effort to elevate the other African languages in South Africa to this status.[785]

The ANC government did not take much notice of such views despite the fact that world-wide the mother tongue is accepted as the best medium of instruction at school. The first years are especially critical for the way in which a child performs later. From the start the ANC used English as the main medium of government communication with the public despite the fact that English mother-tongue speakers formed less than 10 per cent of the population, compared with Afrikaans (13.5 per cent), Xhosa (16 per cent) and Zulu (23.5 per cent).

The ANC adopted an education policy that compelled most black children to receive education in the medium of English from an early stage. It pressured many Afrikaans-medium schools to introduce parallel-medium tuition, which often led to Afrikaans being supplanted by English. It also exerted steady pressure on the Afrikaans universities to expand courses offered in English without supplying additional funds for parallel-medium instruction.

In 2016 and 2017 black students protested on several campuses against 'colonialist' teaching. At Stellenbosch the university authorities granted their demand to phase out Afrikaans in favour of English as the main medium of instruction. As Prah sadly remarks: 'There was hardly any mention of the possibility of utilising African languages as languages of education and instruction.'[786]

A changing university environment

During the 1990s the position of Afrikaans as a university language with a secure foundation changed radically. The National Party irreversibly lost power and, with it, control over the state. A constitution was adopted that provided for eleven official languages, which everyone knew was impracticable.

For the ANC the main objective was finding a formula for elevating English to the position of *primus inter pares*. Article 29(2) of the Constitution makes provision for students to receive education in the official language of their choice, but this is contingent on equity and practicality, and the need to address past injustices. This left the door wide open for imposing English as the medium of instruction. Afrikaans was also challenged by the steady spread in the Western world of English as the language in which the most important articles and books appear.

At university level Afrikaans suddenly experienced far greater threats than most people had expected. Among the factors contributing most to the marginalisation of Afrikaans were (a) the introduction of a ranking system for lecturers and universities, (b) a change in the state's formula for funding, (c) a sharp increase in black student numbers and (d) government hostility to Afrikaans.

The introduction of the rating system

During the 1980s a system of peer evaluation was introduced for researchers. The architect in South Africa was Jack de Wet, an Afrikaner academic who taught at Oxford University for nearly thirty years, and was highly regarded internationally as a mathematician and theoretical physicist. After his retirement he returned to South Africa and was soon asked by a government body to report on the state of research in the natural sciences and engineering.

De Wet was shocked by the great brain drain as top researchers left South African universities because of inadequate research funding by the state. His report recommended a rating system in the form of 'track-record evaluation' of researchers. This was accepted by the National Research Foundation and soon extended to the social sciences and humanities in 2002.

The report introduced a five-tier system of rankings. At the top was an A rating awarded to researchers accepted by the international community as leaders in their fields without any measure of doubt. At the bottom was a category for researchers whose recent work did not merit support. Almost all the researchers in the top two categories published in English and did so mostly in international journals. Researchers finding themselves in the lower categories would soon discover that the taps for research funding had been turned off.

After two rounds of assessment, De Wet's team combined the findings for engineering and natural sciences and then published a table of the quality of research at the different universities. The table was topped by the four liberal, English-medium universities, all scoring a mark of more than 8. The bottom three, all scoring less than 2, were Stellenbosch, Pretoria and Potchefstroom. Halfway between these Afrikaans universities and the English universities at the top stood the University of the Free State with a score of 4.75.

De Wet had particularly harsh words for Stellenbosch University. He said: 'It gets the cream of Afrikaans schools and the university is located in a beautiful setting. But it is an open question if this potential would ever be realised.' To drive home his point he referred to a researcher at the University of Cape Town (UCT) who compared the atmosphere for research on the campus to the best in the world.[787]

At Stellenbosch it was a major shock for the staff and students to see themselves second last. It had always regarded itself as the leading Afrikaans university and almost on a par with UCT. Now it suddenly found itself far below UCT and well below the University of the Orange Free State, which it never regarded as its peer. The ratings were not only a matter of prestige but they also generated revenue for the universities.

The importance that Afrikaans universities in particular suddenly came to attach to the ranking system was indeed extraordinary. Flip Smit, an alumnus of SU who served as Vice-Chancellor of the University of Pretoria during the 1990s, would later make a perceptive remark on the reason for this. 'The scars of the scientific isolation of universities in the apartheid era ran deep. Especially the ex-Afrikaans universities fell over their feet to embrace internationalisation. Perhaps that is why they went overboard in their attempts to climb in the ranking system and thus demonstrate that their institution was on its way to achieving international status.'[788]

In 2017 Smit warned against the obsession of leading South African universities with the ranking system. The list published by the Centre for World University Rankings showed that between 2016 and 2017 the ranking of the top South African universities all fell by twenty points or more. Between 2015 and 2017 the leading South African universities fell as follows: University of the Witwatersrand to 176th, University of Cape Town to 265th, University of Stellenbosch to 329th, University of Pretoria to 697th.

Philip Altbach and Ellen Hazelkorn, recognised scholars in the study of university performance, sounded a similar warning: the ranking system perverts the true function of a university, namely to transfer the knowledge and skills that graduates need in the communities they will one day serve.[789]

The greatest loser in the process was Afrikaans as a medium of instruction and academic publication. Scholars soon realised that it was to their advantage to publish in English. The English journals often had more prestige and in some fields there was a shortage of referees for Afrikaans articles. Between 1990 and 2002 the proportion of Afrikaans titles in academic journals dropped from 14 per cent to 5 per cent.[790] Most of the Afrikaans articles were published by Potchefstroom University (25 per cent). Stellenbosch was last at 11 per cent.

A changed formula for funding

In the 1980s the state provided 60 per cent of the funding for universities, while student fees contributed approximately 30 per cent. This started to change in the late 1980s. A growing part of the budget is now composed of the funds that university researchers generate. In 2017 the sources of revenue for Stellenbosch University were made up as follows: state (37 per cent), student fees (24 per cent), grants and contracts (26 per cent), private donations (7 per cent), and services and products (4 per cent).

The revenue generated by the so-called third stream (grants and contracts) encouraged management and staff to believe that the decision about the language of tuition should be left to their discretion. Financial considerations had to become ever more important.

Attracting more English staff and students

To improve its rankings and receive more revenue, some of the ex-Afrikaans universities, particularly SU, quietly waived the requirement that staff had to demonstrate or acquire the ability to teach in Afrikaans before receiving a permanent appointment. In 2016 SU admitted in court that 200 of its lecturers (almost a fifth) were unable to teach in Afrikaans. Most of them were appointed to boost the university's research credentials.

In the case of SU, the policy yielded dramatic results. Between the mid-1980s, when De Wet's findings became known, and 2003, when the NRF's 2003 rankings were published, the position of SU rose from second from the bottom on the list of South African universities to second place.

By 2017 SU was the most productive university in the country as judged by the number of research publications and the number of master's and doctoral degrees awarded. It has 14 A-rated researchers, the fourth-highest among South African universities.

Accommodating an influx of non-Afrikaans students

Another factor working against Afrikaans was the effect of two migrations. One was the flight to the ex-Afrikaans universities of white English-speaking students from the English-medium liberal universities, which had enrolled large numbers of black students and whose administration had become weaker in some cases.

The second migration was the flight of black students from the so-called bush universities, established under the apartheid system, to the previously white universities. Their numbers were supplemented by the large army of unemployed youth. In 2016 it was estimated that 57 per cent of blacks between the ages of 15 and 34 were without a job. Some went to university simply to keep themselves occupied. Many black students support their families, especially those who live in the rural areas. Every year universities have to write off millions of rands as a result of students not paying their fees.

About half of the black students leave university without a qualification.[791] But it is not only black students who leave without qualifying: 55 per cent for all students (and 45 per cent for residential universities) leave the universities without a degree.

Black students whose parents receive an income of less than R300,000 per year are admitted free. Fees, books and food are all received free. It was President Zuma who acted as the great liberator, thereby hanging a millstone around his successor's neck.

Universities have lowered their admission standards drastically. The number of black students who were accepted rose faster than the number of pupils who passed matric.

The participation rate of the different communities as a percentage of students in the age group 18–24 is as follows: white 55 per cent, black 17 per cent, and coloured 15 per cent. Although the coloured community makes up 9 per cent of the country's population, they form only 6 per cent of the South African student population. The coloured share of the total student population who received degrees between 1970 and 2010 dropped from 10 per cent to 6 per cent. Table 16.3 shows a twelvefold increase in the number of black students enrolled at all the universities.

Table 16.3: Student population figures

	Blacks	Coloureds	Indians	Whites	Total
1986	54,997	13,552	21,838	177,744	277,115
2014	679,800	60,716	53,611	166,172	969,154

Black students not only hope to obtain a degree but also to improve their command of English. Several scholars have pointed out that English has acquired its hegemonic position in most of the world because of its stratification function. Phillipson's general observation is very valid for South Africa.[792] The black middle class use English to secure jobs and privileges, and those of their children, by sending them to good schools where they learn to speak standard English. It is very hard for poor black children who have gone to a township school to compete against a peer who has gone to a private or ex-Model C school where parents pay considerable fees.

The use of English as a medium for students who do not speak it at home has come at a high price. In 2015 the Children's Institute at UCT reported that after graduating from school, students from township schools are at least five years behind their classmates from a more privileged background. In 2016 South Africa's Statistician General, Pali Lehohla, expressed 'horror' at the difference between the failure rates of blacks, who had been taught in their second language, and whites, who received mother-tongue instruction. In the 1980s for every black graduate there were 1.2 white graduates. 'Currently [in 2015],' he continued, 'for every black person who graduates from university there are six white people who make it through successfully.'[793]

Official hostility to Afrikaans

The South African Constitution failed to define what it means by an official language. On paper South Africa has eleven official languages, which are theoretically on a par with each other. In practice English is far superior to the other languages. The government acknowledges Afrikaans and English as languages of instruction at university level; at the same time, however, while rejecting the idea of single-medium Afrikaans universities, it approves of single-medium English universities.

In 2002 a minister described Afrikaans universities as running counter 'to the end goal of a transformed higher education system'. The statement was later repudiated, but the important point is that while condoning parallel medium, the government provided no funding for such instruction.

Parallel medium was unpopular among teaching staff because they were not paid for the extra lectures. Dual medium suffered from the defect that there was no strong pressure on either students or lecturers to become proficient in Afrikaans.

The lack of political protection

In its rise as a language during the twentieth century, Afrikaans could count on the state to enforce the constitutional provisions with respect to the two official languages. After 1994 the ball game changed dramatically. While Presidents Mandela and Ramaphosa were proficient in Afrikaans, many cabinet ministers and top civil servants were not. Some were openly hostile to Afrikaans.

When the fortunes of the NP started to wane, most Afrikaans-speakers flocked to the Democratic Party, which swallowed the bulk of the NP in 1999 to become the Democratic Alliance (DA). Both Tony Leon and Helen Zille as DA leaders did not hesitate to take up the cudgels for Afrikaans if bureaucrats or university principals undermined it. Leon even received a complaint from Dr Chris Brink, SU Vice-Chancellor, when he spoke up for the right of students to receive their tuition in Afrikaans at Stellenbosch. Brink accused Leon of meddling in the internal affairs of the university. After Zille stepped down as leader, the DA's support for the retention of Afrikaans at Stellenbosch seemed to dwindle despite the fact that Afrikaans-speakers form the single biggest bloc in the party.

The electoral system is a factor that is often underestimated in the language question. The Westminster constituency-based system makes it possible to exert strong pressure on candidates contesting a seat in a university town. The electoral system now used in South Africa removes such pressure. The PR electoral system produces what is called the 'suspended state', which is prevalent in much of Africa.

'Laponce's law' at work

Although Afrikaners lost power in 1994, it is baffling that the universities in general have made such a poor effort to retain Afrikaans as medium of instruction while also, with one or two exceptions, failing to promote scholarly work in Afrikaans. One of the reasons is the Afrikaners' loss of control over both the government and state, which could authoritatively decide which universities should take responsibility for Afrikaans. In the absence of such a system there was a strong temptation to simply use the easiest route in the choice of the policy of instruction.

There are at present 171,000 white students of whom slightly more than half are Afrikaans. Purely in demographic terms, and assuming that the interests of students come first, it is not far-fetched to assume that two or three thriving Afrikaans-medium universities could have been established.

Dr Jakes Gerwel, former Vice-Chancellor of the University of the Western Cape and Director-General of the President's office in Nelson Mandela's time, tried in 2001 to persuade the vice-chancellors of the five universities still offering a fair amount of Afrikaans-medium instruction to single out two Afrikaans universities to which a special responsibility for maintaining Afrikaans could be assigned. They would have to report annually to Parliament on the way they executed this responsibility. No agreement was reached: every vice-chancellor wanted to 'preserve' Afrikaans in his own way. What it boiled down to was a determination on the part of each to keep their share of the Afrikaans market without offering anything in return that would ensure the survival of Afrikaans.

Instead, most universities opted for parallel or dual medium despite the dire warning of Jean Laponce, a French Canadian scholar, who described the phenomenon of language displacement in a book that came out in 1987. Laponce wrote: 'A bilingual school and university system generally has only the appearance of equality. Even when it is balanced at the level of courses it is in fact balanced in favour of the dominant language, which dominates the environment outside the school. Bilingualism in education is thus generally a bilingualism of transition, which in the long run facilitates linguistic assimilation.'[794]

At Pretoria and Stellenbosch, where most Afrikaans-speaking students were enrolled, English inexorably began to displace Afrikaans in exactly the way Laponce predicted. At Pretoria a new policy of parallel-medium teaching was announced with the proviso that Afrikaans would only be used if there were sufficient numbers for an Afrikaans stream. The declining share of students at Pretoria who expressed a preference for Afrikaans tuition is shown in Table 16.4.

Table 16.4: Proportion of Afrikaans students at UP preferring Afrikaans

1995	71%
1999	59%
2004	44%
2010	38%
2015	18%
2017	Afrikaans tuition abolished

At SU the position of Afrikaans declined rapidly after the appointment in 2001 of Dr Chris Brink as Vice-Chancellor. The contest for the position had nearly deadlocked between two candidates. Dr Rolf Stumpf, who narrowly lost, held the view that the existence and development of SU had been mainly determined by the Afrikaans community and that no higher-level development could occur without the Afrikaans-speaking community's active co-operation. As regards the issue of diversity, he said: 'I have always believed that Stellenbosch should remain an Afrikaans university from a national-diversity perspective – diversity clearly implies much more than just race and gender. Language coupled with culture are also important considerations for diversity.'

By contrast Dr Chris Brink, who was appointed in the end, scoffed at the notion that the university had a special duty to transmit a particular culture – indeed, he coined the term 'Orania of the mind' (Orania is an all-Afrikaner homeland founded in a remote part of the country) to denigrate the idea of a university committed to single-medium Afrikaans tuition.

He also expressed the conviction that a limited English offering could be imported, but promised that with his 'good management' Afrikaans would remain the most important medium of instruction. But Brink, enthusiastically backed by Edwin Hertzog, chairman of the University Council, tried to manage the language policy without language-proficiency conditions, rules and supervision, which predictably led to the large-scale undermining of Afrikaans.

The main medium of instruction was the so-called T-option (the bilingual option), according to which both languages were intermittently used in the same class. There were no requirements for language proficiency, no monitoring of the rule that Afrikaans had to be used at least 50 per cent of the time, no feedback from students, no obligation on the part of the lecturer to report to the head of department or the dean on the functioning of the system. Van Zyl Slabbert, who would later become Chancellor of the university, correctly called this method of teaching a 'pedagogical absurdity'.

In 2006 Laponce was asked about the future of Afrikaans at SU. He took one look at the policy and then correctly predicted: 'Afrikaans will survive on the SU campus but only as a decoration.'[795] Despite this, Afrikaans students remained loyal to Afrikaans for a considerable period. In the only opinion poll that the SU management requested from an independent, outside body (the Schlemmer report of 2008), more than 80 per cent of Afrikaans-speakers and approximately 40 per cent of English-speakers indicated a preference for predominantly Afrikaans-medium tuition.

Instead of using the report as a basis for language policy, management proceeded by doubling the intake of white English-speaking students between 2008 and 2016 from 7,000 to 14,000 (nearly half of the total undergraduate body). Coloured English-speaking student numbers increased three times from 613 to 2,134. By contrast white Afrikaans-speaking students stayed in a range from 7,000 to 8,000, while coloured Afrikaans students increased only slightly from 1,364 to 1,513. Recruiters from UCT have little doubt that the flight to Stellenbosch had much to do with the fact that the traditional English campuses have become increasingly black.

SU not only took in increasing numbers of English-language students but also flouted its own policy that lecturers had to become proficient in Afrikaans.

In 2016 the SU admitted that over 200 lecturers were unable to provide tuition in Afrikaans.

A managerial conception of the university

On university councils, especially that of Stellenbosch, a growing number of business people sit who consider universities as a business enterprise rather than an academic or cultural institution. In the case of Stellenbosch, business people like Edwin Hertzog, Chair of the University Council, in alliance with the Vice-Chancellor, Chris Brink, between 2002 and 2008 used the so-called T-option (switching languages in the same lecture period) to enable English to make vast inroads. Notable exceptions on the SU Council were Koos Bekker, GT Ferreira and Ritzema de la Bat. In 2005 Bekker published an article in *Die Burger* in which he wrote that it would constitute a form of 'spinelessness' if Stellenbosch was to allow English to elbow out Afrikaans. Ferreira twice offered to fund a proper study of the financial implications of turning the university into a parallel-medium institution. The management ignored the offer.

In 2016 the SU accepted a new draft policy in terms of which English would become the predominant language of instruction and medium of communication. I sent a copy of the draft policy, together with the critical comments of a group of alumni of which I am a member, to JM Coetzee, the Nobel Prize-winner for literature. Coetzee replied: 'My sympathies are all on your side. The crucial fact, for me, is that the official Taalbeleid document does not once use the word "kultuur". The university management seems to conceive of language as an instrumental communication system without any culture-bearing role.'[796]

The University Council of Stellenbosch has been ineffective in preserving Afrikaans as a medium of instruction and communication. As a body, it is far too large (close to 30 members) and the majority are employees of the university or government representatives, who were happy to support the switch to English.

So far, the hope that the courts would ensure there would be some place for Afrikaans tuition at university level has been disappointed. A court ruled against a challenge to the University of Pretoria's abolition of parallel medium on the grounds that Afrikaans tuition constitutes a form of privilege since it gives Afrikaans-speakers a pedagogic advantage over speakers of other African languages.[797]

In the case brought against Stellenbosch University's language policy of 2016, which makes English the default language of tuition, the Cape High Court ruled that there was no evidence that this would lead to the displacement of Afrikaans. This despite the fact that the policy stipulates that Afrikaans could be used as a language of tuition only if two conditions were met: the availability of a lecturer proficient in Afrikaans and a request expressed by most students for Afrikaans tuition.

The Convocation of Alumni has been the only statutory body at SU that has demanded a solid, sustainable, full status for Afrikaans. This does not mean the exclusion of English, but rather that the medium of English should not undermine and ultimately destroy Afrikaans. The demand is motivated by the following considerations: Afrikaans is indisputably the most effective medium of instruction for those with Afrikaans as mother tongue. Afrikaans schools are dependent upon teachers who have studied for their degrees and teacher's diplomas in Afrikaans. Above all, SU has a special responsibility for empowering coloured Afrikaans-speakers, who are the most disadvantaged community in terms of participating in tertiary education. They have the lowest participation rate and the lowest through-put rate at university of all communities. The regression started in 1990 when the University of the Western Cape switched from Afrikaans to English medium.

At the University of the Free State, Afrikaans survived in a parallel-medium structure until 2016, but the Afrikaans stream was abolished because of a claim, advanced by the university administration, that parallel medium promoted racism. The Constitutional Court concurred despite no evidence being led to that effect.

At Potchefstroom instant interpretation was offered in the classroom for students who could not understand Afrikaans lectures. It has seemed to work well, but a proposal is now on the table that most students have to be black within four years. This will inexorably put English in a hegemonic position.

To an important extent the movement Solidarity has come to fill the gap left by the disappearance of Afrikaans-medium universities. In a short period of time it has made remarkable strides to set up a private institution for higher education using distance teaching.

Afrikaans as medium at schools

In 1993 there were 1,396 schools that used Afrikaans as the only medium of instruction. By 2005 the figure had shrunk to 839.[798] The present figures are not known, but the general impression is that over the past twelve years there has been a further sharp decline in single-medium schools. FEDSAS, the federation of school governing bodies, only has figures for schools in which Afrikaans is used as a medium of instruction. The Western Cape has the highest proportion (76 per cent), followed by the Northern Cape (56 per cent); then come Free State and Gauteng (14 per cent and 12 per cent respectively).

Most Afrikaner parents still send their children to Afrikaans schools. Of the approximately half a million Afrikaner pupils, 51 per cent were in Afrikaans single-medium schools, 34 per cent in the Afrikaans stream of a parallel-medium school, and 15 per cent in English schools.

Afrikaans pupils do exceptionally well. In 2016 just over 50,000 Afrikaans children wrote matric. Although schools that use Afrikaans as a single or dominant medium make up only 10.6 per cent of all schools, they deliver 21 per cent of those school-leavers admitted for a bachelor's degree. Afrikaans schools produced a third of the 8,070 students who received a distinction for maths in the matric examination in 2016. Paul Roos Gymnasium in Stellenbosch fared best. The matric pass rate of Afrikaans schools is 90 per cent compared with the country average of 71 per cent.[799]

A crisis in the coloured community

In sharp contrast to this sterling achievement of white Afrikaans-speakers stands the continuing crisis in the education of coloured children and students. More than half of coloured children received their school education in English although the home language of 80 per cent of the community in 2016 was Afrikaans.

Coloured people have the lowest participation rate at university level and the lowest through-put rate. Coloured students fared poorly in a study that the Council on Higher Education commissioned in 2013. Its task was to probe the success rate of the different groups in studying for bachelor's degrees during the period 1970–2010. The percentage of white and Indian students awarded bachelor's degrees rose from 18 per cent to 29 per cent. The figure for black students dropped from 11 per cent to 9 per cent and that of coloured students declined from 10 per cent in 1970 to 6 per cent in 2010. The main reason for this poor performance is the lack of schools and a university where they can complete their studies in Afrikaans.[800]

The intake of coloured students at SU has stagnated. Between 2004 and 2017 it increased from 1,329 to 1,433. In the same period the numbers of white English-speakers swelled from 2,384 to 54,658. Although blacks form only 11 per cent of the undergraduate student body at SU, the university has decreed that all lectures are to be available in English. Afrikaans is only used if the majority in the class demands it and if an Afrikaans-speaking lecturer is available.

There are signs that the performance of the coloured group is deteriorating further. These figures underline the importance of mother-tongue education. SU's decision to choose English as the dominant mode of instruction will greatly compound the educational problems experienced by the Afrikaans-speaking section of the coloured community.

The future of Afrikaans as a public language vitally depends on overcoming the demographic challenges it faces. Flip Smit's demographic projections point to the present 2.7 million Afrikaners declining to 1.8 million in 2030 – to just under 2 per cent of the population – and to 1 million in 2050 (1 per cent of the population). In comparison, the present coloured Afrikaans-speaking population stands at 3.2 million and is projected to grow much faster than the Afrikaners. The future of Afrikaans is literally in coloured hands, and so is the future of the Afrikaners.[801]

Conclusion

Present-day Afrikaans-speakers are responsible for transferring Afrikaans as a fully developed language to the next generation. They have a special responsibility to the less affluent Afrikaans-speakers, of whom most live in the rural Western Cape. Joseph Ratzinger, who became Pope Benedict XVI in 2005, made this striking comment: 'People can change their identity but cannot escape their responsibility.' In 2017 *Rapport* newspaper published an account of an exchange between Johan Theron, a member of the SU Council elected by Convocation, and Wim de Villiers, the Vice-Chancellor. This exchange revealed that, notwithstanding De Villiers's public statements to the contrary, he had concluded that Stellenbosch had to use English as the dominant medium of instruction because it was the 'easiest option'.[802]

With a fifth of the lecturing staff publicly stating that they were unable to teach in the medium of Afrikaans, the university has landed itself in an untenable situation. Can the situation be turned around? Strong and far-seeing leadership is needed in management and the University Council to do so. But leadership and courage are two elements that seem to be sorely lacking.

BOOKS BY HERMANN GILIOMEE

1974	*Die Kaap tydens die eerste Britse bewind*
1979	*The Rise and Crisis of Afrikaner Power / Afrikanermag: Opkoms en toekoms* (co-author Heribert Adam)
1982	*The Parting of the Ways: South African Politics, 1976–1982*
1982	*The Shaping of South African Society, 1652–1820 / 'n Samelewing in wording: Suid-Afrika, 1652–1820* (co-editor Richard Elphick)
1983	*Afrikaner Political Thought: vol. 1: 1780–1850 – Documents and Analyses* (co-author André du Toit)
1985	*Up Against the Fences: Poverty, Passes and Privilege in South Africa* (co-editor Lawrence Schlemmer)
1989	*From Apartheid to Nation-Building* (co-author Lawrence Schlemmer)
1989	*Negotiating South Africa's Future* (co-editor Lawrence Schlemmer)
1990	*The Elusive Search for Peace: South Africa, Israel and Northern Ireland* (co-editor Jannie Gagiano)
1994	*The Bold Experiment: South Africa's New Democracy* (co-editors Lawrence Schlemmer and Sarita Hauptfleisch)
1999	*The Awkward Embrace: One-Party Domination and Democracy in Industrialising Countries* (co-editor Charles Simkins [e-book])
2001	*Kruispad: Die toekoms van Afrikaans as openbare taal* (co-editor Lawrence Schlemmer)
2003	*The Afrikaners: Biography of a People / Die Afrikaners: 'n Biografie*
2006	*'n Vaste plek vir Afrikaans: Taaluitdagings op kampus* (co-author Lawrence Schlemmer)
2007	*New History of South Africa / Nuwe geskiedenis van Suid-Afrika* (co-editor Bernard Mbenga)
2007	*Nog altyd hier gewees: Die storie van 'n Stellenbosse gemeenskap*
2012	*The Last Afrikaner Leaders: A Crucial Test of Power / Die laaste Afrikanerleiers: 'n Opperste toets van mag*
2015	*Buhr van die Bokveld: 'n Bloemlesing uit die werk van Johann Buhr* (compiler)
2016	*Historian: An Autobiography / Historikus: 'n Outobiografie*
2018	*Die Afrikaners: Verkorte en aangevulde uitgawe* *'Always been here': The story of a Stellenbosch community*

REFERENCES

Introduction
1. Jon Lewis, 'The Germiston By-Election of 1932', P. Bonner (ed.), *Working Papers in Southern African Studies* (Ravan Press, Johannesburg, 1981), pp. 97-120.
2. JH Hofmeyr, 'Introduction', in Edgar Brookes et al., *Coming of Age: Studies in South African citizenship and politics* (Maskew Miller, Cape Town, 1930), pp. 6-9.
3. Richard Elphick, *The Equality of Believers: Protestant missions and the racial politics of South Africa* (University of KwaZulu-Natal Press, Scottsville, 2012), pp. 222-37.
4. An earlier, eccentric use of the word 'apartheid' is recorded by Irving Hexham, The Irony of Apartheid (Edward Mellen Press, Toronto, 1981), p. 188.
5. *Die Transvaler*, 19 April 1945.
6. In the late 1980s I had the opportunity to interview actors on both sides of the conflict. See Hermann Giliomee and Jannie Gagiano, eds., *The Elusive Search for Peace: Power and privilege in South Africa, Northern Ireland and Israel* (Oxford University Press, Cape Town, 1990).

Chapter 1
7. J Morgan Kousser, *The Shaping of Southern Politics: Suffrage, restriction and the establishment of the one party South, 1880–1910* (Yale University Press, New Haven, 1974).
8. Alexis de Tocqueville, *Democracy in America* (Schocken Books, New York, 1961), vol. I, p. 50.
9. C Vann Woodward, *The Strange Career of Jim Crow* (Oxford University Press, New York, 1974).
10. C Vann Woodward, 'Herrenvolk Democracy', *New York Review of Books*, 5 March 1981.
11. Cited by Kousser, *The Shaping of Southern Politics*, p. 262.
12. Vernon Lane Wharton, *The Negro in Mississippi, 1856–1890* (Harper and Row, New York, 1965), pp. 214-15.
13. C Vann Woodward, *Origins of the New South, 1877–1913* (University of Louisiana Press, Baton Rouge, 1971), pp. 342-3.
14. Woodward, *Origins of the New South*, p. 330.
15. Kousser, *The Shaping of Southern Politics*, pp. 202-5.
16. Woodward, *Strange Career of Jim Crow*, pp. 168-9.
17. Donald Horowitz, 'Ethnic Identity', in Nathan Glazer and Daniel P Moynihan, eds., *Ethnicity: Theory and experience* (Harvard University Press, Cambridge, 1975), pp. 123-4, 137-8.
18. GD Scholtz, *Die ontwikkeling van die politieke denke van die Afrikaners* (Perskor, Johannesburg, 1977), vol. IV, pp. 70-2.
19. This is the thesis of an illuminating study by David Berger, 'White Poverty and Government Policy in South Africa 1892–1934', PhD dissertation, Temple University, 1983.

20 Cape of Good Hope Parliament, *Debates*, 1894, pp. 345-6.
21 RE van der Ross, *The Rise and Decline of Apartheid: A study of political movements among the coloured people of South Africa, 1880–1885* (Tafelberg, Cape Town, 1986), p. 72.
22 Gavin Lewis, *Between the Wire and the Wall: A history of South African 'Coloured' politics* (David Philip, Cape Town, 1987), p. 164.
23 G Pretorius, *Man van die daad: 'n Biografie van Bruckner de Villiers* (HAUM, Cape Town, 1959), pp. 114-15.
24 Ian Golden, *Making Race: The politics and economics of coloured identity in South Africa* (Maskew Miller Longman, Cape Town 1987), p. 12.
25 A correspondent of *The Clarion* said that one would have a quarrel on one's hands 'if one addressed a coloured in a Cape Town street as Hotnot even if that person had three-quarters Hotnot blood in his veins' (26 April 1919, p. 15). An editorial in *Die Burger*, 20 November 1925, took the view that 'the coloured and also the Malay have developed over generations into a separate race. The term coloured should not be taken to mean the bastard – the child of the degenerate white father and native mother.'
26 James Rose Innes, *Autobiography* (Cape Town, 1949), p. 3.
27 *Cape Times*, 5 May 1877, editorial.
28 *Die Burger*, 20 June 1929.
29 Thelma Shifrin, 'New Deal for the Coloured People: A study of national party policies towards the Coloured people 1924–1929', BA Hons. dissertation, University of Cape Town, 1962, p. 10.
30 WK Hancock and J van der Poel, eds., *Smuts Papers* (Cambridge University Press, Cambridge, 1966), vol. II, p. 375.
31 *APO*, 21 March 1910.
32 Lewis, *Between the Wire and the Wall*, p. 50.
33 Golden, *Making Race*, p. 35.
34 M Adhikari, 'Protest and Accommodation: Ambiguities in the racial politics of the APO', *Kronos*, 20 (1993), p. 95.
35 *APO*, 15 August 1910.
36 *APO*, 24 May 1909.
37 For a further discussion of this remarkable column, see Hein Willemse, 'Stereotyping and Politics in "Straatpraatjes", 1902–1922', seminar paper, Department of History, University of Cape Town, 1993.
38 *APO*, 16 July 1910.
39 *Hertzog-toesprake* (Perskor, Johannesburg, 1977), vol. III, pp. 90-1.
40 Scholtz, *Die ontwikkeling van die politieke denke*, vol. VI, p. 464; Shifrin, 'New Deal', pp. 18-22.
41 Malan's remarkable series of editorials on Afrikaner and coloured poverty are reprinted in the pamphlet *Die groot vlug* and well summarised in CFJ Muller, *Sonop in die suide: Geboorte en groei van die Nasionale Pers, 1915–1948* (Nasionale Boekhandel, Cape Town, 1990), pp. 632-7.
42 *Hertzog-toesprake*, vol. IV, pp. 235-6.
43 Lewis, *Between the Wire and the Wall*, pp. 122-5.
44 *The Clarion*, 19 September 1919, p. 10.
45 *The Clarion*, 5 April 1919.
46 *The Clarion*, 12 April 1919.
47 *The Clarion*, 19 August 1919.
48 *The Clarion*, 26 April 1919.

49 *The Clarion*, 17 December 1919, editorial.
50 *The Clarion*, 3 May 1919.
51 *The Clarion*, 3 May 1919.
52 *The Clarion*, 5 February 1921.
53 *The Clarion*, 29 January 1920.
54 *The Clarion*, 24 May 1919.
55 University of Stellenbosch, Malan MS Collection, 1/1/1, Undated Correspondence.
56 *Die Bond*, 27 February 1926.
57 Lewis, *Between the Wire and the Wall*, pp. 128-39.
58 Lewis, *Between the Wire and the Wall*, p. 126.
59 *Die Burger*, 19 June 1924, editorial.
60 Shifrin, 'New Deal', p. 15.
61 Scholtz, *Ontwikkeling van die politieke denke*, vol. VII, p. 305.
62 Gert Pretorius, *Bruckner de Villiers: Man van die daad* (HAUM, Cape Town, 1959), p. 117.
63 Lewis, *Between the Wire and the Wall*, pp. 126-7, 133-4.
64 Lewis, *Between the Wire and the Wall*, p. 162.
65 U.G. 54/1937, *Report of the Commission of Inquiry regarding the Cape Coloured Population*, p. 57.
66 U.G. 54/1937, *Report of the Commission of Inquiry*, pp. 62-9.
67 Lewis, *Between the Wire and the Wall*, p. 132.
68 *Die Burger*, 12 April 1929, p. 7; *Die Burger*, 22 May 1929, p. 6.
69 U.G. 54/1937, *Report of the Commission of Inquiry*, p. 126.
70 U.G. 54/1937, *Report of the Commission of Inquiry*, p. 15.
71 Cited in Marion Lacey, *Working for Boroko* (Ravan Press, Johannesburg, 1981), p. 71.
72 *Die Burger*, 23 May 1929, p. 6.
73 *Die Burger*, 16 May 1929, citing *Cape Times*, 14 November 1928, editorial.
74 House of Assembly *Debates*, Joint Sitting, 12-15 February 1929, col. 169.
75 JH le Roux and PW Coetzer, *Die Nasionale Party, 1924–1934* (INEG, Bloemfontein, 1980), p. 349.
76 Hancock and Van der Poel, *Smuts Papers*, vol. V: 1991–1934, pp. 368-9.
77 GD Scholtz, *Die ontwikkeling van die politieke denke van die Afrikaner*, vol. VII, p. 305.
78 Hancock and Van der Poel, *Smuts Papers*, vol. V: 1919–1934, p. 401.
79 Arthur Barlow, *Almost in Confidence* (Juta, Cape Town, 1952), pp. 210-12.
80 House of Assembly *Debates*, Joint Sitting, 1929, col. 168.
81 Shifrin, 'New Deal', p. 38.
82 House of Assembly *Debates*, Joint Sitting, 1929, cols. 176-83.
83 *Die Burger*, 6 March, 5 April, 30 April, 2 May and 23 May 1929.
84 Barlow, *Almost in Confidence*, p. 210.
85 Shifrin, 'New Deal', p. 62.
86 Van der Ross, *Rise and Decline of Apartheid*, p. 72.
87 House of Assembly *Debates*, Joint Sitting, 1929, col. 175.
88 *Die Burger*, 5 September 1929.
89 *Cape Times*, 5 September 1929.
90 It stipulates that the prospective coloured voter 'must follow in his daily life the habits of a coloured person or a European, generally associated with coloured persons or Europeans and have a standard of living conforming to that of European civilisation'. See CM Tatz, *Shadow and Substance in South Africa: A study in land and franchise policies affecting Africans, 1910–1960* (University of Natal Press, Pietermaritzburg, 1962), pp. 46-7.

91 House of Assembly *Debates*, 1930, cols. 1523-4.
92 Lewis, *Between the Wire and the Wall*, p. 147.
93 *Die Burger*, 2 May 1929, p. 7.
94 Pretorius, *Man van die daad*, p. 98.
95 *Die Burger*, 5 September 1929.
96 Barlow, *Almost in Confidence*, p. 210; JHH de Waal, *Die lewe van David Christiaan de Waal* (Cape Town, 1928), p. 307.
97 Heribert Adam and Hermann Giliomee, *Ethnic Power Mobilized: Can South Africa change?* (Yale University Press, New Haven, 1979), pp. 120-7.
98 Alf Ries and Ebbe Dommisse, *Broedertwis* (Cape Town: Tafelberg, 1982), p. 112. For an extended discussion see Hermann Giliomee, '"Broedertwis": Intra-Afrikaner conflicts in the transition from apartheid', *African Affairs*, 91 (1992), pp. 339-64.
99 Mike McGrath and Andrew Whiteford, 'Disparate Circumstances', *Indicator*, 11 (1994), pp. 47-51.
100 For analyses of the reasons which prompted the government to negotiate, see F van Zyl Slabbert, *The Quest for Democracy* (Penguin, Johannesburg, 1992); Hermann Giliomee, 'South Africa's Transition to Democracy', *Political Science Quarterly* (forthcoming).
101 *Debates of Parliament*, Joint sitting, 20 June 1991, cols. 13556-8, 13651.
102 *Die Burger*, 19 June 1924 and 5 September 1929.
103 *Cape Times*, 8 March 1994, p. 2.
104 *Launching Democracy, II*, a poll carried out for the Institute of Multi-Party Democracy, February 1994.
105 Lewis, *Between the Wire and the Wall*, p. 143.
106 Van der Ross, *Rise and Decline of Apartheid*, p. 81.
107 Interview with Richard van der Ross, 20 September 1994.
108 *Rapport*, 20 March 1994.
109 Interview with Carel Greyling, 21 September, 1994. I deal with the NP campaign in Andrew Reynolds, ed., *The South African Election of 1994* (David Philip, Cape Town, 1994), pp. 43-71.
110 George M Frederickson, *The Black Image in the White Mind: The debate over Afro-American character and destiny, 1817–1940* (Harper, New York, 1971), pp. 256-82.

Chapter 2
111 Hexham, *The Irony of Apartheid* (Edward Mellen, Toronto, 1981), p. 188.
112 R Davenport and C Saunders, *South Africa: A modern history* (Macmillan, London, 2000), p. 373.
113 'Dawie', *Die Burger*'s columnist, discussed the issue on 24 March and 14 April 1951. The speech is published as 'Die ideale van ons kerk in sendingwerk', *Die NG Kerk en die Naturellevraagstuk* (Nasionale Pers, Bloemfontein, 1929), pp. 22-5. I wish to thank Rick Elphick for pointing me to the document.
114 L Louw (comp.), *Dawie, 1946–1964* (Tafelberg, Cape Town, 1965), p. 49.
115 *House of Assembly Debates (HAD)*, 1944, col. 75; *Die Burger*, 8 May 1944; Louw, *Dawie*, p. 48.
116 A Keppel-Jones, *Friends or Foes?* (Shuter and Shooter, Pietermaritzburg, 1949), p. 48.
117 Davenport and Saunders, *South Africa*, p. 373.
118 M Legassick, 'Legislation, Ideology and Economy in Post-1948 South Africa', *Journal of Southern African Studies*, 1, 1 (1974), pp. 9-10.
119 D O'Meara, *Volkskapitalisme: Class, capital and ideology in the development of Afrikaner nationalism, 1934–1948* (Cambridge University Press, Cambridge, 1983), pp. 171-7.

120 D Posel, *The Making of Apartheid* (Clarendon Press, Oxford, 1997).
121 AJ Gregor, *Contemporary Radical Ideologies* (Random House, New York, 1968), p. 221.
122 A Norval, *Deconstructing Apartheid Discourse* (Verso, London, 1996), p. 67.
123 S Dubow, *Scientific Racism in Modern South Africa* (Cambridge University Press, Cambridge, 1995), pp. 246-83.
124 NP van Wyk Louw, *Versamelde prosa* (Tafelberg, Cape Town, 1986), vol. l, pp. 411-529.
125 From 1924–1945, 1945–1954 and 1954–1977 respectively.
126 Cited by Ivor Wilkins, *Sunday Times*, 19 April 1981.
127 The source of the data is a survey conducted and published by the Cape Town-based Institute for Reconciliation and Justice (www.ijr.org.za). It was undertaken at the end of 2000 and beginning of 2001, and involved 3,727 interviews conducted in the language of choice of the respondent.
128 TD Moodie, *The Rise of Afrikanerdom* (University of California Press, Berkeley, 1974), pp. ix, 15.
129 P Furlong, *Between Crown and Swastika: The impact of the radical right on the Afrikaner nationalist movement in the fascist era* (Witwatersrand University Press, Johannesburg, 1991), pp. 102, 224-6.
130 See *Die OB*, particularly the columns for which Meyer was responsible; Moodie, *The Rise of Afrikanerdom*, pp. 225-31.
131 A du Toit, 'The Problem of Intellectual History in (Post) Colonial Societies: The case of South Africa', *Politikon*, 18, 2 (1991), p. 15.
132 GD Scholtz, *Die ontwikkeling van die politieke denke van die Afrikaner* (Perskor, Johannesburg, 1984), vol. 8, p. 158.
133 Scholtz, *Ontwikkeling*, vol. 8, p. 252.
134 G Carter, *The Politics of Inequality* (Thames and Hudson, London, 1958), p. 78.
135 S Patterson, *The Last Trek* (Routledge, London, 1958).
136 P van den Berghe, *Race and Racism* (Wiley, New York, 1967), p. 109. See also H Adam and H Giliomee, *Ethnic Power Mobilised* (New Haven, Yale University Press, 1979), pp. 25-32.
137 Furlong, *Between Crown and Swastika*, p. 211.
138 The influence of neo-Calvinism on Afrikaner nationalism is exaggerated in Hexham, *Irony of Apartheid*. For Malan's views, see his son's memoir in the University of Stellenbosch Library (hereafter USL), DF Malan collection.
139 A good starting point for this important topic is JJ Broodryk, 'Stellenbosse akademici en die politieke problematiek in Suid-Afrika, 1934–1948', MA dissertation, University of Stellenbosch, 1991.
140 R Millar, 'Science and Society in the Early Career of HF Verwoerd', *Journal of Southern African Studies*, 19 (1993), p. 646.
141 E Stals, 'Die geskiedenis van die Afrikaner Broederbond, 1918–1994' (unpublished manuscript, 1998), pp. 133-41.
142 LJ du Plessis, 'Die Naturellevraagstuk', *Koers*, 8, 1 (1940), pp. 5-9.
143 BM Schoeman, *Die Broederbond en die Afrikaner-politiek* (Aktuele Publikasies, Pretoria, 1982), pp. 27-30.
144 Stals, 'Geskiedenis van die AB', pp. 203-8.
145 R Elphick, 'Missions and Afrikaner Nationalism' (unpublished paper, 1999). See also his 'Missiology, Afrikaner Nationalism, and the Road to Apartheid', presented at Currents in World Christianity symposium; 'Missions, Nationalism, and the End of Empire', Queen's College, Cambridge, 6-9 September 2000, forthcoming in a volume edited by B Stanley (Grand Rapids, Eerdmans).

146 S Dubow, 'Afrikaner Nationalism, Apartheid and the Conceptualisation of "Race"', *Journal of African History* (1992), p. 213.
147 H Bradford, *A Taste of Freedom: The ICU in rural South Africa, 1924–1930* (Ravan Press, Johannesburg, 1987), p. 4.
148 HA Roux, *De Ethiopische Kerk* (n.p., 1905).
149 *Die NG Kerk in die OVS*, pp. 34-5.
150 R Elphick, 'Evangelical Missions and Racial Equalisation in South Africa, 1890–1914' (unpublished paper, 1999).
151 Preface to *Die NGK in die OVS*, p. x.
152 Du Plessis, 'Die ideale van ons kerk in sendingwerk', pp. 22-5.
153 This is reproduced as Appendix 2 in JA Lombard, 'Die sendingbeleid van die NGK van die OVS', PhD dissertation, University of the North, 1985, pp. 308-13.
154 University of Stellenbosch Theological School Library (hereafter USTSL), 'NG Sendingraadnotules', unpublished minutes, p. 98.
155 JG Strydom, 'Die rasse-vraagstuk in Suid-Afrika', in Federasie van Calvinistiese Studenteverenigings (comp.), *Koers in die krisis* (Pro Ecclesia, Stellenbosch, 1941), vol. 3, p. 245.
156 USL, DF Malan Collection, Account of DF Malan's reply to the Transvaal delegation, 5 February 1947.
157 G van der Watt, 'GBA Gerdener: Koersaanwyser in die Nederduitse Gereformeerde Kerk se sending en eukemene', PhD dissertation, University of the Orange Free State, 1990, p. 292.
158 *Op die Horison*, 9, 1 (1947), pp. 1-2; Van der Watt, 'Gerdener', p. 292.
159 GBA Gerdener, *Reguit koers gehou* (NG Kerk Uitgewers, Cape Town, 1951), p. 102.
160 This and the previous paragraph are based on USTSL, Minutes of the Federale Sendingraad van die NGK, 1944, pp. 3-4; 1947, pp. 137-41.
161 *Verslag van die Kleurvraagstuk-kommissie van die HNP* (1947), p. 9. (Later references will be to the Sauer report.)
162 Kinghorn, 'Groei van 'n teologie', pp. 110-11.
163 Elphick, 'Missions and Afrikaner Nationalism'.
164 UG 54/1937, *Verslag van die kommissie van ondersoek insake die Kaapse kleurling*, vol. 3, pp. 3163-71; G Lewis, *Between the Wire and the Wall: A history of South African 'Coloured' politics* (David Philip, Cape Town, 1987), pp. 159-69.
165 PW Coetzer and JH le Roux, *Die Nasionale Party, IV: 1934–1940* (INEG, Bloemfontein, 1986), p. 57.
166 HB Thom, *Die geloftekerk en ander studies* (Nasionale Pers, Cape Town, 1949).
167 W Eiselen, 'Die aandeel van die blanke in afsonderlike ontwikkeling', *Journal of Racial Affairs* (1965); Moodie, *The Rise of Afrikanerdom*, p. 275.
168 PJ Coertze, FJ Language and BIC van Eeden, *Die oplossing van die Naturellevraagstuk in Suid-Afrika* (Publicité, Johannesburg, 1943).
169 J Conrad, *Heart of Darkness* (Könemann, Cologne, 1999), p. 52.
170 Kinghorn, 'Die groei van 'n teologie', pp. 92-6.
171 Du Plessis, 'Die Naturellevraagstuk in Suid-Afrika', p. 5.
172 JC Steyn, *Penvegter: Piet Cillié van Die Burger* (Tafelberg, Cape Town, 2002), pp. 68-72. See also the views of Cillié's predecessor, PA Weber, 'Die Burger – Sy stryd, invloed en tradisie', in JP Scanell, ed., *Keeromstraat 30* (Nasionale Boekhandel, Cape Town, 1965), pp. 18-38.
173 The article was re-published by the *Journal of Racial Affairs*, 1, 6 (1954), pp. 45-7. See also Adam and Giliomee, *Ethnic Power Mobilised*, pp. 61-82.
174 JM Coetzee, 'The Mind of Apartheid', *Social Dynamics*, 17, 1 (1991), p. 30.
175 A Hoernlé, *South African Native Policy* (University of the Witwatersrand Press, Johannesburg, 1939), pp. 149-68.

176 Van Wyk Louw, *Versamelde prosa*, vol. 1, pp. 502-6.
177 NP van Wyk Louw, 'Inleiding', in DP Botha, *Die opkoms van ons derde stand* (Human & Rousseau, Cape Town, 1960), p. viii. I elaborate on this in 'Apartheid, *Verligtheid* and Liberalism', in J Butler et al., eds., *Democratic Liberalism in South Africa* (David Philip, Cape Town, 1987), pp. 363-83.
178 For analyses of Louw's ideas, see in particular JJ Degenaar, *Moraliteit en politiek* (Tafelberg, Cape Town, 1976), pp. 55-91; G Olivier, *NP van Wyk Louw* (Human & Rousseau, Cape Town, 1992); M Sanders, 'Complicities: On the intellectual', PhD dissertation, Columbia University, 1998; and JC Steyn, *Van Wyk Louw* (Tafelberg, Cape Town, 1998). The interpretations of Degenaar and Steyn are largely positive. For an effective response to Olivier's jaundiced view, see JC Kannemeyer, *Ontsyferde stene* (Inset, Stellenbosch, 1996), pp. 62-76.
179 A du Toit, *Sondes van die vaders* (Rubicon, Cape Town, 1982).
180 I elaborate on some of these issues in my 'Critical Afrikaner Intellectuals and Apartheid,' *South African Journal of Philosophy*, 19, 4 (2000), pp. 307-20; for criticism, see H Giliomee, *The Afrikaners: Biography of a people* (Hurst and Co., London, 2003), pp. 447-86.
181 Louw, *Dawie*, p. 48.
182 The quotes are from K Robinson, *The Dilemmas of Trusteeship* (Oxford University Press, London, 1965), pp. 22, 65.
183 *HAD*, 1944, cols. 6697-9.
184 *HAD*, 1944, col. 6713.
185 EJG Janson, '*Die Burger* en die kleurlingstem, 1943–1948', MA dissertation, Unisa, 1987, pp. 77-8.
186 N Rhoodie, *Apartheid and Racial Partnership in Southern Africa* (Academica, Pretoria, 1968), p. 53.
187 Patterson, *The Last Trek*, p. 253.
188 JP Brits, '"The Voice of the People": Memoranda presented in 1947 to the Sauer Commission', *Kronos*, 22 (2000), pp. 61-83; JP Brits, *Op die vooraand van apartheid* (Unisa, Pretoria, 1994), pp. 80-108.
189 *Sauer Report* (1947).
190 Posel, *The Making of Apartheid*, p. 60.
191 JP Heiberg, 'Dr AL Geyer as Suid-Afrika se Hoë Kommissaris in die Verenigde Koninkryk', PhD dissertation, University of Stellenbosch, 2001, pp. 211-13.
192 AM Keppel-Jones, 'The Political Situation in South Africa' (paper presented to the Royal Institute for International Affairs, 27 March 1947).
193 S Dubow, *Racial Segregation and the Origins of Apartheid in South Africa* (London: Macmillan, 1989), p. 178.
194 Nelson Mandela, *Long Walk to Freedom* (London, Little Brown, 1994), p. 104.
195 JP Brits in communication with Willem Kleynhans, the largest private collector of election material, 23 March 2002. See also Brits, Letter to the Editor, *Beeld*, 8 July 1999.

Chapter 3

196 Michael Walzer, *The Company of Critics: Social criticism and political commitment in the twentieth century* (Basic Books, New York, 1988), pp. 234-5. For a more philosophical statement, see his *Interpretation and Social Criticism* (Harvard University Press, Cambridge, 1987).
197 Walzer, *The Company of Critics*, p. 232.
198 Walzer, *The Company of Critics*, p. 70.

REFERENCES

199 Martin Buber, *Israel and the World: Essays in a time of crisis* (Schocken, New York, 1963), p. 248.
200 Martin Buber, *A Land of Two Peoples: Martin Buber on Jews and Arabs*, ed. Paul R Mendes-Flohr (Oxford University Press, Oxford, 1983), p. 223.
201 Martin Buber, 'Hebrew Humanism', in Arthur Herzberg, ed., *The Zionist Idea* (Atheneum, New York, 1972), pp. 457-63.
202 Martin Buber, 'From an Open Letter to Mahatma Gandhi (1939)', *The Zionist Idea*, p. 463.
203 Buber, 'Open Letter to Gandhi', pp. 463-4.
204 Buber, 'Open Letter to Gandhi', p. 465.
205 Albert Memmi, quoted by Michael Walzer, in 'Commitment and Social Criticism: Camus's Algerian War', *Dissent* (Fall 1984), p. 427.
206 Walzer, *The Company of Critics*, p. 150.
207 Albert Camus, *Resistance, Rebellion and Death* (Alfred A Knopf, New York, 1961), p. 141.
208 Camus, *Resistance, Rebellion and Death*, pp. 113-14.
209 Walzer, *The Company of Critics*, p. 145.
210 Cited by Walzer, *The Company of Critics*, p. 151.
211 Ivo Banac, 'Political Change and National Diversity', *Daedalus*, 119, 1 (1990), pp. 141-59.
212 *Washington Post*, 19 October 1992, pp. A16-A18.
213 Henry Katzew, *Apartheid and Survival* (Simondium Publishers, Cape Town, 1965), p. 42.
214 NP van Wyk Louw, *Liberale nasionalisme* (Nasionale Boekhandel, Cape Town, 1958), p. 58.
215 Louw, *Liberale nasionalisme*, p. 53.
216 Louw, *Liberale nasionalisme*, p. 67.
217 Louw, *Liberale nasionalisme*, p. 63.
218 Louw, *Liberale nasionalisme*, p. 108.
219 Louw, *Liberale nasionalisme*, pp. 106-9.
220 Louw, *Liberale nasionalisme*, p. 105.
221 Deborah Posel, *The Making of Apartheid, 1948–1961: Conflict and compromise* (Clarendon Press, Oxford, 1991), pp. 50-8, 126-7.
222 See the discussion of the report by Ashford, Adam, *The Politics of Official Discourse in Twentieth-Century South Africa* (Clarendon Press, Oxford, 1990), pp. 149-94.
223 HA Fagan, *Our Responsibility* (Universiteit Uitgewers, Stellenbosch, 1959), p. 44. This book was also published in Afrikaans under the title *Ons verantwoordelikheid*.
224 Fagan, *Our Responsibility*, p. 45.
225 Fagan, *Our Responsibility*, p. 54.
226 Fagan, *Our Responsibility*, p. 92.
227 Fagan, *Our Responsibility*, p. 93.
228 TE Dönges, in *Die Transvaler*, 17 December 1952.
229 AN Pelzer, ed., *Verwoerd Speaks: Speeches, 1948–1966* (APB Publishers, Johannesburg, 1966), p. 121.
230 J Kinghorn, ed., *Die NG Kerk en apartheid* (Macmillan, Johannesburg, 1986).
231 NP van Wyk Louw, 'Introduction to DP Botha', in *Die opkoms van die derde stand* (Human & Rousseau, Cape Town, 1960).
232 For critical assessments by two Afrikaans-speaking intellectuals, see RE van der Ross, *Onvoldoende liberalisme*, NP van Wyk Louw Memorial Lecture, Randse Afrikaanse Universiteit, 1986; Gerrit Olivier, *NP van Wyk Louw: Literatuur, filosofie, politiek* (Human & Rousseau, Cape Town, 1992).
233 Donald Horowitz, *Ethnic Groups in Conflict* (University of California Press, Berkeley, 1986), pp. 179–80.

234 Brian Urquhart, *Hammarskjöld* (Bodley Head, London, 1973), p. 498.
235 CEW Simkins, 'Agricultural Production in the African Reserves of South Africa, 1918–1969', *Journal of Southern African Studies*, 7 (1981), pp. 256-83.
236 See *Die Burger*, 'Dawie' column' and 'Terug na ons geloof in vryheid' (6 June 1964), reprinted in Louis Louw, ed., *Dawie* (Tafelberg, Cape Town, 1965), pp. 285-90.
237 *Die Burger*, 4 July 1970, editorial.
238 Willem de Klerk, 'The Concepts "Verkramp" and "Verlig"', in NJ Rhoodie, ed., *South African Dialogue* (McGraw Hill, Johannesburg, 1972), pp. 520-31.
239 Cited by Deborah Posel, 'The Language of Domination, 1978–1983', in Shula Marks and Stanley Trapido, eds., *The Politics of Race, Class and Nationalism in Twentieth Century South Africa* (Longman, London, 1987), p. 435.
240 Robert Schrire, *Adapt or Die: The end of white politics* (Ford Foundation, New York, 1991), pp. 37-56.
241 *Sunday Times*, 13 March 1979.
242 Dan Jacobson, 'Among the South Africans', *Commentary*, 65, 3 (1978), pp. 32-48.
243 Heribert Adam and Hermann Giliomee, *Ethnic Power Mobilized: Can South Africa change?* (Yale University Press, New Haven, 1979), p. 14.
244 Cited by Degenaar, *Voortbestaan in geregtigheid*, p. 32.
245 *Die Burger*, 13 November 1976, 'Dawie' column.
246 *Die Burger*, 10 November 1976, 'Dawie' column. See also the column of 6 November 1976.
247 G van N Viljoen, *Ideaal en werklikheid* (Tafelberg, Cape Town, 1978), pp. 31-3.
248 Louw, *Liberale nasionalisme*, pp. 62-3.
249 G van N Viljoen, 'Die kwaliteit van ons oorlewing', *Aambeeld*, 6, 1 (1978), pp. 4-5.
250 Viljoen, *Ideaal en werklikheid*, p. 33.
251 Viljoen, *Ideaal en werklikheid*, pp. 16, 31-3, 40-1, 62.
252 Still, the question of numbers haunted the leadership. Botha reportedly ordered the withdrawal of troops from Angola rather than lose 300 men.
253 G van N Viljoen, '"Wat is 'n volk?": Die aktualiteit van Van Wyk Louw se riglyne vir die nasionalisme', in FIJ van Rensburg, ed., *Oopgelate kring* (Tafelberg, Cape Town, 1982), p. 141.
254 Viljoen, '"Wat is 'n volk?"', p. 23.
255 Viljoen, '"Wat is 'n volk?"', p. 25.
256 *Die Burger*, 13 July 1978.
257 Andre P Brink, *Literatuur in die strydperk* (Human & Rousseau, Cape Town, 1985), p. 155.
258 Breyten Breytenbach, *End Papers* (McGraw Hill, New York, 1986), p. 237; Walzer, *The Company of Critics*, p. 217.
259 BB Lasarus (pseud. Breyten Breytenbach), *'n Seisoen in die Paradys* (Perskor, Johannesburg, 1976), p. 121 (my translation).
260 Breyten Breytenbach, *True Confessions of an Albino Terrorist* (Straus Giroux, New York, 1983), pp. 354-5.
261 Breytenbach, *End Papers*, p. 56.
262 Walzer, *The Company of Critics*, p. 219 observes that since his release, Breytenbach seemed to resent the sharing in the shame, adding 'perhaps he feels that the years in prison has burned the shame out of him'.
263 Lasarus, (pseud. Breyten Breytenbach), *'n Seisoen in die Paradys*, p. 126.
264 *Die Suid-Afrikaan* (Fall 1986), p. 12.
265 He cited the comment of Heinz Kloss, a German-American authority who called the

language movement 'an outstanding achievement' (JC Steyn, 'Die wederopstanding van die Bose Boer', *Aambeeld*, 8, 1 (1980), p. 5.
266 JC Steyn, *Tuiste in eie taal* (Tafelberg, Cape Town, 1980), pp. 452-3.
267 André du Toit, *Die sondes van die vaders* (Rubicon, Cape Town, 1982), p. 26.
268 Du Toit, *Sondes van die vaders*, p. 32.
269 Michael Walzer, *Interpretation and Social Criticism* (Harvard University Press, Cambridge, 1987), pp. 38-9, 54-9.
270 JJ Degenaar, *Voortbestaan in geregtigheid* (Tafelberg, Cape Town, 1980), pp. 1-5. See also his 'Die betekenis van NP van Wyk Louw vir my eie denke', *Standpunte*, 37, 5 (1984), pp. 49-59.
271 Degenaar, *Voortbestaan in geregtigheid*, p. 11.
272 F van Zyl Slabbert and David Welsh, *South Africa's Options* (David Philip, Cape Town, 1979), pp. 90, 170.
273 EG Lombard, 'Elite-houdings oor onderhandeling in Suid-Afrika', MA dissertation, University of Stellenbosch, 1991.
274 Quoted in 'The Deadly Silence of Church Leaders', *Star International Weekly*, 15-21 October 1992.
275 Francis Fukuyama, *The End of History and the Last Man* (The Free Press, New York, 1992), pp. xi-xxiii, 168-91.
276 Interview, David Frost with De Klerk, broadcast on 14 February 1993 (official transcript issued by the office of the State President).
277 *Rapport*, 8 May 1994, p. 21.
278 For a full discussion, see Hermann Giliomee, 'Democratization in South Africa', *Political Science Quarterly* (forthcoming).

Chapter 4
279 Interview by author, 3 May 1999.
280 *Cape Times*, 8 July 1986.
281 D O'Meara, *Forty Lost Years: The apartheid state and the politics of the National Party 1948–1994* (Ravan Press, Johannesburg, 1996), pp. 120, 141.
282 B Fine et al., *The Political Economy of South Africa* (Witwatersrand University Press, Johannesburg, 1996), p. 148.
283 TK McGraw, *Prophet of Innovation: Joseph Schumpeter and creative destruction* (Belknap Press, Cambridge, 2007).
284 D Horowitz, *Ethnic Groups in Conflict* (University of California Press, Berkeley, 1985), pp. 185-228.
285 T Mbeki, Reply of the President of South Africa, 2 September 2003, http://www.anc.org.za/ show.php?doc=ancdocs/history/mbeki/2003/tm0902.html.
286 I Emsley, *The Malaysian Experience of Affirmative Action* (Human & Rousseau, Cape Town, 1996).
287 J van der Westhuizen, *Adapting to Globalisation: Malaysia, South Africa, and the challenges of ethnic redistribution with growth* (Praeger, Westport, 2002).
288 J Jesudason, *Ethnicity and the Economy: The state, Chinese business and multi-nationals in Malaysia* (Oxford University Press, Singapore, 1989), p. 11.
289 Mahathir bin Mohamad, *The Malay Dilemma* (Asia Pacific Press, Singapore, 1970), p. 44.
290 *The Strait Times*, 29 March 2003; see also *Asia Week*, 17 March 2000 and 29 February 2002.
291 JL Sadie, *The Fall and Rise of the Afrikaner in the South African Economy* (University of Stellenbosch Annale, Stellenbosch, 2002).

292 JL Sadie, 'The Afrikaner in the South African Economy', paper prepared for the Canadian Commission on Bilingualism and Biculturalism, 1996.
293 S Pauw, *Die beroepslewe van die Afrikaner in die stad* (Pro Ecclesia, Stellenbosch, 1946).
294 AJ Albertyn et al., *Kerk en stad* (Pro Ecclesia, Stellenbosch, 1947).
295 G Pretorius, *Bruckner de Villiers* (HAUM, Cape Town, 1959).
296 CFJ Muller, *Sonop in die suide: Geboorte en groei van die Nasionale Pers* (Nasionale Boekhandel, Cape Town, 1990).
297 A Ehlers, 'Die Helpmekaarbeweging in Suid-Afrika', MA dissertation, University of Stellenbosch, 1986.
298 WPG Koen, 'Sanlam tussen die twee wêreldoorloë', DPhil dissertation, University of South Africa, 1986.
299 JL Sadie, 'Die ekonomiese faktor in die Afrikaner-gemeenskap', in HW van der Merwe, ed., *Identiteit en Verandering* (Tafelberg, Cape Town, 1974), p. 96.
300 D Welsh, 'The Political Economy of Afrikaner Nationalism', in A Leftwich, ed., *South Africa: Economic growth and political change* (Allison and Busby, London, 1974).
301 Sadie, 'Die ekonomiese faktor in die Afrikaner-gemeenskap', p. 96.
302 Volkskas, *Die bank van oom Bossie* (Volkskas, 1978).
303 A Wessels, *Plaasseun en nyweraar* (Perskor, Johannesburg, 1987), p. 40.
304 WP Esterhuyse, *Anton Rupert* (Tafelberg, Cape Town, 1986), pp. 24-5, 55.
305 H Giliomee, 'The Afrikaner Economic Advance', in H Adam and H Giliomee, eds., *Ethnic Power Mobilized: Can South Africa change?* (Yale University Press, New Haven, 1979); TJ Steenkamp, ''n Ekonomiese ontleding van sosio-politieke groepvorming met spesiale verwysing na die Afrikaner', DPhil dissertation, University of South Africa, 1989; TJ Steenkamp, 'Discrimination and the Economic Position of the Afrikaner', *SA Journal of Economic History*, 5, 1 (1990); RG Stokes, 'The Afrikaner Industrial Entrepreneur and Afrikaner Nationalism', *Economic Development and Cultural Change*, 22, 4 (1974).
306 MC O'Dowd, 'An Assessment of the English-speaking South African's Contribution to the Economy', in André de Villiers, ed., *English-speaking South Africa Today* (Oxford University Press, Cape Town, 1976), p. 149.
307 CGW Schumann, *Die ekonomiese posisie van die Afrikaner* (Nasionale Pers, Cape Town, 1940), p. 118.
308 Sadie, *The Fall and Rise of the Afrikaner in the South African Economy*; H Giliomee, *The Afrikaners: Biography of a people* (University of Virginia Press, Charlottesville, 2003), pp. 352-3.
309 EP du Plessis, *'n Volk staan op* (Human & Rousseau, Cape Town, 1964), pp. 95, 121; G Verhoef, 'Nationalism and Free Enterprise in Mining: The case of Federale Mynbou, 1952–1965', *South African Journal of Economic History*, 10, 1 (1995), pp. 93-4.
310 Du Plessis, *'n Volk staan op*, pp. 112-13; Sadie, 'Die ekonomiese faktor in die Afrikaner-gemeenskap', pp. 88-97.
311 Du Plessis, *'n Volk staan op*, pp. 104-12.
312 J Scannell, *Uit die volk gebore: Sanlam se eerste 50 jaar* (Nasionale Boekhandel, Cape Town, 1968), p. 46.
313 Giliomee, *The Afrikaners*, p. 439.
314 E Dommisse, *Anton Rupert* (Tafelberg, Cape Town, 2005), p. 89.
315 G Carter, *The Politics of Inequality: South Africa since 1948* (Thames and Hudson, London, 1958), p. 259.
316 C Feinstein, *An Economic History of South Africa* (Cambridge University Press, Cambridge, 2005), pp. 127-350.

317 *The Star*, 14 July 1941.
318 *Cape Argus*, 15 August 1946.
319 GD Scholtz, *Die ontwikkeling van die politieke denke van die Afrikaner*, vol. 8 (Perskor, Johannesburg, 1984), pp. 61-5.
320 Volksraad-debatte, 1941, pp. 6367-8.
321 O'Meara, *Forty Lost Years*, p. 122.
322 D O'Meara, *Volkskapitalisme: Class, capital and ideology in the development of Afrikaner nationalism, 1934–1948* (Cambridge University Press, Cambridge, 1983), p. 194.
323 G Verhoef, 'A History of Federale Mynbou' (unpublished manuscript, 1991), p. 6.
324 *Cape Argus*, 15 August 1946.
325 *Cape Argus*, 29 May 1948.
326 Pauw, *Die beroepslewe van die Afrikaner in die stad*, pp. 188-9.
327 K Owen, 'Dropping Out', *Business Day*, 30 April 1999.
328 G Shaw, 'Educated Dreamer Lacked True Vision', *Cape Times*, 21 November 2008.
329 L Marquard, *Peoples and Policies of South Africa* (Oxford University Press, London, 1969).
330 Marquard, *Peoples and Policies of South Africa*, p. 105.
331 R Davies, *Capital, State and White Labour in South Africa* (Harvester Press, Brighton, 1979), p. 298.
332 WH van den Bos, 'An Investigation into Resignation of Officers from the South African Air Force (Permanent Force) during the Period 1946–1971', MA dissertation, University of South Africa, 1978, p. 155.
333 I Evans, *Bureaucracy and Race: Native administration in South Africa* (University of California Press, Berkeley, 1997), p. 87.
334 GR Berridge, 'The Ethnic Agent in Place: English-speaking civil servants and nationalist South Africa, 1948–57', *Intelligence and National Security*, 4, 1 (1989).
335 D Posel, 'Whiteness and Power in the South African Civil Service', *Journal of Southern African Studies*, 25, 1 (1999), pp. 104-7.
336 S van Wyk, 'Die huidige beroepsposisie van die Afrikaner in die stad', DPhil diss., University of Pretoria, 1967; Giliomee, 'The Afrikaner Economic Advance', p. 165.
337 FAK, *Verslag van die Tweede Ekonomiese Volkskongres* (FAK, Bloemfontein, 1950), p. 8.
338 FAK, *Verslag van die Tweede Ekonomiese Volkskongres*, p. 8.
339 JA Lombard, 'Die ekonomiese ontwikkeling van die Afrikaner', in PV de Pienaar, ed., *Kultuurgeskiedenis van die Afrikaner* (Nasionale Boekhandel, Cape Town, 1968), p. 130.
340 *Die Transvaler*, 1 September 1937.
341 ELP Stals, 'Geskiedenis van die Afrikaner-Broederbond, 1918–1994' (unpublished MS, 1998), pp. 573-840.
342 S Patterson, *The Last Trek* (Routledge and Kegan Paul, London, 1957), p. 1710.
343 Verhoef, 'A History of Federale Mynbou', p. 67; JDF Jones, *Through Fortress and Rock: The story of Gencor, 1895–1995* (Jonathan Ball, Johannesburg, 1995), pp. 32-3.
344 Verhoef, 'Nationalism and Free Enterprise in Mining', p. 106.
345 Interview by author, 14 May 1999.
346 *Financial Mail*, 17 June 1983, Supplement.
347 J Nattrass, *The South African Economy* (Oxford University Press, Cape Town, 1981), p. 119.
348 B Bunting, *The Rise of the South African Reich* (Penguin, London, 1969), p. 388.
349 O'Meara, *Forty Lost Years*, pp. 140-1.
350 Interview with Pepler Scholtz, 12 March 1999.
351 Interview with senior Old Mutual manager, 12 March 1999.
352 Interview with Marinus Daling, 21 March 1999.
353 Esterhuyse, *Anton Rupert*, pp. 24-5.

354 Interview with author, 12 February 1999.
355 Dommisse, *Anton Rupert*, p. 116.
356 Du Plessis, *'n Volk staan op*, pp. 182-8.
357 J Howell, 'Enkele grepe', in WJ Verwoerd (comp.), *So onthou ons hom: Verwoerd* (Protea, Pretoria, 2001), p. 219.
358 C Engelbrecht, *Van akker tot eik: Die verhaal van Volkskas* (Heer Drukkers, Pretoria, 1981), pp. 433-4.
359 Interview Pieter Morkel, 9 April 1992. Conrad Strauss, who joined Standard Bank in 1963 and served as CEO from 1978 to 2000, confirmed these points in two communications to the author, 22 March 1999 and 20 August 2008.
360 Email communication with Nallie Bosman (CEO of ABSA, 1998–2004), 2 October 2008.
361 Email communication from Adam Jacobs, senior manager Volkskas, 31 August 2008.
362 Communication from Conrad Strauss, 20 August 2008.
363 B Schoeman, *Die Broederbond in die Afrikaner-politiek* (Aktuele Publikasies, Pretoria, 1982), p. 34.
364 D Richard, *Moedswillig die uwe* (Perskor, Johannesburg, 1985), p. 73.
365 S Pienaar, *Getuie van groot tye* (Tafelberg, Cape Town, 1979), pp. 45-6.
366 Richard, *Moedswillig die uwe*, p. 180.
367 Richard, *Moedswillig die uwe*, p. 179.
368 D Richard, *Asof dit gister was* (Perskor, Johannesburg, 1998).
369 Richard, *Asof dit gister was*, p. 308.
370 DP de Villiers to author, 28 May 1999 (letter deposited in Naspers Archives).
371 DP de Villiers to author, 28 May 1999 (letter deposited in Naspers Archives).
372 Du Plessis, *'n Volk staan op*, p. 237.
373 D Welsh, 'Urbanisation and Afrikaner Nationalism', *Journal of Modern African Studies*, 7, 2 (1969), p. 271.
374 Scannell, *Uit die volk gebore*.
375 Engelbrecht, *Van akker tot eik*, p. 216.
376 A Grundlingh, 'Are We Afrikaners Getting Too Rich?: Cornucopia and the change in Afrikanerdom in the 1960s', *Journal of Historical Sociology*, 21, 2/3 (2008).
377 H Serfontein, *Die verkrampte aanslag* (Human & Rousseau, Cape Town, 1970), p. 55.
378 Stals, 'Geskiedenis van die Afrikaner-Broederbond', p. 405.
379 *Die Volksblad*, 22 August 1969.
380 *Financial Mail* supplement, 14 July 1967.
381 *Financial Mail*, 19 June 1970.
382 Stokes, 'The Afrikaner Industrial Entrepreneur and Afrikaner Nationalism'; A Wassenaar, *Assault on Private Enterprise* (Tafelberg, Cape Town, 1977).
383 F Fukuyama, *Trust: The social virtues and the creation of prosperity* (Free Press, New York, 1995), p. 44.

Chapter 5

384 This chapter builds on two previous contributions: H Giliomee, 'A Note on Bantu Education', *South African Journal of Economics*, 77, 1 (2009), pp. 190-8, and H Giliomee, 'Bantu Education: Destructive intervention or part reform?', *New Contree*, 65 (December 2012), pp. 67-86. This contribution responds to comments on the latter article by Charles Simkins, Servaas van der Berg and Sean Archer, and incorporates material from an unpublished article by Jan Sadie. These scholars are in no way accountable for the views I express here.

385 A Luthuli, *Let My People Go* (Fount Paperbacks, London, 1962), pp. 176-7.
386 E Walker, *A History of Southern Africa* (Longmans Green, London, 1975), p. 900.
387 G Carter, *The Politics of Inequality: South Africa since 1948* (Thames and Hudson, London, 1958), pp. 104-5.
388 Carter, *The Politics of Inequality*, pp. 102-3.
389 J Hyslop, '"A Destruction Coming In": Bantu Education as a response to social crisis', in P. Bonner et al., eds., *Apartheid's Genesis, 1935–1962* (Ravan Press, Johannesburg, 1993), pp. 393-410.
390 TRH Davenport and C Saunders, *South Africa: A modern history* (Macmillan, London, 2000), p. 674. Compare this with TRH Davenport, *South Africa: A modern history* (Macmillan, Johannesburg, 1987), p. 375.
391 JL Sadie, 'Economic-Demographic Aspects of School Education in South Africa' (unpublished paper).
392 Email message from Charles Simkins to author, 12 August 2014.
393 C Kros, *The Seeds of Separate Development: Origins of Bantu Education* (Unisa Press, Pretoria, 2010), pp. 114-16.
394 *The Citizen*, 23 July 2012.
395 *Sunday Times*, 29 July 2012.
396 *SA Times*, 25 July 2012.
397 *Sunday Times*, 9 December 2012, 'So many questions', by Chris Barron.
398 *Die Burger*, 17 November 2012, p. 13.
399 CS le Roux, 'Post-graduate Education Students' Oral History Research: A review of retired teachers, experiences and perspectives of the Bantu Education system', *Yesterday and Today*, 8 December 2012.
400 Communication by a conference participant to author, 7 September 2012.
401 News24, 16 November 2016.
402 Davenport and Saunders, *South Africa*, p. 674.
403 *Cape Times*, 18 May 1939.
404 J Hyslop, *The Class Room Struggle: Policy and resistance in South Africa* (University of Natal Press, Pietermaritzburg, 1993), pp. 8-11.
405 RFA Hoernlé, *South African Native Policy and the Liberal Spirit* (Witwatersrand University Press, Johannesburg, 1939), p. 18.
406 J Rousseau, 'Iets oor Bantoe-onderwys', in WJ Verwoerd (comp.), *Verwoerd: So onthou ons hom* (Praag, Pretoria, 2001), p. 175.
407 R Elphick, *The Equality of Believers: Protestant missionaries and the racial politics of South Africa* (University of KwaZulu-Natal Press, Scottsville, 2012), pp. 290-1.
408 Elphick, *The Equality of Believers*, pp. 288-95.
409 Rousseau, 'Iets oor Bantoe-onderwys', p. 172.
410 AN Pelzer, ed., *Verwoerd Speaks* (APB Publishers, Johannesburg, 1968), p. 83.
411 D Posel, *The Making of Apartheid* (Clarendon Press, Oxford, 1997), p. 186.
412 *Financial Mail*, 14 July 1967, Supplement, p. 43.
413 Hyslop, *The Class Room Struggle*, pp. 4-5.
414 Carter, *The Politics of Inequality*, pp. 102-3.
415 R Millar, 'Science and Society in the Early Career of HF Verwoerd', *Journal of Southern African Studies*, 19, 4 (1993), pp. 636-46.
416 For a discussion see C Marx, 'Hendrik Verwoerd's Long March to Apartheid: Nationalism and racism in South Africa', in M Berg and S Wendt, eds., *Racism in the Modern World: Historical perspectives on cultural transfer and adaptation* (Berghahn Books, New York, 2011), pp. 281-302.

417 Pelzer, *Verwoerd Speaks*, pp. 28-30.
418 H Giliomee and B Mbenga, eds., *New History of South Africa* (Tafelberg, Cape Town, 2007), pp. 420-32.
419 HB Thom, *DF Malan* (Tafelberg, Cape Town, 1980), p. 279.
420 H Giliomee and L Schlemmer, *From Apartheid to Nation-Building* (Oxford University Press, Cape Town, 1989), p. 119.
421 G van de Wall, 'Verwoerd, die hervormer', in Verwoerd, *Verwoerd*, p. 166.
422 Hyslop, '"A Destruction Coming In"', pp. 393-410.
423 Interview by author of Dirk Meiring, Director-General of Education and Training during the early 1990s, 21 December 2013.
424 Rousseau, 'Iets oor Bantoe-onderwys', p. 172.
425 Interview by author with Dirk Meiring, 16 December 2012.
426 Communication to author by Prof. Flip Smit, a demographer who was previously Vice-Chancellor, University of Pretoria, 25 June 2012.
427 See discussion in the next section in which source references confirm this observation.
428 JW Fedderke, R de Kadt and J Lutz, 'Uneducating South Africa: The failure to address the need for human capital', *International Review of Education*, 46, 3 (2000), pp. 257-8.
429 Fedderke et al., 'Uneducating South Africa', p. 259.
430 Fedderke et al., 'Uneducating South Africa', p. 262.
431 J Burger, *The Black Man's Burden* (Victor Gollancz, London, 1944), p. 171.
432 L Marquard and J Lewin, *The Native in South Africa* (University of Witwatersrand Press, Johannesburg, 1948), p. 76.
433 F Wilson, *Dinosaurs, Diamonds and Democracy* (Umuzi, Cape Town, 2009), p. 88.
434 Rousseau, 'Iets oor Bantoe-onderwys', p. 172.
435 M Horrell, *Bantu Education to 1968* (South African Institute of Race Relations, Johannesburg, 1968), p. 72; Rousseau, 'Iets oor Bantoe-onderwys', p. 177.
436 Horrell, *Bantu Education to 1968*, pp. 58-9, 71.
437 K Hartshorne, *Crisis and Challenge: Black education 1910–1960* (Oxford University Press, Cape Town, 1992), p. 41.
438 C Kros, 'Deep Rumblings: ZK Matthews and African education before 1955', *Perspectives in Education*, 12, 1 (1990), p. 35.
439 P Walshe, *The Rise of African Nationalism in South Africa* (University of California Press, Berkeley, 1971), pp. 150-2.
440 TD Moodie, *The Rise of Afrikanerdom* (University of California Press, Berkeley, 1975), p. 272.
441 JD Shingler, 'Education and Political Order in South Africa, 1902-1960', PhD dissertation, Yale University, 1973, pp. 279-80.
442 Cited by D Braam, 'A boost for mother-tongue education', *Mail & Guardian*, 16 March 2012.
443 M Wilson, 'The Growth of Peasant Communities', in M Wilson and LM Thompson, eds., *Oxford History of South Africa* (Oxford University Press, Oxford, 1971), vol. 2, pp. 79-80.
444 Elphick, *The Equality of Believers*, p. 290.
445 Rousseau, 'Iets oor Bantoe-onderwys', p. 175.
446 J Kane-Berman, *Soweto: Black revolt, white reaction* (Ravan Press, Johannesburg, 1978), pp. 12-16.
447 K Heugh, 'Languages, Development and Reconstructing Education in South Africa', *International Journal of Educational Development*, 19 (1999), pp. 301-2.

448 K Heugh, 'Multilingual Education Policy in South Africa Constrained by Theoretical and Historical Disconnection', *Annual Review of Applied Linguistics*, 33 (2013).
449 Heugh, 'Languages, Development and Reconstructing Education', pp. 301-13.
450 Heugh, 'Multilingual Education Policy in South Africa'.
451 CH Feinstein, *An Economic History of South Africa* (Cambridge University Press, Cambridge, 2005), p. 243.
452 Hartshorne, *Crisis and Challenge*, p. 42.
453 Email message from Charles Simkins to author, 12 August 2014.
454 Rousseau, 'Iets oor Bantoe-onderwys', pp. 172-3.
455 Fedderke et al., 'Uneducating South Africa', p. 262.
456 Giliomee and Schlemmer, *From Apartheid to Nation-Building*, p. 118.
457 This was communicated several times to the author by Dr Gerrit Viljoen, who became the minister responsible for black education in 1980.

Chapter 9

458 C Naudé, 'Walg-video beklemtoon behoefte aan leierskap', *Die Burger*, 4 March 2008.
459 LA Barnard and JA Stemmet, 'PW Botha's Rubicon Speech of 15 August 1985', *Journal for Contemporary History*, 27, 1 (2002), pp. 119-35.
460 FW de Klerk, *Die laaste trek – en 'n nuwe begin* (Human & Rousseau, Cape Town, 1998), p. 121; CA Crocker, *High Noon in Southern Africa* (Norton, New York, 1992), p. 275.
461 A van Wyk, 'Chris Heunis: Onderskatte voorloper van hervorming', *Die Burger*, 4 February 2006.
462 R Renwick, *Unconventional Diplomacy in Southern Africa* (Macmillan, London, 1997), p. 110.
463 E Dommisse, *Anton Rupert: 'n Lewensverhaal* (Tafelberg, Cape Town, 2005), p. 369.
464 K van Wyk and D Geldenhuys, *Die Groepsgebod in PW Botha se politieke oortuigings* (RAU, Johannesburg, 1987), p. 47.
465 D de Villiers and J de Villiers, *PW* (Tafelberg, Cape Town, 1984), p. 367.
466 C Alden, *Apartheid's Last Stand: The rise and fall of the South African security state* (Macmillan, London, 1996), pp. 41-50.
467 Renwick, *Unconventional Diplomacy*, p. 114.
468 Interviews with two neurologists who studied the scan, 20 March 2008.
469 Interview, J Roux, 30 November 2007. Roux had specialised in clinical psychology.
470 Interview, M Malan, 9 February 2008.
471 Interview, J Roux, 30 January 2008.
472 A Ries and E Dommisse, *Leierstryd* (Tafelberg, Cape Town, 1990), p. 45.
473 L Schlemmer, 'Message Received: Now let us face these realities', *Sunday Times*, 18 August 1985.
474 Market and Media Research poll of 1988 reported in H Giliomee and L Schlemmer, *From Apartheid to Nation-Building* (Oxford University Press, Cape Town, 1989), p. 156.
475 Institute of Contemporary History (ICH), University of Free State, Gerrit Viljoen papers, Extraordinary meeting of the State Security Council, 18 July 1985; Circular to members, August 1985.
476 Interview, RF Botha, 30 November 2007.
477 Interview, JH (Koos) van der Merwe, 3 April 2008.
478 Interview, M Malan, 9 February 2008.
479 Email communication from J van der Merwe, 24 March 2008.
480 S Huntington, *Political Order in Changing Societies* (Yale University Press, New Haven, 1968), p. 359.

481 N Machiavelli, *The Prince* (Penguin Books, London, 1961), p. 51.
482 N Machiavelli, *The Discourses* (Penguin Books, London, 1970), p. 132; JM Coetzee, *Diary of a Bad Year* (Harvill Secker, London, 2007), p. 18 citing *The Discourses*, sections 20, 23.
483 D O'Meara, *Forty Lost Years: The apartheid state and the politics of the National Party, 1948–1994* (Ohio University Press, Athens, 1996), p. 263.
484 V Bogdanor, ed., *The Blackwell Encyclopaedia of Social Science* (Blackwell, London, 1991), p. 267.
485 Huntington, *Political Order*, pp. 346-7.
486 S Huntington, 'Reform and Stability in a Modernising, Multi-Ethnic Society', *Politikon*, 8 (1981), p. 11.
487 Huntington, *Political Order*, p. 347.
488 B Pottinger, *The Imperial Presidency: PW Botha – The first ten years* (Southern, Johannesburg, 1988), p. 82.
489 Interview, F Cloete, 20 December 2007.
490 Interview, J van Tonder, 11 January 2008.
491 Machiavelli, *The Discourses*, p. 156.
492 Parliamentary debates, 25 January 1985, col. 6.
493 A Lijphart, *Power-Sharing in South Africa* (Institute of International Studies, Berkeley, 1985), p. 67.
494 F van Zyl Slabbert and D Welsh, *South Africa's Options* (David Philip, Cape Town, 1979), pp. 67, 133.
495 H Giliomee, 'The Botha Quest: Sharing power without losing control', *Leadership SA*, 2, 2 (1983), pp. 27-35.
496 De Villiers and De Villiers, *PW*, pp. 210-11.
497 A Ries and E Dommisse, *Broedertwis* (Tafelberg, Cape Town, 1982), p. 112.
498 *Die Burger*, 29 July 1979.
499 *Die Burger*, 27 August 1981.
500 *Die Burger*, 23 February 1982.
501 Ries and Dommisse, *Broedertwis*, p. 115.
502 Email: JH van der Merwe (MP for the Conservative Party) to H Giliomee (researcher), 6 April 2008.
503 *Die Burger*, 21 August 1982.
504 *South Africa International Quarterly*, 16, 2 (1985), p. 111.
505 De Klerk, *Die laaste trek*, p. 118.
506 De Klerk, *Die laaste trek*, p. 138.
507 Van Wyk, 'Chris Heunis'.
508 Interview, AH van Wyk, 6 May 2008.
509 Crocker, *High Noon*, p. 115.
510 Interview, RF Botha, 30 November 2007.
511 Interview, J van Tonder, 11 January 2008.
512 Interview, F Cloete, 20 December 2008.
513 Interview, J van Tonder, 11 January 2008.
514 De Klerk, *Die laaste trek*, p. 119.
515 Parliamentary debates, 25 January 1985, cols. 11-16.
516 Interview with C Heunis reported by Alden, *Apartheid's Last Stand*, pp. 199-201.
517 Interview, W Breytenbach, 20 November 2007; interview, AH van Wyk, 7 May 2008.
518 Daan Prinsloo, *Stem uit die wildernis* (Vaandel Publishers, Mossel Bay, 1997), p. 211.
519 Interview with D Prinsloo, 30 January 2008.

520 Interview with J Roux, 6 May 2008; interview with Dawie de Villiers, 6 May 2008.
521 Prinsloo, *Stem uit die wildernis*, p. 309.
522 Verbatim extract from cabinet minutes, published in *Sunday Times*, 28 August 1994.
523 J Heunis, *Die binnekring* (Jonathan Ball, Johannesburg, 2007), p. 78.
524 Interview, C Heunis by J Heunis, n.d.
525 Interview, AH van Wyk, 9 May 2008.
526 De Klerk, *Die laaste trek*, p. 120.
527 Unabridged manuscript of D Prinsloo, later published as *Stem uit die wildernis*, p. 1362.
528 *Sunday Times*, 11 August 1985.
529 Interview, RF Botha, 30 November 2007.
530 Interview, AH van Wyk, 6 May 2008.
531 D Prinsloo, *Stem uit die wildernis*, p. 215.
532 Interview, F van Zyl Slabbert, 1 August 2007.
533 *Beeld*, 22 June 2007.
534 For a discussion of Botha's speeches at the party congresses, see Prinsloo, *Stem uit die wildernis*, pp. 211-15.
535 Interview, CH Heunis by J Heunis, 2005.
536 Interview, D Steward, 21 April 2008.
537 Email from C von Hirschberg, 20 April 2008.
538 Email from C von Hirschberg, 28 April 2008.
539 Email from C von Hirschberg, 30 April 2008.
540 *Sunday Star*, 6 October 1985.
541 Interview, AH van Wyk, 7 May 2008; P Sullivan, 'Why PW Jibbed at His Rubicon', *Sunday Star*, 6 October 1985.
542 Interview, M Malan, 8 February 2008.
543 This view is held by F van Zyl Slabbert and a senior NP leader.
544 Unabridged manuscript of D Prinsloo, later published as *Stem uit die wildernis*, p. 1362.
545 *The Star*, 22 September 1985.
546 Crocker, *High Noon*, p. 275.
547 Interview, D Steward, 21 April 2008.
548 Emails from W Scholtz (diplomat stationed in Vienna), 15 April 2008, 23 July 2008.
549 Interview, N van Heerden (senior Foreign Affairs official), 6 May 2008.
550 De Klerk, *Die laaste trek*, p. 121.
551 Email from Daan Prinsloo, 16 March 2008.
552 Email from Daan Prinsloo, 16 March 2008.
553 Interview, T Ehlers, 7 June 2008. On 9 August 1985 the *New York Times* published a report under the heading 'US and South Africa aides meet in Vienna over "serious situation"'. It stated that White House and State Department officials disclosed information about the confidential meeting only after persistent questioning by journalists. Pik Botha, however, dismisses the possibility that this could have prompted the President to decide on a hard-line speech rather than appear to act under American pressure. He points out that the President did not take serious notice of what appeared in foreign papers. Newspapers in South Africa reported on his visit to Europe for which he had received the President's permission (interview, 10 June 2008).
554 Interview with AH van Wyk, 7 July 2007.
555 A Botha, 'Notes on the Heunis Papers', Institute for Contemporary Archives, Bloemfontein, 16 January 2007; Heunis, *Binnekring*, pp. 84-5.
556 The State President's Durban Manifesto. This document, which was not signed and not

dated, was the formal input from the Department of Foreign Affairs for the President's speech. A copy is lodged in the library of the University of Stellenbosch. Pik Botha discussed this document in detail in "'n Feitelike resensie van J Heunis se Die binnekring', *Beeld, 21 June 2007.*

557 This paragraph is based on Prinsloo, *Stem uit die wildernis,* pp. 346-7.
558 *Die Burger,* 14 August 1985.
559 P Waldmeir, *Anatomy of a Miracle* (Vintage, New York, 1997), p. 54.
560 *Weekend Argus,* 10 August 1985.
561 Interview, T Ehlers, 7 June 2008.
562 Prinsloo, *Stem uit die wildernis,* p. 346.
563 Pottinger, *The Imperial Presidency,* p. 330.
564 Prinsloo, *Stem uit die wildernis,* p. 343.
565 Heunis, *Binnekring,* p. 82; interview, Chris Heunis by J Heunis, 2005.
566 Interview, C Heunis by J Heunis, n.d.
567 Waldmeir, *Anatomy of a Miracle,* p. 54.
568 Verbatim text of the speech, issued by the NP Information Office, 15 August 1985.
569 Email from D Steward, 3 May 2008.
570 Verbatim text of the speech, NP Information Service, 15 August 1985.
571 Schlemmer, 'Message Received', *Sunday Times,* 18 August 1985.
572 Prinsloo, *Stem uit die wildernis,* p. 345.
573 *The Citizen,* 17 August 1985.
574 Cited by W Jordaan, *Beeld,* 19 August 2005.
575 *Los Angeles Times,* 18 August 1985.
576 ANC response to PW Botha's Rubicon speech, 16 August 1985, http://www.anc.org.za/ancdocs/pr/1980s/pr850816.html.
577 CH Feinstein, *An Economic History of South Africa* (Cambridge University Press, Cambridge, 2005), pp. 228-9.
578 Waldmeir, *Anatomy of a Miracle,* p. 56.
579 H Giliomee, 'Surrender without Defeat', SA Institute of Race Relations Topical Papers, Johannesburg, 1997.
580 De Klerk, *Die laaste trek,* p. 123.
581 Renwick, *Unconventional Diplomacy,* p. 110.
582 M Robinson, 'The Politics of Successful Governance Reforms: Lessons of design and implementation', *Commonwealth and Comparative Politics,* 45, 4 (2007), pp. 521-48.

Chapter 10
583 Mark Sanders, *Complicities: The intellectual and apartheid* (Duke University Press, Durham, 2002), p. 135.
584 Breyten Breytenbach, *The True Confessions of an Albino Terrorist* (Taurus, Johannesburg, 1984), pp. 216-17.
585 Breytenbach, *The True Confessions of an Albino Terrorist,* p. 60.
586 M Walzer, *The Company of Critics: Social criticism and political commitment in the twentieth century* (Basic Books, New York, 1988), p. 219.
587 Breyten Breytenbach, *End Papers* (Faber & Faber, London, 1986), p. 237.
588 Francis Galloway, *Breyten Breytenbach as openbare figuur* (HAUM, Pretoria, 1990), p. 283; Walzer, *The Company of Critics,* p. 222.
589 Breytenbach, *The True Confessions of an Albino Terrorist,* p. 60.
590 Breytenbach, *The True Confessions of an Albino Terrorist,* p. 61.

591 Breytenbach, *The True Confessions of an Albino Terrorist*, pp. 325, 327.
592 Walzer, *The Company of Critics*, p. 222.
593 JM Coetzee, *Stranger Shores: Essays, 1986–1999* (Vintage Books, London, 2001), p. 306.
594 Breyten Breytenbach, *Return to Paradise* (Faber & Faber, London, 1993), p. 123.
595 Breytenbach, *End Papers*, pp. 167-80.
596 Breytenbach, *End Papers*, pp. 198-9.
597 Breytenbach, *End Papers*, p. 188.
598 *Rapport*, 13 April 1986.
599 Galloway, *Breyten Breytenbach as openbare figuur*, pp. 236-8.
600 Breytenbach, *End Papers*, p. 12.
601 JM Coetzee, *Doubling the Point* (Harvard University Press, Cambridge, 1992), pp. 377-8.
602 Coetzee, *Stranger Shores*, p. 314.
603 *South African Digest*, 1986.
604 F van Zyl Slabbert, *The Other Side of History* (Jonathan Ball, Johannesburg, 2006), p. 46.
605 Graham Leach, *The Afrikaners: Their last great trek* (Macmillan, London, 1989), p. 149.
606 Galloway, *Breyten Breytenbach as openbare figuur*, p. 261.
607 African National Congress, 'Paris-Dakar Meeting' (unpublished MS, 1987, Mayibuye Centre, University of the Western Cape).
608 African National Congress, 'Paris-Dakar Meeting', pp. 67-9.
609 African National Congress, 'Paris-Dakar Meeting', pp. 67-8.
610 André du Toit, 'Beginning the Debate', *Die Suid-Afrikaan*, 11 (1987), pp. 18-20.
611 African National Congress, 'Paris-Dakar Meeting', pp. 6-7.
612 Slabbert, *The Other Side of History*, p. 76.
613 Anthea Jeffery, *People's War: New light on the struggle for South Africa* (SA Institute of Race Relations, Johannesburg, 2009).
614 Leach, *The Afrikaners*, p. 156.
615 African National Congress, 'Paris-Dakar Meeting', p. 13.
616 African National Congress, 'Paris-Dakar Meeting', p. 16.
617 D Steward, interview with author, 23 May 2008.
618 African National Congress, 'Paris-Dakar Meeting', pp. 18-19, 70.
619 M Staniland, 'Democracy and Ethno-centrism', in Patrick Chabal, ed., *Political Domination in Africa* (Cambridge University Press, Cambridge, 1986), p. 70.
620 Theo Hanf, 'The Prospects of Accommodation in Communal Conflicts', in Hermann Giliomee and Lawrence Schlemmer, eds., *Negotiating South Africa's Future* (St Martin's Press, New York, 1989), pp. 108-9.
621 Galloway, *Breyten Breytenbach as openbare figuur*, p. 283; Walzer, *The Company of Critics*, p. 222.
622 Eli Kedourie, 'One-man-one-vote', *South Africa International*, 18, 7 (1987), p. 1.
623 Richard Sklar, 'Democracy in Africa', in Patrick Chabal, *Political Domination in Africa*, p. 25.
624 African National Congress, 'Paris-Dakar Meeting', pp. 26-34, 75.
625 African National Congress, 'Paris-Dakar Meeting', p. 11.
626 Martin Meredith, *The State of Africa: A history of fifty years of independence* (Free Press, London, 2005), p. 379.
627 African National Congress, 'Paris-Dakar Meeting', p. 72.
628 Alex Boraine, *A Life in Transition* (Zebra, Cape Town, 2008), p. 154.
629 African National Congress, 'Paris-Dakar Meeting', p. 26.
630 African National Congress, 'Paris-Dakar Meeting', p. 72.

631 Jacques Kriel, 'The Human Face of Dakar', *Frontline*, July 1987, p. 23.
632 African National Congress, 'Paris-Dakar Meeting', p. 23.
633 Hermann Giliomee and Lawrence Schlemmer, *From Apartheid to Nation-Building* (Oxford University Press, Cape Town, 1989).
634 African National Congress, 'Paris-Dakar Meeting', p. 23.
635 P Jordan, 'Why Won't Afrikaners Rely on Democracy?', *Die Suid-Afrikaan*, 13 (1988), pp. 24-9.
636 Charles Taylor, 'The Dynamics of Democratic Exclusion', *Journal of Democracy*, 9, 4 (1998), p. 148.
637 Pierre van den Berghe, 'Introduction', in P van den Berghe, ed., *The Liberal Dilemma in South Africa* (St Martin's Press, New York, 1979), p. 7.
638 Chris Louw, 'SA pers oopgevlek', *Die Suid-Afrikaan*, 11 (1987).
639 *Debatte van die Parlement*, 17, 1987, cols. 2469-70, 2514.
640 Walzer, *The Company of Critics*, p. 211.
641 C Truehart, 'JM Coetzee: Voices of Afrikaner conscience', *International Herald Tribune*, 28 November 1990.
642 Breyten Breytenbach, *Return to Paradise* (Faber & Faber, London, 1993), p. 215.

Chapter 12

643 Cited by F van Zyl Slabbert in *Die Suid-Afrikaan*, August 1988, p. 23.
644 Jannie Gagiano, 'Meanwhile Back on the "Boereplaas"', *Politikon*, 13 (1986), pp. 3-21.
645 Jannie Gagiano, 'Ruling Group Cohesion', in Hermann Giliomee and Jannie Gagiano, *The Elusive Search for Peace: South Africa, Israel, Northern Ireland* (Oxford University Press, Cape Town, 1990), p. 196.
646 Anna Starcke, *Survival: Taped interviews with South Africa's power elite* (Tafelberg, Cape Town, 1978), pp. 66, 71.
647 *Cape Times*, 17 September 1987, p. 10.
648 Chester Crocker, *High Noon in Southern Africa: Making peace in a rough neighborhood* (Norton, New York, 1992), p. 491.
649 *Mayibuye*, November 1992.
650 *New York Times*, 10 November 1996.
651 *Sunday Times*, Business Supplement, 10 September 1996, p. 1.
652 *Financial Times*, 18 July 1994.
653 Peter F Alexander, *Alan Paton: A biography* (Oxford University Press, New York, 1994), pp. 273, 299-300, 401.
654 Dan O'Meara, *Forty Lost Years: The apartheid state and the politics of the National Party, 1948–1994* (Ravan, Johannesburg, 1996), p. 463.
655 Walker Connor, 'Nation-Building or Nation-Destroying?', *World Politics*, 24, 3 (1972), pp. 319-55.
656 Steven Friedman, 'Elite Unlikely to Make Sacrifices', *Business Day*, 24 June 1996.
657 Heribert Adam, 'Cohesion and Coercion', in Giliomee and Gagiano, *The Elusive Search for Peace*, p. 236.
658 Pierre Hugo, 'Towards Darkness and Death', in Pierre Hugo, *Perspectives on South Africa* (Die Suid-Afrikaan, Cape Town, 1989), p. 255; Chris de Kock, 'Movements in South African Mass Opinion and Party Support to 1993', in RW Johnson and Lawrence Schlemmer, *Launching Democracy in South Africa: The first open election, 1994* (Yale University Press, New Haven, 1996), p. 45.
659 Lawrence Schlemmer, 'The Domestic Contexts' (unpublished paper, 1995).

660 *Financial Times*, 26 May 1993.
661 Lawrence Schlemmer, *Social Research in a Divided Society* (University of Natal Press, Pietermaritzburg, 1973), p. 15.
662 HA Fagan, *Our Responsibility* (Universiteit Uitgewers, Stellenbosch, 1959), p. 93.
663 Lewis Gann, 'Liberal Interpretations of South African History', *Rhodes-Livingstone Journal* (1959), pp. 40-58.
664 NP van Wyk Louw, *Liberale nasionalisme* (1958); reprinted in *Versamelde prosa* (Tafelberg, Cape Town, 1986), vol. I, p. 505.
665 Hugo, 'Towards Darkness and Death', pp. 237-63; Alexander, *Alan Paton*, p. 264.
666 De Kock, 'Movements in South African Mass Opinion', p. 37.
667 Charles Simkins, *Reconstructing South African Liberalism* (South African Institute of Race Relations, Johannesburg, 1987), pp. 60-1.
668 Most of these figures are derived from a series of publications by Mike McGrath, whose work is based on analyses of the 1975 and 1991 censuses. See also my chapter on the Afrikaner economic advance in Heribert Adam and Hermann Giliomee, *Ethnic Power Mobilized: Can South Africa change?* (Yale University Press, New Haven, 1979), pp. 145-76.
669 Milan Kundera, 'The Czech Wager', *New York Review of Books*, 22 January 1981, p. 21.
670 For a perceptive article on this issue by an Afrikaans journalist, see Ton Vosloo, 'Is die Afrikaner die dodo van Suid-Afrika?', *Buurman* (September–November 1981), pp. 7-8.
671 Louw, *Versamelde prosa*, pp. 457-8.
672 Donal Harman Akenson, *God's Peoples: Covenant and land in South Africa, Israel and Ulster* (Cornell University Press, Ithaca, 1992).
673 Hermann Giliomee, 'Broedertwis: Intra-Afrikaner conflicts in the transition from apartheid', *African Affairs*, 91 (1992), p. 347.
674 Merle Lipton, *Capitalism and Apartheid: South Africa, 1910–1986* (Wildwood House, Aldershot, 1986), pp. 51-61.
675 For an extended discussion see Hermann Giliomee, '"Survival in Justice": An Afrikaner debate over apartheid', *Comparative Studies in Society and History*, 35, 3 (1994), pp. 527-48.
676 John Kane-Berman, *The Silent Revolution* (South African Institute of Race Relations, Johannesburg, 1990).
677 For a succinct overview see Patrick McGowan, 'The "New" South Africa: Ascent or descent in the world system', *South African Journal of International Affairs*, 1, 1 (1993), pp. 35-61.
678 Lawrence Schlemmer, 'South Africa's National Party Government', in Peter Berger and Bobby Godsell, eds., *A Future South Africa* (Human & Rousseau, Cape Town, 1988), pp. 27-8.
679 Mike Louw, interview, 21 November 1994.
680 Samuel Huntington, 'Reform and Stability in a Modernising, Multi-Ethnic Society', *Politikon*, 8 (1981), p. 11.
681 *Sunday Times*, 28 August 1994, p. 26.
682 Unpublished document of the Afrikaner Broederbond, c. July 1986.
683 Akenson, *God's Peoples*, pp. 385-6.
684 See, for instance, Heribert Adam and Kogila Moodley, *South Africa without Apartheid* (Maskew Miller Longman, Cape Town, 1986).
685 Padraig O'Malley, ed., 'Ramaphosa and Meyer in Belfast' (McCormack Institute, University of Massachusetts, 1996, mimeo).
686 De Kock, 'Movements in South African Mass Opinion', pp. 39-40; Hermann Giliomee and Lawrence Schlemmer, *From Apartheid to Nation-Building* (Oxford University Press, Cape Town, 1990), pp. 156-7; and unpublished research by Schlemmer.

687 Arend Lijphart, 'Prospects for Power-Sharing in the New South Africa', in Andrew Reynolds, ed., *Election 1994: South Africa* (David Philip, Cape Town, 1994), p. 229.
688 Michael Bratton and Nicholas van de Walle, 'Neopatrimonial Regimes and Political Competition in Africa', *World Politics*, 46, 1 (1994), pp. 454-89.
689 Alf Ries and Ebbe Dommisse, *Broedertwis* (Tafelberg, Cape Town, 1982), pp. 111-12.
690 *Sunday Star*, 17 March 1990.
691 *Die Burger*, 31 March 1990.
692 Steven Friedman, *The Long Journey: South Africa's quest for a negotiated settlement* (Ravan Press, Johannesburg, 1993), p. 157.
693 I am basing this on the forthcoming study of Patti Waldmeir, *Anatomy of a Miracle*.
694 For an extended critique of this school see Walker Connor, *Ethnonationalism* (Princeton University Press, Princeton, 1994) and Donald Horowitz, *Ethnic Groups in Conflict* (University of California Press, Berkeley, 1985).
695 FW de Klerk, 21 January 1997; copy issued by his office.

Chapter 13

696 De Klerk phrased his decision as follows in a speech given in London: 'The decision to surrender the right to national sovereignty is certainly one of the most painful any leader can be asked to make. Most nations are prepared to wage war and catastrophe rather than surrender this right. Yet this was the decision we had to take. We had to accept the necessity of giving up on the ideal on which we have been nurtured and the dream for which so many generations had struggled for and for which so many of our people have died.'

Chapter 14

697 A succinct articulation of this view in Parliament was given by AI Malan, father of a future Minister for Defence, cited in H Giliomee, *The Afrikaners: Biography of a people* (Tafelberg, Cape Town, 2003), p. 486.
698 A Drury, *A Very Strange Society: A journey to the heart of South Africa* (Michael Joseph, London, 1968), p. 451.
699 P van den Berghe, *South Africa: A study in conflict* (Wesleyan University Press, Middletown, 1965), p. 262.
700 RW Johnson, *How Long Will South Africa Survive?* (Macmillan, London, 1977).
701 H Adam, *Modernising Racial Domination: South Africa's political dynamics* (University of California Press, Berkeley, 1971), pp. 15-17.
702 RW Johnson, *How Long Will South Africa Survive? The looming crisis* (Jonathan Ball, Johannesburg, 2015), p. 11.
703 S Robinson, Review of RW Johnson's *How long will South Africa survive?*, *Sunday Times* (London), 16 August 2015.
704 H Giliomee, *The Last Afrikaner Leaders: A supreme test of power* (Tafelberg, Cape Town, 2012), pp. 316-17.
705 A Jeffery, *People's War: New light on the struggle for South Africa* (Jonathan Ball, Johannesburg, 2009), pp. xxxiii–xxxiv.
706 M Plaut, 'CIA Assessments of South Africa's Transition: How accurate were they?' (available at ever-fasternews.com, accessed on 20 November 2011), first posted 22 July 2007.
707 JL Sadie, 'The Political Arithmetic of the South African Population', *Journal of Racial Affairs* (July 1950), p. 152; JL Sadie, 'The Political Arithmetic of Apartheid', in P Hugo, ed., *South African Perspectives* (Die Suid-Afrikaan, Cape Town, 1989), pp. 150-7.

708 H Giliomee, 'Afrikaner Politics, 1977-1987', in J Brewer, *Can South Africa Survive? Five minutes to midnight* (Macmillan, London, 1989), pp. 108-35.
709 A Toynbee, 'History's Warning to Africa', *Optima*, 9, 2 (1959), pp. 55-6.
710 J Hatch, *The Dilemma of South Africa* (Dennis Dobson, London, 1953), p. 93.
711 J Robertson, *Liberalism in South Africa, 1948–1963* (Oxford University Press, Oxford, 1971), p. x.
712 N Mandela, *Long Walk to Freedom: The autobiography of Nelson Mandela* (MacDonald Purnell, Randburg, 1994), p. 105.
713 AN Pelzer, ed., *Verwoerd Speaks* (APB, Johannesburg, 1966), pp. 14, 24.
714 S Ellis, *External Mission: The ANC in exile* (Jonathan Ball, Johannesburg, 2012), pp. 17-18; I Filatova and A Davidson, *The Hidden Thread: Russia and South Africa in the Soviet era* (Jonathan Ball, Johannesburg, 2013), pp. 300-1.
715 T Lodge, *Mandela: A critical life* (Oxford University Press, Oxford, 2006), pp. 68-70.
716 N Mandela, 'Nelson Mandela to Hendrik Verwoerd' (available at www.nelsonmandela.org).
717 Lodge, *Mandela*, pp. 104-5.
718 Mandela, *Long Walk to Freedom*, pp. 260-6.
719 Ellis, *External Mission*, pp. 17-18.
720 Filatova and Davidson, *The Hidden Thread*, pp. 300-1; I Filatova, 'Mandela and the SACP: Time to close the debate' (available at www.politicsweb.co.za, 24 June 2015, accessed on 20 September 2015).
721 Ellis, *External Mission*, pp. 16-17; R Malan, 'The Real Story of Nelson Mandela and the Communists', *The Spectator* blogs, 10 December 2013.
722 N Mandela, 'Manuscript of Nelson Mandela's autobiography' (available at www.nelsonmandela.org, accessed on 1 May 2015).
723 Ellis, *External Mission*, p. 33.
724 RW Johnson, *The First Man, the Last Nation* (Jonathan Ball, Johannesburg, 2004), p. 109.
725 N Alexander, *An Ordinary Country* (University of Natal Press, Pietermaritzburg, 2002), pp. 46-9.
726 N Mandela, 'Manuscript of Nelson Mandela's autobiography', p. 302.
727 H Giliomee, interview, P Swanepoel, 29 January 2014.
728 Email: Jamie Miller to H Giliomee, 7 February 2015. Miller's book on John Vorster will appear shortly.
729 Alexander, *An Ordinary Country*, p. 47.
730 N Mandela, 'Nelson Mandela and the Bantustans' (available at www.politicsweb.co.za, accessed on 14 May 2012), republication of Nelson Mandela, 'Clear the Obstacles and Confront the Enemy', c.1974.
731 Email: N Barnard to H Giliomee, 26 February 2015.
732 Letter, B Pogrund to the editor, *Mail & Guardian*, 3 February 2015.
733 *Weekly Mail*, 16 February 1990.
734 H Giliomee and L Schlemmer, *From Apartheid to Nation-Building* (Oxford University Press, Cape Town, 1989), p. 156.
735 M Louw, interview, P Waldmeir, 29 May 1995, Manuscripts Collection, University of Stellenbosch.
736 For an account of these talks, see N Barnard, *Geheime rewolusie: Geheime van 'n spioenbaas* (Tafelberg, Cape Town, 2015), pp. 176-84.
737 N Barnard, 'NIS wou sonder middelman na ANC gaan', *Die Burger*, 18 February 1992.
738 H Ebrahim, *The Soul of a Nation: Constitution-making in South Africa* (Oxford University Press, Cape Town, 1998), p. 447.
739 N Mandela, interview, H Giliomee, 1 March 1992.

740 Barnard, *Geheime rewolusie*, pp. 215-20.
741 P Waldmeir, interview, PW Botha, 1 March 1995.
742 Email: N Barnard to H Giliomee, 26 February 2015.
743 P Waldmeir, *Anatomy of a Miracle: The end of apartheid and the birth of a new South Africa* (Norton, New York, 1997), p. 148.
744 R Renwick, *Mission to South Africa: Diary of a revolution* (Jonathan Ball, Johannesburg, 2015), p. 107.
745 Renwick, *Mission to South Africa*, p. 109.
746 Renwick, *Mission to South Africa*, p. 126.
747 Giliomee, *The Last Afrikaner Leaders*, p. 368.
748 Jeffery, *People's War*, pp. 496-511.
749 I de Villiers, *Strooidak en toring* (Umuzi, Cape Town, 2009), p. 195.
750 O'Malley Archives, interview, Colin Eglin, 3 August 1992.
751 O'Malley Archives, interview, Lawrence Schlemmer, 2 October 1992.
752 Waldmeir, *Anatomy of a Miracle*, pp. 231-2.
753 J Heunis, *Die binnekring* (Jonathan Ball, Johannesburg, 2007), p. 150.
754 *Die Burger*, 31 March 1990.
755 De Villiers, *Strooidak en toring*, p. 200.
756 J van Rooyen, *Hard Right: The new white power in South Africa* (IB Tauris, London, 1994); D Welsh, 'Rightwing terrorism in South Africa', *Terrorism and Political Violence*, 7, 1 (1995), pp. 239-64.
757 H Giliomee, interview, G Meiring, 11 November 2002.
758 D Cruywagen, *Brothers in War and Peace: Constand and Braam Viljoen and the birth of a new South Africa* (Zebra Press, Cape Town, 2014), pp. 224-5.
759 CJ Friedrich, *Man and His Government* (McGraw-Hill, New York, 1963), pp. 159-79.
760 M Gladwell, *David and Goliath: Underdogs, misfits and the art of battling giants* (Allen Lane, London, 2013), pp. 197-213.
761 F Dyson, 'How to be an Underdog, and Win', *New York Review of Books*, 21 November 2013, pp. 22-3.
762 J Gagiano, 'Ruling Group Cohesion', in H Giliomee and J Gagiano, *The Elusive Search for Peace: South Africa, Northern Ireland and Israel* (Oxford University Press, Cape Town, 1989), p. 197.
763 H Giliomee, interview, C Heunis, 15 December 2002.
764 H Giliomee, interview, N Barnard, 25 February 2015.
765 H Giliomee, interview, FW de Klerk, 2 May 1990.
766 H Giliomee, *The Afrikaners: Biography of a people* (Virginia University Press, Charlottesville, 2003), p. 635.
767 L Schlemmer, 'Factors in the Persistence or Decline of Ethnic Group Mobilisation: A conceptual review and case study of cultural group responses among Afrikaners in post-apartheid South Africa', PhD dissertation, University of Cape Town, 1999.
768 Johnson, *How Long Will South Africa Survive?*, pp. 72-3.
769 *Rapport*, 29 March 2015.
770 A Jammine, quoted in 'Business Times', *Sunday Times*, 10 May 2015.

Chapter 15
771 Children's Institute, University of Cape Town, 'Child Gauge Report', 2015.
772 'Why Universities Should Quit the Ratings Game', *University World News*, 442 (January 2017).

Chapter 16

773 Heinz Kloss, *The Unfolding of Afrikaans in Its Germanic, African and World Context* (University of the North, Pietersburg, 1977), p. 10.
774 Cited in Hermann Giliomee et al., *Die toekoms van Afrikaans as openbare taal* (Tafelberg, Cape Town, 2001), p. 117.
775 Stephen Wurm, 'Strategies for Language Maintenance and Revival', in David and Myra Bradley, eds., *Language Endangerment and Language Maintenance* (Routledge, London, 2002), p. 15.
776 JFW Grosskopf, 'Die nuwe Stellenbosch', *Het Gedenkboek van het Victoria-Kollege* (Nasionale Pers, Cape Town, 1918), pp. 177-8.
777 André du Toit and Hermann Giliomee, *Afrikaner Political Thought: Analysis and documents, 1780–1850* (University of California Press, Berkley, 1982.)
778 James Bryce, *Impressions of South Africa* (Macmillan, London, 1899), p. 314.
779 MCE van Schoor and JJ van Rooyen, *Republieke en Republikeine* (Nasionale Boekhandel, Cape Town, 1960), p. 109.
780 Pieter Duvenage, *Afrikaanse Filosofie: Perspektiewe en dialoë* (Sun Press, Bloemfontein, 2016). See also the extended review of this book by Johann Rossouw first published on the website Litnet Akademies, 22 March 2016.
781 George Schopflin, 'Nationalism and National Minorities in East and Central Europe', *Journal of International Affairs*, 45, 1 (1991), p. 52.
782 Jean Laponce, *Languages and Territories* (University of Toronto Press, Toronto, 1987), pp. 72-3.
783 I owe this insight to Robert Ross, who has written revealingly on nineteenth-century Cape history.
784 Kole Omotoso, *Season of Migration to the South* (Tafelberg, Cape Town, 1994), p. 114.
785 Sonja Loots, *Rapport*, 18 September 2017.
786 Kwesi Kwaa Prah, 'The Challenge of Language in Post-apartheid South Africa', first published on the website LitNet on 22 March 2018.
787 Hermann Giliomee, 'In gesprek met Jack de Wet oor ons universiteite', *Die Suid-Afrikaan*, 4 (1985), pp. 8-11.
788 Flip Smit, 'Van isolasie na ranglyste', Netwerk24, 22 July 2017.
789 'Why Universities Should Quit the Ratings Game', *University World News*, 442 (January 2017).
790 Johan Mouton, 'Afrikaans as wetenskapstaal in Suid-Afrika', *Tydskrif vir geesteswetenskappe*, 45, 3 (2005), p. 370.
791 Flip Smit, 'Die aard, wese en rol van die Suid-Afrikaanse universiteite in 'n ontwikkelende land' (unpublished paper, 2017).
792 Robert Phillipson, *Linguistic Imperialism* (Oxford University Press, Oxford, 1992), p. 35.
793 News24, 16 November 2016.
794 Laponce, *Languages and Territories*, p. 234.
795 Hermann Giliomee and Lawrence Schlemmer, *'n Vaste plek vir Afrikaans: Taaluitdagings op kampus* (Sunmedia, Stellenbosch, 2007), pp. 253-6.
796 Communication, 16 April 2016.
797 Judgment in the case of Afriforum and Solidariteit versus the University of Pretoria, High Court Gauteng Division, 3 December 2017.
798 Giliomee and Schlemmer, *Vaste plek vir Afrikaans*, p. 242.
799 Data provided by Dr Flip Smit, 26 August 2017.
800 The above two paragraphs are based on a communication from Dr Smit, 12 July 2017.

801 Tim du Plessis, 'Afrikaans se toekoms is in bruin hande', *Beeld*, 27 August 2017.
802 Pieter Malan, '"Engels is maklikste" sê prof Wim al lankal', *Rapport*, 23 August 2017. See also the interview with De Villiers on the video 'Die ander kant' posted by Mercy Kannemeyer, uploaded on YouTube on 21 February 2017.

INDEX

Abdurahman, Abdullah 10-13, 18, 29, 47
Adam, Heribert 37, 270-271
African National Congress (ANC) 27-30, 66, 74, 80, 84, 116, 118-119, 121, 126, 130, 169-171, 174, 179, 184-185, 187, 198, 200, 202-217, 228, 232, 238-239, 241, 249, 253-254, 256-265, 267, 271-272, 274-289, 291-293, 301, 310-311
African Political Organisation (APO) 10-11, 13-14, 16-17, 21, 28-29
Afrikaans vii, xi, 9, 11, 14-15, 25-27, 29-30, 76-77, 84, 86-89, 243-245, 304-325
   and arts festivals 308-309
   and language battle at Stellenbosch University xi, 297-304, 312, 318-322, 324
   and the law 304-307
   as 'high-culture' (science, arts and humanities) 245-246, 307, 314, 318-322, 324
   as instrument of de-colonisation 305
   as public language & medium of instruction at schools, universities xi, 26, 29, 75, 130-133, 135, 259, 297-302, 304-314, 317-325
   as mother tongue of coloureds xi, 11, 15-16, 26, 68, 77, 208, 300, 305, 309, 320, 322-323
   as mother tongue of whites 9, 14, 25-27, 50, 144, 300, 316-323
   as official language 130, 135, 213, 245, 266, 298, 302, 304-305, 316
Afrikaans business 83-84, 86-89, 93-94, 105, 108, 111-112
Afrikaans churches viii, 32, 34, 36, 41-42, 44-46, 55, 67-68, 80, 255
Afrikaans literature 131, 163, 300, 304, 306-309
Afrikaanse Nasionale Bond (ANB) 16-19, 23-25, 28-29
Afrikaanse Pers Bpk ix, 108
Afrikaner Broederbond (AB) 25, 36-38, 40-41, 49, 52, 57, 89, 92-93, 99, 112, 140, 255

Afrikaner nationalism vii, ix, 9, 35-36, 56, 61, 73, 100, 132-134, 160, 207, 214-215, 220
Afrikaans press and media 37, 75, 82, 108-112, 177, 216, 243, 245, 308
Afrikaner Bond 7, 16
Afrikaner volkstaat 263, 293
Alexander, Neville 130, 278, 280
Altbach, Philip 301, 313
Annale (Stellenbosch University) 305
apartheid viii-xi, 25-30, 32-58, 62-69, 71-73, 76-82, 96, 115, 117-119, 131-132, 134, 140, 142-144, 147-148, 150-153, 155, 157, 160, 163, 166, 169, 176, 184-187, 191, 194-195, 197-200, 202-208, 210-212, 215, 217, 231-232, 237, 239-242, 244, 246-248, 253, 255-256, 260, 263, 265-266, 268-275, 280-282, 285-286, 292, 299, 309, 312, 314
Anglo American Corporation 83, 100-102, 107
Anglo-Boer War viii, 52, 63, 267, 304
Apprenticeship Act (1921) 19
Archives Yearbook for South African History 307
armed struggle 207, 209-210, 239, 277-278
Ayandele, Emmanuel 309-310

Bantu Education 110, 115-122, 126-127, 129-135, 251
Barlow, Arthur 22
Barnard, Niël 174, 283-286, 291
Beeld, Die 109
Bekker, Koos 303, 321
Benvenisti, Meron 220
Berlin Wall, fall of 171, 258, 285, 291
Biko, Steve 140-141, 204
Black Consciousness Movement 204
Boesak, Allan 166
Bond, Die 17
Boraine, Alex 177, 207-208, 213
Bosman, JJ 89
Botha, Fanie 107, 178
Botha, Louis 10, 71, 139
Botha, MC 110

INDEX

Botha, Pik 180, 184-187, 189-196, 198, 238
Botha, PW x, 72, 75, 111, 147-152, 154-155, 159, 167-172, 174-175, 177-178, 180-198, 200-201, 206, 225-226, 228, 241-242, 248, 254-255, 281-285, 291-292, 298
Breytenbach, Breyten 58-59, 77-78, 163, 202-208, 211-213, 215, 217, 308
Brink, Chris 316-319
Brink, CB 95
Buber, Martin 58-60, 62
Bunting, Brian 104
Burger, Die 9, 12, 14, 16, 18-20, 23, 32, 34, 36-39, 54, 56-57, 63, 70, 194, 216, 259, 287, 303, 320, 329
Burton, John 229
Buthelezi Commission 182, 200, 231
Buthelezi, Mangosuthu 166, 182, 186, 198, 239, 253-254

Camus, Albert 58-61, 77-78, 218
Cape Argus 49, 201
Cape Times 9, 20
Cape, The 89
Carlton Conference 150, 154
Carter, Gwendolen 37, 116, 123
Cillié, Piet 34, 49, 63, 70-71, 73, 139
Clarion, The 14-17, 329
Clark, W Marshall 97
Cloete, Fanie, 172, 174, 181
Coertze, PJ 39, 48
Coetzee, JM 50, 206, 217, 320
Coetzer, WB 95, 100-101
Coloured Representative Council (CRC) 161-162
Comprehensive Anti-Apartheid Act (1985) 199
Connor, Walker 241, 253
Conservative Party (CP) 71-72, 156, 170-171, 174, 178, 216, 252
consociationalism 176, 212, 257
Constitution, American 70
Constitution of 1996, South African 184-187, 190, 240, 242, 259, 264-267, 276, 286, 288-290, 311, 316
Constitution, Tricameral (1983) 27, 153-166, 177, 184, 254
Constitution, Union of South Africa (1909) vii, 3, 9, 96, 298, 304
Constitutional Court x, 297, 321
Ćosić, Dobrica 61

Cottesloe Conference 67
Council on Higher Education 323
Crocker, Chester 189-190, 195, 201, 222, 239
Cronjé, Geoff 34, 37-38, 57

Dagbreekpers 108-110
Dakar conference with ANC (1987) 202, 207-209, 212-213, 216-217
Daling, Marinus 105-106
Davenport, TRH 32, 116
Davidson, Apollon 278
De Beers Consolidated Mines 101
De Cuéllar, Pérez 170
Degenaar, JJ 78-79
De Klerk, FW x, 30, 70, 81, 167, 172, 180-181, 184-185, 191, 197, 201, 241-242, 253, 255, 257-259, 261-266, 270, 272, 284-293, 352
De Klerk, Willem 70, 147, 151, 157-158
Democratic Party (DP) 28, 30, 287, 317
De Tocqueville, Alexis 3, 225
De Villiers, Bruckner 8, 13, 17, 23, 25, 38
De Villiers Commission 123
De Villiers, Dawie 30, 183
De Villiers, Izak 287, 289
De Villiers, Wim 297, 324
De Waal, JHH 13, 16, 26
De Waal, Marius 301
De Wet, Jack 311-312, 315
De Wet, JC 307
Diederichs, Nic 37-38, 57, 99
Dieper reg, Die 62
Distillers Corporation 94
Dönges, Eben 37, 92, 95, 274
Drury, Allen 270
Dual Mandate 53
Dubow, Saul 34, 37, 56
Du Pisani, André 213
Du Plessis, Barend 27-28, 180, 192, 196, 271
Du Plessis, Fred 83
Du Plessis, JC x, 32, 42-43
Du Plessis, Johannes 41, 47
Du Plessis, LJ 36, 92
Dutch Reformed Church viii, 32, 34, 36, 41-42, 44-46, 55, 67, 80, 255
Du Toit, André 36, 53, 78, 209
Dyson, Freeman 290

Eerste Ekonomiese Volkskongres (1939) 92, 98, 112

Ehlers, Ters 192, 195
Eiselen, Werner 48-49, 97, 115-118, 122, 129, 135
Ellis, Stephen 277-278
Elphick, Richard 41, 46, 122
End Papers 202, 217
Erasmus Commission 145
Erasmus, Frans 38, 97
Ethnic Groups in Conflict 84, 218

Fagan, HA 65-66
Federale Mynbou 100-101
Federale Volksbeleggings (FVB) 93-95, 104, 113
Federation of Governing Bodies of South African Schools (FEDSAS) 323
Ferreira, GT 320
Filatova, Irina 277-278
Financial Mail 113, 123
franchise, disfranchisement of coloureds vii, ix, 3-4, 10, 21-26
Franchise Laws Amendment Act (1931) 24
Freedom Charter 211-212, 309
Freedom Front 290
Free Market Foundation 212
Frontline 208
Fukuyama, Francis 81, 113
Furlong, P 35-37

Gagiano, Jannie 221
Gamiet, Azared 23
Gandhi, Mahatma 60
Gann, Lewis 243
Geldenhuys, Deon 165
Gellner, Ernest 245
Gelyke Kanse/Equal Opportunities 302
Gencor 102
General Mining 100-102, 271
Gerdener, GBA 34, 39, 45-46, 48, 54-55
Gerwel, Jakes 317
Geyer, Albert 34, 38-39, 56
Gini coefficient 104
Good Hope Conference 150
Gorbachev, Mikhail 171, 265
Gramsci, Antonio 58
Gray, JL 95
Gregor, AJ xiii, 33
Grosskopf, JFW 39, 299, 305
group areas policy 151, 155, 161, 163

Hailey, Lord 39
Hammarskjöld, Dag 69
Hanf, Theodor 163, 211, 222, 224
Harmel, Michael 275
Hartshorne, Ken 129
Hazelkorn, Ellen 301, 313
Herstigte Nasionale Party (HNP) 71
Hertzog, Albert 40, 142
Hertzog, Dirk 90
Hertzog, Edwin 319-320
Hertzog, JBM vii, ix, 12-13, 18, 20-22, 24-25, 39, 50, 139, 156
Heugh, Kathleen 131
Heunis, Chris 148, 172-174, 177-178, 180-187, 189, 192, 195-196, 200, 226, 291
Heunis, Jan 187, 196, 288
Hexham, Irving 32
Hoernlé, Alfred 49, 51, 56, 64, 121
Hofmeyr, JH vii-viii, x
Hofmeyr, Willie 38, 51, 56, 88-89
homeland policy of National Party (Bantustans) 49, 64, 65, 69-70, 81, 106, 116, 123-126, 134-135, 142, 153, 165, 177, 179, 181-186, 191-192, 196, 198, 226, 246, 248, 275, 278, 280
Horowitz, Donald 6-7, 25, 68, 84, 218
Horrell, Muriel 129
How Long Will South Africa Survive? 270
Huisgenoot, Die 63
Huntington, Samuel 157, 173-174, 176, 181, 218, 224, 254
Hurter, Jan 112
Hutt, WH 95
Hyslop, Jonathan 116, 120

Immorality Act 155
Index Medicus 307
Industrial and Commercial Workers' Union of Africa 42
influx control 33, 150-151, 157, 165, 166, 185, 197
Information Scandal 145
Inkatha 208-209, 219, 286
Innes, James Rose 9
Institute for a Democratic Alternative for South Africa (Idasa) 207-212, 214, 216
Institute of Race Relations 80, 129, 293
Institute for Reconciliation and Justice 35
Iron and Steel Corporation (Iscor) 91, 250
Ismael, Anwar 30

INDEX

Jaster, Robert 143
Jeffery, Anthea 286
Jesudason, James 85
job reservation 71, 75, 251
Johannesburg Stock Exchange 93, 238, 240
Johnson, RW 270-271, 293
Jooste, Marius 110
Jordan, Pallo 210, 213
Kabwe Conference 171
Kant, Immanuel 78
Katzew, Henry 63
Kaunda, Kenneth 143, 145
Kedourie, Eli 212
Keeromstraat clique 108
Keppel-Jones, Arthur 33, 56
Kerkbode, Die 36
Kestell, JD 91, 113
Keys, Derek 271
Khomeini, Ayatollah 140
Kissinger, Henry 280
Kleurling Versekeringsmaatskappy 17
Kloss, Heinz 300, 304
Kohl, Helmut 183, 188, 190
Kousser, J Morgan 4
Krog, Antjie 308
Kruger, Jimmy 139, 141
Kubayi, Mmamoloko 119
Kundera, Milan 245

Labour Party 8, 18
Labour Party (Coloured) 162-163
Land Bank 18
Langenhoven, CJ 298
Language Endangerment and Language Maintenance 299
Language, FJ 48
language policy of national government 316-317
Laponce, Jean 317-319
Leadership SA 147
Legassick, M 33
Le Grange, Louis 180
Le Grange, W 24
Lehohla, Pali 119-120, 300, 315
Leon, Tony 316-317
Lewin, Julius 128
Liberal Dilemma in South Africa, The 216
liberal nationalism 34, 50, 53
Lijphart, Arend 173, 176, 257
Lipset, Seymour Martin 4, 28

Lojale verset 62
Lombard, Ivan 41
Long Walk to Freedom, A 277, 278, 284
Louw, Chris 216
Louw, Eric 109
Louw, Leon 212
Louw, Mike 254
Louw, MS (Tinie) 84, 89, 93, 95
Louw, NP van Wyk ix-x, 34, 50-53, 62-65, 68, 74-79, 214-216, 243, 246-247, 308
Lugard, Lord 53
Luthuli, Albert 116, 274, 277

Machiavelli, Niccolò 172, 174-176, 188, 196
Malan, DF ix, 12, 17, 23-26, 32, 35-39, 44, 47-48, 50, 53-54, 98, 108, 125, 274, 329
Malan, FS 298
Malan, Magnus 72, 169, 171, 174-175, 189
Malay Dilemma, The 85
Malherbe, Rassie 172
Mamdani, Mahmood 300, 310
Mandela, Nelson x, 30, 56, 182, 184-186, 189-191, 193-194, 197-198, 209-210, 239-240, 257-262, 270-271, 274-291, 293-294, 316-317
Mangope, Lucas 142
Marais, Jannie 88, 298
Marquard, Leo 96, 128
Matthews, ZK 121, 129
Mayibuye 239
Mbeki, Govan 278
Mbeki, Thabo 84, 207, 209, 292
McFarlane, Robert 189
Mchunu, Senzo 119
Meiring, Dirk 129
Meiring, George 289-290
Merriman, John X 7
Meyer, Piet 36-38, 57
Meyer, Roelf 253, 256, 288
Mill, John Stuart 53
Milner, Alfred 52, 63
Milošević, Slobodan 61
Mitterrand, Danielle 207
Mitterrand, François 188
M-Net 111
Mohamad, Mahathir bin 85-86
Moodie, TD 35-36
Morkel, Pieter 107
Motlanthe, Kgalema 119
Motshekga, Angie 119

Mugabe, Robert 143
Mulder, Connie 72
Muzorewa, Abel 143

Nasionale Pers (Naspers) 37-38, 88, 108-111, 174
Nasson, Bill 299
National Democratic Revolution (SACP) 278
National Party (NP) vii, ix-x, 4, 12-13, 15-18, 20-30, 35-38, 40, 44, 46, 50, 54-56 , 61-63, 65, 67, 69-74, 80, 82-83, 88, 96-99, 103, 105, 107-108, 110, 114, 120, 125, 132, 134, 140, 149, 152, 154-156, 158, 160, 166-168, 170-171, 173, 175, 177-178, 181, 189, 196-197, 199-200, 202, 210, 215, 221, 228, 237-239, 241-245, 247-248, 252-253, 257-267, 270, 274, 276, 279, 285-288, 293, 296, 305, 311, 316
National Research Foundation (NRF) 312, 315
Native Representative Council (NRC) 120, 124-125
Nattrass, J 103
Neame, LE 49
Nel, MC de Wet 32
Nelson, Joan 269, 299
neo-colonialism in teaching 309-311
New Economic Policy (NEP, Malaysia) 84-85
New Order 35-36
Nickel, Herman 189
Nkomo, Joshua 143
Non-European Unity Movement 116
Norval, A 33-34, 37
Nyerere, Julius 143

Oates, William 5
O'Dowd, MC 90-91
Okhela 204
Old Mutual 105-106
Olivier, Nic 39, 162
O'Meara, Dan 33, 37, 104
Omotoso, Kole 310
O'Neill, Terence 225-226
Op die horison 45
Opkoms van die derde stand, Die 68
Oppenheimer, Ernest 100
Oppenheimer, Harry 100, 150
Optima 272
Orwell, George 58
Ossewabrandwag (OB) 35-36, 50, 141

Owen, Ken 237
Oxford History of South Africa 130

Pact government (1924-1932) 18-19, 23-26, 91
Pahlavi, Reza (Shah of Iran) 174
Pan Africanist Congress (PAC) 211
Panorama 109
Parkinson's Law 6
Pascal's wager 245
Paton, Alan 140, 240, 243
Patriot, Die 72
Patterson, S 37
Perskor 108, 110-111
Pienaar, Schalk 73
Pirow, Oswald 35
Political Domination in Africa 212
Pogrund, Benjamin 282
Poole, Evered 97
Posel, Deborah 33
power-sharing 145, 175-178, 180, 182, 187, 190, 195-196, 198, 200, 211-212, 238-239, 249, 252, 257, 259-260, 262, 264, 266, 272, 285-287, 289
Power-sharing in South Africa 176
Prah, Kwesi Kwaa 309, 311
Prince, The 172
Prins, Gwyn 159
Prinsloo, Daan 183, 195-196
Progressive Federal Party (PFP) 79, 162, 176-178, 220
Prohibition of Mixed Marriages Bill (1949) 37
Purified National Party ix, 25
Ramaphosa, Cyril 256, 288, 316
Ramphele, Mamphela 118
ranking system of universities 301, 311-314
Rapport 205, 266, 287, 289, 297
Ratzinger, Joseph (see Benedict XVI)
Rautenbach, Ig 172
Reagan, Ronald 171, 188, 222
Reddingsdaadbond (RDB) 94
Rembrandt 90, 94, 99, 106-107, 112
Renwick, Robin 167, 169, 200, 285-286
Rhodes, Cecil John 21
Rhoodie, Nic 32
Richard, Dirk 110
Rive, Louis 111
Robinson, Kenneth 53
Rossouw, J Grainger 16
Rousseau, Joubert 127
Roux, Jannie 169

INDEX

Rubicon speech x, 167-172, 178, 180, 185, 186-187, 189-190, 194, 197-201, 282
Rupert, Anton 83-84, 90, 93-94, 99, 106, 114, 167

Sadie, Jan 39, 89, 98, 101, 117, 342
Sanlam 13, 38, 83, 88-89, 92-95, 100-102, 104-106, 108, 111-112, 240
Sanlam: Uit die volk gebore – Sanlam se eerste 50 jaar 112
Santam 88
Sasbank 93
Sauer Commission 46, 50, 55
Sauer, Paul 23, 38, 53-54
Saunders, C 32, 116
Schlemmer, Lawrence 115, 210-211, 213-214, 287, 292, 304, 319
Schoeman, Karel 308
Schoeman, PJ 39
Scholtz, Pepler 105, 112
Scholtz, Werner 190
Schumann, CGW 91, 100
Schumpeter, Joseph 84, 89, 114
Sebe, Lennox 185
Selborne, Lord 9-10
separate amenities policy 150
Serfontein, Hennie 208
Sharpeville massacre 67, 276
Shepherd, RWH 121-122, 130
Simkins, Charles 115, 117-118, 132, 162, 342
Sites, Paul 220, 222
Sithole, Ndabaningi 143
Sklar, Richard 212
Slabbert, Frederik van Zyl 34-35, 79-80, 166, 176, 186, 202, 206, 207-208, 210, 216-217, 292, 319
Slovo, Joe 239, 278, 292
Smit, Flip xi, 312-313, 323
Smith, Ian 143, 145, 245, 259
Smuts, Genl. Jan vii, ix, 10, 18, 21-23, 45, 50, 56, 96, 139, 156
Solarz, Stephen 196
Solidarity movement 322
Sondes van die vaders, Die 78
Soros, George 207
South African Bureau of Racial Affairs (SABRA) 65
South African Communist Party (SACP) 104, 170, 187, 203-204, 277-279, 283, 285, 292-293

South African Mining and Engineering Journal 100
South African Outlook 121
South African Party (SAP) vii, 10-11, 18, 20-21, 28-29
South Africa's Options 80
Soweto uprising (1976) 71, 76, 131, 141, 142, 246, 248, 252, 280
Special Cabinet Committee (SCC) 179-184, 254
Spicer, Michael 101
Stals, Ernst 41
Staniland, M 211
Star, The 37, 94
Stellenbosch University ix, xi, 23, 221, 297-298, 300, 305, 312-321
Sterrewag meeting (1985) 187-188, 191-192, 196, 201
Steward, Dave 187, 190, 197
Steyn, Jaap 77-78
Stoker, HG 36-37
'Straatpraatjes' (Street talk) 11
Strange Career of Jim Crow, The 3
Strijdom, JG 36, 40, 108, 125, 134, 141
Strydom, JG (Valie) 42-45
Study of History, A 272
Stumpf, Rolf 318
Suid-Afrikaan, Die 208
Sullivan, Peter 188
Sunday Times 185, 187
Suzman, Helen 243
Swanepoel, Piet 279

Tabata, IB 116
Tambo, Oliver 179, 198, 228, 274
Tegniek 106
Thatcher, Margaret 183, 188, 190, 195
Theron, Johan 324
Thirion, Chris 286
Thom, HB 39, 48
Tlhabi, Redi 118
Tolstoy, Leo 290
Tomlinson Commission 57, 65, 70
T-option of language instruction (Stellenbosch University) 319-320
total onslaught ideology 71, 75, 169, 248, 281
Toynbee, Arnold 272-273, 276, 281, 292
Transvaler, Die xiii, 38, 99
Treason Trial 275, 293
Treurnicht, Andries (AP) 27, 72, 171, 177-178

Trew, Tony 208
Troup, Freda 118
True Confessions of an Albino Terrorist, The 202, 204, 213, 217
Trust Bank 112
Truth and Reconciliation Commission (TRC) 35
Tutu, Desmond 277
Tweede Ekonomiese Volkskongres (1950) 107

Uithaalder, Piet 11
Umkhonto we Sizwe (MK) 271, 277
Union Corporation 102
Unionist Party 11
United Afrikaner League (UAL) 13-14
United Democratic Front (UDF) 170, 174, 179, 209
United Party (UP) ix, 36, 44, 65, 94, 96, 120-121, 123, 155

Vaderland, Die xiii
Van den Bergh, Hendrik 141, 144
Van den Berghe, Pierre 37, 216, 232, 270
Van den Bos, WH 97
Van der Merwe, Johan 171
Van der Merwe, Koos 178
Van der Merwe, PJ 306
Van der Merwe, Stoffel 181
Van der Ross, Richard 23, 29-30
Van der Westhuizen, Pieter 174
Van Eeden, Barney 39, 48
Van Heerden, Etienne 308
Van Heerden, Neil 190
Van Niekerk, Gerhard 320
Van Niekerk, Marlene 308
Van Ryneveld, Pierre 97
Van Tonder, Joh 172, 175, 181,
Van Wyk, Andreas 167, 172, 180
Van Wyk, JJ 165
Vargas, Getúlio 172
Veldsman, NR 19, 23
Venter, Eben 308
Verhoef, G 101
Verwoerd, HF ix, 34, 36, 38-40, 47, 49, 56-57, 65, 67-70, 92, 99, 107-110, 112, 116, 118-120, 122-130, 134-135, 139, 141-142, 147, 151, 169, 274-277, 293

Verwoerd Speaks 123
Viljoen, Constand 263, 289-290
Viljoen, Gerrit 73-75, 180-181, 194, 258, 285
Viviers, Jack 174
Volkskas ix, 89-90, 92-94, 107-108, 112
Voltaire 76
Von Hirschberg, Carl 188, 193
Von Ranke, Leopold 306
Voortbestaan in geregtigheid 78
Voortrekkerpers 108
Vorster, BJ 69, 139-145, 151, 154, 169, 172, 178, 246, 248, 279-281
Vosloo, Ben 172

Waldmeir, Patty 199, 266
Walker, Eric 116
Walzer, Michael 58-59, 77-78, 204, 217
Warneck, Gustav 43, 45
Wassenaar, Andreas 84, 100, 112
Weber, Phil 34, 39
Welsh, David 80, 176
Wentzel, Tos 195
Wessels, Albert ix, 90
When Smuts Goes 56
White Paper on Defence (1977) 71
Wiehahn Commission 144
Wilcocks, RW 39, 47
Williams, Abe 29
Wilson, Monica 130
Winterbach, Ingrid 308
Women's Enfranchisement Bill (1930) 24
Woods, Donald 140
Woodward, C Vann 3-4, 6, 164
World Council of Churches 67
Wright, Harrison 37
Wurm, Stephen 299, 305

Xiao-ping, Deng 170

Zille, Helen 316-317
Zuma, Jacob 118, 315